FAMILY AND CHILD WELL-BEING AFTER WELFARE REFORM

FAMILY AND CHILD WELL-BEING AFTER WELFARE REFORM

DOUGLAS J. BESHAROV
EDITOR

TRANSACTION PUBLISHERS
NEW BRUNSWICK (U.S.A.) AND LONDON (U.K.)

First paperback printing 2004
Copyright © 2003 by Transaction Publishers, New Brunswick, New Jersey.

This book is printed on acid-free paper that meets the American National Standard for Permanence of Paper for Printed Library Materials.

Library of Congress Catalog Number: 2003044788
ISBN: 0-7658-0188-4 (cloth); 0-7658-0845-5 (paper)
Printed in the United States of America

Library of Congress Cataloging-in-Publication Data

Family and child well-being after welfare reform / edited by Douglas J. Besharov.
    p. cm.
Includes bibliographical references and index.
ISBN 0-7658-0845-5 (alk. paper)
    1. Welfare recipients—United States. 2. Child welfare—United States.
3. Poor families—United States. 4. Problem families—United States.
5. Public welfare—Government policy—United States. I. Besharov,
Douglas J.

HV699F243 2003
362.7'0973—dc21

2003044788

*To Jerry M. Wiener,
friend and teacher*

Contents

Figures

Tables

Boxes

Acknowledgments

This volume reflects the knowledge and good judgment of many people. Eugene Lewit and Margie K. Shields at the David and Lucile Packard Foundation provided early encouragement and critical support for the development of this book. Substantial support from the Smith Richardson Foundation and the American Enterprise Institute helped turn the original papers into this publication. Peter Germanis, my dear and valued colleague, skillfully reviewed the papers for content and suggested substantive and editorial changes.

Staff at the University of Maryland and the American Enterprise Institute performed the essential administrative, editing, and fact-checking tasks with great care and good humor. Betsy Allen helped organize the initial effort and lined up the authors. Eric Weingart, Christina Imholt, and Kerri Smith, with the assistance of Caroline Polk and Susan Freis, edited the papers and developed the typographic design. Anne Shi, Christopher Brown, and Patrick Ruffini perfected the graphic design and produced the figures. Anne Schneider, our editor at Transaction Publishers, kept us on schedule and encouraged us to aim for the highest quality publication.

Most of all, we are indebted to the authors themselves, who have made this an informative and thought-provoking volume that promises to strengthen future efforts to monitor the well-being of low-income families and their children.

Family and Child Well-Being after Welfare Reform is one in a series of reports from the Committee to Review Welfare Reform Research, a project of the University of Maryland's Welfare Reform Academy. The committee was formed to help the public, other scholars, practitioners, and policymakers understand research on welfare reform and apply its lessons. Its purpose is to assess the quality and relevance of the most significant evaluation studies, identifying those findings that are sufficiently well-grounded to be regarded as credible.

The committee members, experts in evaluation and related social science fields, are Robert F. Boruch, University of Pennsylvania;

James J. Heckman, University of Chicago; Robinson G. Hollister, Swarthmore College; Christopher Jencks, Harvard University; Glenn C. Loury, Boston University; Peter H. Rossi, University of Massachusetts (Amherst); Isabel V. Sawhill, the Brookings Institution; Thomas C. Schelling, University of Maryland; and James Q. Wilson, Pepperdine University.

Douglas J. Besharov
May 2003

1

Introduction

Douglas J. Besharov and Peter Germanis

Between March 1994 and July 2001, welfare rolls fell an amazing 59 percent from their historic high of 5.1 million families. How much of this decline was the result of welfare reform and how much was the result of other factors, such as the strong economy? What were the effects of the decline on low-income families? About a quarter billion dollars is being spent on studies and surveys designed to answer these and other questions. Unfortunately, we are unlikely to get more than a modest amount of the information sought.

This book is titled *Family and Child Well-Being after Welfare Reform*, even though the common formulation is "child well-being." The word *family* was added to the title in recognition of the family's preeminent role in protecting and fostering the well-being of children and in recognition that well-functioning families are likely to be more successful in doing so.

After one chapter on welfare reform and the caseload decline and another chapter assessing the research on welfare reform's impact, the volume reviews some of the key areas of family and child well-being: income and expenditures; cohabitation and child well-being; fatherhood, cohabitation, and marriage; teenage sex, pregnancy, and nonmarital births; child maltreatment and foster care; housing conditions and homelessness; child health; nutrition, food security, and obesity; crime and juvenile delinquency; drug use; and mothers' work and child care.

Each chapter addresses a series of questions: Can existing surveys and other data be used to measure trends in the area? How might they be improved? What key indicators should be tracked? What are the initial trends after welfare reform? What other information or approaches would be helpful? These specific-topic chapters

1

are followed by a description of the activities of the U.S. Department of Health and Human Services (HHS) to monitor broadly the well-being of low-income children and their families.

The final chapter summarizes what will and will not be learned from existing studies; emphasizes the importance of high-quality, ongoing data for monitoring the well-being of low-income families; describes several options for improving selected data sources; and recommends randomized experiments to assess the impact of specific welfare reform provisions.

Welfare Reform and the Caseload Decline

The 1996 welfare reform law, the Personal Responsibility and Work Opportunity Reconciliation Act (PRWORA), replaced the Aid to Families with Dependent Children program (AFDC) with the Temporary Assistance for Needy Families program (TANF). Between March 1994 (two years before the passage of PRWORA) and June 2001, the welfare rolls fell an amazing 59 percent from their historic high of 5.1 million families.[1] Around July of 2001, caseloads stopped declining in most states and started rising again, presumably because of the weakening economy. But, although about ten states experienced caseload increases of 10 to 20 percent in the next year, at least as of June 2002, the nationwide rise has been surprisingly modest.[2]

In "Welfare Reform and the Caseload Decline" (chapter 2), Douglas J. Besharov, a resident scholar at the American Enterprise Institute (AEI) and a professor at the University of Maryland School of Public Affairs, and Peter Germanis, assistant director of the university's Welfare Reform Academy, trace what is known about the large decrease in welfare recipiency and what families are doing after they leave welfare. The authors' main data sources are the Current Population Survey (CPS), the Survey of Income and Program Participation (SIPP), state administrative data on welfare submitted to HHS, and state "leaver studies" (see boxes 1.1 and 1.2).

Besharov and Germanis describe how a number of respected researchers have used econometric models to estimate how much of the decline was caused by welfare reform compared with other factors. That research suggests that 35 to 45 percent of the decline resulted from the strong economy, 20 to 30 percent stemmed from massive expansion in aid to the working poor, up to 5 percent came from an increase in the minimum wage, 25 to 35 percent resulted from welfare reform, and 5 to 10 percent came from the erosion in the real value of benefits. The authors express each factor as a range, to reflect the uncertainty surrounding the estimates, but they nevertheless conclude that these percentages accurately reflect the relative importance of each factor to the decline in caseloads.

Box 1.1
Multipurpose Sources of Welfare Data

The **Consumer Expenditure Survey (CE)** is an ongoing survey of about 7,500 households (5,000 before 1999) designed by the Bureau of Labor Statistics (BLS) and conducted by the Census Bureau. Each family is surveyed for five consecutive quarters regarding their purchases during the previous three months. The survey also includes information on the income and demographic characteristics of participating families.

The **Current Population Survey (CPS)** is a monthly survey of about 60,000 households (up from 50,000 before July 2001) sponsored jointly by the Census Bureau and BLS. The data are collected by the Census Bureau. Although the main purpose of the survey is to collect data on employment-related outcomes, each March a supplement to the CPS (with a sample of 78,000 households, beginning in 2001) collects detailed information on the nation's families, including family income, poverty status, living arrangements, and participation in government and welfare programs. Additional supplements focus on food security, fertility and marital history, and other topics.

The **Decennial Census** is the complete enumeration of the nation's population, conducted by the Census Bureau every decade since 1790. The "short form" of the survey (sent to five of every six households) is used to collect information about each housing unit and basic demographic information for all household members. A subset of the population is asked more detailed questions on the "long form" (sent to one of every six households), including questions about the demographic, economic, and social circumstances of the sample and about the characteristics of the participants' housing.

The **Survey of Income and Program Participation (SIPP)** is a longitudinal survey conducted by the Census Bureau. The 1996 panel had 36,700 participating households, which are interviewed twelve times over a four-year period. The survey provides detailed information on the demographic characteristics of participating families and their income, labor force participation, participation in government and welfare programs, living arrangements, and other factors. Topical modules conducted periodically have covered issues such as child care, child support, disability, and support from nonhousehold members.

Box 1.2
State-Based Welfare Data

States are required to submit detailed administrative data to the federal government for most major programs, such as Temporary Assistance for Needy Families (TANF), food stamps, and Medicaid. The data can include program aggregates, such as caseloads and total spending, as well as detailed information about the characteristics of public assistance recipients, including their age, sex, race or ethnicity, income, employment, and the number and characteristics of other people living in the home. The *TANF Annual Report to the Congress* and other HHS materials, for example, are based on state administrative data on caseload size and welfare recipient characteristics submitted by all states to HHS.

Leaver studies are state studies of families leaving welfare that are based on surveys or administrative data. They attempt to track the employment, earnings, welfare receipt, and other outcomes of families leaving welfare. The studies vary considerably in the scope and completeness of their data, the length of their follow-up, and the comprehensiveness of their questions. As a result, many analysts limit the use of such studies to those that meet certain minimum criteria. For example, the U.S. General Accounting Office (GAO) summarized only those studies that achieved a 70 percent response rate or included a nonresponse analysis indicating that the nonrespondents were similar to the respondents. Many of the leaver studies also examine specific issues, such as use of child care, use of health care services, and homelessness.

According to Besharov and Germanis, welfare offices have been transformed from places where mothers are signed up for benefits (with almost no questions asked beyond those concerning eligibility) to places where mothers are helped, cajoled, and pressured to get a job—or to rely on others for support. This dual approach is reflected in case outcomes: Survey research of those who have left welfare ("leavers") suggests that only about 50 to 60 percent seem to be working regularly, often in low-paying jobs. The other 40 or 50 percent are just leaving—some to work eventually, but more immediately to move in with (or to be supported by) family, friends, or boyfriends. (Besharov and Germanis note that several studies of leavers suggest that even those who have "barriers" to employment are leaving the rolls at a high rate.) Most welfare leavers report that they are as well off or better off after leaving than while on welfare, but a significant minority report being worse off.

Besharov and Germanis point out that many nonworking mothers who have left welfare could be initiating new co-residency arrangements or falling back on preexisting ones (together with other sources of support). Many observers focus on cohabitation, but Besharov and Germanis describe a far more extensive economic and social network comprising other shared living arrangements. According to SIPP data, for example, in 1990, before the declines in welfare caseloads, 37 percent of welfare mothers lived with other adults—18 percent with their parents, 6 percent with a boyfriend, and 13 percent with others.[3]

When welfare reform was first debated, many people feared that it would hurt the poor, especially children. But according to Besharov and Germanis, as well as most of the other contributors to this volume, little evidence suggests that—as of now—welfare reform has caused widespread additional hardship, such as substantial decreases in incomes, increased homelessness, or more foster care placements. But, the incomes of the poorest single mothers may have declined, at least in the immediate aftermath of welfare reform. Because of various methodological problems, Besharov and Germanis conclude that substantially better data are needed to assess the situation of single mothers and their children.

Assessing Welfare Reform's Impact

About a quarter billion dollars is being spent on studies and surveys specifically designed to monitor and evaluate "welfare reform." Can these surveys and studies determine how much of the caseload decline was due to welfare reform? Can they determine welfare reform's impact on low-income children and their families? If not, can they at least tell us about the well-being of children after welfare reform?

In "Assessing Welfare Reform's Impact" (chapter 3), Peter H. Rossi, a professor emeritus at the University of Massachusetts at Amherst, describes the four major research projects assessing welfare reform, programs that account for more than half the spending in the area: the Survey of Program Dynamics (SPD), the National Survey of America's Families (NSAF), the Project on Devolution and Urban Change (UC), and the Child Impact Waiver experiments being funded by the federal government (see box 1.3). He concludes that these studies cannot provide a reliable assessment of welfare reform's impact on children and families because it is too late to construct a valid control or comparison group with which to measure the "counterfactual," or what would have happened in the absence of welfare reform.

Box 1.3
Welfare Reform Evaluative Studies

The **National Survey of America's Families (NSAF)**, part of the Urban Institute's Assessing the New Federalism project, is a nationwide survey of 44,000 households in 1997 and 42,000 households in 1999, with an additional survey completed in 2002. The New Federalism project is intended to provide researchers with resources to monitor and assess the consequences of program changes and fiscal developments. Thus, the NSAF captures information on the economic, health, and social well-being of children, adults under age sixty-five, and their families. Although the survey is national in scope, the focus is on thirteen states that together account for about half the nation's population. The 1997 survey was intended to be a snapshot of family life on the eve of major policy changes, most notably welfare reform, with subsequent surveys capturing the period after welfare reform.

The **Survey of Program Dynamics (SPD)**, conducted by the Census Bureau, is a national longitudinal survey that was authorized by the 1996 welfare reform law to evaluate the impact of welfare reform. The SPD is an extension of the 1992 and 1993 panels of the SIPP and will follow the same households for ten years, from 1992 to 2001. It collects detailed information on the socioeconomic characteristics of participating households, including family composition, program participation, and employment and earnings. Because the survey is longitudinal, researchers will be able to examine transitions on and off welfare programs. In some years, the survey includes special questions related to child and adolescent well-being. The SPD started with 50,000 households in 1992–1993 (as the SIPP), but attrition and budget restrictions have substantially reduced the sample.

The **Project on Devolution and Urban Change (UC)**, conducted by the Manpower Demonstration Research Corporation (MDRC), is studying the aftermath of welfare reform in four large cities (Cleveland, Los Angeles, Miami, and Philadelphia). The project has several components, including ethnographic studies in poor neighborhoods, implementation studies examining how welfare agencies implemented the new law, and studies assessing the impact of welfare reform on local social agencies and businesses. In each city, 1,000 single mothers who received AFDC in 1995 were interviewed in 1998 on such topics as their experience with welfare, their labor market participation, and the well-being of household members, especially children. The survey achieved a response rate of 79 percent. A follow-up survey of these mothers was conducted in 2002, with a response rate of 80 to 83 percent of the first-wave respondents. Since 1992, detailed administrative data covering welfare receipt and employment and earnings have also been collected.

The **Child Impact Waiver Experiments** are five experiments funded by HHS that began before enactment of national welfare reform to test alternatives to the old AFDC program. States were granted waivers to try such experiments only if they established rigorous, random-assignment experiments to measure the impact of their new policies. Many of the waiver projects resembled the TANF programs. HHS supported expansions of evaluations in five states (Connecticut, Florida, Indiana, Iowa, and Minnesota) to include additional measures of child well-being. The studies concentrated on families with children between ages five and twelve.

Rossi cautions that none of the studies should be used to make causal statements about the impact of welfare reform on the condition of low-income children. Before-and-after studies, he explains, cannot convincingly distinguish the effects of welfare reform from other changes occurring at the same time, including improvements in the economy and expansions in other social programs, such as the Earned Income Tax Credit (EITC). On the other hand, Rossi notes:

> [S]ome attempts to estimate the net effects of PRWORA generally, or TANF specifically, may turn out to be more than merely suggestive, especially when findings are strong, consistent, and robust. For example, despite the weaknesses cited above, if analysis using NSAF data were to find that states with more generous earnings disregards had relatively higher caseloads (holding other interstate differences constant), and that such effects were muted when combined with a strict time limit or work requirement, then the findings could be regarded as supporting a causal inference—if they held up under different specifications and were confirmed in comparable analyses in the SPD and UC data sets, as well as in the Child Impact Waiver Experiments. Such a convergence of findings across data sets, however, is not likely to occur often.

Rossi also notes that response rate problems plague both the SPD and the NSAF. In the SPD, only 50 percent of the original sample responded in the years between 1998 and 2001.[4] "Especially worrisome is that even higher percentages of low-income households stopped cooperating," he says. Rossi concludes that the rates will not be high enough to satisfy most researchers. In the first NSAF survey, response rates were only 65 percent for families with children and only 62 percent for families without children.[5] Rossi characterizes those rates as "average for well-run national telephone surveys," but he warns that "'average' may not be good enough for surveys that are highly policy relevant." Moreover, in the second survey, the response rates dropped to 62 percent and 59 percent, respectively.[6] (They were apparently lower for low-income families.)

Moreover, given the variation in state welfare regimes, Rossi says, "TANF cannot be evaluated as a national program; only state TANF programs can be evaluated." Because each state has its own unique welfare program and because the programs are evolving over time, it will be difficult to estimate the effects of welfare reform generally. Cross-state comparisons are also problematic because of the difficulty of controlling for socioeconomic differences among the states and target populations as well as the difficulty of characterizing state welfare reform policies.

Although NSAF's large samples for each of thirteen states might enable it to examine how families in states with different TANF plans have fared, the decline in welfare rolls has considerably reduced the number of welfare families in the survey taken after TANF went into effect. The resultant small sample sizes of welfare recipients within each state will restrict the ability of analysts to estimate the impact of welfare reform, especially subgroup differences at the level of individual states. State samples of welfare recipients are even smaller in the SPD. (An obvious move, according to Rossi, would be to enlarge sample sizes of other ongoing national surveys to provide adequate state sample sizes.)

The first survey in the MDRC's UC achieved what Rossi termed a "very good" response rate of 79 percent. The second survey, conducted between March and September 2001, was limited to those who responded to the first survey and achieved response rates that ranged from about 80 percent to 83 percent, depending on the site, or about two-thirds of the original sample. The project should provide a rich picture regarding the characteristics and circumstances of the most vulnerable families. Unfortunately, because the study is limited to selected poor neighborhoods in four cities, the findings cannot be generalized to the broader welfare population nationally or even to other urban neighborhoods.

Rossi also summarizes the Child Impact Waiver experiments, five randomized experiments of state welfare reform programs, with funding from the federal government, that compare each state's welfare reform plan with the old AFDC program. According to Rossi, "The importance of these experiments is considerable." He believes that the experiments come closest to testing the impact of welfare reform but points out that they, too, suffer from problems such as a lack of generalizability, failure to isolate control groups from some elements of welfare reform, and an inability to capture entry effects.

Given the response rate and other limitations of the four major studies described above, can the larger surveys conducted by the Census Bureau and the specialized surveys conducted by other federal agencies be used to measure the well-being of low-income children and families? In effect, the remainder of the volume addresses this question in its various dimensions.

Income and Expenditures

Welfare reform could affect family income in several ways. If it encourages families to leave welfare for work or couples to marry, family income may rise. If it pressures families to leave before they are ready or otherwise penalizes them, family income may decline. What has happened to the financial well-being of low-income mothers after welfare reform?

In "Income and Expenditures" (chapter 4), Richard Bavier, a policy analyst at the U.S. Office of Management and Budget, traces changes in child poverty and the incomes of unmarried female-headed families with children from the period before welfare reform through the next three or four years. For his analysis, he uses three long-standing federal surveys: the CPS, the SIPP, and the Consumer Expenditure Survey (CE) (see box 1.1).

Immediately following the 1996 welfare reform law, welfare rolls fell much more sharply than would have been predicted on the basis of the historical relationship between caseloads and the economy (and other factors), a result suggesting that welfare reform played a significant role in the caseload decline. According to Bavier, before 1997, changes in both child poverty rates and welfare caseloads were closely linked to economic factors, such as unemployment rates and real wage levels. Child poverty rates continued to maintain their historical relationship to changes in the economy and other variables (except for 1999). Welfare caseloads, however, fell much more sharply between 1997 and 1999 than would have been expected on the basis of improvements in the economy, changes in the number of female-headed households with children, and other factors that influence welfare participation.

The poorest female-headed families experienced an initial drop in income after the passage of PRWORA, but between 1998 and 2000, their incomes rose about 15 percent to their highest level ever. But with the weakening economy, they fell back in 2001. Bavier uses the CPS and the SIPP to explore the income changes among female-headed families. He finds that between 1995 and 1998, families in the bottom quintile experienced a decline in annual family income of about $617 (in 2001 dollars), or about 7.4 percent. Between 1998 and 2000, however, family income increased $1,160 to its highest level. But it then declined by $1,073 between 2000 and 2001. He finds a similar pattern using the SIPP, with an initial decline of 9.1 percent in average monthly income for the bottom quintile between 1995 and 1997, followed by two years in which incomes grew. Family income also declined between 1999 and 2001. (No SIPP data were available for 2000.)

In contrast to the up-and-down trends in income experienced by low-income, female-headed families, consumption data suggest a steady improvement in their well-being throughout the 1995 to 2000 period. For example, according to Bavier, the CE indicates that quarterly spending by the poorest female family heads grew steadily. It increased 9.4 percent between 1995 and 1998, and 14.7 percent between 1995 and 2000—suggesting that the group's economic situation was improving. Differences in how the surveys are conducted and what they seek to measure account for some of this inconsistency, cautions Bavier, so that the differences in the three surveys should make us hesitant to draw firm conclusions about how welfare reform has affected female-headed families in the bottom quintile.

Cohabitation and Child Well-Being

Co-residency (living with relatives, boyfriends, and other adults) is an important source of support for low-income, female-headed families, as described by Besharov and Germanis. How extensive is co-residency? According to Bavier, in March 2000, 32 percent of single mothers with children under age eighteen had other adults living with them, 15 percent lived in a relative's home, and 4 percent lived in a nonrelative's home. Less than one-half lived with no other adults.[7] In fact, between 1994 and 2000 cohabitation among couples with children under fifteen seems to have risen by at least a third, or another 400,000 couples.[8] (There is no detectable increase in marriage rates.) This support helps explain why so many mothers have been able to leave welfare without working and without becoming homeless. What are the economic, social, and developmental consequences of this change in single mothers' living arrangements?

In "Cohabitation and Child Well-Being" (chapter 5), Wendy D. Manning, an associate professor in Bowling Green State University's Department of Sociology, summarizes what is known about cohabitation and its effects on children. She describes how some people view "cohabiting-couple" households (that is, unmarried couples cohabiting with a biological child of at least one of the adults) as a two-parent family form and that one of the major goals of the 1996 welfare reform law was to encourage the formation and maintenance of two-parent families. The main sources of data she uses are the CPS, the Decennial Census, the SIPP, the National Survey of Families and Households (NSFH), and the National Survey of Family Growth (NSFG) (see boxes 1.1 and 1.4).

Box 1.4
Data on Fertility and Family Living Arrangements

The **National Survey of Families and Households (NSFH)** is a survey of nearly 13,000 people ages nineteen and older conducted by researchers at the Center for Demography and Ecology at the University of Wisconsin–Madison from 1987 to 1988. It collected information on respondents' fertility, marriage and cohabitation histories, and child outcomes. A five-year follow-up survey in 1992–1994 targeted a sample of the original cohort and added spouses and children in selected age groups. A third survey was conducted in 2001–2002.

The **National Survey of Family Growth (NSFG),** a survey of nearly 11,000 women ages fifteen to forty-four conducted by the National Center for Health Statistics (NCHS), collects current information on childbearing, factors affecting childbearing (such as family planning), and related aspects of maternal and child health. The NSFG was conducted in 1995 and between February 2002 and February 2003, when, for the first time, men were included in the survey.

The **Vital Statistics Cooperative Program (VSCP)** is run by NCHS and is based on 100 percent of the birth certificates nationally. It includes information on all births (including health outcomes) by marital status, race, age, and educational attainment of mothers, both by state and nationally.

Manning reports that, according to the 1990 Decennial Census, 2.2 million children (3.5 percent of all children) were in a cohabiting-couple household. This estimate is only a point-in-time estimate, however. According to other estimates, about 38 percent of all children will spend some part of their childhood in a cohabiting-couple household. For African-American families, the estimate is even higher: 55 percent. Manning points out that 54 percent of the children in cohabiting-couple households live with just one biological parent, which she calls cohabiting-partner households. In many cases, these families are more akin to stepfamilies than to two-parent families with two biological parents.

Manning discusses the positive and negative aspects of cohabitation for children. The most obvious benefits are that a child has two potential caregivers and income providers. Indeed, the poverty rate for children living in such relationships falls dramatically once the income of the cohabitor is included. Many children born into a cohabiting relationship remain in a stable union (either subsequent

marriage or continued cohabitation). According to Manning, however, children in cohabiting-partner households are more likely to
have lower levels of academic performance and greater behavioral
problems than those in intact families.

Manning summarizes the mixed effects of cohabitation as follows: "Cohabitation may be advantageous for children by providing two potential caretakers and income providers, but it may be
disadvantageous for children because of the relatively short duration, informal nature of cohabiting unions, and other factors." She
concludes that a great need exists for additional data and recommends further study of patterns of cohabitation and their impact on
children. She particularly recommends more research on income-
sharing among cohabiting-couple households, on the effects of transitions into and out of cohabiting relationships on child well-being,
and on the way that cohabiting families are treated under the new
welfare reform law.

Fatherhood, Cohabitation, and Marriage

PRWORA encouraged states to develop programs designed to promote "the formation and maintenance of two-parent families." As
Manning explains in the previous chapter, cohabitation is a rapidly
growing living arrangement, and some even argue that it is the
equivalent of marriage. Others counter that such households are an
extremely weak family form. What are the differences in child well-
being when children have nonresident fathers, cohabiting fathers,
and married fathers? What role does public policy have in promoting healthy marriages and strong families?

In "Fatherhood, Cohabitation, and Marriage" (chapter 6), Wade
F. Horn, HHS Assistant Secretary for Children and Families, summarizes the importance of fathers to child well-being. He explains
that "fatherlessness is a significant risk factor for poor developmental outcomes for children." This connection has led some observers
to view cohabitation as a substitute or at least an alternative to marriage.

Horn argues, however, that marriage is the best option for children and that cohabitation is a weak family structure compared with
marriage. Children in households with married parents do better on
almost every measure of child well-being, even after controlling for
income. Many cohabiting parents break up, and even those who
marry are more likely to divorce than are couples who marry before

having children. As a result, 75 percent of children born to cohabiting couples will have their parents separate before age sixteen, compared with just one-third of children born to married parents. Outcomes for children whose fathers leave may actually be worse than for those who have had a continuously absent father. Many cohabiting men are not the biological fathers of the children involved, a factor that makes the children more vulnerable to physical and sexual abuse. Thus, encouraging cohabitation may do more harm than good, says Horn.

Although Horn acknowledges that more research is needed to guide policymakers, he asserts that the government can do many things to promote healthy marriages. He points out that welfare and tax policies often penalize marriage by reducing household income for those who marry. Moreover, he asserts, government officials are often reluctant to bring up the topic, which "sends the not-so-subtle message that marriage is neither expected nor valued." One way to fix this, according to Horn, is for hospitals to ask about both paternity establishment and marriage. Couples that are not married could then be referred to various services, such as premarital education. Horn also recommends that public policy stop penalizing marriage through its various tax and benefit programs. He argues, "It seems patently unfair to promote the value of marriage and then impose a financial penalty of between $2,000 and $8,000 on couples who get married."

State welfare officials should do more to "promote the employment of low-income men so that they are seen as better 'marriage material,'" Horn continues. One way to do this would be to expand their participation in various welfare-to-work programs and thus increase not only their employability, but their marriageability. Finally, because many low-income fathers and mothers lack the skills to be parents, he suggests that states encourage religious and civic organizations to offer marriage and parenting enrichment courses for low-income parents.

Teenage Sex, Pregnancy, and Nonmarital Births

Child poverty is strongly associated with single parenthood and family breakdown. Hence, a major objective of the 1996 welfare reform bill was to reduce nonmarital childbearing (especially among teenagers) and to promote marriage. To do this, the law imposes new requirements on teen parents (raising the cost of early childbearing), gives states funds for abstinence education programs, and authorizes bonuses to states that are most effective in reducing nonmarital childbearing without increasing abortion.

In "Teenage Sex, Pregnancy, and Nonmarital Births" (chapter 7), Isabel V. Sawhill, a senior fellow at the Brookings Institution, describes recent trends in teenage sex, pregnancy, and nonmarital births. Her main sources of data are the CPS and the Vital Statistics Cooperative Program (VSCP) (see boxes 1.1 and 1.4).

Sawhill begins by describing the high proportion of children living in single-parent families and showing how this arrangement contributes to child poverty. Between 1970 and 1996, for example, poverty rose from 15 to 20 percent of all children. Virtually all this increase stemmed from the growth of single-parent families. Moreover, a shift in the composition of single parents, so that a greater number are never-married mothers, exacerbated poverty and welfare dependency. In the 1960s and 1970s, the growth in single parenthood was largely attributable to increases in divorce; in the 1980s and 1990s, however, the growth was largely driven by nonmarital births.

Sawhill links the increased number of nonmarital births to three factors: "later marriage, a higher birth rate among young unmarried women, and a lower birth rate among older married women." Echoing the earlier discussion by Manning, she describes how marriage is being replaced by less stable family or household structures. Some research suggests that about half the mothers who give birth out of wedlock are cohabiting with the fathers and another 30 percent are "romantically involved" with those men. Sawhill notes, "Past research suggests that such ties are not very durable."

Sawhill describes how nonmarital childbearing appears to have leveled off and shows that teen births had been declining even before welfare reform, largely because of a decline in sexual activity and an increase in contraception. She cites five possible reasons for this change in behavior: (1) a growing awareness of AIDS and other sexually transmitted diseases; (2) more conservative attitudes about sexual behavior; (3) the availability of more effective forms of contraception, such as Norplant and Depo-Provera; (4) a strong economy, which gives young people more employment opportunities; and (5) welfare reform and increased aid to the working poor, which have greatly increased the financial returns to single mothers who take a low-paying job. She points out that in 1986, a single mother was only a little better off going to work than being on welfare but, by 1997, she was able to double her income by doing so.

Sawhill believes that it is too early to determine whether the welfare law's emphasis on reducing nonmarital and teen childbearing has had an effect, but she notes that employment rates have risen for young unmarried mothers. She concludes, "Work is, I would suggest, a great contraceptive."

Child Maltreatment and Foster Care

Opponents of the 1996 welfare reform law were concerned that some provisions, such as mandatory work, benefit sanctions, and time limits, would lead to more child maltreatment and an increase in foster care placements. Those provisions might, for example, lead some single mothers to leave welfare and live with a boyfriend who might become physically or sexually abusive, especially if he is not the biological father. Foster care placements might increase if mothers who lose their benefits have no income and no place to live.

In "Child Maltreatment and Foster Care" (chapter 8), Richard J. Gelles, a professor at the University of Pennsylvania School of Social Work, reports what is known about the incidence of child maltreatment and foster care placement rates since welfare reform. He relies on four major sources of data: *Current Trends in Child Abuse Reporting and Fatalities: Results of the 1998 Annual Fifty State Survey*, the National Child Abuse and Neglect Data System (NCANDS), the National Incidence Survey of Reported and Recognized Child Maltreatment (NIS), and the Voluntary Cooperative Information System (VCIS) (see box 1.5).

According to Gelles, many of the data sets contain incomplete and inaccurate data. Nevertheless, he says, collectively they "present a rough portrait of maltreated children and their placements." NCANDS data, for example, indicate an increase in the reported number of such children from 2.6 million in 1990 to nearly 2.8 million in 2000. But, the rate of *confirmed* child maltreatment peaked in 1993, rising from 13.4 per 1,000 children in 1990 to 15.3 per 1,000 children in 1993, and has since declined to 12.2 per 1,000 children in 2000 (up slightly from 11.8 per 1,000 children in 1999). The sharpest declines occurred in the two years after 1996. Gelles notes that the rate of victimization in 1999 was the lowest it has been since the NCANDS data collection began in 1990. The number of child fatalities, however, has remained roughly constant in recent years.

Box 1.5
Data on Child Maltreatment and Foster Care

Current Trends in Child Abuse Reporting and Fatalities: Results of the 1998 Annual Fifty State Survey is based on an annual national survey conducted by Prevent Child Abuse America (formerly the National Committee to Prevent Child Abuse), a private, nonprofit organization.

The **National Child Abuse and Neglect Data System (NCANDS)** is an annual survey of child abuse reporting and child abuse fatalities from states that voluntarily submit data to the HHS Office of Child Abuse and Neglect. (In 1998, all states submitted at least some data.)

The **National Incidence Survey of Reported and Recognized Child Maltreatment (NIS)**, conducted by HHS's Office of Child Abuse and Neglect, surveys more than 5,600 professionals who have contact with suspected cases of child maltreatment in a stratified sample of counties. It collects data on the incidence of child abuse and neglect and has detailed information on the characteristics of affected children. Surveys were conducted in 1979–1980, 1986, and 1993.

The **State Automated Child Welfare Information System (SACWIS)** is a federal effort that will collect aggregate and case-level data on children in out-of-home care.

The **Voluntary Cooperative Information System (VCIS)** is a voluntary survey of the states regarding the characteristics of children in foster care and adoptive care. It was conducted annually by the American Public Human Services Association (APHSA) from 1982 through 1995, when slightly more than half the states responded to the survey.

The **Adoption and Foster Care Analysis and Reporting System (AFCARS)**, which replaced the VCIS, is a federal effort that will eventually collect data from all the states on all children in foster care for whom the state child welfare agency has responsibility for placement, care, or supervision.

According to Gelles, foster care placements increased steadily throughout the 1990s. Researchers at the Urban Institute, however, attribute the growth in foster care since 1987 to factors independent of welfare reform.[9] One factor, for example, is the increasing reliance on "kinship care," a practice in which extended family members care for children when their parents are unable to do so and that is widely thought to increase caseloads.

On this basis, Gelles concludes that "no evidence indicates that welfare reform legislation has produced an increase or decrease in child maltreatment reports, child abuse and neglect fatalities, or the number of children placed in foster care." He is careful to qualify his conclusion, because of the limited and weak data available and because welfare reform may not really have an impact until after families begin reaching the federally imposed five-year time limit in 2001.

Housing Conditions and Homelessness

Another concern expressed by critics of welfare reform was that homelessness would increase—particularly among families that lost their welfare benefits as a result of a sanction or time limit. Even if families do not become homeless, it was feared that a decline in income might increase the risk that they live in substandard or over-crowded housing conditions or spend a larger share of their income on housing, at the expense of meeting other needs.

In "Housing Conditions and Homelessness" (chapter 9), John C. Weicher, Assistant Secretary for Housing/Federal Housing Administration Commissioner at the U.S. Department of Housing and Urban Development, discusses trends in homelessness and housing conditions. His main sources of data are the American Housing Survey (AHS) and special surveys on homelessness (see box 1.6). Because of the dearth of post-1996 data, he focuses on trends before welfare reform.

In regard to homelessness, Weicher explains that few reliable data are available, so that estimates of the total number of homeless people are problematic. He estimates that about 600,000 people are home-less in an average week, and that the estimate can vary over the

---

Box 1.6
Surveys on Housing and Homelessness

The **American Housing Survey (AHS)** is a survey of about 50,000 households conducted biennially by the Census Bureau for the U.S. Department of Housing and Urban Development. It provides information on the quality and quantity of the nation's housing stock as well as the socio-economic characteristics of household members. Topics include housing costs, the physical condition and age of units, available equipment (such as a heating system), residential mobility, neighborhood services, and needed improvements for all types of public and private housing in various locations.

Special surveys on homelessness. Most such surveys are limited in geographic scope and miss individuals not served by homeless programs.

course of a year. The most recent national data are for 1996 and serve as a baseline from which to observe trends. At present, virtually no evidence indicates that homelessness has increased (or decreased) since the passage of welfare reform.

Weicher addresses changes in housing conditions that might affect child well-being: adequacy, overcrowding, and affordability. Using data from the AHS, he finds that "by almost every objective measure, housing quality steadily improved through 1995 for virtually every identifiable demographic group of interest" since 1974.

Weicher reports that according to the AHS, in 1995, 2 percent of very low-income renter households (127,000) lived in housing with severe physical problems, down from 7 percent in 1978. Furthermore, Weicher points out, the incidence of overcrowding (defined as more than one person per room in a housing unit) was 8 percent (527,000) in 1995, down from 11 percent in 1978. Although housing quality seems to have improved steadily for low-income renters, Weicher notes that affordability has decreased. In 1995, 30 percent of low-income renters with children (1.9 million) paid more than half their incomes for rent (up from 28 percent in 1978).

Weicher notes that the apparent decline in affordability is not large (two percentage points between 1978 and 1995) and that there may be problems with the data. The data on affordability reveal a different trend from the data on quality and space. The increased rent burden may reflect improvements in housing quality, but even if so, low-income families may have little left over for other purchases after paying the rent.

Child Health

Welfare reform could affect the health of low-income children either positively or negatively. Employment that leads to higher incomes or better functioning families could result in better health by improving nutrition, housing, child care, and health-related behaviors. But lower incomes, greater stress on parents, or the loss of health insurance could be detrimental to children.

In "Child Health" (chapter 10), Lorraine V. Klerman, a professor at Brandeis University's Heller School for Social Policy and Management, describes the difficulty of measuring welfare reform's impact on children's physical and mental health by using existing data sources and suggests additional approaches to consider. She relies on the following data sources: the Behavior and Risk Factor Surveillance System (BRFSS); the CPS;[10] the Medical Expenditure Panel Survey (MEPS); the National Health Interview Survey (NHIS); the National Health and Nutritional Examination Survey (NHANES); the National Hospital Discharge Survey (NHDS); the National Household Survey of Drug Abuse (NHSDA); the National Immunization Survey; the State and Local Area Integrated Telephone Survey (SLAITS); the VSCP; and the Youth Risk Behavior Surveillance System (YRBSS) (see boxes 1.1, 1.4, 1.7, and 1.10).

Klerman believes that using current federal data sources to measure the impact of welfare reform on children's health will be difficult for several reasons. First, most children are relatively healthy, even though the health of low-income children is worse by almost every indicator than is the health of more well-to-do children. Thus, changes in health status, if they occur, will be difficult to detect, especially in the short term. On the other hand, changes in health insurance status, which can affect health care utilization and status, should be easier to detect.

Second, according to Klerman, each of the data sources she lists has deficiencies that make them of limited use in assessing the impact of welfare reform on child health. "[N]one are totally adequate to the task of assessing the impact of welfare reform" because, she explains, most do not have information on welfare status and some do not even have an indicator of economic status more generally. Moreover, most have relatively small samples of the population of interest—that is, low-income families—and suffer from low response rates (particularly among those most likely to have been affected by welfare reform). Also, state-level data are not usually available, but they are needed for any analysis, given the differences in implementation of welfare reform across states.

Measuring the impact of welfare reform on health, according to Klerman, would require data sets with the following characteristics: information on health before the implementation of reform to detect time changes; periodic data collection, again to show changes over time; oversampling of special populations, including the poor and minorities; state-level data; a good response rate; valid indicators of socioeconomic status, including past and present welfare status; and improved measures of child health. The traditional measures of child health status are deaths, illnesses, and injuries. Because these measures, with a few exceptions, such as asthma, are already on the decline, using them to measure the impact of welfare reform is diffi-

---

Box 1.7
Surveys on Children's Health

The **Behavior Risk Factor Surveillance System (BRFSS)** is a state-based system that collects information on the prevalence of risk behaviors among adults, some of which can influence child health. The system is operated by the National Center for Chronic Disease Prevention, Centers for Disease Control and Prevention (CDC).

The **Medical Expenditure Panel Survey (MEPS)** is a nationally representative survey of health care use, expenditures, sources of payment, and insurance coverage for the population. It surveys about 10,000 people or households over a 2.5-year period. The survey is co-sponsored by the Agency for Health Care Research and Quality (AHRQ) and the National Center for Health Statistics (NCHS).

The **National Health Interview Survey (NHIS)** is a continuing, nationwide survey of about 43,000 households that collects information about illnesses, injuries, chronic conditions, utilization of health care services, and other health topics. The survey is sponsored by NCHS and carried out by the Census Bureau. Topical modules are conducted periodically and cover subjects such as adult or child health-related behaviors.

The **National Health and Nutritional Examination Survey (NHANES)** collects data on about 34,000 people age two months and older. The data are based on surveys and direct physical examinations and cover a range of health conditions. The survey is designed by NCHS and conducted by the Census Bureau.

The **National Hospital Discharge Survey (NHDS)** is an annual survey of patients discharged from a selected sample of hospitals. The survey was designed by NCHS and is carried out with the assistance of the Census Bureau. It collects information on reasons for hospitalization but asks few questions about family characteristics. Moreover, unlike population-based surveys, it is a facility-based survey, so it captures only information on the health problems of health care users.

The **National Immunization Survey** collects data on the immunization coverage of more than 30,000 children ages nineteen to thirty-five months from across the United States. The survey is a collaborative effort between NCHS and the CDC and Prevention National Immunization Program.

The **State and Local Area Integrated Telephone Survey (SLAITS)** is a multipurpose survey developed by NCHS to collect information on health insurance coverage, access to care, health status, and utilization of services as well as welfare-related topics.

The **Youth Risk Behavior Surveillance System (YRBSS)** is a survey of about 16,000 students in grades nine to twelve in about 150 schools. It is conducted by the National Center for Chronic Disease Prevention with Westat, Inc., and Macro International. The survey monitors six areas of health-risk behaviors among youth, including those that contribute to unintentional and intentional injuries, tobacco use, alcohol and other drug use, unintended pregnancy and sexually transmitted diseases, unhealthy diets, and physical inactivity.

cult. New measures of physical and mental health functioning are needed to complement studies of health-related behaviors and medical care access or utilization.

Because no currently available national data set possesses all the desired characteristics, Klerman believes that information on the impact of welfare reform will be obtained largely from the independent studies of low-income and welfare families that are funded by the federal government, some states, and foundations. Many use a common set of child health and well-being measures developed with the help of Child Trends, Inc., which will allow comparisons across sites. Because the surveys focus on the welfare population, which is also a population at high risk for health problems, they are more likely than national studies to detect the impact of welfare reform on the physical and mental health of children and their parents. In addition, Klerman recommends expanding the NHIS to collect more data on children or administer new surveys that would be sensitive to the health problems of low-income children.

Nutrition, Food Security, and Obesity

If welfare reform results in less income to current and former recipients, they might compensate by cutting back on food, especially healthy foods (which tend to be more expensive). In addition, if program differences make it more difficult for eligible families to receive food stamps, the children may suffer. What have been the trends in food stamp receipt, hunger, nutrition, and related health outcomes since the passage of welfare reform?

In "Nutrition, Food Security, and Obesity" (chapter 11), Harold S. Beebout, a senior fellow at Mathematica Policy Research, Inc., and chief information officer at the Child and Family Services Agency, District of Columbia, reviews what is known about nutrition, food security, and obesity. He relies on the following data sources: the Continuing Survey of Food Intake for Individuals (CSFII), the CPS, the NHANES, and state administrative data reported to the U.S. Department of Agriculture (see boxes 1.1, 1.7, and 1.8).

Beebout first examines the forces behind the dramatic decline in food stamp rolls, which dropped by 9.1 million (35 percent) between August 1995 and July 2000. He describes how the welfare reform law (PRWORA) restricted eligibility, particularly for able-bodied adults who have no children and who work less than twenty hours per week. He adds that many legal immigrants were disquali-

---

Box 1.8
Surveys on Nutrition and Hunger

The **Continuing Survey of Food Intake for Individuals (CSFII)** is a survey of more than 15,000 people of all ages conducted periodically by the U.S. Department of Agriculture's Agricultural Research Service. The survey is intended to monitor the nutritional adequacy of American diets and includes information on dietary intake and participation in food programs. The survey was conducted in 1985–1986 (2 years), 1989–1991 (3 years), 1994–1996 (3 years), and 1999–2002 (3 years).

---

fied under the legislation as well. But, he notes, these changes explain only about 20 percent of the food stamp decline. Most of the decline occurred among households with children, many of which still appear to be eligible for benefits. He suggests two possibilities for the large impact on this group:

- Efforts to divert families from welfare have also caused them to leave the food stamp program, perhaps because families do not realize that they remain eligible.

- The relatively low benefit amounts for working families have discouraged many of them from applying for benefits.

Beebout concludes that if families know that they are eligible for the Food Stamp Program but choose not to participate, "current policies and program operations may be appropriate," but because participation rates vary substantially from state to state, he concludes that the data do "give rise to concern that some states are offering greater access to food assistance than others."

Beebout explores the question of whether welfare reform has affected food insecurity and hunger. He recognizes that the relationship between these measures and health status is uncertain. According to Beebout, "These food security measures have been criticized because they are based on the perceptions of respondents and thus have an unclear relationship to more objective measures of nutrition or health status." Nevertheless, he points out, "Between 1995 and 2001, no appreciable change occurred in these measures for low-income households or for households as a whole."

Beebout also describes troubling trends in overweight and obesity among adolescents in low-income families, calling it "a high-priority problem with serious long-term consequences." Low-income adolescents have double the rate of obesity than the rest of the adolescent population, making them vulnerable to diabetes, high blood pressure, and other health problems.

Beebout recommends additional research, including: (1) conducting case studies to determine how highly vulnerable families—those with little or no income—are faring; (2) examining why some states have high levels of food stamp participation for welfare leavers while others do not; (3) expanding state-level samples in surveys to measure child well-being at the state level; (4) examining how food insecurity relates to other measures of well-being; and (5) directing more attention to the dietary and health behaviors of children.

Crime and Juvenile Delinquency

Crime and violence have perhaps the most immediate impact on children, who are often the direct victims of street crime and indirect victims through effects on parents and relatives. Can the impact of welfare reform on crime be measured? If so, how?

In "Crime and Juvenile Delinquency" (chapter 12), Lawrence W. Sherman, a professor at the University of Pennsylvania's Department of Sociology, describes how changes in criminal and other dysfunctional behaviors could be measured. He relies on data from the National Crime Victimization Survey and the Uniform Crime Reporting System (see box 1.9). Sherman describes how criminal behavior tends to be concentrated in inner-city neighborhoods. He contends that "it is misleading to compare homicide rates across cities or to look at national homicide rates without disaggregating them by the factors that are most strongly correlated with their existence." Although individual characteristics, such as age, race, and income, are important, he notes that "the effects of those characteristics are magnified by location and space."

Sherman argues that if we want to understand the effects of welfare reform on a range of behaviors, including crime, data collection should focus on high-poverty areas—where such behaviors are concentrated. For example, the city of Baltimore has a homicide rate of about 40 per 100,000, or about forty times the rate for the rest of Maryland. Furthermore, most of those homicides occur in East Baltimore, where the homicide rate is probably about 200 to 300 per 100,000. Sherman laments that homicide rates are not reported to the FBI at the neighborhood level and emphasizes that those data should be collected to understand how our policies are working.

Box 1.9
Data on Crime

Juvenile Offenders and Victims: 1999 National Report, published by the Office of Juvenile Justice and Delinquency Prevention, uses FBI and other data sources to track changes in the rates of juvenile crime and of juveniles in correctional facilities.

The **National Crime Victimization Survey** is conducted twice annually by the Census Bureau for the Bureau of Justice Statistics. A nationally representative survey of the population, it focuses on collecting information on the characteristics of victims (age twelve or older) and offenders and the circumstances surrounding incidents of violence. Victims are interviewed twice each year for two years.

The **Uniform Crime Reporting System** is a compilation of crime statistics voluntarily reported to the FBI by police agencies. The main categories include murder-homicide, assault, robbery, rape, burglary, larceny-theft, motor vehicle theft, and arson. The data are standardized by the FBI and published in *Crime in the United States*.

According to Sherman, any assessment of welfare reform's impact on crime and other behaviors must "get below the national and city-level data and zero in on where the problems are most heavily concentrated." Indeed, he writes, "The goal of reporting 'national' rates of crime and arrests interferes with good measurement of problems in hard-to-serve populations." He explains, "Examining a subgroup organized by space and then by the demographic categories of age, gender, and race within those spatial areas would perhaps be the most informative way to investigate many kinds of questions."

Sherman recommends that data collection focus on "hot spots" and the measurement of problems among high-risk populations. Specifically, he recommends financial support for monthly data transfers for poverty areas and the creation of a monitoring system for a small number of poverty areas that would merge data from many sources, including data on crime, misconduct, welfare use, employment, educational achievement, pregnancy, and so on.

Drug Use

Drug use can hamper welfare reform efforts by making it more difficult for welfare recipients to go to work and leave welfare. Drug use can also interfere with effective parenting and adversely affect child well-being. What is known about the extent of drug use among welfare mothers and its impact on dependency?

In "Drug Use" (chapter 13), Peter Reuter, a professor at the University of Maryland School of Public Affairs and Department of Criminology, examines substance abuse and addiction among welfare and low-income mothers. His main data sources are the Arrestee Drug Abuse Monitoring (ADAM) program, the Drug Abuse Warning Network (DAWN), Monitoring the Future (MTF), and the NHSDA (see box 1.10).

Box 1.10
Data on Drug Use

The **Arrestee Drug Abuse Monitoring (ADAM)** program is an ongoing voluntary survey of randomly selected arrestees in thirty-five urban areas. The survey, which is conducted by the National Institute of Justice, collects information about the prevalence and types of drug use among arrestees and includes drug testing as part of the survey effort.

The **Drug Abuse Warning Network (DAWN)**, sponsored by the Substance Abuse and Mental Health Services Administration, is an ongoing national survey of hospitals (604 in 1997) that have a twenty-four-hour emergency department (ED). The survey collects information on the number of drug-related ED episodes and the specific drugs involved.

Monitoring the Future is an annual survey of about 50,000 eighth, tenth, and twelfth graders conducted by the Survey Research Center of the Institute for Social Research at the University of Michigan under the sponsorship of the National Institutes of Health (NIH). It collects information on students' behaviors, attitudes, and values.

The **National Household Survey on Drug Abuse (NHSDA)** is a nationally representative annual survey of about 70,000 individuals age twelve and older. Sponsored by NIH, it is designed to provide estimates of illicit drug use over time.

Reuter describes the changing patterns of drug use in the general population. He explains that drug use increased rapidly in the late 1970s, declined in the 1980s, and remained relatively flat in the 1990s. The patterns, however, are driven largely by changes in marijuana use. The pattern of frequent use of more dangerous drugs, such as cocaine, is somewhat different. The heavy use of cocaine—especially crack cocaine—peaked during the late 1980s. By the early 1990s, the number of new addicts had fallen dramatically, although not many heavy users discontinued their use. As a result, the stock of frequent users held constant through much of the 1990s and only recently began to decline as more users discontinued their use or died.

Reuter also explores the patterns of drug use among welfare families, before and after PRWORA. He observes that before PRWORA, a widespread perception existed that substance abuse was a major factor contributing to welfare dependency. He notes that one influential report asserted that 27 percent of AFDC mothers were substance abusers (including alcohol), three times the rate for mothers not receiving AFDC. But, other studies, including several that used the same data source, reported much lower levels of substance abuse, generally under 10 percent. The likely reason for the disparity in estimates is differences in definitions, with the highest estimate based on a broad definition that classified anyone who had used marijuana in the past month as a drug abuser or drug dependent.

Since the passage of PRWORA, Reuter explains, the focus of research has been on the role of drug use as a barrier to leaving welfare. The research suggests that the prevalence of drug use is even lower than suggested by earlier estimates, with both national and state data pointing to estimates that less than 5 percent of welfare recipients are drug dependent. Reuter concludes, "the weight of the very imperfect evidence is that abuse of illicit drugs affects only a modest share of welfare clients, even after the sharp declines post PRWORA." Nevertheless, he adds, "welfare participation provides an important venue for identifying and helping poor mothers with drug problems."

Mothers' Work and Child Care

Welfare reform could have its most immediate impact on child well-being through child care. If a mother works, someone needs to take care of her children. What is known about the utilization of child care and early childhood development programs and their impact on children?

In "Mothers' Work and Child Care" (chapter 14), Julia B. Isaacs, director of the Division of Data and Technical Analysis of the HHS Office of Planning, discusses the main data sources that HHS uses to measure the availability and quality of child care for low-income families: the CPS;[11] the SIPP;[12] the National Household Education Survey (NHES); the NSAF; state administrative data collected by the federal government that include aggregate numbers of children receiving subsidies as well as some of the characteristics of those subsidies, such as type of provider and age of child; and state leaver studies (see boxes 1.1, 1.2, 1.3, and 1.11).[13]

Box 1.11
Data on Child Care

The **National Household Education Survey (NHES)** is an annual survey of about 60,000 households sponsored by the National Center for Education Statistics (NCES). It includes information about "child care arrangements for children in third grade or below, including details about the language of the provider, sick child care, and distance between the care and home and job—data not found in other national surveys."

Isaacs describes the strengths and weakness of the child care data in the main national surveys. The SIPP provides information about child care utilization patterns and costs, but it is not released in a timely manner. For example, the child care data collected in the spring of 1997 were not published until the summer of 2002, too late to inform the welfare reform reauthorization debate. The CPS provides detailed information regarding the employment patterns of parents, but it does not provide direct information about child care arrangements. CPS data have been used by HHS to estimate the potential need for child care and child care subsidies. The NHES provides detailed information about child care for young children and about child care providers, but it does not collect detailed data on family income. Finally, the NSAF provides data on child care arrangements that can be linked to various measures of child well-being, but as Rossi observes, it is plagued by low response rates. Isaacs explains that an obvious advantage of all four data sources is that they provide nationally representative data; unfortunately, they provide limited information at the state and local level.

Isaacs then discusses federal and state administrative data that provide information on child care subsidized through various federal programs, primarily through the Child Care Development Fund (CCDF). In an average month in 2000, Isaacs writes, 1.75 million children up to age thirteen received subsidized child care. (Using the CPS data described above, she estimates that 9 to 10 million children were eligible for subsidies, which would rise to between 15 and 16 million children if all states set their income limits at the federal maximum of 85 percent of state median income.) She indicates that the data can provide information on the characteristics of children in child care and the setting of that care. A strength of the data is that they cover all children receiving subsidies, so small sample sizes are not a problem. But, the data can provide no information on unsubsidized child care or care provided by other state programs.

Isaacs also summarizes the findings from a series of HHS–funded leaver studies that examined child care utilization patterns and subsidy usage for families that left welfare. She reports that 41 to 65 percent of employed leavers who used nonparental child care relied on relatives and siblings as the primary providers, while just 8 to 36 percent relied on center-based care. Only about half of leavers reported paying for care, and only about 15 to 25 percent reported receiving a government subsidy. Isaacs explains that the low utilization of subsidized care may reflect the "heavy use of unpaid care, problems posed by applications procedures and administrative paperwork, and lack of knowledge of subsidy eligibility." She also cautions that the data should be viewed as suggestive, since some studies had low response rates and the studies generally did not focus on child care.

Isaacs concludes that the quality of child care data has improved in recent years but that "many unanswered questions" remain. Among the biggest challenges are obtaining good data on informal arrangements, the quality of child care settings, and representative state and local data.

Activities of the U.S. Department of Health and Human Services

As the above demonstrates, no single data source or study will answer the many questions surrounding the well-being of low-income children and their families that have arisen in the aftermath of welfare reform. The federal government—and HHS in particular—funds most of the surveys and data sources described in this volume. What role can HHS play in developing and maintaining a comprehensive data system and a policy-relevant research agenda?

In "Activities of the U.S. Department of Health and Human Services" (chapter 15), Don Winstead, HHS Deputy Assistant Secretary of Human Services Policy, and Ann McCormick, a social science analyst at HHS, describe HHS's efforts to improve existing data systems and create new ones to advance our understanding of "the condition of the low-income population before and after welfare reform." Their main sources of data are the SPD; the SIPP; and state-based administrative data on programs such as TANF, food stamps, and Medicaid (see boxes 1.1, 1.2, and 1.3).

Winstead and McCormick confirm the seriousness of the problems that the other authors raise about various national, state, and local data sets, such as attrition and the inability to capture "the new variation in programs across the country." They describe some of HHS's efforts to deal with those problems. For example, HHS is working with the Census Bureau to match Social Security records "with samples of adult welfare recipients and non-recipients from Census surveys to help assess employment and earnings patterns and outcomes on the basis of baseline characteristics." HHS is also examining several options to enhance longitudinal tracking capabilities with reliable state samples.

Winstead and McCormick also discuss the advantages and disadvantages of administrative data. On one hand, for example, administrative data presumably contain information on all program participants, a great advantage for studying subgroups and small geographic areas. In many states, administrative data are available for periods both before and after welfare reform, allowing researchers to examine how welfare reform may have led to various outcomes. On the other hand, administrative data may be inaccurate or incomplete; in addition, they often lack information on what happens after people leave the program. Winstead and McCormick explain that one promising approach for dealing with some of these problems is to link data across programs. For example, welfare records could be linked to unemployment insurance records, thereby permitting the tracking of mothers leaving welfare for work.

Winstead and McCormick note that President Bush's welfare reauthorization proposed improving the well-being of children as an overarching purpose of TANF. They describe several of the administration's efforts designed to improve program accountability, including the establishment of state-specific performance goals aimed at improving the well-being of children. To support these efforts, HHS would conduct research and provide technical assistance.

Conclusion

Two questions motivated much of the research after welfare reform: (1) How much of the caseload decline was due to welfare reform? and (2) How can researchers best determine the impact of welfare reform and monitor the well-being of low-income children and families? Collectively, the chapters in this volume examine these two important questions.

In the "Conclusion" (chapter 16), Douglas J. Besharov and Peter H. Rossi summarize the major findings of this volume. The main sources of data they discuss, besides the chapters in this volume, are the Current Population Survey (CPS), the Survey of Income and Program Participation (SIPP), the National Survey of America's Families (NSAF), the Survey of Program Dynamics (SPD), the Project on Devolution and Urban Change (UC), and the Child Impact Waiver Experiments (see boxes 1.1 and 1.3).

Besharov and Rossi conclude that little will be learned from existing research about the causes of the caseload decline and welfare reform's impact on family and child well-being. They explain that, except in rare instances, the design of nonexperimental studies (such as the NSAF, the SPD, and the UC) cannot credibly isolate the impact of welfare reform from other forces that may have influenced the caseload, such as the economy and expanded aid to the working poor. In addition, many of the studies have other weaknesses that further limit their usefulness, such as "unrepresentative samples, low response rates or high attrition rates, and limited external validity (that is, generalizability)." For example, the response rates of the SPD and the NSAF are so low that neither survey may be very useful—even for measuring the well-being of families and children. The UC project relies on sophisticated modeling that will be difficult to accomplish and, even if successful, will only detect very large impacts; its findings are likely to be suggestive, at best. And, although the Child Impact Waiver Experiments have a relatively strong research design, their findings are not generalizable beyond the states studied.

Nevertheless, argue Besharov and Rossi, even though it is too late to measure the impact of welfare reform overall, an overriding need exists to monitor the well-being of low-income families and children. "Society has a deep and abiding interest in how they are doing—regardless of the cause." For example, a sudden increase in homelessness among children, whether or not due to welfare reform, could signal a need for remedial action. (Such monitoring could also identify gaps in research.)

Besharov and Rossi also express concern about plans for new surveys to monitor child and family well-being. Besides the difficulties always encountered in developing new surveys, they argue, welfare reform's "real impact" may take a decade or more to fully materialize. Hence, monitoring efforts should be likewise long-term, which suggests using "well-established and on-going, national surveys" such as the CPS and the SIPP. They note, however, that these surveys may need to be strengthened. In regard to the CPS and the SIPP, for example, serious consideration should be given to expanding sample size, improving response rates, reducing underreporting, and enhancing their capacity for supporting longitudinal research. To examine outcomes not captured by the larger national surveys, Besharov and Rossi also recommend greater use of other specialized surveys and administrative data (as described in this volume's various chapters).

Randomized experiments could also be helpful in suggesting how welfare programs affect well-being. HHS is currently conducting four major, multi-year experiments on employment retention and advancement services, enhanced services for the hard-to-employ, rural welfare-to-work strategies, and efforts to build strong families. Besharov and Rossi believe that it would have been preferable to test the "major—and still problematic—aspects of TANF," such as mandatory work ("workfare") and time-limited benefits. But the decision has been made not to do so, and at this time no funding is available for additional large-scale experiments. Unfortunately, the funded is studies also do not provide a common set of services, so their findings cannot be compared or combined across sites. As a result, they "will lack sufficient generalizability to help identify welfare policies that enhance child and family well-being."

Besharov and Rossi conclude by warning that we should expect divergent research findings on a host of issues. Hence, any assessment of the well-being of children and families must be based on the analysis of multiple studies, with careful attention to each study's data and methodology. The limitations of some studies will be obvious, such as when comparisons are based on arbitrarily selected time frames. The defects of other studies will not be so clear, and resolving differences across studies may require a long and contentious debate. Besharov and Rossi would encourage discussion of competing analyses, so that researchers can learn from each other and policy analysts can learn how to better design programs. But this will not be an easy or short-term effort. "Persistence, open-mindedness, and a sharp eye will surely be needed. But disadvantaged children and families deserve no less."

Notes

1. U.S. Department of Health and Human Services, Administration for Children and Families, "Aid to Families with Dependent Children Caseload Data: Average Monthly Numbers for Fiscal and Calendar Years 1994," available from: http://www.acf.dhhs.gov/programs/opre/afdc/1994.xls, accessed November 13, 2002; and U.S. Department of Health and Human Services, Administration for Children and Families, "Temporary Assistance for Needy Families: Total Number of Families," in *ACF Data and Statistics*, 2001, available from: http://www.acf.dhhs.gov/news/stats/families.htm, accessed January 7, 2002.
2. Douglas J. Besharov, "Welfare Rolls: On the Rise Again," *Washington Post*, July 16, 2002. See also Elise Richer, Hedieh Rahmanou, and Mark Greenberg, *TANF Caseloads Declined in Most States in Second Quarter, But Most States Saw Increases over the Last Year* (Washington, D.C.: Center for Law and Social Policy, October 1, 2002), available from: http://www.clasp.org/DMS/Documents/1033487945.66/caseload_2002_Q2.pdf, accessed October 13, 2002.
3. Calculated from data presented in Rebecca A. London, "The Interaction Between Single Mothers' Living Arrangements and Welfare Participation," *Journal of Policy Analysis and Management* 19 (2000): 93–117; and personal communication from Rebecca London, April 5, 2000.
4. The 1992–1993 Survey of Income and Program Participation (SIPP) began with 50,000 households. The 1997 Survey of Program Dynamics (SPD) "bridge survey" was limited to the 38,000 households that completed all of their earlier SIPP interviews (about 73 percent of the original sample). The response rate to the bridge survey was 82 percent, yielding a sample of 30,125 interviewed households. As a result, the cumulative response rate at that point was just 59 percent. Budget constraints then forced the Census Bureau to reduce the sample to 18,500 in 1998. It then oversampled low-income households, using weights to attempt to maintain national representativeness. (This change does not affect the measured response rate.) The 1998 SPD suffered more attrition, resulting in a cumulative response rate of 50 percent. The response rate remained at 50 percent in 1999, as the Census Bureau made special efforts, including incentive payments, to bring some nonrespondents back into the sample. After the Census Bureau added a financial incentive, the response rates stopped dropping and stabilized at 50 percent.
5. These rates were achieved only after substantial additional efforts that may have introduced other methodological complications to the analysis.
6. In their response to Rossi, the Urban Institute researchers argue that comparisons with other surveys should be based on an alternative weighted response rate that is slightly higher (about 70 percent for the 1997 survey). But, even using this measure, the 1999 response rate fell to about 64 percent. See Kenneth Finegold and Fritz Scheuren, comments on "Ongoing Major Research on Welfare Reform: What Will Be Learned," by Peter H. Rossi, in *Family Well-Being after Welfare Reform*, edited by Douglas J. Besharov, 2002, available from: http://www.welfareacademy.org/pubs/familywellbeing/familywellbeing-ch3rossi.pdf, accessed November 22, 2002.
7. Special tabulations from the March 2000 Current Population Survey provided by Richard Bavier.
8. U.S. Census Bureau, "Unmarried-Couple Households, by Presence of Children: 1960 to Present," June 29, 2001, available from: http://www.census.gov/population/socdemo/hh-fam/tabUC-1.txt, accessed October 16, 2002.
9. Shelley Waters Boots and Rob Geen, *Family Care or Foster Care? How State Policies Affect Kinship Caregivers*, New Federalism: Issues and Options for States, A-34 (Washington, D.C.: Urban Institute, July 1999).

10.   The March supplement collects information on the health insurance coverage of the population.

11.   Although the survey does not collect information on child care, it does collect extensive information on the labor force participation of family members with children, which provides an indication of the need for child care.

12.   A special topical module collects information on child care utilization patterns and child care costs.

13.   Many leaver studies include questions about the patterns and costs of child care utilization.

References

Besharov, Douglas J. 2002. "Welfare Rolls: On the Rise Again." *Washington Post.* July 16.

Boots, Shelley Waters, and Rob Geen. 1999. *Family Care or Foster Care? How State Policies Affect Kinship Caregivers.* New Federalism: Issues and Options for States. A-34. Washington, D.C.: Urban Institute. July.

Finegold, Kenneth, and Fritz Scheuren. 2002. Comments on "Ongoing Major Research on Welfare Reform: What Will Be Learned," by Peter H. Rossi. In *Family Well-Being after Welfare Reform.* Edited by Douglas J. Besharov. Available from: http://www.welfareacademy.org/pubs/familywellbeing/familywellbeing-ch3rossi.pdf. Accessed November 22, 2002.

London, Rebecca A. 2000. "The Interaction Between Single Mothers' Living Arrangements and Welfare Participation." *Journal of Policy Analysis and Management* 19: 93–117.

Richer, Elise, Hedieh Rahmanou, and Mark Greenberg. 2002. *TANF Caseloads Declined in Most States in Second Quarter, But Most States Saw Increases over the Last Year.* Washington, D.C.: Center for Law and Social Policy. October 1. Available from: http://www.clasp.org/DMS/Documents/1033487945.66/caseload_2002_Q2.pdf. Accessed October 13, 2002.

U.S. Census Bureau. 2001. "Unmarried-Couple Households, by Presence of Children: 1960 to Present." June 29. Available from: http://www.census.gov/population/socdemo/hh-fam/tabUC-1.txt. Accessed October 16, 2002.

U.S. Department of Health and Human Services, Administration of Children and Families. "Aid to Families with Dependent Children Caseload Data: Average Monthly Numbers for Fiscal and Calendar Years 1994." Available from: http://www.acf.dhhs.gov/programs/opre/afdc/1994.xls. Accessed November 13, 2002.

———. 2001. "Temporary Assistance for Needy Families: Total Number of Families." In *ACF Data and Statistics.* Available from: http://www.acf.dhhs.gov/news/stats/families.htm. Accessed January 7, 2002.

2

Welfare Reform and the Caseload Decline

Douglas J. Besharov and Peter Germanis

Passage of the welfare reform law of 1996 abruptly reversed sixty years of federal welfare policy. The Temporary Assistance for Needy Families program (TANF) ended the legal entitlement to benefits, mandated that a large percentage of recipients work, and imposed a five-year time limit on the receipt of federally funded benefits. Since then, welfare caseloads have fallen sharply, and the percentage of single mothers working has risen dramatically. And despite the concerns of many—on the left and the right—there has not been a substantial increase in material hardship. In fact, for most single mothers, incomes have risen.

By June 2001, welfare rolls had fallen 59 percent from their historic high of 5.1 million families in March 1994.[1] That translates into about 9 million parents and children who are no longer forced to rely on welfare.[2] Beginning in July 2001, however, caseloads stopped declining and started rising, presumably because of the weakening economy. Nevertheless, at least as of June 2002, the national rise has been modest, although about ten states experienced caseload increases of from 10 to 20 percent in that year.[3]

It suited the purposes of both the Clinton administration and the Republican Congress, which had jointly passed the original bill in 1996, to claim that "welfare reform" caused this dramatic decline in welfare rolls—and that over two million former recipients are now working because of the new law. That claim is not quite true. The strong economy and massively increased aid to the working poor almost certainly had more impact on the plight of the poor than welfare reform per se. Moreover, as many as 40 percent of the mothers who left welfare are not working regularly but are instead relying on support from boyfriends, family members, friends, or other governmental and private programs.[4]

Both liberals and conservatives have found it convenient to ignore this reality: Conservatives, because it gives more credit to the "Clinton economy" and the former president's success in expanding aid to the working poor and less credit to Republican welfare reform; and liberals, because it suggests that many welfare recipients did not really "need" governmental benefits in the first place. But the failure to be clear about the reason for the decline in the welfare rolls not only prevents an accurate accounting of the law's impact but also fails to clarify what needs to be done in the next phases of welfare reform.

Welfare's Rise and Fall

For nearly sixty years, it seemed to most analysts that welfare rolls could only grow. With the exception of a few short-lived declines, the rolls grew from 147,000 families in 1936 to about five million in 1994—from less than 1 percent of all American families with children to about 15 percent (see figure 2.1).[5]

Between 1963 and 1973, caseloads increased by a striking 230 percent—not because of a bad economy (unemployment was actually quite low during most of this period) nor simply because of an increase in the breakdown of the family (both divorce and illegitimacy were rising, though not nearly as fast as caseloads) (see figure 2.1). Rather, the increase was largely the result of both programmatic changes that made it easier for income-eligible families to receive benefits and the destigmatization of being on welfare. Where welfare agencies once discouraged applicants by pressing them to seek other means of support or by imposing a grueling eligibility process, the obstacles to enrollment were now lowered. New York City's rolls more than doubled in eight years (from 1966 to 1973) under liberal mayor John Lindsay—rising 145 percent, from 101,233 to 247,915.[6] The same liberalization was taking place across the nation, as welfare came to be seen more as a right than as a temporary safety net. Some of the drive behind this national movement was undoubtedly the long overdue repeal of Jim Crow–like rules in the South that kept African-American mothers off welfare.

After this liberalization, caseloads stayed roughly steady for almost fifteen years. They rose again, by 34 percent, between 1989 and 1994, largely because of the weak economy. (In some places, the impact of the recession was particularly severe: In the two years preceding New Hampshire's 1992 presidential primary, the rolls in

Figure 2.1
Welfare's Growth and Decline, 1936–2002

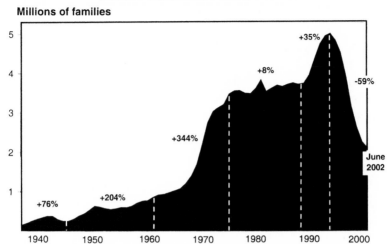

Sources: For 1936–1999, U.S. Department of Health and Human Services, Administration for Children and Families, "Temporary Assistance for Needy Families (TANF) 1936–1999," in *ACF Data and Statistics,* 2000, available from: http://www.acf.dhhs.gov/news/stats/ 3697.htm, accessed April 29, 2002; for 2000 and 2001, U.S. Department of Health and Human Services, Office of Planning, Research, and Evaluation, *Temporary Assistance for Needy Families Program (TANF): Fourth Annual Report to Congress* (Washington, D.C.: U.S. Department of Health and Human Services, April 2002), pp. II-13 and II-15, table 2:1a and table 2:1b, "TANF: Total Number of Families, Fiscal Year 2000," and "TANF: Total Number of Families, Fiscal Year 2001," available from: http://www.acf.dhhs.gov/programs/ opre/ar2001/chapter02.pdf, accessed May 23, 2002; and for 2002, Elise Richer, Hedieh Rahmanou, and Mark Greenberg, *TANF Caseloads Declined in Most States in Second Quarter, But Most States Saw Increases Over the Last Year* (Washington, D.C.: Center for Law and Social Policy, October 1, 2002), available from: http://www.clasp.org/DMS/Documents/ 1033487945.66/caseload_2002_Q2.pdf, accessed October 13, 2002.

that state rose by about 80 percent,[7] which perhaps helps to explain why welfare reform became such a prominent aspect of Bill Clinton's campaign that year.) But there were other important causes: a spike in out-of-wedlock births among some groups; an increase in immigrant applications for means-tested benefits, either for themselves or their American-born children; five years of outreach efforts to get single mothers to sign up for Medicaid (and, therefore, welfare benefits); and an increase in child-only cases, perhaps caused by the spread of crack addiction among mothers and by an increase in cases of parental disability.

Regardless of what caused rolls to rise in the past, they rarely fell back very far. Thus, no one predicted the huge reduction in the welfare rolls between March 1994 and July 2001. Twenty-three states have had declines of over 60 percent; two states have reported declines of 85 percent or more.[8]

Some of these reported declines, however, exaggerate the actual reductions in welfare dependency. Some declines, for example, involve shifting cases from federal welfare programs to state-only programs. In California, for example, most two-parent welfare families—about 50,000—were moved to a separate state program and are no longer counted as part of the overall welfare caseload. Thus, the state's reported caseload decline of 46 percent would be only 40 percent if the welfare cases transferred to its new program for two-parent families were counted.[9]

Another factor that artificially reduces caseloads is the increased use of "diversion payments" made before an applicant is actually placed on welfare. Some states use these payments to such an extent that they amount to a substitute for short periods on welfare. About half the states give lump-sum payments of up to about $2,000 (usually one time only) to help parents with temporary needs—instead of putting them on welfare.[10] In many states, these payments are designed to help a mother get or keep a job, but, in others, they are more similar to a short-term alternative to welfare. In Virginia, for example, welfare applicants may receive a cash payment equal to 120 days of assistance (about $1,200 for a family of three), which makes them ineligible for welfare for 160 days.

These payments can be an attractive alternative to regular welfare because recipients are not subject to work requirements, and the assistance usually does not count toward the time limit for benefits. They also make welfare rolls seem lower than they actually are. In the eight states that we surveyed, for example, diversion payments reduced the measured size of caseloads by about 1 to about 5 percent.[11]

These points, however, are minor quibbles. Indeed, almost everywhere, welfare rolls are way down, and work is way up. For example, never-married mothers—the group most prone to long-term welfare dependency—were 43 percent more likely to be working in 2001 than in 1994: 65 percent versus 46 percent.[12] But what is responsible for the decline in welfare and the increase in work?

The End of Welfare as We Knew It

In 1992, Barbara Sabol, then New York City's welfare commissioner, visited two of her own welfare offices dressed in a "sweatshirt, jeans, and scarf or wig." She told the welfare workers she needed a job in order to care for her children, but regardless of how hard she tried, she could not get the workers to help her find a job.[13]

The same year, candidate Bill Clinton showed that he was a New Democrat by ambiguously promising to "end welfare as we know it." After the election, his administration granted many waivers to states that, among other things, toughened work requirements and imposed partial time limits on benefits—measures that ultimately culminated in the Republican-inspired 1996 welfare reform law (TANF).[14]

Because the Republican bill bore a superficial resemblance to what Clinton proposed, both sides were able to claim credit for reforming welfare; however, the changes in welfare were largely based on the Republican plan. While both bills placed time limits on benefits, the Clinton proposal added an entitlement to a subsequent public job. The Republican bill, which had no such entitlement, also transformed the program into a capped block grant, which gave states an incentive to cut caseloads because they got to keep any unexpended funds.

Today, Sabol would find that welfare workers are eager to find jobs for their clients. Across the nation, the culture of welfare offices has changed, from places where mothers are signed up for benefits (with almost no questions asked) to places where they are helped, cajoled, and, yes, even pressured to get a job or rely on others for support. The U.S. General Accounting Office described the change this way: "Under states' welfare reform programs, participation requirements are being imposed sooner than under JOBS [the old welfare regime], with many states requiring participation in job search activities immediately upon application for assistance. Before reform, recipients could wait months—or even years—before being required to participate, and many never were required to participate because of the lack of sufficient services and staff."[15]

Many welfare offices are now "job centers," where workers help applicants and recipients find employment. Depending on the office, these centers can teach resume-writing and interviewing skills; provide access to word processors, fax machines, telephones, and even clothes; offer career counseling and financial-planning services; and refer individuals to employers who have specific job openings. In a survey of Texas welfare recipients who left rolls, over 60 percent said that the welfare agency "gave me the kind of help I needed."[16]

Some of this is boosterism, plain and simple, with welfare workers giving young mothers the moral support they often need. As one worker said, "Some of these women never thought that they could get a job. We give them the confidence to try." Nonetheless, the assistance also can be quite concrete. Besides large expansions in Medicaid and child care, many states provide cash assistance to families on welfare to help them leave or stay off the rolls. These payments range from a few hundred dollars to over $2,000. For example, Texas provides stipends to help such families pay for employment-related expenses such as transportation, education, and training.[17] Virginia gives transportation allowances for up to one year after an individual leaves welfare.[18] And about a dozen states have created or expanded Earned Income Tax Credit (EITC)–like tax credits that low-income families can use for any purpose.[19]

In a real break from the past, however, few welfare agencies seem to focus their efforts on job training. Administrative data from the states indicate that only about 5 percent of adult welfare recipients are in some sort of formal job-training program (including vocational programs).[20] Instead, agencies now emphasize immediate job placement and on-the-job work experience. Not only does this give much-needed work experience to mothers, it also adds to the pressure to leave welfare or not even apply for it in the first place.

Welfare reform also has a sharper edge, however. In most places, the application process for welfare has a new element: diversion. Diversion is a straightforward effort to keep families off welfare. It is encapsulated in two simple questions now asked of welfare applicants: Have you looked for a job? Can someone else support you? Many welfare agencies now maintain a bank of phones that applicants must use to call as many as twenty potential employers before they can even apply for benefits. When told of these requirements, many applicants simply walk out the door.

In New York City's job centers, for example, all applicants are encouraged to look for work (and are offered immediate cash support for child care) or to seek support from relatives or other sources. Those who still decide to apply for welfare are required to go through a thirty-day assessment period during which they complete the application process and undergo a rigorous job-readiness and job-search regimen involving many sessions at the job center and other offices. At the end of this period, eligible, able-bodied adults who choose to receive assistance are required to participate in the city's workfare program. New York City officials estimated that the percentage of mothers entering these job centers who eventually enrolled fell by

about 40 percent, from about one-half to about one-third of applicants.[21]

The Hassle Factor

Being on welfare has also changed, but not as much as many
people think. When Congress was considering welfare reform, most
analysts expected the states to institute large, mandatory work programs in order to satisfy the bill's "participation" requirements. However, because those requirements were established in relation to 1995
welfare caseloads,[22] the sharp decline in the rolls since then has
obviated the need for such programs—and few places beyond Ohio,
New Jersey, Wisconsin, and New York City have established them.

Instead, almost all states require recipients to sign "self-sufficiency
agreements" describing their plan for becoming self-sufficient within
a specified time frame. Iowa, for example, requires all able-bodied
recipients without infant children to develop and sign a Family Investment Agreement. Failure to sign or comply with this agreement
can result in immediate and complete termination of cash assistance.
In 1998, about 10 percent of those who began this process apparently had their benefits terminated for failure to sign or comply with
the agreement.[23]

In addition, most states now impose on recipients various behavior-
related rules (such as requiring parents to have their children immu-
nized from disease and to send them to school). In a few states,
mothers and fathers must attend parenting skills classes as a condition of receiving assistance. Failure to comply with these requirements may result in a reduction of benefits; in about thirty-seven
states, benefits may even be completely terminated.[24] Most states
begin with a partial reduction in benefits—generally, about one-third
of the welfare grant—as a tool to enforce compliance with program
requirements. When this is insufficient to ensure cooperation, however, an increasing number of states have resorted to full-family sanctions. (In seven states, continued non-compliance can result in a
lifetime ban on public assistance.)[25]

According to administrative data, in 2000, 6.3 percent (or 133,000)
of the 2.1 million families who left welfare did so after a sanction.[26]
In some states, the percentage was over 30 percent.[27] The national
data may understate the impact of sanctions, since in some states,
welfare recipients who are at risk of a long-term sanction may voluntarily close their cases so that they can reapply if they need to do

so later. On the other hand, some mothers apparently do not respond to a sanction notice after they get a job or decide to leave welfare.

These and other new requirements raise what economists would call the "cost" of being on welfare. By a rough calculation that assumes that recipients value their time at the minimum wage, these kinds of requirements can reduce the advantage of being on welfare versus working by about 50 percent. In very low-benefit states, the advantage can fall to zero.

This amounts to the reintroduction of one aspect of applying for welfare—hassle—and it clearly leads some welfare recipients to seek other ways of supporting themselves. When these new requirements are explained to them, applicants often say things such as, "I guess I might as well get a real job" or "I might as well move back home." Or they just walk out of the office—or stop responding to warnings that they will lose their benefits if they do not participate in work-related activities.

In the 1996 Texas survey of former recipients, about one-quarter of respondents said that important factors for leaving were either "unfriendly caseworkers" or "new program requirements."[28] And in a survey of those who left welfare in South Carolina between January and March of 1997, 60 percent said they felt hassled, and 13 percent said that is why they left.[29] About one-third said that the state's welfare program "wants to get rid of people, not help them."[30] A similar survey was conducted in Wisconsin for those who left welfare in 1998, and the results were about the same.[31] (Of course, hassle may have led others to leave welfare, though they may have cited some other reason, such as finding a job.)

These are dramatic changes in welfare, and it is natural to assume that they are responsible for recent caseload declines. However, welfare reform has coincided with the strongest economy in at least three decades, coupled with an unprecedented increase in aid to the working poor. The increased returns for low-skilled work are probably as responsible for the decline in welfare—perhaps more so.

Work Pays

"A rising tide lifts all boats," as President John F. Kennedy said.[32] Until the recent economy slowdown that started in 2000, the strong economy, most experts agree, played a key role in the caseload declines. In 1994, two years before the welfare law was enacted, the rolls had already started falling; this decline also occurred before the welfare waivers that allowed some states to "get tough" on welfare recipients could have much impact. The weak economic conditions that helped drive up welfare rolls during the presidency of George H. W. Bush ended a few months before he left office (not soon enough, of course, to affect the election). Between January 1993 and November 1999, the economic news was truly remarkable: Real per capita gross domestic product rose about 25 percent in real dollars, 20 million new jobs were created, the employment-to-population ratio (64.3 percent) was the highest ever, and the unemployment rate (4.1 percent) was at its lowest level since 1970.[33]

Most relevant to the welfare decline has been the increase in average real earnings, especially among low-wage workers. For example, since the second quarter of 1996, weekly earnings for full-time workers have grown 5.3 percent.[34] The gains for low-income, full-time workers have been even larger: 7.0 percent for those at the twenty-fifth percentile of earnings, and 8.5 percent for those at the tenth percentile of earnings.[35]

Also helping to reduce caseloads has been the progress in fulfilling Clinton's promise "to make work pay." Both Democratic and Republican Congresses have supported—to varying degrees—Clinton's initiatives for massive increases in governmental aid to low-income, working families with children. Spending on them now far exceeds what was spent on the old Aid to Families with Dependent Children (AFDC) program. Between 1993 and 1999 alone, a conservative estimate is that total aid to low-income, working families increased by nearly $40 billion a year, from about $33 billion to about $72 billion (in 2001 dollars).[36] At its height, combined federal and state spending on AFDC never exceeded $30 billion.

The EITC, for example, provides a cash subsidy to low-income working parents. Between 1993 and 1999, total expenditures on the EITC rose $12 billion, from $19 billion to $31 billion (in 2001 dollars). The increases for particular groups were striking: For example, the income supplement for a single mother (with two children) working at the minimum wage more than doubled, rising from about $1,700 to about $3,900 per year.

Child care aid has also expanded, becoming all but an entitlement for those families leaving welfare. Total annual federal and related state child care expenditures rose from $8 billion to over $15 billion (in 2001 dollars) in the same years, providing child care slots for well over 1 million additional children. Gaps in coverage remain, and take-up rates may be lower than the rates advocated by many experts (although the latter is probably because so many parents already have access to government-subsidized child care or have other family members who can care for their children). In any event, subsidized child care is obviously helping many low-skilled and low-earning mothers to be employed.

Medicaid eligibility, too, has been substantially expanded. While Medicaid was once limited primarily to families receiving welfare, sequential expansions for pregnant women and children (beginning in the mid-1980s) have taken eligibility to between 100 percent and 250 percent of the poverty line (depending on the child's age and the state program). The welfare reform law gave states the authority to expand coverage for adults, and some have done so. As a result, total Medicaid and related health care costs for low-income working families with children rose from $6 billion in 1993 to $26 billion in 1999 (in 2001 dollars)—making millions more children (and sometimes families) eligible. The absence of health care coverage is not an insuperable barrier to work for healthy mothers with healthy children, but for those mothers who live with chronic illnesses or care for sick children, the threat of losing coverage can be a substantial disincentive to leave welfare.

President Clinton also managed to push through the Republican-controlled Congress a two-stage increase in the minimum wage—from $4.25 an hour to $4.75 an hour on October 1, 1996, and then to the current $5.15 an hour on September 1, 1997.

Explaining the Decline

A number of respected researchers have used econometric models to estimate how much of the caseload decline was caused by welfare reform itself, compared with the economy and increased aid to low-income families.[37] The models they used, unfortunately, are extremely sensitive to the assumptions and variables incorporated, making their findings imprecise and variable. Looking across all the studies, and discounting the weakest ones, the most reasonable conclusion is that, although welfare reform was an important factor in reducing caseloads (accounting for 25 to 35 percent of the decline), the economy was probably more important (35 to 45 percent of the decline), and expanded aid to low-income, working families (primarily through the EITC) was almost as important as welfare reform (20 to 30 percent). (Some studies also find that the failure to increase welfare benefits, a twenty-five-year trend, reduced rolls another 5 to 10 percent.) (See box 2.1.)

Box 2.1 Explanations for Declining Welfare Caseloads 1994–1999	
Economy	35 to 45 percent
Aid to the working poor	20 to 30 percent
Minimum wage increases	0 to 5 percent
Welfare reform	25 to 35 percent
Erosion of benefits	5 to 10 percent

Placing too much confidence in the results of such econometric models is always questionable. These studies have many weaknesses, including the failure to include all policy changes, such as heightened child-support enforcement. Most also fail to consider partially independent demographic factors such as declines in out-of-wedlock births, drug abuse, crime, and immigration. Nevertheless, these studies were carefully conducted, and their results are roughly consistent. Therefore, it seems reasonable to conclude that these studies correctly reflect the approximate contribution of these four factors— the economy, aid to the working poor, minimum wage increases, and welfare reform—to the decline in caseloads.

It is possible that welfare reform has played a more substantial role by interacting with the strong economy and providing more generous aid to the working poor to encourage more single mothers to find jobs. By this way of thinking, the strong economy and more generous aid are necessary but not sufficient conditions for making the transition from welfare to work—with welfare reform providing the needed motivation for people to seek jobs or to enlist the support of others who have jobs. After all, we have had strong economies in the past without concomitant welfare declines; sometimes, welfare rolls have even risen. In other words, the impact of each of the factors may be greater than would otherwise be the case if each had occurred alone. For example, David Ellwood, professor at Harvard University's John F. Kennedy School of Government, comes to just this conclusion: "Administrative [welfare] changes interact with the economy and the availability of other benefits. States appear far more willing to sanction people or refuse them aid if jobs are perceived to be relatively plentiful."[38]

This appealing thought blurs the policy distinctions among welfare reform, aid to the working poor, and a strong economy. We would be happy if the caseload decline were a combined effect of the interaction among these factors, but even states that have not implemented "get tough" welfare reform have experienced large declines in welfare caseloads. Thus, unless there are giant spillover effects from one state to another, welfare reform, the economy, and aid to the working poor are independent and major forces drawing down caseloads. Even so, it is immensely fortunate for welfare recipients—and politicians—that all three came together at roughly the same time.

The results of randomized welfare experiments seem to confirm that the caseload decline is only partially due to welfare reform. Starting in earnest in 1992, states were granted waivers from the old AFDC rules, but only if they established rigorous, random-assignment experiments to measure the impact of their new policies. Many of these new policies bear a close resemblance to the program restrictions in new-style state welfare regimes, such as establishing tougher work requirements, placing time limits on benefits, and linking benefits to immunization and school attendance. The experiments also reflect many of the expansions in benefits that characterize welfare reform, such as liberalized earnings disregards (which allow working recipients to keep more of their benefits), resource limits, transitional benefits, and eligibility for two-parent families. About ten of these experiments have yielded findings that provide an indirect measure of welfare reform's impact on caseloads.

Across all ten of these waiver studies, and regardless of the varying combination of program components, the difference between the experimental and control groups is rarely more than a few percentage points. The biggest declines in welfare receipt due to welfare reform do not exceed fifteen percentage points or so, and often over two or three years. This does not mean that welfare reform's contribution to the decline is only 15 percent. We recognize that these randomized experiments are an imperfect measure of welfare reform's potential impact because they do not capture either its role in discouraging people from going on the rolls ("entry effects") or its broader impact on personal and agency behavior (partly through a change in community values).[39] The point is that no rigorously evaluated program of welfare reform has ever had an impact even remotely comparable to what has happened to national welfare caseloads.

Indeed, sometimes the group receiving the "reformed" welfare services was less likely to leave the rolls. This is due to the fact that most of the waiver experiments, like most state-implemented welfare reforms, include components that both decrease caseloads (such as work mandates) and increase them (such as the expansion of earnings disregards).[40] Thus, Minnesota's "welfare reform," which expanded the state's earnings disregard, asset limits, and two-parent eligibility for benefits, while imposing modest work requirements, increased caseloads by almost 5 percent for long-term recipients (after twenty-one months).[41]

Leaving Welfare without Working

In addition to the often unappreciated contribution of the economy and aid to the working poor, another significant aspect of the caseload decline is that so many mothers seem to be leaving welfare without taking jobs.

The best sources of data about families who have left welfare are surveys of former welfare recipients ("leaver studies")[42] that have been conducted by various states and by the Urban Institute.[43] Although all of these studies have some weaknesses, such as low response rates and insufficiently detailed information, the best studies tell almost the same story: Between 50 and 65 percent of those who have left welfare were employed at the time they were surveyed (and 60 to 85 percent had been employed at some point since leaving). Of those who were working, about 70 to 80 percent seemed to be working full-time, earning about $6 to $8 per hour (or about $900 to $1,300 per month) (see figure 2.2). The remainder worked fewer hours and thus earned less money. (Many studies, however, exclude the 20 to 30 percent of leaver families that have returned to welfare, which tends to minimize the difficulty that some mothers face in finding work.)

Broader measures of employment are consistent with this high level of non-work among leavers—and also suggest that many of the single mothers who did not go on welfare are also not working. For example, between March 1994 and March 2001, the number of employed single mothers with children under age eighteen increased by 1.1 million (from 5.712 million to 6.827 million).[44] During the same period, welfare caseloads (almost all of which include single mothers) fell by 3 million (from 5.098 million to 2.127 million). Even if the entire 1.1 million increase in the number of single mothers working in this period represented those who were previously on welfare (or who would have gone on welfare during that time),

Figure 2.2
What Are Welfare Leavers Doing? 1997–2000

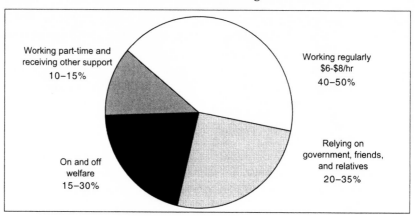

Source: Author's estimate based on Robert A. Moffitt, *From Welfare to Work: What the Evidence Shows*, Policy Brief no. 13 (Washington, D.C.: Brookings Institution, January 2002), p. 5, available from: http://www.brook.edu/wrb/publications/pb/pb13.pdf, accessed February 12, 2002; Gregory Acs and Pamela Loprest, *Final Synthesis Report of Findings from ASPE "Leavers" Grants* (Washington, D.C.: Urban Institute, November 27, 2001), available from: http://aspe.hhs.gov/hsp/leavers99/synthesis02/, accessed October 16, 2002; Christine Devere, *Welfare Reform Research: What Do We Know About Those Who Leave Welfare?* (Washington, D.C.: Congressional Research Service, March 2001); Julia B. Isaacs and Matthew R. Lyon, "A Cross-State Examination of Families Leaving Welfare: Findings from the ASPE–Funded Leaver Studies," paper presented at the National Association for Welfare Research and Statistics, Chicago, August 2000 (revised November 2000); and U.S. General Accounting Office, *Welfare Reform: Information on Former Recipient Status* (Washington, D.C.: Government Printing Office, April 1999).

this would still amount to only about one-third of the caseload decline.

Some mothers who have left welfare, of course, may not be reporting their employment. A four-city study conducted in the early 1990s by researchers Kathryn Edin, an associate professor in the University of Pennsylvania Department of Sociology and Population Studies Center, and Laura Lein, a senior lecturer at the University of Texas at Austin School of Social Work, found that about 30 percent of low-income working mothers and about 50 percent of welfare mothers did not report work.[45] But there is no reason that the percentage of individuals not reporting work should have grown in recent years. If anything, the expansions in earnings disregards and the EITC should have encouraged more low-income mothers to report their employment.

Thus, only about 50 to 60 percent of the mothers who have left welfare (and have stayed off) seem to be working regularly (with *regularly* defined as at least almost full-time for a long period of time, generally over six months). The surprisingly large number of individuals leaving without work has been all but ignored by most commentators, including severe critics of welfare reform. Yet this has profound implications for the economic and social conditions of low-income families.

Other Sources of Support

How could so many mothers have left welfare without working? Work requirements and heightened levels of hassle would be expected to cause mothers to leave welfare for work, even for relatively low-paying work. But why would mothers leave welfare without having jobs? The burdens placed on them hardly seem a sufficient reason for them to abandon the only means of support for themselves and their children.

The leaver studies suggest the answer: These mothers have other sources of support besides welfare. In South Carolina, for example, nonworking leavers were almost twice as likely as working leavers to have other sources of support—including other forms of governmental assistance, such as Social Security (13 percent versus 6 percent) or Supplemental Security Income (SSI) (20 percent versus 8 percent); free housing from a parent or relative (15 percent versus 10 percent); another adult in the home to help with the bills (17 percent versus 7 percent); or help from someone outside the home (22 percent versus 8 percent).[46] A study of former recipients in Milwaukee conducted by the Hudson Institute and Mathematica Policy Research, Inc., found that over two-thirds of all the mothers who left welfare received help (such as transportation assistance, a place to stay, or food) from family or friends. Those leavers who were not working were about 15 percent more likely to be receiving such help (72 percent versus 63 percent).[47]

Most leaver studies do not separately identify the sources of support for working and nonworking mothers, but they nevertheless reflect the importance of other household members or income sources. In Iowa, after families were dropped from welfare, they were about 33 percent more likely to be relying on others for a place to stay (25 percent versus 33 percent).[48] Similarly, in Florida, where families have begun to lose welfare benefits because of a time limit, one-third of those who hit the time limit either moved or had a different living arrangement, such as adding another household member to help with the expenses.[49] Finally, in Connecticut, 43 percent of the families who left welfare because of the state's twenty-one-month time limit reported living with at least one other adult, six months after the termination of benefits.[50] (No comparison data are available for the period before the time limit was imposed.)

When welfare reform was being debated in 1996, many experts predicted that as mothers were pushed off welfare, such "co-residency" or "doubling-up" arrangements would increase. So far, there has been no detectable increase in marriage rates, although, since 1994, cohabitation seems to be up by at least a third, or another 400,000 couples with children under fifteen.[51] Opinion, of course, is mixed about whether that is progress.

Mothers have another way to leave welfare without working: They can fall back on *preexisting* co-residency arrangements (together with other sources of support). On the basis of a study by Rebecca London, a research associate at the University of California, Santa Cruz, Center for Social Justice, Tolerance, and Community, which used data from the Survey of Income and Program Participation, we calculate that, in 1990, before the declines in welfare caseloads, at least 37 percent of welfare mothers lived with other adults: 18 percent with their parents, 6 percent with a boyfriend, and 13 percent with others.[52]

These findings may seem surprising, but for many years now, the welfare system has largely ignored household income in such co-residency arrangements. Depending on the situation, the income of the grandparents with whom a welfare mother was living would not be considered (for example, if the mother was an adult herself); and the man-in-the-house rule (which denied benefits to households with a cohabiting male) was abandoned years ago.[53]

When faced with the newly established work and behavioral requirements, it seems likely that mothers who had other sources of support sufficient to permit them to forgo welfare (predominantly those living in households with adequate economic resources) simply left welfare without looking for work. This would be nothing new. For example, in the Teenage Parent Demonstration, about 11 percent of the young mothers left welfare rather than comply with the program's requirements, explains Rebecca Maynard, a professor at the University of Pennsylvania Graduate School of Education, "primarily because they had other means of support and so left welfare rather than participate."[54]

As suggested by the leaver studies, it also helps that many of these mothers are still receiving other governmental benefits—primarily food stamps and housing assistance—which are often much more valuable than the basic welfare payment. (The continued availability of Medicaid also encourages mothers to leave welfare without finding work, even if the family does not sign up for coverage until someone takes ill.) On their own, nonworking mothers cannot subsist on only these benefits, but by living with others (or getting support from others) they can get by.

This is particularly the case in low-benefit states where it may simply no longer "pay" to be on welfare. In Alabama, for example, in 1999, the welfare benefit for a family of three was just $164 per month, compared with a food stamp allotment of $329. (Moreover, the food stamp benefit comes with virtually no strings attached, whereas cash assistance can be accompanied by work and other behavioral requirements that further reduce its value.) So mothers in low-benefit states can leave welfare and not suffer a complete loss of income, especially if there are other adults in the household with an income.

This makes economic sense. If one assumes that these mothers value their time at the minimum wage or above, then they have little incentive to engage in work activities for twenty to thirty hours per week to avoid a sanction that can be as little as $10 to $50 per week. The added income from complying with these requirements translates into an effective wage of fifty cents to two dollars per hour, which, for most, does not compensate for the lost free time (what economists call leisure) that mothers can use, for example, to care for their children or take a job with unreported income.

Both the economy and aid to the working poor could play roles here, as more households would *become* economically comfortable enough for the mother to leave welfare without working. This would be consistent with earlier patterns. Greg Duncan, a professor at Northwestern University's School of Education and Public Policy, and his colleagues used data from the Panel Study of Income Dynamics (PSID) to determine why mothers left welfare between 1986 and 1991.[55] ("Leaving welfare" was defined as receiving welfare in one year but not in the next year.) They found that about one-half of welfare exits were for work (or a rise in earnings); about one-quarter were due to changes in marital status or living arrangements; about 5 percent occurred because there were no longer children under eighteen living in the household; and the remainder were due to a variety of reasons, such as an increase in other transfer income or a change in the mother's state of residence. About one-third of the earnings-related exits involved an increase in the earnings of an adult *already* in the household other than the mother, thus demonstrating the importance of shared living arrangements.

In Iowa, for example, a survey of families conducted two to four months after their benefits had been terminated for a second time found that only one-third of sanctioned families reported a reduction in their household income (averaging $384 per month), despite the loss of their welfare check.[56] One-half of these families experienced an increase in household income (averaging $758 per month), nearly double their income before the sanction. The primary sources of this additional income were the former recipient's own earnings and an increase in the earnings of other household members—which is, as we have seen, an important alternate source of family support.

These dynamics also explain the behavior of those mothers whom Larry Mead, a professor at New York University's Department of Politics, calls the "happily sanctioned." Such mothers accept less in welfare benefits rather than choose to work or meet other behavioral requirements. In about fourteen states—which account for about half of the national welfare caseload—the sanction for non-compliance is only a partial reduction in benefits; that is, the family's grant is reduced by some percentage, usually representing the mother's share of the grant (about one-third of the welfare check). These mothers may not actually be happy, but since this reduction typically amounts to only one-sixth of their total benefit package, one can see why they willingly make the trade-off.

Assessing "Welfare Reform"

When congressional Republicans were pushing for the enactment of their welfare reform bill in 1996, opponents predicted widespread hardship—including sharp increases in homelessness and in the number of children living in poverty. Happily, no such catastrophe has followed welfare reform. There is no evidence that welfare reform has caused substantial increases in homelessness or in other indicators of extreme hardship, such as foster care placements or substantiated reports of child abuse and neglect. And despite extensive efforts, journalists have found few individual horror stories with which to document the harmful effects of welfare reform. As one administrator said, "We underestimated the ability [of welfare recipients] to get jobs that meet their basic needs—or to get support from other sources."[57]

For a while, it appeared that incomes of the poorest single mothers might be edging down—a sign that welfare reform might be squeezing those at the bottom. A widely disseminated study by Wendell Primus of the Center on Budget and Policy Priorities estimated that, from 1995 to 1997, the bottom quintile of single mothers had experienced an 8 percent drop in income. Even though many of these mothers were not welfare leavers (nor were they likely to have gone on assistance before welfare reform),[58] advocates latched onto this income decline as a sign that welfare reform should be reconsidered. However, after another year of data, Primus's further analysis has reduced the estimated income loss for this group to about 4 percent. In the same period—1995 to 1998—all the other quintiles of income for single mothers rose, with the middle quintile up 7 percent, from $20,617 to $22,063. In a more recent update, Richard Bavier of the United States Office of Management and Budget indicates that, "By 2000, even the bottom quintile had exceeded 1995 peaks."[59] (With the recession of 2001, the incomes of female heads fell back to where they were before the 1995 peak.)

But, if welfare reform has not been the social catastrophe that some predicted, neither has it lifted large numbers of female-headed families out of poverty. While some mothers left welfare for relatively higher paying jobs, others accepted lower paying jobs. Thanks to the EITC and other forms of aid, most of the mothers who left welfare and are now working have more income than they did when they were on welfare, but average earnings are only about $12,000 a year. And as we saw, many mothers simply left welfare without working. And unless these mothers lived with someone earning a great deal more, they probably suffered at least a partial loss of income.

Moreover, some of those who gained income through work may not be immediately better off, since they are also likely to have more expenses. Even if their child care costs are fully covered by public subsidy or family members, mothers leaving welfare still face other work-related expenses, such as transportation and clothing; and by working, they lose the ability to earn additional money off the books.

Thus, their higher incomes come at the price of having to work many hours a week while also raising their children, often on their own.

The data that underlie the foregoing conclusions have many weaknesses. For example, it is difficult to find and count the number of homeless families and individuals, much less to get detailed information on their characteristics. Data on substantiated cases of child maltreatment, for example, are a function of the number of reports received, the ability of the system to investigate them, and the willingness of states to report them. Even the much-cited income data used to measure trends in financial well-being are plagued by numerous problems. Perhaps most significantly, reported welfare receipt in the Current Population Survey (CPS) is over one-third lower than that indicated by administrative records. These surveys also miss much of the income that is earned working off the books or is received from boyfriends or other household members. (Recipients may want to conceal this income from those administering the survey, for fear that it could affect their welfare eligibility.)

This mixed picture of life after welfare is captured in the before-and-after questions asked in some of the more reliable leaver studies (Mississippi, New Mexico, South Carolina, Virginia, Washington, and Wisconsin).[60] Depending on the study, between 20 and 40 percent of those responding said that life was better while they were on welfare. Conversely, 60 to 80 percent of former recipients said that life is the same or better since they have been off welfare. (Three states asked leavers separately about being better off.[61] In all three, about 55 percent said that they were better off, about 25 percent said that they were doing the same, and about 20 percent said that they were worse off.)

What should we make of these patterns? First, reducing welfare rolls is a tremendous and unprecedented achievement, especially given the apparently small amount of additional hardship. If this result had been guaranteed when welfare reform was being debated in 1996, most opposition would surely have melted away. Indeed, even some past opponents of welfare reform have been quieted by its apparent early success. Nevertheless, the reduction in welfare rolls is not entirely due to welfare reform itself; a robust economy and unprecedented increases in aid to low-income, working families are also responsible for the decline. Many of the mothers who gained ground after leaving welfare can probably thank the latter two factors for their improved situation, and many of those who lost ground probably left assistance because of welfare reform and the added hassle associated with it.

What about those mothers who are now working but not making much more than their previous welfare benefits, or those who are now relying on the support of others rather than on welfare? Robert Haveman, professor at the University of Wisconsin–Madison Department of Economics, says that these mothers are "treading water, but staying afloat."[62]

For most Americans, welfare reform was not just about reducing the rolls; nor was it some silver bullet that would immediately eradicate poverty. Instead, it was about reducing the deep-seated social and personal dysfunctions associated with long-term dependency, thereby ultimately reducing poverty. The success of welfare reform on this measure will depend on whether the low-paying jobs taken by many leavers lead to better jobs, whether the household arrangements (and other sources of support) that have allowed mothers to leave welfare without working prove supportive and nurturing, and whether the eventual result is less dysfunctional behavior among parents and better outcomes for children. We may need a generation to find out.

In the meantime, real challenges to welfare reform are looming. The easy, early reduction in welfare rolls not only has lulled policymakers and the public into complacency but also has obscured what still needs to be done to complete the task of welfare reform. As we have seen, only part of the caseload decline can be attributed to welfare reform. No one knows what will be the full impact of a sustained economic downturn. Moreover, the single mothers who have already left welfare are predominantly those with the best earning potential—or those with the best sources of outside support. The single mothers who currently remain on welfare do not have nearly the same choices (or opportunities). Many will require increased public and private assistance to leave welfare—and many will be unable to do so.

For the latter, some kind of long-term support will undoubtedly be needed, and yet these are the very families against whom the federal time limit on benefits will fall most heavily. And for them, it seems clear that new approaches that deal with personal problems and weaknesses will be required. Government-run programs are unlikely to provide the mix of support, discipline, and inspiration that is needed, and it is here that we expect welfare agencies to turn increasingly to the agents of civil society, including faith-based programs.

Little work is being done to prepare for either of these eventualities. And yet, mishandled, either one could undermine continued public support for work-oriented welfare policies. Making the needed adjustments will require ingenuity, resources, and time to build experience and political support. But the process cannot begin without policymakers being clear-minded about what welfare reform has and has not accomplished thus far.

Notes

1. U.S. Department of Health and Human Services, Administration for Children and Families, "March 1994," in *Aid to Families with Dependent Children Caseload Data*, 2001, available from: http://www.acf.dhhs.gov/programs/opre/afdc/1994.xls, accessed January 7, 2002; and U.S. Department of Health and Human Services, Administration for Children and Families, "Temporary Assistance for Needy Families: Total Number of Families," in *ACF Data and Statistics,* 2001, available from: http://www.acf.dhhs.gov/news/stats/families.htm, accessed October 22, 2002.

2. U.S. Department of Health and Human Services, Administration for Children and Families, 2001, "March 1994"; and U.S. Department of Health and Human Services, Administration for Children and Families, "Temporary Assistance for Needy Families: Total Number of Recipients," in *ACF Statistics,* 2001, available from: http://www.acf.dhhs.gov/news/stats/recipients.htm, accessed January 7, 2002.

3. Elise Richer, Hedieh Rahmanou, and Mark Greenberg, *TANF Caseloads Declined in Most States in Second Quarter, But Most States Saw Increases over the Last Year* (Washington, D.C.: Center for Law and Social Policy, October 2002), available from: http://www.clasp.org/DMS/Documents/1033487945.66/caseload_2002_Q2.pdf, accessed October 13, 2002.

4. Authors' estimate based on Gregory Acs and Pamela Loprest, *Final Synthesis Report of Findings from ASPE "Leavers" Grants* (Washington, D.C.: Urban Institute, November 27, 2001), available from: http://www.aspe.hhs.gov/hsp/leavers99/synthesis02/#HI, accessed October 16, 2002; Christine Devere, *Welfare Reform Research: What Do We Know About Those Who Leave Welfare?* (Washington, D.C.: Congressional Research Service, March 2001); Gregory Acs and Pamela Loprest, *Initial Synthesis Report of the Findings from ASPE's "Leavers" Grants* (Washington, D.C.: Urban Institute, January 2001); Julia B. Isaacs and Matthew R. Lyon, "A Cross-State Examination of Families Leaving Welfare: Findings from the ASPE–Funded Leaver Studies," paper presented at the National Association for Welfare Research and Statistics 40th Annual Workshop, Phoenix, Ariz., August 2000, revised November 2000; and U.S. General Accounting Office, *Welfare Reform: Information on Former Recipient Status* (Washington, D.C.: Government Printing Office, April 1999).

5. U.S. Department of Health and Human Services, Administration for Children and Families, "Temporary Assistance for Needy Families (TANF): 1936–1999," in *ACF Data and Statistics,* 2000, available from: http://www.acf.dhhs.gov/news/stats/3697.htm, accessed December 30, 2001.

6. New York City Human Resources Administration, Office of Program Reporting, Analysis, and Accountability, unpublished data, April 3, 2002; and U.S. Depart-

ment of Health and Human Services, Administration for Children and Families, "Temporary Assistance for Needy Families: 1936–2000," available from: http:// www.acf.dhhs.gov/news/stats/3697.htm, accessed January 7, 2002.

7.   U.S. Department of Health and Human Services, Administration for Children and Families, "1990," in *Aid to Families with Dependent Children Caseload Data*, 2001, available from: http://www.acf.dhhs.gov/programs/opre/afdc/1990.xls, accessed October 22, 2002; U.S. Department of Health and Human Services, Administration for Children and Families, "1991," in *Aid to Families with Dependent Children Caseload Data*, 2001, available from: http://www.acf.dhhs.gov/programs/ opre/afdc/1991.xls, accessed October 22, 2002; and U.S. Department of Health and Human Services, Administration for Children and Families, "1992," in *Aid to Families with Dependent Children Caseload Data*, 2001, available from: http:// www.acf.dhhs.gov/programs/opre/afdc/1992.xls, accessed October 22, 2002.

8.   Authors' calculations based on U.S. Department of Health and Human Services, Administration for Children and Families, *March 1994*, 2001; and U.S. Department of Health and Human Services, Administration for Children and Families, "TANF: Average Monthly Number of Families Fiscal Year 2001," in *ACF Data and Statistics*, 2002, available from: http://www.acf.dhhs.gov/news/stats/ familiesL.htm, accessed October 24, 2002.

9.   Authors' calculation from data collected by the State of California and the U.S. Department of Health and Human Services, Administration for Children and Families, "September, 2000" in *Aid to Families with Dependent Children Caseload Data*, 2001, available from: http://www.acf.dhhs.gov/programs/opre/afdc/2000.xls, accessed October 22, 2002.

10.   Kathleen Maloy, LaDonna Pavetti, Peter Shin, Julie Darnell, and Lea Scarpulla-Nolan, *A Description and Assessment of State Approaches to Diversion Programs and Activities under Welfare Reform* (Washington, D.C.: Center for Health Policy Research at the George Washington University Medical Center, 1998).

11.   Authors' calculations based on a 1999 telephone survey of the following states: Arizona, Arkansas, Colorado, Florida, Iowa, Texas, Utah, and Virginia.

12.   Bureau of Labor Statistics, table 15. "Presence and Age of Own Children of Civilian Women 16 Years and Over, by Employment Status and Marital Status," various years, unpublished data.

13.   Telephone interview by Douglas Besharov with Barbara Sabol, March 24, 2000; *see also* Alison Mitchell, "Posing as Welfare Recipient, Agency Head Finds Indignity," *New York Times*, February 5, 1993.

14.   The Personal Responsibility and Work Opportunity Reconciliation Act of 1996 (PRWORA) replaced the Aid to Families with Dependent Children (AFDC) program with the Temporary Assistance for Needy Families (TANF) program.

15.   U.S. General Accounting Office, *States Are Restructuring Programs to Reduce Welfare Dependence* (Washington, D.C.: Government Printing Office, June 1998), p. 38.

16.   Carol Nemir, Richard Sanders, and Don Warren, *Why People Leave Welfare: Reasons Former Clients Give for the Decline in Welfare Caseloads in Texas*, Legislative Council Research Division Issue Brief (Austin, Tex.: Texas Legislative Council, 1997), p. 5.

17.   Eileen Sweeney, Liz Schott, Ed Lazere, Shawn Fremstad, Heide Goldberg, Jocelyn Guyer, David Super, and Clifford Johnson, *Windows of Opportunity: Strategies to Support Families Receiving Welfare and Other Low-Income Families in the Next Stage of Welfare Reform* (Washington, D.C.: Center on Budget and Policy Priorities, January 2000), p. 8.

18.   Ibid., p. 11.

19.   Ibid., p. 9.
20.   U.S. Department of Health and Human Services, Office of Planning, Research, and Evaluation, *Temporary Assistance for Needy Families (TANF) Program: Fourth Annual Report to Congress* (Washington, D.C.: U.S. Department of Health and Human Services, April 2002), III-100, available from: http://www.acf.dhhs.gov/programs/opre/ar2001/indexar.htm, accessed October 13, 2002.
21.   Personal communication from Andrew Bush, former deputy administrator of New York City's Human Resources Administration, May 17, 2000.
22.   The requirements include a caseload reduction credit, which provides for a reduction in the participation rate based on the percentage decline in caseloads since 1995. (In fact, forty-three states faced an "adjusted" participation rate of 10 percent or less in 2000—compared with a statutory rate of 40 percent—and thirty-one states had caseload declines so large that they did not have to place anyone in a work activity.)
23.   Authors' calculation from data submitted by Ann Wiebers, welfare reform waiver coordinator for the Iowa Department of Human Services, Division of Economic Assistance, to Peter Germanis, November 1998.
24.   U.S. General Accounting Office, *State Sanction Policies and Number of Families Affected* (Washington, D.C.: Government Printing Office, March 2000), p. 17.
25.   Ibid.
26.   U.S. Department of Health and Human Services, Office of Planning, Research, and Evaluation, p. X-244.
27.   Ibid.
28.   Nemir et al., 1997, p. 4.
29.   South Carolina Department of Social Services, Division of Program Quality Assurance, *Survey of Former Family Independence Program Clients: Cases Closed during January through March 1997* (Columbia, S.C.: South Carolina Department of Social Services, 1997), p. 6.
30.   Ibid., p. 16.
31.   State of Wisconsin, Department of Workforce Development, *Survey of Those Leaving AFDC or W-2 January to March 1998, Preliminary Report* (Madison, Wisc.: Department of Workforce Development, 1998).
32.   John F. Kennedy, *Public Papers of the Presidents of the United States: John F. Kennedy, January 1 to December 31, 1962* (Washington, D.C.: Government Printing Office, 1962), p. 626.
33.   Council of Economic Advisers and the Office of the Chief Economist, *Twenty Million Jobs: January 1993–November 1999* (Washington, D.C.: Council of Economic Advisers, December 1999), pp. 1 and 3.
34.   Ibid., p. 6.
35.   Ibid.
36.   See also Congressional Budget Office, *Policy Changes Affecting Mandatory Spending for Low-Income Families Not Receiving Cash Welfare* (Washington, D.C.: Congressional Budget Office, September 1998). The Congressional Budget Office (CBO) studied the growth in federal spending due to policy changes (for example, holding the effects of other factors, such as population growth and unemployment, constant) of five programs: Medicaid, SCHIP (State Children's Health Insurance Program), the EITC, the portion of the child credit for low-income families, and child care. Adding state spending and converting the estimate to 2001 dollars results in an estimated $58 billion increase in spending between 1984 and 1999 due solely to policy changes. About half of this increase occurred since 1993.
37.   Council of Economic Advisers, *The Effects of Welfare Policy and the Economic Expansion on Welfare Caseloads: An Update* (Washington, D.C.: Government Printing Office, August 1999); Robert A. Moffitt, *The Effect of Pre–PRWORA*

Waivers on AFDC Caseloads and Female Earnings, Income, and Labor Force Participation (Baltimore, Md.: Johns Hopkins University, 1999); David Figlio and James Ziliak, "Welfare Reform, the Business Cycle, and the Decline in AFDC Caseloads," paper presented at the Joint Center for Poverty Research Conference "Welfare Reform and the Macroeconomy," Washington, D.C., November 1998; Geoffrey Wallace and Rebecca Blank, "What Goes Up Must Come Down? Explaining Recent Changes in Public Assistance Caseloads," paper presented at the Joint Center for Poverty Research Conference "Welfare Reform and the Macroeconomy," Washington, D.C., November 1998; Marianne Page, Joanne Spetz, and Jane Millar, *Does the Minimum Wage Affect Welfare Caseloads?* (San Francisco: Public Policy Institute of California, June 1998); Alberto Martini and Michael Wiseman, *Explaining the Recent Decline in Welfare Caseloads: Is the Council of Economic Advisers Right?* (Washington, D.C.: Urban Institute, 1997); Council of Economic Advisers, *Explaining the Decline in Welfare Receipt, 1993–1996* (Washington, D.C.: Government Printing Office, May 1997); and Stacy Dickert, Scott Houser, and John Scholz, "The Earned Income Tax Credit and Transfer Programs: A Study of Labor Market and Program Participation," *Tax Policy and the Economy* 9 (1995): 1–50.

38.   David T. Ellwood, *The Impact of the Earned Income Tax Credit and Social Policy Reforms on Work, Marriage, and Living Arrangements* (Cambridge, Mass.: John F. Kennedy School of Government, Harvard University, November 1999), p. 12.

39.   Normally, program impacts are measured in terms of the difference in average outcomes between the experimental and the control groups. A properly planned and implemented randomized experiment should result in experimental and control groups that have comparable characteristics and that are exposed to the same outside forces, such as economic conditions and social environments. The purpose of the randomization is to exclude the influence of all outside factors, so that any subsequent differences in outcomes between the two groups can be attributed to the prescribed intervention. That means that, in a time of general caseload declines, both experimental and control groups will see rapid declines in welfare receipt. The impact of welfare reform is the total decline in the experimental group minus the control group.

Consider Florida's Family Transition Program (FTP), which was rigorously evaluated in one county: Welfare receipt fell by 75 percent among those in the FTP group three years after enrolling in the program (Dan Bloom, Mary Farrell, James Kemple, and Nandita Verma, *The Family Transition Program: Implementation and Three-Year Impacts of Florida's Initial Time-Limited Welfare Program* [New York: Manpower Demonstration Research Corporation, April 1999], p. 163). But, because it also fell by 60 percent for those in the control group, the experimental-control difference of fifteen percentage points represents the impact of Florida's welfare reform. (Conversely, if the caseload had fallen faster in the control group than in the experimental group, this would suggest that welfare reform had a caseload-increasing impact.)

This estimate is not directly comparable to the caseload decline in the county where the program was tested, because the overall caseload is affected by a constant flow of entries and exits, whereas the caseload changes reported above are for a cohort entering the program about three years earlier. Thus, the caseload can only decline, because no new people are added. Nevertheless, the findings are suggestive of the impact on the overall caseload.

40.   The expansion of earnings disregards allows recipients to keep a larger portion of their earnings without losing benefits. (In seventeen states, for example, a family of three can earn over $12,000 a year and still retain at least some benefits.) Although

a disregard encourages some mothers to start working, it encourages others to stay on welfare while also working. Thus, a generous disregard probably increases caseloads by as much as 10 or 15 percent. (Some would argue that earnings disregards also build self-confidence about working by allowing mothers to combine work and welfare.)

41.   Cynthia Miller, Virginia Knox, Patricia Auspos, Jo Anna Hunter-Manns, and Alan Orenstein, *Making Welfare Work and Work Pay: Implementation and Eighteen-Month Impacts of the Minnesota Family Investment Program* (New York: Manpower Demonstration Research Corporation, October 1997).

42.   Although the caseload decline may also be influenced by fewer entrants, the data to assess these numbers and the reasons for non-entry are not available. Thus, we rely on the leaver studies as a proxy for assessing what is happening as a result of the broader caseload decline.

43.   Acs and Loprest, *Final Synthesis*, 2001; Devere, 2001; Acs and Loprest, *Initial Synthesis*, 2001; Isaacs and Lyon, 2000; and U.S. General Accounting Office, 1999.

44.   Bureau of Labor Statistics, unpublished data, various years.

45.   Kathryn Edin and Laura Lein, *Making Ends Meet: How Single Mothers Survive Welfare and Low-Wage Work* (New York: Russell Sage Foundation, 1997), pp. 150–151.

46.   South Carolina Department of Social Services, Office of Program Reform, Evaluation, and Research, *Comparison Between Working and Non-Working Clients Whose Cases Were Closed Between January and March 1997* (Columbia, S.C.: South Carolina Department of Social Services, March 1998), p. 7.

47.   Rebecca Swartz, Jacqueline Kauff, Lucia Nixon, Tom Fraker, Jay Hein, and Susan Mitchell, *Converting to Wisconsin Works: Where Did Families Go When AFDC Ended in Milwaukee?* (Madison, Wisc.: Hudson Institute and Mathematica Policy Research, Inc., 1999), p. 66.

48.   Lucia Nixon, Jaqueline Kauff, and Jan Losby, *Second Assignments to Iowa's Limited Benefit Plan* (Washington, D.C.: Mathematica Policy Research, Inc., August 1999), table C.20, "Housing Moves and Homelessness."

49.   Dan Bloom, Mary Farrell, James Kemple, and Nandita Verma, *The Family Transition Program: Implementation and Three-Year Impacts of Florida's Initial Time-Limited Welfare Program* (New York: Manpower Demonstration Research Corporation, April 1999), p. 94.

50.   Jo Anna Hunter-Manns and Dan Bloom, *Connecticut Post–Time Limit Tracking Study: Six-Month Survey Results* (New York: Manpower Demonstration Research Corporation, January 1999), p. 8.

51.   Between 1994 and 2000, the number of unmarried couples with children under fifteen increased from 1.270 million to 1.675 million. See U.S. Census Bureau, *Families and Living Arrangements: Historical Time Series* (Washington, D.C.: U.S. Census Bureau, June 2001), table UC-1, "Unmarried-Couple Households, by Presence of Children: 1960 to Present," available from: http://www.census.gov/population/socdemo/hh-fam/tabUC-1.txt, accessed October 16, 2002.

52.   Rebecca London, "The Interaction Between Single Mothers' Living Arrangements and Welfare Participation," *Journal of Policy Analysis and Management* 19 (1) (2000): 93–117; and personal communication from Rebecca London, April 5, 2000.

53.   Under the old Aid to Families with Dependent Children (AFDC) program, the income of stepparents (and the parents of minor parents) was generally counted toward the income of an AFDC family, after allowing for three deductions: the first $90 of earned income; the amount of the state's "need standard" for the stepparent (or grandparent) and other dependents who were not in the AFDC unit; and the

amount paid by the stepparent (or grandparent) to other legal dependents outside the home (for example, for child support or alimony). This could result in the reduction of assistance or even ineligibility in some cases. A number of states received waivers to increase these income disregards, thus expanding eligibility and benefits for those with such living arrangements.

In the early years of AFDC, many states denied benefits to mothers who cohabited with a man. The Supreme Court struck down the so-called "man-in-the-house" rule in 1968, and the income of the cohabitor was generally not counted, unless there was evidence of an explicit contribution from the man to the mother for the support of her family. (If the cohabiting male was the biological father of at least one of the mother's children, the family could be considered only for the AFDC–Unemployed Parent program).

54. Rebecca A. Maynard, "Paternalism, Teenage Pregnancy Prevention, and Teenage Parent Services," in *The New Paternalism: Supervisory Approaches to Poverty,* edited by Lawrence Mead (Washington, D.C.: Brookings Institution Press, 1997), p. 28.

55. U.S. Department of Health and Human Services, Office of Assistant Secretary for Planning and Evaluation, *Indicators of Welfare Dependence: Annual Report to Congress* (Washington, D.C.: Government Printing Office, October 1998), table 8b, "Percentage of First AFDC Spell Endings Associated with Specific Events."

56. Nixon, Kauff, and Losby, 1999, p. C32.

57. Private conversation with Douglas J. Besharov.

58. Unpublished data produced by Wendell Primus and Richard Bavier indicate that, even in 1995, only about half of all families in the bottom quintile received AFDC. This suggests that other forces may partially explain the low incomes of some families at the bottom of the income distribution. For example, some families may have low incomes because they are self-employed and experience a temporary period of low income. Or, some may have been female heads at the time of the survey, but in a different type of family in the preceding year. Thus, their low income and non-participation in welfare may be because they faced very different circumstances in the preceding year. And others may be living with another adult and simply do not need welfare. Clearly, more information is needed about the characteristics of this group, but since about half of the families in the bottom quintile have traditionally not relied on cash welfare, attributing an income decline in this quintile to welfare reform is just speculation.

59. Bavier, chap. 4, this volume.

60. See, for example, Jesse Beeler, Bill Brister, Sharon Chambry, and Anne McDonald, *Tracking of TANF Clients: First Report of a Longitudinal Study: Mississippi's TANF State Program* (Jackson, Miss.: Center for Applied Research, Millsaps College, January 28, 1999, revised); MAXIMUS, *New Mexico Longitudinal Study: Results of the First Year Follow-Up Surveys* (Washington, D.C.: MAXIMUS, April 2000); South Carolina Department of Social Services, Office of Program Reform, Evaluation, and Research, 1998; South Carolina Department of Social Services, Division of Program Quality Assurance, 1997; Carole Kuhns, Anne Gordon, Roberto Agodini, and Renee Loeffler, *The Virginia Closed Case Study: Experience of Virginia Families One Year after Leaving Temporary Assistance for Needy Families* (Falls Church, Va.: Center for Public Administration and Policy at the Virginia Polytechnic Institute and State University, November 1999); DSHS Economic Services Administration, Division of Program Research and Evaluation, *Washington's TANF Single Parent Families after Welfare: Management Reports and Data Analysis* (Olympia, Wash.: State of Washington, January 1999); State of Wisconsin, Department of Workforce Development, 1998; and Swartz et al., 1999.

61.   The states were New Mexico, Virginia, and Washington.
62.   Robert Haveman, "What Happens When People Leave Welfare?" paper presented at
the American Enterprise Institute/Brookings Institution seminar on welfare reform,
Washington, D.C., July 16, 1999.

References

Acs, Gregory, and Pamela Loprest. 2001. *Final Synthesis Report of Findings from ASPE's
"Leavers" Grants.* Washington, D.C.: Urban Institute. November 27.
———. 2001. *Initial Synthesis Report of the Findings from ASPE's "Leavers" Grants.*
Washington, D.C.: Urban Institute. January.
Bavier, Richard. 2001. "Material Well-Being." In *Family Well-Being after Welfare Reform.*
Edited by Douglas J. Besharov. Available from: http://www.welfareacademy.org/pubs/
familywellbeing/familywellbeing-ch4bavier.pdf. Accessed November 4, 2002.
Beeler, Jesse, Bill Brister, Sharon Chambry, and Anne McDonald. 1999. *Tracking of
TANF Clients: First Report of a Longitudinal Study: Mississippi's TANF State Program.*
Revised. Jackson, Miss.: Center for Applied Research, Millsaps College. January 28.
Bloom, Dan, Mary Farrell, James Kemple, and Nandita Verma. 1999. *The Family Transi-
tion Program: Implementation and Three-Year Impacts of Florida's Initial Time-
Limited Welfare Program.* New York: Manpower Demonstration Research Corpora-
tion. April.
Brauner, Sarah, and Pamela Loprest. 1999. *Where Are They Now? What States' Studies of
People Who Left Welfare Tell Us.* Washington, D.C.: Urban Institute. May.
Bureau of Labor Statistics. Various years. table 15. "Presence and Age of Own Children of
Civilian Women 16 Years and Over, By Employment Status and Marital Status." Un-
published data.
Congressional Budget Office. 1998. *Policy Changes Affecting Mandatory Spending for
Low-Income Families Not Receiving Cash Welfare.* Washington, D.C.: Congressional
Budget Office. September.
Council of Economic Advisers. 1997. *Explaining the Decline in Welfare Receipt, 1993–
1996.* Washington, D.C.: Government Printing Office. May.
———. 1999. *The Effects of Welfare Policy and the Economic Expansion on Welfare
Caseloads: An Update.* Washington, D.C.: Government Printing Office. August.
Council of Economic Advisers and the Office of the Chief Economist. 1999. *Twenty
Million Jobs: January 1993–November 1999.* Washington, D.C.: Council of Eco-
nomic Advisers. December.
Devere, Christine. 2001. *Welfare Reform Research: What Do We Know about Those Who
Leave Welfare?* Washington, D.C.: Congressional Research Service. March.
Dickert, Stacy, Scott Houser, and John Scholz. 1995. "The Earned Income Tax Credit and
Transfer Programs: A Study of Labor Market and Program Participation." *Tax Policy
and the Economy* 9: 1–50.
DSHS Economic Services Administration, Division of Program Research and Evaluation.
1999. *Washington's TANF Single Parent Families after Welfare: Management Reports
and Data Analysis.* Olympia, Wash.: State of Washington. January.
Edin, Kathryn, and Laura Lein. 1997. *Making Ends Meet: How Single Mothers Survive
Welfare and Low-Wage Work.* New York: Russell Sage Foundation.
Ellwood, David T. 1999. *The Impact of the Earned Income Tax Credit and Social Policy
Reforms on Work, Marriage, and Living Arrangements.* Cambridge, Mass.: John F.
Kennedy School of Government, Harvard University. November.
Figlio, David, and James Ziliak. 1998. "Welfare Reform, the Business Cycle, and the
Decline in AFDC Caseloads." Paper presented at the conference "Welfare Reform and
the Macroeconomy." Washington, D.C. October.

Haveman, Robert. 1999. "What Happens When People Leave Welfare?" Paper presented at the American Enterprise Institute/Brookings Institution seminar on welfare reform. Washington, D.C. July 16.

Hunter-Manns, Jo Anna, and Dan Bloom. 1999. *Connecticut Post-Time Limit Tracking Study: Six-Month Survey Results.* New York: Manpower Demonstration Research Corporation. January.

Isaacs, Julia B., and Matthew R. Lyon. 2000. "A Cross-State Examination of Families Leaving Welfare: Findings from the ASPE–Funded Leaver Studies." Paper presented at the National Association for Welfare Research and Statistics 40th Annual Workshop. Phoenix, Ariz. August. Revised November 2000.

Jencks, Christopher, and Joseph Swingle. 2000. "Without a Net: Whom the Welfare Law Helps and Hurts," *American Prospect* 3 (January): 37–41.

Kennedy, John F. 1962. *Public Papers of the Presidents of the United States: John F. Kennedy, January 1 to December 31, 1962.* Washington, D.C.: Government Printing Office.

Kuhns, Carole, Anne Gordon, Roberto Agodini, and Renee Loeffler. 1999. *The Virginia Closed Case Study: Experience of Virginia Families One Year after Leaving Temporary Assistance for Needy Families.* Falls Church, Va.: Center for Public Administration and Policy at the Virginia Polytechnic Institute and State University. November.

London, Rebecca. 2000. "The Interaction between Single Mothers' Living Arrangements and Welfare Participation." *Journal of Policy Analysis and Management* 19 (1): 93–117.

Loprest, Pamela. 1999. *Families Who Left Welfare: Who Are They and How Are They Doing?* Washington, D.C.: Urban Institute.

Maloy, Kathleen, LaDonna Pavetti, Peter Shin, Julie Darnell, and Lea Scarpulla-Nolan. 1998. *A Description and Assessment of State Approaches to Diversion Programs and Activities under Welfare Reform.* Washington, D.C.: Center for Health Policy Research at the George Washington University Medical Center.

Martini, Alberto, and Michael Wiseman. 1997. *Explaining the Recent Decline in Welfare Caseloads: Is the Council of Economic Advisers Right?* Washington, D.C.: Urban Institute.

MAXIMUS. 2000. *New Mexico Longitudinal Study: Results of the First Year Follow-Up Surveys.* Washington, D.C.: MAXIMUS. April.

Maynard, Rebecca A. 1997. "Paternalism, Teenage Pregnancy Prevention, and Teenage Parent Services." In *The New Paternalism: Supervisory Approaches to Poverty.* Edited by Lawrence Mead. Washington, D.C.: Brookings Institution Press.

Miller, Cynthia, Virginia Knox, Patricia Auspos, Jo Anna Hunter-Manns, and Alan Orenstein. 1997. *Making Welfare Work and Work Pay: Implementation and Eighteen-Month Impacts of the Minnesota Family Investment Program.* New York: Manpower Demonstration Research Corporation. October.

Mitchell, Alison. 1993. "Posing as Welfare Recipient, Agency Head Finds Indignity." *New York Times.* February 5.

Moffitt, Robert A. 1999. *The Effect of Pre–PRWORA Waivers on AFDC Caseloads and Female Earnings, Income, and Labor Force Participation.* Baltimore, Md.: Johns Hopkins University.

Nemir, Carol, Richard Sanders, and Don Warren. 1997. *Why People Leave Welfare: Reasons Former Clients Give for the Decline in Welfare Caseloads in Texas.* Texas Legislative Council Research Division Issue Brief. Austin, Tex.: Texas Legislative Council.

New York City Human Resources Administration. Office of Program Reporting, Analysis, and Accountability. 2002. Unpublished data. April 3.

Nixon, Lucia, Jaqueline Kauff, and Jan Losby. 1999. *Second Assignments to Iowa's Limited Benefit Plan.* Washington, D.C.: Mathematica Policy Research, Inc. August. Table C.20. "Housing Moves and Homelessness."

Page, Marianne, Joanne Spetz, and Jane Millar. 1998. *Does the Minimum Wage Affect Welfare Caseloads?* San Francisco: Public Policy Institute of California. June.

Richer, Elise, Hedieh Rahmanou, and Mark Greenberg. 2002. "TANF Caseloads Declined in Most States in Second Quarter, But Most States Saw Increase Over the Last Year." Washington, D.C.: Center for Law and Social Policy. October. Available from: http://www.clasp.org/DMS/Documents/1033487945.66/caseload_2002_Q2.pdf. Accessed October 13, 2002.

South Carolina Department of Social Services, Division of Program Quality Assurance. 1997. *Survey of Former Family Independence Program Clients: Cases Closed during January through March 1997.* Columbia, S.C.: South Carolina Department of Social Services.

South Carolina Department of Social Services, Office of Program Reform, Evaluation, and Research. 1998. *Comparison Between Working and Non-Working Clients Whose Cases Were Closed between January and March 1997.* Columbia, S.C.: South Carolina Department of Social Services. March.

State of Wisconsin, Department of Workforce Development. 1998. *Survey of Those Leaving AFDC or W-2 January to March 1998, Preliminary Report.* Madison, Wisc.: Department of Workforce Development.

Swartz, Rebecca, Jacqueline Kauff, Lucia Nixon, Tom Fraker, Jay Hein, and Susan Mitchell. 1999. *Converting to Wisconsin Works: Where Did Families Go When AFDC Ended in Milwaukee?* Madison, Wisc.: Hudson Institute and Mathematica Policy Research, Inc.

Sweeney, Eileen, Liz Schott, Ed Lazere, Shawn Fremstad, Heide Goldberg, Jocelyn Guyer, David Super, and Clifford Johnson. 2000. *Windows of Opportunity: Strategies to Support Families Receiving Welfare and Other Low-Income Families in the Next Stage of Welfare Reform.* Washington, D.C.: Center on Budget and Policy Priorities. January.

U.S. Census Bureau. 2001. *Families and Living Arrangements: Historical Time Series.* Washington, D.C.: U.S. Census Bureau. Table UC-1. "Unmarried-Couple Households, by Presence of Children: 1960 to Present." Available from: http://www.census.gov/population/socdemo/hh-fam/tabUC-1.txt. Accessed October 16, 2002.

U.S. Department of Agriculture, Office of Analysis, Nutrition, and Evaluation. 1999. *Who is Leaving the Food Stamp Program? An Analysis of Caseload Changes from 1994 to 1998.* Alexandria, Va.: Department of Agriculture, Food and Nutrition Service. August. Table 3.

U.S. Department of Health and Human Services, Administration for Children and Families. 2000. "Temporary Assistance for Needy Families (TANF): 1936–1999." In *ACF Data and Statistics.* Available from: http://www.acf.dhhs.gov/news/stats/3697.htm. Accessed December 30, 2001.

———. 2000. "Change in TANF Caseloads: Total TANF families and recipients." In *ACF Data and Statistics.* Available from: http://www.acf.dhhs.gov/news/stats/caseload.htm. Accessed December 28, 2001.

———. 2001. "1990." In *Aid to Families with Dependent Children Caseload Data.* Available from: http://www.acf.dhhs.gov/programs/opre/afdc/1990.xls. Accessed October 22, 2002.

———. 2001. "1991." In *Aid to Families with Dependent Children Caseload Data.* Available from: http://www.acf.dhhs.gov/programs/opre/afdc/1991.xls. Accessed October 22, 2002.

———. 2001. "1992." In *Aid to Families with Dependent Children Caseload Data.* Available from: http://www.acf.dhhs.gov/programs/opre/afdc/1992.xls. Accessed October 22, 2002.

———. 2001. "March 1994." In *Aid to Families with Dependent Children Caseload Data.* Available from: http://www.acf.dhhs.gov/programs/opre/afdc/1994.xls. Accessed October 22, 2002.

————. 2001. "September 2000." In *Aid to Families with Dependent Children Caseload Data*. Available from: http://www.acf.dhhs.gov/programs/opre/afdc/2000.xls. Accessed October 22, 2002.

————. 2001. "Temporary Assistance for Needy Families: Total Number of Recipients." In *ACF Statistics*. Available from: http://www.acf.dhhs.gov/news/stats/recipients.htm. Accessed January 7, 2002.

————. 2002. "TANF: Average Monthly Number of Families Fiscal Year 2001." In *ACF Data and Statistics*. Available from: http://www.acf.dhhs.gov/news/stats/familiesL.htm. Accessed October 24, 2002.

————. 2002. "Temporary Assistance for Needy Families: 1936-2000." In *ACF Data and Statistics*. Available from: http://www.acf.dhhs.gov/news/stats/3697.htm. Accessed January 7, 2002.

U.S. Department of Health and Human Services, Office of Assistant Secretary for Planning and Evaluation. 1998. *Indicators of Welfare Dependence: Annual Report to Congress*. Washington, D.C.: Government Printing Office. October. Table 8b. "Percentage of First AFDC Spell Endings Associated with Specific Events."

————. 1999. *Temporary Assistance for Needy Families (TANF) Program: Third Annual Report to Congress*. Washington, D.C.: Government Printing Office. August.

U.S. Department of Health and Human Services, Office of Planning, Research, and Evaluation. *Temporary Assistance for Needy Families (TANF) Program: Fourth Annual Report to Congress*. Washington, D.C.: U.S. Department of Health and Human Services. 2002. Available from: http://www.acf.dhhs.gov/programs/opre/ar2001/indexar.htm. Accessed October 13, 2002.

U.S. General Accounting Office. 1998. *States Are Restructuring Programs to Reduce Welfare Dependence*. Washington, D.C.: Government Printing Office. June.

————. 1999. *Welfare Reform: Information on Former Recipient Status*. Washington, D.C.: Government Printing Office. April.

————. 2000. *State Sanction Policies and Number of Families Affected*. Washington, D.C.: Government Printing Office. March.

Wallace, Geoffrey, and Rebecca Blank. 1998. "What Goes Up Must Come Down? Explaining Recent Changes in Public Assistance Caseloads." Paper presented at the conference "Welfare Reform and the Macroeconomy." Washington, D.C. October.

3

Assessing Welfare Reform's Impact

Peter H. Rossi

Although few tears were shed over the death of the Aid to Families with Dependent Children program (AFDC), both advocates and opponents of the 1996 welfare reform law were concerned about how the new law would affect low-income families. Advocates worried that welfare reform might not reduce welfare dependency by moving families off the welfare rolls. Opponents worried that low-income families would be plunged into deeper poverty and that the children of the poor would suffer greatly. Fueled by these concerns, several major research projects were started and ongoing projects modified in order to provide empirical data on the changes wrought by the Temporary Assistance for Needy Families program (TANF) and other reforms mandated by the Personal Responsibility and Work Opportunity Reconciliation Act of 1996 (PRWORA).

This chapter assesses the prospects of the four major research projects designed to provide empirically based findings about how well low-income families fared before and after PRWORA, how those prospects varied from state to state, and whether those trends can be credibly attributed to PRWORA.[1] The four research programs and their major weaknesses are as follows.

The *Survey of Program Dynamics (SPD)*, a Census Bureau extension of the Survey of Income and Program Participation (SIPP), is a longitudinal survey consisting of repeated interviews of a national sample of households from several years before PRWORA to several years after enactment. The SPD oversamples low-income households.[2]

The SPD's most attractive feature is its promise to provide longitudinal data on national samples of households for five years before and after the enactment of PRWORA. However, the most serious problem facing the SPD is a low response rate, with just 50 percent of the original sample responding in 1998 and 1999. Especially worrisome is that even higher percentages of low-income households stopped cooperating. Furthermore, it is likely that less than one-quarter of the sample will produce complete longitudinal data covering all or even most of the interviews over the ten-year period. The Census Bureau undertook efforts to reach and obtain the cooperation of the nonresponding households, hoping to raise the response rates to above 60 percent. However, the response rate did not rise, but remained steady in 2000 and 2001, at 50 percent, after the Census Bureau introduced a $40 incentive payment. Even with these efforts to reduce attrition, the rates will not be high enough to satisfy most researchers.

The *Assessing the New Federalism* project, being conducted by the Urban Institute, is examining the devolution shifting many welfare programs from the federal to the state level.[3] Administrative studies will describe the changes in health and welfare systems in each state and take an intensive look at thirteen states both before and after PRWORA. Much of the Urban Institute project will center on a pre–PRWORA survey[4] and several post–PRWORA national household sample surveys—the National Survey of America's Families (NSAF), being conducted by Westat, Inc.—with subsamples large enough to support precise estimates for each of the thirteen states in which intensive administrative studies are being undertaken. The NSAF also oversamples households at 200 percent or less of the poverty level to support detailed findings for low-income families.

The NSAF is a series of nationally representative surveys conducted in 1997 and 1999, with a third survey completed in the fall of 2002, to permit comparisons between households before and after welfare reform. Response rates for the first NSAF survey were average for well-run national telephone surveys: 65 percent for families with children and 62 percent for families without children. But "average" may not be good enough for surveys that are highly policy relevant. Moreover, in the 1999 survey, the response rates dropped to 62 percent and 59 percent, respectively.[5] NSAF staff have attempted to compensate for low response rates by weighting the data. The large samples for each of the thirteen states also make it possible to examine how families in states with different TANF plans have fared. The decline in welfare rolls, however, has considerably reduced the number of welfare families in the survey taken after TANF went into effect. The small sample sizes within each state will restrict the ability of analysts to estimate the impact of welfare reform, especially subgroup differences at the level of individual states.

The *Project on Devolution and Urban Change (UC)*, being conducted by the Manpower Demonstration Research Corporation (MDRC), consists of intensive studies of poor households in four major cities: Cleveland, Miami, Philadelphia, and Los Angeles.[6] Using administrative data, the program participation and earnings of cohorts of poor households entering the Food Stamp or AFDC/TANF programs at given points in time are being tracked before and after TANF went into effect. In addition, it includes surveys of a sample of AFDC/TANF households, intensive studies of the TANF programs in the four cities, institutional analyses, and ethnographic studies within selected poor neighborhoods.

MDRC's UC focuses on welfare recipients in four major cities, combining administrative data from 1992 to 2001 with surveys of welfare mothers who were on the rolls in 1995. Response rates for the first survey in 1997 were very good, averaging 79 percent across the four sites. A second survey was conducted between March and September 2001, with response rates that ranged from 80 percent to 83 percent for the wave 1 respondents, depending on the site, or about two-thirds of the original sample. The project should provide a rich—and textured—picture of the characteristics and circumstances of the most vulnerable families in the cities studied. However, the findings cannot be generalized to the broader welfare population nationally or even to other urban neighborhoods.

The *Child Impact Waiver Experiments*, sponsored by the U.S. Department of Health and Human Services (HHS), consist of five randomized waiver experiments with measures of effects on children in projects referred to as the Child Impact Waiver Experiments.[7] The five waiver experiments began before PRWORA and compare randomly selected families that have been receiving welfare benefits under the old AFDC rules (control-group families) with randomly selected families that received benefits under the waivers (experimental-group families). The waiver provisions being studied resemble quite closely the TANF provisions enacted by the states being studied. Because these are among the best of the waiver experiments and will provide information on effects on children, for the purposes of this chapter, they are considered a fourth major research project. The five states and the contractors involved are Florida (MDRC), Minnesota (MDRC), Connecticut (MDRC), Iowa (Mathematica Policy Research, Inc.), and Indiana (Abt Associates Inc.).

The importance of these experiments is considerable. Because the experiments resemble each state's TANF program and are evaluated by using a rigorous methodology, they represent perhaps the best attempt at measuring the impact of welfare reform in selected states. Although the projects all rely on the universally preferred randomized experiments, generalizing findings to other states is clearly hazardous. It also is not clear whether the experimental conditions were maintained with fidelity. Given the widespread publicity accompanying welfare reform, it is possible that control-group families may not have been subjected to AFDC rules and that such families did not fully realize that their welfare benefits were not subject to state TANF rules.

This review is based on various published documents and on many more unpublished memoranda, proposals, drafts of papers, and questionnaires intended to be used in the field. *Because some of these projects are still in operation, this review should be regarded as a description of work still in progress.*

Estimating Welfare Reform's Impact Will Be Difficult

The four research projects each have several objectives, including describing how public welfare changed under PRWORA, describing how low-income families fared before and after welfare reform, and estimating the net effects of welfare reform. Findings bearing on these three topics will undoubtedly be met with great interest. The question that most interests the policy community, though, is: What have been the net effects of TANF on the employment and well-being of low-income households?

The "gold standard" design for estimating net effects is the randomized experiment. Only the Child Impact Waiver studies are experiments; they provide good impact estimates for the five TANF–like programs, but the extent to which those findings will be able to be generalized to the nation as a whole is limited. (They will also be unable to provide information on entry effects.) The other three research projects provide nonexperimental data that cannot support estimates of net effects that are as credible.

Urban Change, Survey of Program Dynamics, and Assessing the New Federalism

The net effects of a program are estimated by measuring relevant outcomes among program participants and comparing those outcomes with what would have been measured had the subjects not experienced the program. In a literal sense, such comparisons are impossible. The best approximation is achieved by conducting randomized experiments, in which subjects are randomly assigned to different groups that either experience the program or serve as controls from which the program is withheld. The conditions to which the control groups are subjected are known as *counterfactuals*. Because the assignment to experimental and control groups is random, the two groups are expected to differ only by chance. Hence, measures of outcome that differ between the two groups to an extent greater than what can be expected from chance can be reasonably attributed to the effects of the program.[8]

In all three of the prospective research projects this chapter reviews, the main contrasts that will be available will be between how households were faring before 1997 under AFDC and their condition living under TANF. Of course, the studies also can be used as cross-sections. For example, NSAF data on the thirteen states can theoretically be used to estimate the effects of state TANF plan differences on the well-being of poor households. Or children in TANF families can be compared with children in comparable non–TANF families. Such analyses can hardly ever be credible and are certainly far inferior to even before-and-after analyses. Accordingly, they are not discussed in detail in this chapter.

These before-and-after research designs are perhaps the best designs possible under the conditions existing when the research programs were formulated—the projects had to get rapidly underway before PRWORA was enacted, but only after it was clear that some sort of welfare reform was inevitable. Consequently, the design options were limited. Nevertheless, the findings resulting from such designs are widely viewed by evaluators as subject to many credibility problems. The two most serious problems are:

- The client population may change as a consequence of TANF. Indeed, the welfare rolls began to decline in 1994, several years before the enactment of PRWORA, hinting that the composition of welfare clientele under TANF might be different in important respects compared with AFDC clientele. At least some of the decline in caseloads appears to result because some families that might be eligible for benefits have decided not to apply for them. Such "entry effects" cannot easily be studied or even detected, let alone the conditions of those families that were "deterred" from applying for welfare.

- Before-and-after designs are not able to distinguish convincingly the effects of interventions from other changes occurring at the same time. For example, the studies may detect a significant increase in employment of single mothers after TANF, but that increase may result from increased employment opportunities created by a tighter labor market. Changes in other programs, such as the Earned Income Tax Credit (EITC), or changes in the federal minimum wage also may affect employment.

Some of the difficulties in estimating TANF effects lie in the nature of the reforms themselves. Within quite broad limits, each state can develop its own version of welfare reform. For example, some states have quite generous income disregards, whereas others are less generous; some have quite short time limits on eligibility, but other states permit longer periods of eligibility. Some have imposed family caps, which involve not increasing income maintenance payments when children are born after initial eligibility. And so on.[9]

In effect, TANF cannot be evaluated as a national program; only state TANF programs can be evaluated. In addition, one can expect within-state variation in implementation, especially in such states as California or New York, where welfare is administered by local political jurisdictions (for example, counties) with substantial local discretion. Even in state administered programs, TANF plans permit considerable discretion to "street-level bureaucrats" in implementation, potentially leading to within-state heterogeneity.

Further complicating evaluation is the mixed nature of welfare reform components. Within each state, TANF is designed as a package of interventions, typically consisting of several provisions, some of which can be expected to have quite opposite effects. For example, generous earned income disregards may make employment quite attractive, leading to higher household incomes for some households, but sanctions imposed for noncompliance with work provisions may serve to reduce income for other households. Accordingly, if a research project judges a state's program to be effective, it will be quite impossible to attribute those effects to any specific provision in the "bundle" that constitutes that state's version of TANF because only the bundle can be evaluated.[10] Furthermore, the effects of some provisions may be counterbalanced by the opposite effects of other provisions to the extent that the bundle may appear to have had no effects. The consequence is that it will be difficult, if not impossible, to discern which elements of each state's TANF bundle are contributing (and how much) to success or failure.

Not only the state bundles but also the names given them vary. Although "Temporary Assistance for Needy Families" is the title given in the federal legislation to the successor to AFDC, many states have given different titles to their versions. This diversity produces difficulties for national surveys. It will be hard to write questions about TANF program participation in national surveys so that they are understood properly by respondents. This difficulty may be one of the main reasons that the Census Bureau's estimates of TANF participation using the Current Population Survey (CPS) increasingly have departed in recent years from counts obtained from administrative data.

TANF will take some years to settle into a relatively steady state. HHS published final regulations in 1999; accordingly, each state's plans did not begin to take final form until that year. Nevertheless, many states wrote their versions without benefit of the federal regulations and had to change them to conform to the final federal regulations. Implementation failures and modifications undoubtedly will occur in some states' TANF programs. For example, several states have experienced difficulties in training front-line personnel, who under AFDC primarily determined welfare eligibility, to take on the task of facilitating client movement to employment.[11] As a result, the versions of TANF experienced in the first few years will change after a few years of trial and error. All three research projects are designed to measure what happens in the first few years of PRWORA and may therefore be measuring early versions of those programs rather than what will appear after the programs have settled down. Of course, determining how long such a period of adjustment will take is problematic.

It is also possible that some or all of the state PRWORA plans may never reach a steady state but will change continually over time. In addition, Congress may alter provisions in PRWORA, forcing changes on the states. Although evaluation of a frequently changing program can be undertaken, interpreting findings will be quite difficult.

Even if TANF functions as its authors expected, its fate depends heavily on forces outside the influence of the program. In particular, moving TANF clients into jobs cannot succeed unless jobs for which clients can be considered are available in the economy and unless the child care industry provides enough slots to meet the needs for child care. To be sure, the states might provide public-sector positions if the labor market does not offer private-sector employment, but arranging for and financing public-sector jobs will be difficult and expensive. Much more problematic is whether the child care industry can provide slots for the increased demand at prices that are affordable under state subsidies as well as meet quality standards. Unfortunately, none of the research projects plans to collect data directly relevant to those issues. For example, the sample surveys will collect data on respondents' child care arrangements, but no studies of child care markets are planned.[12]

Finally, issues of what should be regarded as criteria of success and when measurement should be undertaken remain. TANF has multiple goals as well as the potential to produce unanticipated and unwanted effects. The key outcome of greatest interest concerns the extent to which welfare clients will move off the rolls, obtain employment, and thereby be better off. Because clients are expected to be better off when employed, researchers are interested in the earnings of those who move into employment. Because some analysts have predicted that children will be worse off under PRWORA, they also have considerable interest in measures of child well-being. Accordingly, it is appropriate to ask whether each of the projected studies has planned to collect data relevant to the important outcomes that PRWORA is intended to effect.

The available outcome measures are restricted to those that can be obtained by the data collection modes used. For example, the quality of child care used by the households studied cannot be measured directly, only through the reports of household respondents.[13] Nor is it possible to measure directly other important outcomes, such as the quality of parent-child relationships or the cognitive abilities of children.

Some effects can be expected to appear relatively quickly, but others can be expected to occur after several years or longer. If TANF increases employment and earnings, such effects should appear within the first two years or so, whereas effects on the developmental trajectories of children may take a much longer period of time to detect. Steadiness of employment also requires observations over longer periods of time, whereas determining whether clients have found employment might require only a single interview. No one can expect that initial earnings of new entrants in the labor force will be high: It will take time to observe what shape earnings will take over time.

Child Impact Waiver Experiments

Relating the five waiver experiments to TANF presents somewhat different problems. Because each is a randomized experiment, the studies avoid all the difficulties stemming from nonrandomized designs, as described above. The waiver studies should produce unbiased estimates of the net effects of the waiver provisions involved in each case compared with the prewaiver AFDC programs in place in that state. The families in the experimental and control groups experience the same historical events and trends, so results will be independent of, say, trends in the local economy and labor market.

Using the waiver experiment findings to judge the effects of TANF, however, is problematic. First, although the waiver provisions being tested were fairly close to the TANF programs enacted in the five states involved, some differences exist, especially in time limits.[14] Accordingly, ascertaining the implications of waiver experiment findings for TANF must be judgment calls, advanced through argumentation and clearly subject to dispute.

Second, the waiver experiments are plagued by some of the same problems affecting the prospective studies. In particular, four of the plans were bundles of provisions that could not be separately evaluated, the exception being the Minnesota experiment.[15] The experiments also are studies of welfare reform in its earliest years.

Third, the subjects enrolled in the waiver experiments may have become increasingly unrepresentative of all welfare families over time. For example, the members of the households were five years older at the end of a five-year-long experiment—and likely to be older than current welfare clients. Any changes in the characteristics of welfare clients enrolled after PRWORA would not be detected. Moreover, entry effects cannot be studied.

Fourth, maintaining the integrity of the waiver experiments was difficult. In particular, it is essential that the control-group families were subject to AFDC rules throughout the time periods of the experiments. It also is essential that they knew that they were under such rules. PRWORA and TANF have received so much general publicity in the mass media that control-group families may not have known that time limits, family caps, and other TANF rules did not apply to them. In addition, control-group families were typically a small proportion of the total welfare caseload, and welfare personnel mistakenly may have applied the wrong rules to such families. That this is a very real danger can be seen in the failure to maintain the fidelity of treatments for both the control group and the experimental group in the New Jersey waiver experiment evaluating that state's Family Development Program.[16] A central feature of the New Jersey program was a family cap, under which family benefits were not increased when children conceived after enrollment were born to mothers enrolled in the plan. Despite the fact that the control group was not under the family cap rule, it was found that the benefits of more than a score of control-group families had not been increased after the birth of children. In addition, a survey of control-group families found that few knew that the family cap rules did not apply to them. Given these findings, it was clear that the experimental conditions had been violated to the extent that the resulting data can hardly be regarded as valid.[17]

The research organizations running the waiver experiments were fully aware of the need to be vigilant in maintaining the integrity of the experimental and control groups. Some placed safeguards in the management information systems software, which blocked inappropriate actions with regard to the participating families. All were determined to provide reminders to participating families about the relevant rules to which they were subject. Perhaps these measures succeeded in maintaining fidelity in treatments—but perhaps not.

What Will Be Learned

This section describes what can be learned from the studies reviewed. It first considers the three prospective research projects, then the Child Impact Waiver Experiments.

The Condition of Low-Income Families

The three prospective PRWORA research projects have already cost more than $170 million, and millions more will be spent over the next few years. Between 1996 and 2002, the New Federalism Project spent $84 million,[18] the SPD spent $76 million,[19] and UC spent $13 million.[20] Assuming successful completion of data collection for the three projects, what will be learned from them? When released, the descriptive findings undoubtedly will be met with intense public and partisan interest in how the poor are faring under PRWORA.

Subject to the serious limitations summarized above, the studies may be able to provide descriptive findings on the following levels of aggregation:

- *National level.* The Urban Institute's Assessing the New Federalism project and the Census Bureau's SPD will provide findings concerning how American households were doing socioeconomically before and after PRWORA. This will include whether earnings and employment of low-income households have improved or declined and whether children in low-income families are better or worse off in certain respects. The Urban Institute's state database is designed to provide detailed data on how the fifty states used the opportunities offered by devolution to design their particular versions of PRWORA. For example, we should know which states offered generous income disregards, which adopted stricter time limits than those called for in TANF, and which put caps on payments when mothers on TANF had additional children.

- *State level.* Assessing the New Federalism will also provide detailed information on each of thirteen states. The administrative case studies promise to provide rich information on how the states ran AFDC and what changes were made under TANF. Implementation issues also will be studied. The NSAF's sampling design is intended to provide large enough state samples (about 3,000 households in each of the thirteen states) to describe how the circumstances of the poor changed after PRWORA. Comparisons of AFDC and TANF will be made among the states and within each state. The Urban Institute will provide detailed descriptions of PRWORA and TANF plans for each of the thirteen states. The Census Bureau's SPD is not based on a large enough sample to provide data on more than the largest states—perhaps only New York and California—and even then, the samples are quite small.

- *Local level.* MDRC's UC project is concerned with four cities and promises to provide detailed longitudinal descriptions of how several cohorts of poor households changed in employment and program participation over the historical periods before and after TANF. UC will provide descriptions of how TANF was implemented in the cities as well as changes in several poor neighborhoods in all the cities. UC's findings will be especially valuable for learning about how the changes making up PRWORA are being interpreted in practice, with the obvious limitation that such findings are limited to the four urban locales under study.

Taken together, the descriptive information resulting from the three research projects may be valuable. It will be of great interest to find out how various subgroups among low-income households are faring under PRWORA. For example, when TANF participants are cut off from support, either through sanctions or from coming up against time limits, what happens to them? Will job-seeking success be more difficult to achieve among teenage single mothers than among older mothers? Will TANF participants in urban neighborhoods characterized by extreme poverty have different experiences compared with participants living in small towns?

Whether these analyses can be carried out, however, depends on whether the data sets contain enough households in the situations in question. For example, the NSAF surveys do not contain enough TANF participants in many of the thirteen states to sustain subgroup analyses in those states, although the UC study will likely support such analyses in each of the four cities being studied.

Impact data

Conspicuously missing from the discussion above are findings concerning the impact of PRWORA and TANF. They are omitted because the before-and-after designs involved cannot support credible impact analyses. Nevertheless, it can be safely predicted that attempts will be made to estimate the effects of PRWORA and TANF because of widespread interest in policy circles and in the general public.

An obvious approach to impact analysis would be to exploit the longitudinal features of the data sets, contrasting individuals, cohorts, or political jurisdictions before and after PRWORA and TANF were implemented. Because there is reason to believe that many changes affected households during the research period in addition to welfare policy, any analysis must try to take such changes into account. Especially important are macro-level changes in the economy and changes in other programs, such as the EITC. The changes occurring at the micro level may be more difficult to model and take into account. For example, increased earnings of partners and in-kind transfers may make it possible for TANF recipients to leave the program and join other households. Whether such nonwelfare changes can be adequately taken into account in the before-and-after analyses will be problematic. Indeed, it is likely that analysts may come to quite different impact assessments depending on how their statistical models are constructed.

The data sets produced by the three projects also can be analyzed as cross-sections—snapshots taken at particular points in time. A likely strategy will be to contrast households that face different TANF plans or to compare households that are TANF participants with comparable households that are not. In such analyses, the major obstacle to credibility is whether analysts have properly managed to model and adjust for selection biases.

A related approach might be to contrast the clients of different welfare plans on the state, county, or city level. The point of such analyses would be to discern how the features of different plans affect outcomes for households subject to them. The cross-sectional approach is especially fraught with potential for error. As discussed earlier, the TANF plans are bundles that are impossible to "unbundle." It is unlikely that any pairs of jurisdictions exist whose TANF plans differ in just one or even two features. It will be difficult to make a strong case for any impact estimate based on such comparisons.

Although statistical modeling cannot fully compensate for the inherent weaknesses of before-and-after designs, it appears to be the best strategy for the impact analyses of the prospective data sets. Furthermore, such analyses can yield valuable information. When practiced skillfully and sensitively, such analyses can yield quite credible causal statements.[21] Estimates that are consistent across several data sets and are robust under alternative model specifications will be especially credible.

Some attempts to estimate the net effects of PRWORA generally, or TANF specifically, may turn out to be more than merely suggestive, especially when findings are strong, consistent, and robust. For example, despite the weaknesses cited above, if analysis using NSAF data were to find that states with more generous earnings disregards had relatively higher caseloads (holding other interstate differences constant), and that such effects were muted when combined with a strict time limit or work requirement, then the findings could be regarded as supporting a causal inference—if they held up under different specifications and were confirmed in comparable analyses in the SPD and UC data sets, as well as in the Child Impact Waiver Experiments. Such a convergence of findings across data sets, however, is not likely to occur often. Thus, in all likelihood, the nonexperimental studies—the SPD, the NSAF, and the UC—because they must rely on "before-and-after" analyses, will be unable to distinguish between the effects of welfare reform and those of other economic and policy changes that occurred at the same time. The best use of these nonexperimental research projects is to provide descriptive information about what has happened to low-income households and families as they experience TANF.

Child Impact Waiver Experiments

The descriptive information resulting from the waiver experiments likely will not be of much more than local interest. Whatever benefits they may yield will come from impact estimates. To the extent that the changes in the experiments made the experimental conditions equivalent to the TANF plans in those states and control-group conditions were maintained with reasonable fidelity, the experiments will provide the only estimates of TANF effects based on randomized designs that will be available in the near future. The waiver experiments' findings therefore will be of considerable importance.

What Will Not Be Learned

As emphasized in this chapter, a major limitation to before-and-after designs is their inability to distinguish between the effects of historical events or trends and the effects of the program being developed. Accordingly, differences between pre– and post–PRWORA conditions cannot be uniquely attributed to PRWORA. If TANF rolls are much smaller than AFDC rolls, it could be a result of welfare reform or the consequence of other trends occurring in the post–PRWORA period. For example, in the several years before PRWORA, welfare rolls were declining; that trend simply might persist into the post–PRWORA period. Similarly, inequality in the distribution of household income has been increasing over the past decade or so. An increase in income inequality after PRWORA may simply be a continuation of that trend. In short, the findings of the three projects will not reveal much about the overall effects of PRWORA. Of course, this limitation does not apply to the augmented waiver experiments, because they are based on randomized designs.

The decline in welfare rolls also has the effect of considerably reducing the number of welfare families in each of the surveys taken after TANF went into effect. NSAF–I completed interviews with about 2,700 families receiving welfare assistance; the numbers in individual states ranged from 83 in Alabama to 379 in Wisconsin and averaged 188 in the thirteen states.[22] Because the rolls have further declined since 1997, NSAF–II will have considerably smaller sample sizes for welfare families, perhaps as much as 25 percent smaller. The small sample sizes will restrict the ability of analysts to estimate the impact of welfare reform, especially subgroup differences at the level of individual states.

The four projects also have another important limitation: As planned now, none of the research extends much beyond the first few years of PRWORA. For many states, the period covered will be one in which each state will be developing its own version of PRWORA—writing regulations, training staff, and disseminating knowledge of the new system to its clients. For many states, this process will take several years to complete. The "permanent" version of PRWORA may not appear, at the earliest, until beyond the research period. The NSAF and UC second surveys may reflect a stage in the evolution of PRWORA before the transition to the permanent PRWORA versions will have occurred. The waiver experiments ended in the period 1998 through 2000. Accordingly, the versions of PRWORA being studied in the four projects may not look like the PRWORA that exists later in the first decade of the twenty-first century. This timing, however, may have some strengths. For example, if PRWORA has some important unwanted effects—say, a sharp rise in the number of children in abject poverty—it would be useful to know about that as quickly as possible so that countermeasures can be undertaken.

It also is important to keep in mind that research on the effects of PRWORA will not come to an end when the four research projects are completed. Indeed, the projects may be extended: Data collection for NSAF–III was completed in late 2002; SIPP samples may be enlarged to provide more detailed information. New research projects may be funded to carry on when these projects have ended. It is almost certain that interest in learning more about poverty, unemployment, and PRWORA will continue indefinitely into the future.

Although the research projects cover many important outcomes that might be affected by PRWORA, they will not be able to track how the changing conditions of the poor affect child abuse, substance abuse, or housing adequacy because none of the studies plans to measure them. Missing also are measures of social approval or disapproval as experienced from peers, kin, or the larger society. Of course, limitations exist on how many outcomes can be measured with the kinds of survey instruments used, and well-tested, reliable, measurement instruments do not exist for some alternative outcome measures. Furthermore, the research designers may have thought that such areas of behavior were unlikely to be affected by PRWORA. In any event, even if all the studies successfully overcome data collection problems, not all questions concerning the changes accompanying welfare reform will be answered.

Finally, an important limitation arises because a large part of the 1994–2001 decline in enrollment may be a result of "entry effects," wherein fewer eligible families apply for benefits and, perhaps, fewer are able to complete the enrollment process successfully. Anecdotal evidence indicates that some state welfare agencies have made the application process difficult to complete, thereby discouraging prospective applicants. Whatever the cause for the decline, the entry effects preceding and accompanying PRWORA are producing important changes in welfare.

Entry effects can take several forms. In some states, welfare workers are authorized to provide emergency cash payments to people who apply for TANF benefits in exchange for becoming ineligible for TANF benefits for a specified period of time (for example, six months). The payments often are offered when it appears that the applicant may need immediate financial help, such as paying rent arrears or repairing a car, rather than long-term support. Some welfare departments have made applying for TANF a tedious and lengthy process, with the result that some applicants never complete the process. Of course, some eligible families simply may have come to believe that the new work requirements of TANF may be more trouble than the payments are worth and have not applied at all.

The research projects will have various difficulties providing data that directly bear on entry effects. Because the SPD is a longitudinal study, however, it is better designed to study those effects. The SPD can identify eligible families and determine the socioeconomic and employment characteristics of those who do not apply at various points in time in the pre– and post–PRWORA periods.[23] UC and Assessing the New Federalism may be able to study entry effects indirectly by contrasting the composition of enrollees before and after PRWORA. Least able to provide information on entry effects are the five Child Impact Waiver Experiments. The experimental and control groups were formed by randomly allocating people already enrolled at specific points in time and cannot provide information on how the composition of new enrollees subsequently may have changed.

Balancing the Books

The three prospective welfare reform research programs reviewed in this chapter were driven by a concern for collecting the best possible information on how PRWORA would affect poor households. The constraints that had to be met in designing them were formidable. Everyone agreed that to launch randomized experiments after PRWORA started was simply out of the question. Of course, the waiver experiments could be used, although they could provide information on just a few states. Except for administrative data and extending the SIPP, there was no way to collect extensive series of pre–PRWORA observations covering many states. Administrative data did not contain measures of such critically important outcomes as child well-being, and the task of pooling data from states with different data systems was formidable. The SIPP had some child well-being measures, but they were not as extensive as desired. And so on.

To be sure, arguments can be made that each project could be improved, but the improvements would likely result in marginal benefits only. As the saying goes, hindsight is 20/20. Taken together, the three prospective projects may spend about $200 million, and the augmentation of the five waiver experiments will cost more than $13 million more.[24] Given this level of funding, would other strategies have been more productive? For example, would it have been more productive to strengthen the SPD, possibly by making intensive efforts initially to raise response rates, provide for interviews every four months (rather than annual post–PRWORA interviews), and allow for following all the households in the two cohorts? Alternatively, might it have been better to strengthen NSAF–I and NSAF–II by designing them as in-person surveys, which typically experience better response rates than telephone surveys? Would it have been better to provide funds to MDRC to expand its community studies to statewide studies? Any one of those alternatives would probably have led to richer data sets, but none of them would have made estimating the impact of PRWORA any easier.

At this writing, it seems unlikely that these projects will be continued, either because of their problems or because they have run their course. In addition, serious consideration should be given to actions ranging from releasing the data sets with strong warnings about their limitations to suppressing their release entirely. In the final chapter to this volume (chapter 16), Douglas Besharov and Peter Rossi assess these and other projects and recommend what they believe will be a more effective method for monitoring the well-being of families and children after welfare reform.

Notes

1. The five research organizations involved in the projects assessed here—the U.S. Census Bureau, the Manpower Demonstration Research Corporation (MDRC), the Urban Institute, Mathematica Policy Research, Inc., and Abt Associates Inc.— generously made available the materials on which this review is based. I am especially grateful to Daniel Weinberg, Stephanie Shipp, and Michael McMahon (U.S. Census Bureau), Judith Gueron, Gordon Berlin, and Charles Michalopoulos (MDRC), Fritz Scheuren, Kenneth Finegold, Genevieve Kenney, and Anna Kondratas (Urban Institute), and Howard Rolston (U.S. Department of Health and Human Services, HHS), all of whom sent me materials and patiently answered my questions. I circulated earlier versions of this chapter to them, and their comments helped correct errors in my descriptions of the projects. I did not always agree with some of their judgments, but I take them into account in this revision. Some of their detailed comments may be found in Peter H. Rossi, "Ongoing Major Research in Welfare Reform: What Will Be Learned," in *Family Well-Being after Welfare Reform*, edited by Douglas J. Besharov, 2002, available from: http://www.welfareacademy.org/pubs/familywellbeing/familywellbeing-ch3rossi.pdf, accessed November 12, 2002. See Daniel H. Weinberg and Stephanie S. Shipp, comments on Rossi "Ongoing Major Research in Welfare Reform"; Charles Michalopoulos, comments on ibid.; Kenneth Finegold and Fritz Scheuren, comments on ibid.; Howard Rolston, comments on ibid.; and Judith M. Gueron, comments on ibid.
2. For a detailed analysis of the Survey of Program Dynamics (SPD), see Rossi, 2002, pp. 3-32–3-36; and Weinberg and Shipp, 2002, pp. 3-64–3-85.
3. For a detailed analysis of the Assessing the New Federalism Project, see Rossi, 2002, pp. 3-22–3-32; and Finegold and Scheuren, 2002, pp. 3-88–3-102.
4. Although the National Survey of America's Families (NSAF) interviewing took place in 1997, the survey collected information about 1996, covering the period before most Personal Responsibility and Work Opportunity Reconciliation Act of 1996 (PRWORA) provisions went into effect.
5. Editor's note: In their response to Rossi, the Urban Institute researchers argue that comparisons with other surveys should be based on an alternate "weighted" response rate for the 1997 survey that is slightly higher (about 70 percent). But, even using this measure, the 1999 NSAF response rate fell to about 64 percent. See Adam Safir, Fritz Scheuren, and Kevin Wang, *Survey Methods and Data Reliability, 1997 and 1999* (Washington, D.C.: Urban Institute, November 3, 2000), available from: http://www.urban.org/Template.cfm?NavMenuID=24&template=/TaggedContent/ViewPublication.cfm&PublicationID=7955, accessed October 24, 2002.
6. For a detailed description of the UC, see Rossi, 2002, pp. 3-36–3-40; and Michalopolous, 2002, pp. 3-103–3-106.
7. For a detailed description of the Child Impact Waiver Experiments, see Rossi, 2002, pp. 3-40–3-42; and Rolston, 2002, pp. 3-107–3-110.
8. Program net effects are always estimated comparatively. The comparison is between the program being evaluated and the "program" represented by the conditions prevailing in the control group.
9. The diversity that Temporary Assistance for Needy Families (TANF) state plans have developed is described in detail in an Urban Institute report summarizing state plans as of October 1997. See L. Jerome Gallagher, Megan Gallagher, Kevin

Perese, Susan Schreiber, and Keith Watson, *One Year after Federal Welfare Reforms: A Description of State Temporary Assistance for Needy Families (TANF) Decisions as of October 1997*, Occasional Paper no. 6 (Washington, D.C.: Urban Institute, 1998). For more recent information on state plan provisions, see U.S. Department of Health and Human Services, Office of Planning, Research, and Evaluation, *Temporary Assistance for Needy Families (TANF) Program: Fourth Annual Report to Congress* (Washington, D.C.: U.S. Department of Health and Human Services, April 2002), available from: http://www.acf.dhhs.gov/programs/opre/ar2001/indexar.htm, accessed October 13, 2002.

10. In principle, it is possible to study the separate effects of provisions making up a bundle. Factorial experiments using several experimental groups, each consisting of unique combinations of programs, would provide estimates of the relative effectiveness of the separate programs and combinations of programs that make up a bundle. Factorial experiments have been used in the two major income maintenance studies as well as in the housing allowance experiment. For the income maintenance studies, see Peter H. Rossi and Katherine Lyall, *Reforming Public Welfare* (New York: Russell Sage, 1976). For the housing allowance experiment, see Philip K. Robins, Robert G. Spiegelman, Samuel Weiner, and Joseph G. Bell, editors, *A Guaranteed Annual Income: Evidence from a Social Experiment* (New York: Academic Press, 1980); and Joseph Friedman and Daniel H. Weinberg, "Housing Consumption in an Experimental Housing Allowance Program: Issues of Self-Selection and Housing Requirements," unpublished paper, 1980. One of the waiver experiments, described below, had a factorial design.

11. U.S. General Accounting Office, *Welfare Reform: States Are Restructuring Programs to Reduce Welfare Dependency* (Washington, D.C.: Government Printing Office, June 1998).

12. HHS is funding research to be conducted by Abt Associates Inc. on low-income child care markets; the planned survey may provide the needed information.

13. Little empirically based knowledge exists on how to measure the quality of child care.

14. For a description of experimental treatments, see Rossi, 2002, appendix 3-A, pp. 3-57–3-60.

15. In Minnesota, the waiver provisions concerning mandatory services and the financial incentive are tested separately and in combination, making it possible to estimate the effects of each provision separately and in combination.

16. Michael J. Camasso, Carol Harvey, Radha Jagannathan, and Mark Killingworth, *A Final Report on the Impact of New Jersey's Family Development Program: Experimental–Control Group Analysis* (New Brunswick, N.J.: Rutgers University, 1998).

17. The Family Development Program was also assessed by using administrative data on all welfare clients before and after the onset of the program. See Michael J. Camasso, Carol Harvey, Radha Jagannathan, and Mark Killingworth, *A Final Report on the Impact of New Jersey's Family Development Program: Results from a Pre–Post Analysis of AFDC Case Heads from 1990–1996* (New Brunswick, N.J.: Rutgers University, 1998).

18. Personal communication from Alan Weil, director of the Assessing New Federalism Project, to Peter Germanis, December 11, 2002.

19. Personal communication from Daniel Weinberg, chief, Housing and Household Economics Statistics Division, U.S. Census Bureau, to Peter Germanis, December 11, 2002.

20. Personal communication from Charles Michalopoulos, senior research associate, MDRC, to Peter Germanis, October 31, 2002.

21. Over the past decade, considerable thought has gone into how best to analyze nonexperimental data. See James Heckman and Richard Robb, "Alternative Methods for Solving the Problem of Selection Bias in Evaluating the Impact of Treat-

ments on Outcomes," in *Drawing Inferences from Self-Selected Samples,* edited by
H. Wainer (Berlin: Springer-Verlag, 1986); and Paul R. Rosenbaum, *Observational
Studies* (New York: Springer-Verlag, 1995).
22.   By design, the Wisconsin sample was larger than in other states.
23.   In addition, for survey years 1998 to 2002, the SPD asked about reasons for
applying for welfare.
24.   Personal communication from Howard Rolston, director, Office of Planning, Research, and Evaluation in the Administration for Children and Families, HHS, to
Peter Germanis, November 1, 2002.

References

Bavier, Richard. 1998. "An Early Look at the Effects of Welfare Reform." Draft memoran-
dum. Washington, D.C.: Office of Management and Budget.
Brick, Pat Dean. 1999. "A Descriptive Review of Ten Major Surveys." Draft memoran-
dum. Washington, D.C.: Urban Institute.
Brim, Orville G., and David L. Featherman. 1997. "Surveying Midlife Development in the
United States." Unpublished paper, Life Trends, Vero Beach, Fla.
Camasso, Michael J., Carol Harvey, Radha Jagannathan, and Mark Killingworth. 1998. *A
Final Report on the Impact of New Jersey's Family Development Program: Experi-
mental–Control Group Analysis.* New Brunswick, N.J.: Rutgers University.
———. 1998. *A Final Report on the Impact of New Jersey's Family Development Pro-
gram: Results from a Pre–Post Analysis of AFDC Case Heads from 1990–1996.* New
Brunswick, N.J.: Rutgers University.
Connecticut Department of Social Services. 1997. *Child Impact Studies Project.* Hartford:
Connecticut Department of Social Services.
Coulton, Claudia, and Nandita Verma. 1997. *Using Social Indicators to Study Change in
Low-Income Neighborhoods Before and After the Implementation of Welfare Reform.*
MDRC project design paper. New York: Manpower Demonstration Research Corpo-
ration.
Edin, Kathryn. 1997. *Urban Change Project Ethnographic Component.* MDRC project
design paper. New York: Manpower Demonstration Research Corporation.
Edin, Kathryn, and Laura Lein. 1997. *Making Ends Meet: How Single Mothers Survive
Welfare and Low-Wage Work.* New York: Russell Sage Foundation.
Finegold, Kenneth, and Fritz Scheuren. 2002. Comments on "Ongoing Major Research in
Welfare Reform: What Will Be Learned," by Peter H. Rossi. In *Family Well-Being after
Welfare Reform.* Edited by Douglas J. Besharov. Available from: http://
www.welfareacademy.org/pubs/familywellbeing/familywellbeing-ch3rossi.pdf. Ac-
cessed November 12, 2002.
Florida Department of Children and Families. 1997. *Child Impact Studies.* Tallahassee:
Florida Department of Children and Families.
Friedman, Joseph, and Daniel H. Weinberg. 1980. "Housing Consumption in an Experi-
mental Housing Allowance Program: Issues of Self-Selection and Housing Require-
ments." Unpublished paper.
Gallagher, L. Jerome, Megan Gallagher, Kevin Perese, Susan Schreiber, and Keith Watson.
1998. *One Year after Federal Welfare Reforms: A Description of State Temporary
Assistance for Needy Families (TANF) Decisions as of October 1997.* Occasional
Paper no. 6. Washington, D.C.: Urban Institute.
Gueron, Judith M. 2002. Comments on "Ongoing Major Research in Welfare Reform:
What Will Be Learned," by Peter H. Rossi. In *Family Well-Being after Welfare Reform.*
Edited by Douglas J. Besharov. Available from: http://www.welfareacademy.org/pubs/
familywellbeing/familywellbeing-ch3rossi.pdf. Accessed November 12, 2002.

Heckman, James, and Richard Robb. 1986. "Alternative Methods for Solving the Problem of Selection Bias in Evaluating the Impact of Treatments on Outcomes." In *Drawing Inferences from Self-Selected Samples*. Edited by H. Wainer. Berlin: Springer-Verlag: 63–113.

Hollister, Robinson. 1997. "What Works, for Whom? Learning from the Experience of Welfare Reform." *Poverty Research News* (Summer): 3–6.

Indiana Division of Family and Children. 1997. *Child Impact Studies: Operational Phase*. Indianapolis: Indiana Division of Family and Children.

Iowa Department of Human Services. 1997. *An Application for Continuing Funding for the Operational Phase: Iowa Child Impact Study*. Des Moines: Iowa Department of Human Services.

Manpower Demonstration Research Corporation. 1997. "The Institutional Study Design: Urban Change Project." MDRC project design paper. New York: Manpower Demonstration Research Corporation.

Massey, James T., Dan O'Connor, and Karol Krotki. 1997. "Response Rates in Random Digit Dialing (RDD) Telephone Surveys." *Proceedings of the Section on Survey Methods*. Washington, D.C.: American Statistical Association: 707–712.

Michalopoulos, Charles. 2002. Comments on "Ongoing Major Research in Welfare Reform: What Will Be Learned," by Peter H. Rossi. In *Family Well-Being after Welfare Reform*. Edited by Douglas J. Besharov. Available from: http://www.welfareacademy.org/pubs/familywellbeing/familywellbeing-ch3rossi.pdf. Accessed November 12, 2002.

Michalopoulos, Charles, Hans Bos, Robert Lalonde, and Nandita Verman. 1997. *Assessing the Impact of Welfare Reform on Urban Communities: The Urban Change Project and Methodological Considerations*. MDRC project design paper. New York: Manpower Demonstration Research Corporation.

Minnesota Department of Human Services. 1997. *Child Impact Studies: Operational Phase*. St. Paul: Minnesota Department of Human Services.

Quint, Janet. 1997. *Urban Change: Implementation Study Design*. MDRC project design paper. New York: Manpower Demonstration Research Corporation.

Riccio, James A. 1998. *A Research Framework for Evaluating Jobs-Plus, A Saturation and Place-Based Employment Initiative for Public Housing Residents*. New York: Manpower Demonstration Research Corporation.

Robins, Philip K., Robert G. Spiegelman, Samuel Weiner, and Joseph G. Bell. Editors. 1980. *A Guaranteed Annual Income: Evidence from a Social Experiment*. New York: Academic Press.

Rolston, Howard. 2002. Comments on "Ongoing Major Research in Welfare Reform: What Will Be Learned," by Peter H. Rossi. In *Family Well-Being after Welfare Reform*. Edited by Douglas J. Besharov. Available from: http://www.welfareacademy.org/pubs/familywellbeing/familywellbeing-ch3rossi.pdf. Accessed November 12, 2002.

Rosenbaum, Paul R. 1995. *Observational Studies*. New York: Springer-Verlag.

Rossi, Peter. 2002. "Ongoing Major Research in Welfare Reform: What Will Be Learned." In *Family Well-Being after Welfare Reform*. Edited by Douglas J. Besharov. Available from: http://www.welfareacademy.org/pubs/familywellbeing/familywellbeing-ch3rossi.pdf. Accessed November 12, 2002.

Rossi, Peter H., and Katherine Lyall. 1976. *Reforming Public Welfare*. New York: Russell Sage.

Safir, Adam, Fritz Scheuren, and Kevin Wang. 2000. *Survey Methods and Data Reliability, 1997 and 1999*. Washington, D.C.: Urban Institute. November 3. Available from: http://www.urban.org/Template.cfm?NavMenuID=24&template=/TaggedContent/ViewPublication.cfm&PublicationID=7955. Accessed October 24, 2002.

Urban Institute. 1997. *National Survey of America's Families: Questionnaire*. Washington, D.C.: Urban Institute.

———. 1999. *Early Nonresponse Studies of the 1997 National Survey of America's Families.* NSAF Methodology Report no. 7. Washington, D.C.: Urban Institute.

———. 1999. *Survey Methods and Data Reliability.* NSAF Methodology Report no. 1. Washington, D.C.: Urban Institute.

———. 1999. *1997 NSAF Benchmarking Measures of Child and Family Well-Being.* NSAF Methodology Report no. 6. Washington, D.C.: Urban Institute.

———. 1999. *1997 NSAF Response Rates and Methods Evaluation.* NSAF Methodology Report no. 8. Washington, D.C.: Urban Institute.

———. 1999. *1997 NSAF Sample Design.* NSAF Methodology Report no. 2. Washington, D.C.: Urban Institute.

———. 1999. *1997 NSAF Snapshot Survey Weights.* NSAF Methodology Report no. 3. Washington, D.C.: Urban Institute.

Urban Institute Policy and Benefits Staff. 1998. "Comparing the NSAF Results to the Current Population Survey." Internal memorandum. Washington, D.C.: Urban Institute.

U.S. Department of Health and Human Services, Office of Planning, Research, and Evaluation. 2002. *Temporary Assistance for Needy Families (TANF) Program: Fourth Annual Report to Congress.* Washington, D.C.: U.S. Department of Health and Human Services. April. Available from: http://www.acf.dhhs.gov/programs/opre/ar2001/indexar.htm. Accessed October 13, 2002.

U.S. General Accounting Office. 1998. *Welfare Reform: HHS' Progress in Implementing Its Responsibilities.* Washington, D.C.: Government Printing Office.

———. 1998. *Welfare Reform: States Are Restructuring Programs to Reduce Welfare Dependency.* Washington, D.C.: Government Printing Office.

Weinberg, Daniel H., and Stephanie S. Shipp. 2002. Comments on "Ongoing Major Research in Welfare Reform: What Will Be Learned," by Peter H. Rossi. In *Family Well-Being after Welfare Reform.* Edited by Douglas J. Besharov. Available from: http://www.welfareacademy.org/pubs/familywellbeing/familywellbeing-ch3rossi.pdf. Accessed November 12, 2002.

Weinberg, Daniel H., Vicki J. Huggins, Robert A. Kominski, and Charles T. Nelson. 1997. *A Survey of Program Dynamics for Evaluating Welfare Reform.* Paper presented at the Statistics Canada Symposium XIV. Ottawa, Canada.

4

Income and Expenditures

Richard Bavier

This chapter attempts to piece together a coherent picture of recent developments in the economic well-being of children in families headed by an unmarried female by presenting data from several household surveys that tell us about their income and expenditures. The focus is on the period of the greatest change in welfare programs, from the last peak in the poverty rate in 1993 to 2001. Also examined is whether recent directions and magnitudes of change are in line with longer-term trends.

Trends in Poverty

In the 1970s, children replaced those aged sixty-five or older as the poorest age group. Figure 4.1 displays official poverty rates. The poverty thresholds are the official statistical measures, and the income counted is the official income measure, that is, regular pretax money income, including cash government transfers. The data come from the March annual demographic supplement to the Current Population Survey (CPS). The main purpose of this monthly survey of around 50,000 households is to provide monthly unemployment statistics. But once a year respondents are asked a wide array of questions about their income and program participation in the preceding calendar year.

Children residing with female family heads have much higher poverty rates than those living with married couples. As figure 4.2 illustrates, official poverty rates among children with female householders have remained well above the poverty rate of the aged, and rates for children living with couples have remained just below.

Figure 4.1
Poverty Rates for Children and Elderly, 1969–2001

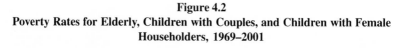

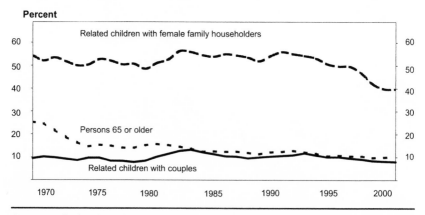

Source: U.S. Census Bureau, "Historical Poverty Tables," table 3, "Poverty Status of People, by Age, Race, and Hispanic Origin: 1959 to 2001," available from: http://www.census.gov/hhes/poverty/histpov/hstpov3.html, accessed November 21, 2002.

Figure 4.2
Poverty Rates for Elderly, Children with Couples, and Children with Female Householders, 1969–2001

Source: Author's calculation from annual March Current Population Survey; U.S. Census Bureau, "Historical Poverty Tables," table 3, "Poverty Status of People, by Age, Race, and Hispanic Origin: 1959 to 2001," and table 10, "Related Children in Female Householder Families, by Poverty Status," available from: http://www.census.gov/hhes/poverty/histpov/hstpov3.html and http://www.census.gov/hhes/poverty/histpov/hstpov10.html, accessed November 21, 2002.

Unfortunately, as figure 4.3 shows, the share of children living with two parents—including stepparents—has been declining steadily. (Intriguingly, this decades-long trend appears to have stopped in the mid-1990s.) When thinking about the well-being of children, therefore, it is often helpful to track measures separately by family type.

Even with unfavorable family composition trends—when a broad income measure and a consistent inflation adjustment are employed—the trend in child poverty over the last two decades is downward. Figure 4.4 displays poverty rates for all children combined again, this time for the period from 1979 to 2001, to illustrate two other points to keep in mind about the familiar image in figure 4.1. The top solid line tracks official poverty rates. A trend line overlays the cyclical ups and downs. Due to a strong improvement in poverty since the mid-1990s, the trend line of official child poverty for the period between 1979 and 2001 finally shows a weak decline.

The bottom lines illustrate two experimental efforts at improvements in the poverty measure. A broader range of income is counted—including noncash food and housing benefits (but not Medicare or

Figure 4.3
Children Living in Two-Parent Families, 1970–2002

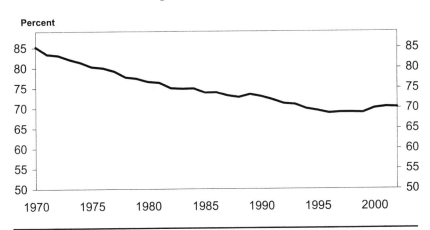

Note: Includes families with two natural, adoptive, or stepparents.
Source: Author's calculation from U.S. Census Bureau, "Families and Living Arrangements," table CH-1, "Living Arrangements of Children Under 18 Years Old: 1960 to Present," available from: http://www.census.gov/population/socdemo/hh-fam/tabCH-1.txt, accessed November 22, 2002.

Figure 4.4
Official and Experimental Poverty Rates for Children, 1979–2001

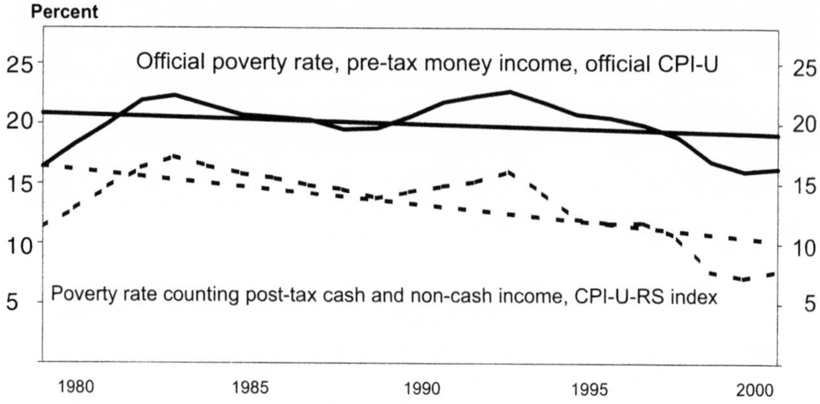

Source: Author's calculations and U.S. Census Bureau, "Poverty Thresholds by Size of Family and Number of Children" available from: http://www.census.gov/hhes/poverty/threshld.html, accessed November 21, 2002.

Medicaid) and the effects of direct taxes. Also, a more consistent inflation index is used to adjust the poverty thresholds forward each year from the late 1960s. Each year, the official poverty thresholds have been increased by the Consumer Price Index for Urban Consumers (CPI-U) to account for inflation and keep thresholds representing a constant level of economic well-being. It is widely recognized now that the official CPI-U overstated inflation in several respects. The poverty thresholds underlying the dotted line on figure 4.4 were inflated each year from 1967 using the experimental (research series) index—CPI-U-RS—published by the Bureau of Labor Statistics.[1] This has the effect of applying later improvements consistently across the whole period.

As can be seen, when a broader definition of income and a more consistent inflation adjustment are used, there is a more pronounced downward trend in poverty among children for the period between 1979 and 2001. This is not widely noted, and two qualifications need to be mentioned.

First, not all this progress was intentional. During this period, some types of income, such as social security benefits, food stamps, and some wages, were indexed each year according to the CPI-U. The intention was to protect these types of income against erosion by inflation. But because the CPI–U overstated inflation, indexed income actually increased in real terms.

Second, the National Research Council (NRC) has recommended a new measure of poverty that would change the poverty thresholds as well as make adjustments to the definition of income.[2] If the NRC proposal or other major changes were adopted, the trends in child poverty might look different.[3] Yet, underneath the ups and downs of the business cycle, the long-term trend in poverty among children appears to be heading gradually downward, despite the increase in the share of children living in family types characterized by higher poverty.

Did Welfare Reform Change This Trend?

We can ask, now, whether the years of the greatest change in cash welfare programs for families with children have seen changes in income and poverty that in any way depart from these longer-term trends. Figures 4.5 and 4.6 suggest that official child poverty rates, at least, are about what we would expect based on historical relationships with civilian unemployment rates and real wage levels. Figure 4.5 displays the familiar official rate in the solid line and rates that would be predicted from an ordinary least-squares regression

Figure 4.5
Child Poverty Rates, Actual and Predicted, 1960–2001

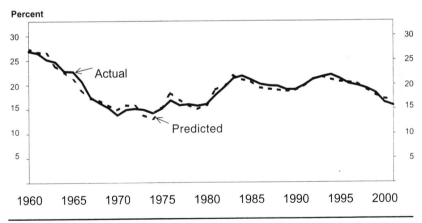

Note: Predicted poverty rates of related children are based on civilian unemployment rate, real wages, and the share of workers in the agricultural sector.

Source: Author's calculations and U.S. Census Bureau, "Historical Poverty Tables," table 3, "Poverty Status of People, by Age, Race, and Hispanic Origin: 1959 to 2001," available from: http://www.census.gov/hhes/poverty/histpov/hstpov3.html, accessed November 21, 2002.

Figure 4.6
Change in Child Poverty Rates, Actual and Predicted, 1960–2001

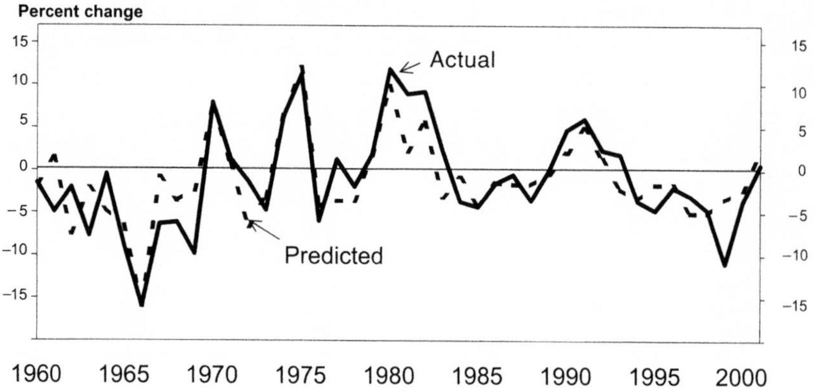

Percent change

Note: Figure shows change in actual official child poverty rates and change predicted by a change in civilian unemployment rate, change in real weekly wages of nonsupervisory and production employees, and a 1966 dummy variable for the CPS allocation and imputation changes.
Source: Author's calculations and U.S. Census Bureau, "Historical Poverty Tables," table 3, "Poverty Status of People, by Age, Race, and Hispanic Origin: 1959 to 2001," available from: http://www.census.gov/hhes/poverty/histpov/hstpov3.html, accessed November 21, 2002.

model in the dashed line. Figure 4.6 tracks actual and predicted annual *changes* in the official child poverty rate. Change models help deal with the fact that the poverty rate in one year is correlated with what the rate was in the previous year. The models are not very sophisticated, but they do a reasonably good job and suggest that recent declines in child poverty are generally consistent with past experience, although the large drop in poverty from 1998 to 1999 on figure 4.6 appears to be greater than the model predicted based on economic factors.

Did Welfare Participation Depart from This Trend?

From 1997 to 1999, welfare caseloads certainly departed from long-term trends, as figure 4.7 shows. Again, the solid line shows the actual year-to-year changes in the average monthly number of families receiving Aid to Families with Dependent Children (AFDC), and now Temporary Assistance for Needy Families (TANF), as reported by the states. The dotted line is the prediction of a model based on annual changes in the number of female householders with children, their employment rate, and the level of welfare benefits. As with the poverty change model, actual caseloads depart from predicted trends mainly in years with significant policy changes not captured by the predictor variables. Beginning with 1997, the factors that did a reasonably good job at predicting annual caseload changes over a long period that included sharp cyclical swings and major program changes suddenly lost their power. Again, like the poverty change model in figure 4.6, by 2000, the relationship appears to have been restored.

Figure 4.7
Change in AFDC/TANF Caseload, Actual and Predicted, 1965–2001

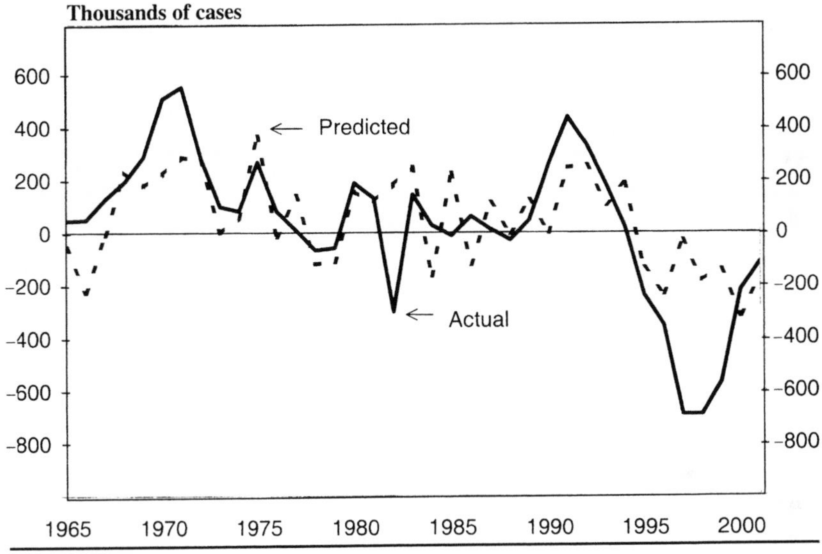

Note: Curves represent the actual and predicted changes in AFDC/TANF average monthly caseloads. The caseload change = (.9783 x change in number of female householders with children) + (-8,214,713 x change in employment rate of female householders with children) + (1,742 x constant dollar change in combined AFDC and food stamp benefits) + (490,187 due to the Omnibus Reconciliation Act in 1981).

Source: Author's calculations, and for 1936–1999, U.S. Department of Health and Human Services, Administration for Children and Families, "Temporary Assistance for Needy Families (TANF), 1936–1999," *ACF Data and Statistics,* 2000, available from: http:// www.acf.dhhs.gov/news/stats/3697.htm, accessed April 29, 2002; for 2000 and 2001, U.S. Department of Health and Human Services, Office of Planning, Research, and Evaluation, *Temporary Assistance for Needy Families Program (TANF): Fourth Annual Report to Congress* (Washington, D.C.: U.S. Department of Health and Human Services, April 2002), pp. II-13 and II-15, tables 2:1a. and 2:1b., "TANF: Total Number of Families, Fiscal Year 2000," and "TANF: Total Number of Families, Fiscal Year 2001," available from: http:// www.acf.dhhs.gov/programs/opre/ar2001/chapter02.pdf, accessed May 23, 2002.

Could the apparent departures reflect mismeasurement? The relationship between employment rates of female family heads and welfare caseloads may have changed. As employment rates among female family heads continue to rise, they are likely to include an increasingly rich mix of mothers who otherwise would be on welfare. As figure 4.8 shows, throughout the 1980s and as late as 1994, the share of female family heads employed when the March CPS was taken remained a little over half. In the next six years, it surpassed two-thirds. An employment rate increase from 60 to 65 percent may involve more welfare mothers than an increase from 50 to 55 percent. However, if the relationship between unemployment rates and child poverty or welfare caseloads changed in the mid-1990s, we would not expect the models to do a good job again beginning in 2000.

Instead of focusing on the percentage of families below the poverty line, we can understand more from a picture of the whole income distribution of such families, and how it has changed recently. This chapter will not say much about the income of couples with children or the small but growing share of children living with unmarried male family heads. Income among these groups appears to be rising all along the distribution. Another very interesting question not addressed here is whether welfare reform could be having an effect on family composition. Rather, this chapter focuses on the

Figure 4.8
Employment of Female Family Heads with Children, 1980-2002

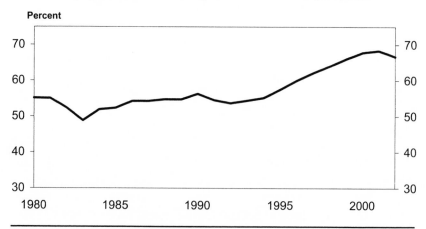

Note: Employment rate from March Current Population Survey.
Source: Author's calculation from U.S. Census Bureau, March Current Population Survey, various years.

group most affected by the replacement of AFDC by TANF—female family heads with children.

Family and Household Income (CPS)

Most female family heads with children have seen considerable income gains since the early 1990s, but the poorest lost most of these in the recession year of 2001. The top of table 4.1 shows the mean *family* income of each fifth of female-headed families with children for years since 1993. Families were ranked from those with the lowest incomes to those with the highest. This distribution was divided into fifths (quintiles), and the average income for each fifth was calculated for each year, then all years were expressed in 2001 dollars.

A significant proportion of female family heads with children in the bottom quintile lived with other unrelated adults. When the income of these others is counted, the economic status of the female family heads looks much better. In the bottom set of rows on table 4.1, the families are the same, and the income concept is the same. But instead of counting only income when creating the quintiles, those bottom rows count the income of everyone in the *household,* whether related or not. Then families are distributed into quintiles based on this household income.

There are several reasonable ways to calculate these kinds of distributional numbers. Table 4.1 counts all female family heads with children and no spouse present, whether they be heads of primary families or what the Census Bureau terms related or unrelated subfamilies. The income concept is the same comprehensive definition mentioned before—regular money income, including net capital gains, plus noncash food and housing benefits and the effect of direct taxes.

Other adjustments can reasonably be made to the Census data when calculating income distributions. Some analysts do not count families that show up with negative income. Some make adjustments to minimize the effects of top-coding, a privacy measure that the Census Bureau takes when it releases data for public use. Some adjust dollar income for family size. In producing table 4.1, adjustments were made for top-coding but not for the other kinds of adjustments.[4]

To add a little texture to the picture in table 4.1, employment and earnings rose both before and after 1995, all along the distribution.

Table 4.1

Family and Household Income for Female Heads of Primary Families, Related Subfamilies, or Unrelated Subfamilies with Children, 1993–2001 (in 2001 dollars)

	1993	1994	1995	1996	1997	1998	1999	2000	2001
Family income[a]									
Bottom quintile	7,138	7,907	8,310	7,980	7,653	7,693	8,080	8,853	7,780
Second quintile	14,041	15,061	15,917	15,585	15,788	16,585	17,028	18,138	17,378
Middle quintile	19,885	21,147	22,147	22,012	22,154	23,541	24,066	24,781	24,582
Fourth quintile	30,032	30,913	32,142	31,371	32,101	33,681	35,025	35,817	35,167
Top quintile	57,422	57,371	61,062	63,407	62,969	64,827	68,597	70,129	71,924
Household income[b]									
Bottom quintile	8,533	9,172	9,703	9,467	9,422	9,433	9,880	10,889	9,568
Second quintile	15,410	16,703	17,485	17,244	17,579	18,311	19,105	20,113	19,455
Middle quintile	22,322	23,922	24,869	24,502	24,876	26,099	27,485	28,290	27,554
Fourth quintile	33,785	35,033	36,316	35,156	36,499	38,231	40,756	41,412	39,793
Top quintile	62,138	63,060	68,142	70,402	69,518	71,442	75,677	77,291	79,604

Note: Due to top-coding, top quintile values are not strictly comparable.

[a]Post-tax, *family* money income plus food and housing noncash benefits (2001 dollars).

[b]Post-tax, *household* money income plus food and housing noncash benefits (2001 dollars).

Source: Author's calculation from U.S. Census Bureau, March Current Population Survey, various years.

And the maximum value of the Earned Income Tax Credit (EITC) was growing at the same time that more female family heads were becoming eligible for it. Reported receipt of other means-tested benefits generally declined. After 1995, the decline was sharper. For the bottom quintile, it was greater than the earnings increase. (Although one should keep in mind that individual families may move up and down the distribution from year to year.)

Data for 1999 and 2000 were more encouraging. By 2000, even the bottom quintile had exceeded the 1995 peaks. Figure 4.9 illustrates that improvements appeared even among the poorest tenth of female family heads with children. However, the recession year of 2001 brought income losses in the bottom quintile. In these CPS data, female family heads at the bottom of the distribution were back where they had been before the 1995 peak.

To summarize the CPS data, female family heads all along the income distribution have seen gains since 1993. In the period from 1995 to 1998, progress in the middle quintiles halted, and the bottom quintile lost income. However, 1998 saw gains by the middle quintiles and continued gains by the top. The bottom quintile finally saw gains again in 1999 and 2000, but they were lost in 2001.

The next question is how much confidence we should put in this picture. Analysts have noted that the bottom of the income distribution includes families with zero or negative incomes and that the

Figure 4.9
Post-Tax Cash and Non-cash Household Income of Female
Family Heads with Children, 1993–2001

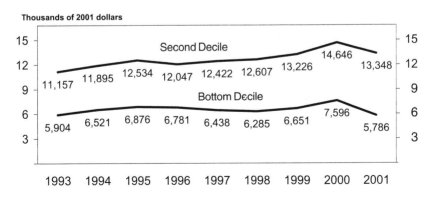

Source: Author's calculation from U.S. Census Bureau, March Current Population Survey, various years.

CPS seems to be missing more welfare recipients than it did only a few years ago. The sample of female family heads in the CPS includes several with negative family incomes and around thirty reporting zero income. About twice that number report annual incomes of less than $1,000. When household income is counted, the numbers are similar. Families do not go through a whole year with zero consumption, so zero or negative incomes must be only part of the story. On the other hand, these sample anomalies are present every year. Unless we have reason to think that the negative incomes and zero incomes exhibit a trend, then year-to-year comparisons in the bottom quintile and decile should tell us something useful about the direction of change.

Data reported by states to the U.S. Department of Health and Human Services show that TANF caseloads have been declining rapidly. The number of persons reporting that they received AFDC/TANF in the March CPS has been declining even faster. So it appears that the March CPS is capturing a shrinking share of cases that remain on the TANF rolls. Household surveys usually find fewer recipients and fewer benefit dollars than welfare program administrative data benchmarks indicate they should. However, after holding at around four-fifths through the late 1980s and early 1990s, the ratio of AFDC/TANF families in the March CPS versus administrative data has fallen below two-thirds. At this point, no one has come forward with a good explanation of this increase in what is called *underreporting* or *failure to report*. Some research is underway. For the present, we have to wonder how table 4.1 would look if there had been no increased failure to report.

Some analysts have sought to correct for this apparent loss of income by adding income back.[5] The difficult part is knowing who is failing to report TANF and so should be credited with additional welfare income. Table 4.1 does not make any adjustment of this kind. Earlier research on underreporting found that the people most likely to fail to report welfare were those who were married when the survey was taken, were no longer receiving the benefits, or were working.[6] We are more likely to find those in the middle and upper quintiles of the distribution, rather than in the bottom quintile.

It is also worth noting that we do not know for sure that the welfare income is not included in table 4.1. Some TANF benefits may be misreported rather than unreported. For example, recipients may report wage subsidies and even workfare benefits as "work for pay" rather than cash welfare. However, given state reports about the number of families participating in these kinds of activities, it does not seem likely that such misreporting could account for much of the apparent increase in failure to report. Fortunately, there are other sources of information that can support or correct the picture in the March CPS.

Monthly Income Data (SIPP)

The Survey of Income and Program Participation (SIPP) provides another perspective on the economic well-being of families. The SIPP is a panel survey that returns to the same sample households every four months and asks questions about monthly personal and family characteristics, income, and labor force and program participation. In addition to core questions asked with each visit (or wave), modules devoted to different topics on different waves gather detailed information on a wide variety of other subjects.

The 1993 SIPP panel started with nearly 20,000 households. Panels starting in 1996 and 2001 began with around 37,000, or nearly the size of the March CPS. A major problem for panel surveys is attrition, and this is the case with the SIPP as well. On the other hand, the recall period is shorter with the SIPP than with the CPS.

Spells of unemployment and other income interruptions mean that monthly data will tend to have a higher proportion of very poor families than annual data. Whatever the income measure, poverty rates that result from testing monthly income against one-twelfth the annual poverty threshold tend to be higher than rates testing annual income against the annual threshold.

A major limitation for our purposes is that the Census Bureau does not yet include estimates of the value of rental assistance or the effect of direct taxes on SIPP public use files. Monthly estimates of income taxes and refundable credits involve difficult conceptual issues. However, with increased employment and increases in the real value of the EITC, the absence of taxes from SIPP data is a serious limitation when it comes to trying to understand what has been happening to the economic well-being of female family heads.

Keeping cautions about the effects of attrition and the absence of rental assistance and taxes in mind, we observe that table 4.2 shows a pattern in SIPP monthly money income plus food stamps in the bottom quintile of female family heads that is similar to the track of annual income in the CPS. As in the CPS, employment increased all along the distribution during this period, while transfer income declined. The net was a downward trend through 1998, with improvement in 1999. We do not have SIPP data for 2000. However, the Census Bureau has released core data from the first wave of the 2001 panel, and that is shown in table 4.2.[7] Family income in the bottom quintile is well below its 1999 level, while household income is about the same as in 1999. In the CPS annual income data in table 4.1, family and household income move more in tandem.

Expenditures (CE)

Income is not the only, or necessarily the best, measure of economic well-being. Table 4.3 displays information about *expenditures* by female unit heads with children from the Consumer Expenditure Survey (CE).[8] The CE is an ongoing survey of around 5,000 sample households that gathers detailed quarterly information about household spending, as well as demographic, employment, and income information. The data in table 4.3 are from the interview part of the survey.

There are some definitional differences. The recall period for the CE is a quarter of a year, rather than a whole year as in the CPS, and for decades the CE has found higher expenditures than income at the bottom of the income distribution. However, we would expect the track of income in the CPS and the SIPP and expenditures in the CE to be generally consistent with each other. Unfortunately, they do not seem to agree when it comes to what happened to the poorest female family heads with children. Table 4.3 shows no decline at the bottom of the spending distribution after 1995, even in the bottom decile. Among female consumer unit heads with children in the CE, expenditures in the bottom quintile increased fairly steadily, while among female family heads with children in the CPS and the SIPP, income fell after 1995 before recovering at the very end of the decade. We do not have CE data for 2001 yet to see whether the dip in the bottom income quintile is mirrored in expenditures.

A Partial Explanation of Differences

The characteristics of female unit heads with children in the CE and the CPS are really quite similar, as table 4.4 illustrates. Some differences are just what would be expected between a survey with a three-month recall and another with an annual recall.

The bottom expenditure and income quintiles are another story. In table 4.5, the African-American share of the bottom quintile of

Table 4.2
Quintiles of Monthly Pre-Tax Money Income Plus Food Stamps, 1993–1999 and 2001 (in 2001 dollars)

	1993	1994	1995	1996	1997	1998	1999	2000	2001
Family income									
Bottom quintile	552	535	548	517	498	497	512	—	432
Second quintile	1,065	1,102	1,114	1,148	1,188	1,241	1,294	—	1,159
Middle quintile	1,629	1,688	1,718	1,805	1,893	1,952	2,040	—	1,894
Fourth quintile	2,567	2,630	2,679	2,827	2,923	3,034	3,193	—	2,942
Top quintile	5,272	5,271	5,363	5,860	5,967	6,205	6,618	—	6,101
Household income									
Bottom quintile	678	655	672	621	602	592	610	—	579
Second quintile	1,225	1,259	1,281	1,310	1,348	1,382	1,445	—	1,381
Middle quintile	1,920	1,976	1,989	2,076	2,137	2,182	2,274	—	2,213
Fourth quintile	3,022	3,020	3,053	3,259	3,273	3,405	3,552	—	3,408
Top quintile	5,886	5,807	5,838	6,427	6,469	6,712	7,112	—	6,796

Note: Due to top-coding, top quintile values are not strictly comparable.
Source: Author's calculation from U.S. Census Bureau, *The Survey of Income and Program Participation*, the 1993, 1996, and wave 1 of the 2001 panels.

Table 4.3

Quarterly Expenditures of Female Unit Heads with Children, 1992–2000 (in 2000 dollars)

	1992	1993	1994	1995	1996	1997	1998	1999	2000
Bottom quintile	2,155	2,099	2,172	2,122	2,246	2,255	2,323	2,413	2,433
Second quintile	3,456	3,466	3,607	3,354	3,570	3,682	3,686	3,794	3,947
Middle quintile	4,779	4,800	4,851	4,575	4,825	5,014	5,004	5,108	5,290
Fourth quintile	6,679	6,541	6,668	6,293	6,763	7,037	6,855	7,110	7,442
Top quintile	13,171	12,324	11,614	12,476	13,005	14,173	13,416	14,188	14,850

Source: Author's calculation from *Consumer Expenditure Survey*, interview data, various years.

Table 4.4

Characteristics of Female Unit Heads with Children, March 1998 Current Population Survey (CPS) and 1997 Consumer Expenditure Survey (CE)

	CPS March 1998	CE 1997
Number of householders	8,822,007	8,400,957
White	62%	58%
Black	35%	39%
Family size	1.8	1.9
With non–SSI cash welfare	23%	18%
With food stamps	33%	31%
With rental assistance	18%	17%
With earnings	82%	65%
Age of head	38 years	39 years
Marital status		
Widowed	9%	11%
Divorced	37%	37%
Separated	15%	18%
Never married	35%	34%

Source: March 1998 Current Population Survey and 1997 Consumer Expenditure Survey.

Table 4.5

Characteristics of Female Unit Heads with Children, Bottom Quintile of Income, March 1998 Current Population Survey (CPS) and Bottom Quintile of Expenditures, 1997 Consumer Expenditure Survey (CE)

	CPS March 1998	CE 1997
White	61%	47%
Black	36%	49%
Family size	3	3.2
Number of children	1.8	1.9
With non–SSI cash welfare	40%	35%
With food stamps	42%	63%
With rental assistance	15%	43%
With earnings	50%	38%
Age of head	35 years	37 years
Marital status		
Widowed	7%	9%
Divorced	25%	20%
Separated	17%	23%
Never married	49%	47%

Source: March 1998 Current Population Survey and 1997 Consumer Expenditure Survey.

spenders is much larger than their share of the bottom income quintile. Spenders in the bottom group are a little older. They are less likely to report earnings, although some of the difference reflects the fact that the CPS shows any earnings during a year, while the CE shows any earnings during a quarter. CE householders are about as likely to report cash welfare, but *much* more likely to be receiving food stamps and especially public housing or Section 8 assistance. It appears that the female householders with the lowest incomes are not necessarily those with the lowest expenditures. Or, if that seems to be the question, that those with the lowest expenditures are not necessarily those with the lowest incomes.

One contributing factor is rental assistance. Both surveys show a little under one-fifth of all female family heads receiving rental assistance, such as public housing or Section 8 certificates and vouchers. The CPS asks about rental assistance at the time of the survey, unlike other program benefits, for which the reference period is the preceding calendar year. So we would expect counts of rental assistance to be fairly similar in the two surveys. However, housing expenditures by CE families in public housing or with Section 8 certificates reflect only spending by the unit out-of-pocket, but not the rental subsidy paid by the local housing agency. This means that nearly half the units in the bottom spending quintile do not reflect total costs for what is, on average, the largest single expenditure category. So it is not surprising that those with subsidized housing are more apt to end up in the bottom quintile of total spending. However, leaving subsidized housing units in the CE out of the calculation does not change the basic pattern in table 4.3.

The apparent disagreement between the income and expenditures survey data leaves us with some uncertainty about what happened among the poorest female family heads with children from 1995 to 1998. And we do not yet have expenditure data for 2001 to see whether expenditures will turn down at the bottom as income did after 2000.

Welfare Leavers

The title of this volume implies that welfare reform may have influenced the economic well-being of families with children, independent of the effects of the economy. If so, the group likely to have been influenced most directly is made up of families that left the welfare rolls in record numbers since the caseload peak of 1994.

Chapter 2 discusses a large number of state-level studies of the experience of welfare leavers. The SIPP provides a national picture of the economic well-being of welfare leavers. Unlike the state-level leaver studies and other special surveys undertaken after enactment of welfare reform, the SIPP also lets us observe the economic well-being of those who left the welfare rolls in years before enactment of reform. So we can answer a very basic descriptive question left open by other leaver studies: Was the economic experience of post-reform leavers very different from pre-reform leavers?

Figure 4.10 traces monthly household pre-tax money income plus food stamps among welfare leavers from the 1993 and 1996 SIPP panels. All leavers in each panel who could be followed for twenty-four post-exit months were included. Leavers were ranked into thirds based on their total income over the twenty-four months. While the income gains of the top third of leavers in the 1996 panel appear steeper than in the 1993 panel, overall, it looks like the economic experience of most post-reform welfare leavers was very similar to pre-reform leavers. Most gains were at the top, but by the second post-exit year, income in the middle was higher than before exit. If the effect of direct taxes, including the EITC, was added, income levels would be higher in every third.

Figure 4.10
Monthly Income of AFDC/TANF Leavers: Thirds Ranked by Post-Exit Income

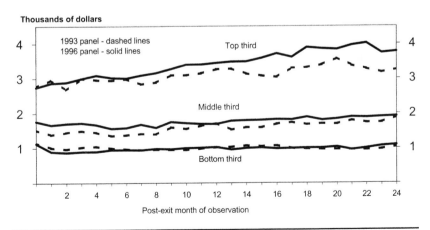

Note: Monthly household pre-tax money income plus food stamps.
Source: Author's calculations from U.S. Census Bureau, *Survey of Income and Program Participation*, the 1993 and 1996 panels.

Figure 4.11
Simulated Monthly Poverty Rates of AFDC/TANF Leavers

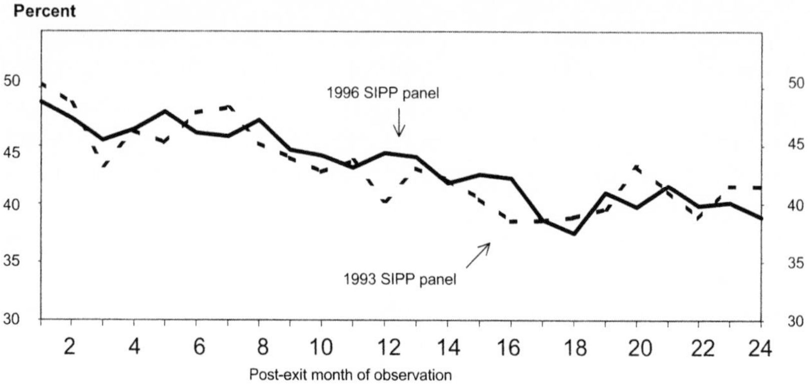

Percent

Note: Poverty measure simulated with monthly household pre-tax money income plus food stamps and one-twelfth poverty threshold.
Source: Author's calculations from U.S. Census Bureau, *Survey of Income and Program Participation*, the 1993 and 1996 Panels.

The similarity of poverty rates among leavers in both SIPP panels, shown in figure 4.11, is striking, and it raises two questions. With a stronger economy in the second half of the decade, would we not expect 1996 panel leavers to do better economically? On the other hand, as more and more families left the welfare rolls, would we not expect that later leavers would have less to offer the labor market than earlier leavers, and so have more economic difficulties?

These are questions that go beyond the focus of this volume. They ask what difference welfare reform made, after controlling for differences in the economy and the characteristics of the welfare leavers. Several attempts have been made to go beyond understanding outcomes—What happened in the years since welfare reform?—and address the question of welfare impacts—What difference did welfare reform make? On the whole, favorable impacts have been found, but should be regarded as preliminary.

Using March CPS data, researchers have found that, controlling for other factors, the enactment of welfare reform increased employment among target populations and reduced welfare participation.[9] As figure 4.7 suggests, more female family heads left welfare and went to work than would have without reform, even allowing for the hot labor market in the late 1990s.

Econometric analysis of SIPP data has also found that many female family heads left welfare *because of* reform. This study concluded that, all else equal—meaning controlling for changes in the economy, the characteristics of leavers, and other factors—post-reform leavers would have had more economic problems than earlier leavers. However, figures 4.10 and 4.11 show that 1996 panel leavers did not do worse than 1993 panel leavers. All else was not equal after August 1996 when the Personal Responsibility and Work Opportunity Reconciliation Act (PRWORA) was enacted. The economy was stronger in the last years of the decade than in the first years. So, while reform may have pushed families off the rolls who would have stayed on welfare even in such a strong economy, the strong economy kept most of them from experiencing more economic difficulties than earlier leavers.[10]

A final note on welfare reform impacts. Earlier discussion of figures 4.6 and 4.7 noted that, after losing their predictive power at some point in the late 1990s, these simple models begin to do a good job again with data for 2000. In that year, changes in TANF caseloads and child poverty appear to resume long-term relationships with a few demographic and economic predictors. The temporary departures from trends on figures 4.6 and 4.7 may reflect the impacts of welfare reform found by the more sophisticated econometric analyses just mentioned. If so, the figures also suggest that the impacts ended in 2000. Due to impacts on year-to-year changes in 1997–1999, caseloads and child poverty rates may remain below the *levels* we would have seen without reform. However, impacts on annual *changes* appear to have ended.

Concluding Observations

Since the poverty crest in 1993, and during a period of great welfare changes and dropping caseloads, income improved for female family heads with children. The combined picture of increased employment, declining caseloads, and falling child poverty is more favorable at this stage than anyone predicted in 1996.

There is some incongruity in the pictures of economic well-being of female family heads with children provided by national income surveys (CPS and SIPP), on the one hand, and a national expenditure survey (CE) on the other. Years immediately after enactment of PRWORA appear to show both income losses and expenditure increases among the poorest families. In the most recent year for which we have data, the recession year of 2001, the poorest female family heads with children appear to have experienced significant income losses that largely erased gains since the early 1990s. We do not have expenditure data for 2001, but in the past such data have provided a more positive picture of the economic well-being of this subpopulation. However, the CE sample is small, and reconciliation of spending numbers with the income numbers remains elusive.

The track of average income and expenditures for quintiles of the distribution of female family heads with children looks something like the fingers of a hand. All three household surveys show at least four fingers pointed up. Where the bottom finger is pointing is unclear. That is one caution while we celebrate widespread progress.

Notes

1.   See Kenneth J. Stewart and Stephen B. Reed, "CPI Research Series Using Current Methods, 1978–98," *Monthly Labor Review* 122 (6) (1999): 29–38. This paper was updated in an April 2001 draft, "CPI Research Series Using Current Methods, 1978–2000," by the authors. See also supplemental tables in Carmen DeNavas-Walt and Robert W. Cleveland, *Money Income in the United States: 2001,* Current Population Reports P60-218 (Washington, D.C.: Government Printing Office, 2002).

2.   Constance F. Citro and Robert T. Michael, editors, *Measuring Poverty: A New Approach* (Washington, D.C.: National Academy Press, 1995).

3.   Kathleen Short, *Experimental Poverty Measures: 1999,* Current Population Reports P60-216 (Washington, D.C.: Government Printing Office, 2001).

4.   One more caution about year-to-year comparisons with the Current Population Survey (CPS). Significant changes in CPS methods were made with the March 1994 CPS (1993 data), and the U.S. Census Bureau cautions about making precise comparisons with earlier years. A new sample design was implemented over a period affecting March 1994 and March 1995, as well. See U.S. Census Bureau, *Income, Poverty, and Valuation of Noncash Benefits: 1993,* Current Population Reports P60-188 (Washington, D.C.: Government Printing Office, 1995).

5.   See Wendell Primus, Lynette Rawlings, Kathy Larin, and Kathryn Porter, *The Initial Impacts of Welfare Reform on the Economic Well-Being of Single-Mother Families* (Washington, D.C.: Center on Budget and Policy Priorities, August 22, 1999).

6.   See Kent H. Marquis and Jeffrey C. Moore, "Measurement Errors in the Survey of Income and Program Participation (SIPP) Program Reports," proceedings of the 1990 Annual Research Conference, U.S. Census Bureau, Washington, D.C., 1990; and Karen Goudreau, Howard Oberheu, and Denton Vaughan, "An Assessment of the Quality of Survey Reports of Income from the Aid to Families with Dependent Children (AFDC) Program," *Journal of Business and Economic Statistics* 2 (2) (1984): 179–186.

7.   Note that 2001 values on table 4.2 reflect only four months, while values for other years reflect twelve months of data.

8.   These expenditure data differ from a similar display in a May 27, 1999, U.S. House of Representatives, Republican Leadership paper, "Welfare Reform Has Already

Achieved Major Successes: A House Republican Assessment of the Effects of Welfare Reform," in two principal ways. First, table 4.2 includes only female consumer unit heads with minor children. Second, the distribution is based on expenditures, rather than on income. Income data in the CE are less complete than in the CPS or the SIPP.

9. Robert F. Schoeni and Rebecca Blank, "What Has Welfare Reform Accomplished? Impacts on Welfare Participation, Employment, Income, Poverty, and Family Structure," National Bureau of Economic Research Working Paper 7627, 2000; and Neeraj Kaushal and Robert Kaestner, "From Welfare to Work: Has Welfare Reform Worked?" *Journal of Policy Analysis and Management* 20 (4) (2001): 699–719.

10. Richard Bavier, "Welfare Reform Impacts in the Survey of Income and Program Participation," *Monthly Labor Review* 125 (11) (November 2002): 23–28.

References

Bavier, Richard. 2002. "Welfare Reform Impacts in the Survey of Income and Program Participation." *Monthly Labor Review* 125 (11) (November): 23–28.

Citro, Constance F., and Robert T. Michael, editors. 1995. *Measuring Poverty: A New Approach.* Washington, D.C.: National Academy Press.

DaNavas-Walt, Carmen, and Robert W. Cleveland. 2002. *Money Income in the United States: 2001.* Current Population Reports P60-218. Washington, D.C.: Government Printing Office.

Goudreau, Karen, Howard Oberheu, and Denton Vaughan. 1984. "An Assessment of the Quality of Survey Reports of Income from the Aid to Families with Dependent Children (AFDC) Program." *Journal of Business and Economic Statistics* 2 (2): 179–186.

Kaushal, Neeraj, and Robert Kaestner. 2001. "From Welfare to Work: Has Welfare Reform Worked?" *Journal of Policy Analysis and Management* 20 (4): 699–719.

Marquis, Kent H., and Jeffrey C. Moore. 1990. "Measurement Errors in the Survey of Income and Program Participation (SIPP) Program Reports." Proceedings of the 1990 Annual Research Conference. U.S. Census Bureau.

Primus, Wendell, Lynette Rawlings, Kathy Larin, and Kathryn Porter. 1999. *The Initial Impacts of Welfare Reform on the Economic Well-Being of Single-Mother Families.* Washington, D.C.: Center on Budget and Policy Priorities. August 22.

Schoeni, Robert F., and Rebecca Blank. 2000. "What Has Welfare Reform Accomplished? Impacts on Welfare Participation, Employment, Income, Poverty, and Family Structure." Working Paper 7627. National Bureau of Economic Research. Boston, Mass.

Sherman, Arloc. 1999. *Extreme Child Poverty Rises Sharply in 1997.* Washington, D.C.: Children's Defense Fund. August 22.

Short, Kathleen. 2001. *Experimental Poverty Measures: 1999.* Current Population Reports P60–216. Washington, D.C.: Government Printing Office.

Stewart, Kenneth J., and Stephen B. Reed. 1999. "CPI Research Series Using Current Methods, 1978–98." *Monthly Labor Review* 122 (6): 29–38.

U.S. Census Bureau. 1995. *Income, Poverty, and Valuation of Noncash Benefits: 1993.* Current Population Reports P60–188. Washington, D.C.: Government Printing Office.

U.S. House of Representatives. Republican Leadership. 1999. *Welfare Reform Has Already Achieved Major Successes: A House Republican Assessment of the Effects of Welfare Reform.* May 27.

5

Cohabitation and Child Well-Being

Wendy D. Manning

Definitions of "family" influence our understanding of children's well-being. This chapter illustrates this point by exploring the distinction between two types of unmarried-mother households: those in which the mother lives only with her children and those in which she is living (cohabiting) with a man who may or may not be the father of her children. Single mothers are typically viewed as unmarried women living alone with their children. Yet they often are living in households with one or more other adults, and they experience a wide variety of household living arrangements. In 1995, for example, 40 percent of unmarried mothers were not living alone.[1]

Differentiating between cohabiting-couple households and other unmarried-mother families is important because the children may have substantially different childhood experiences. Empirical evidence indicates that an unmarried mother's household living arrangements, not just her marital status, have implications for her children's social and economic well-being.[2]

This chapter focuses on children in cohabiting-couple households for two reasons. First, cohabitation represents a two-adult living arrangement that has become a prominent part of children's lives. Traditionally, however, cohabiting unions with children have been treated like one-parent families because the parent and her or his cohabiting partner are not legally married. This approach is problematic because at times children live with both biological parents who are not married but are sharing a residence. Alternatively, children live with one biological parent and the parent's cohabiting partner, somewhat akin to a stepfamily. Using the parents' marital status as a basis for making conclusions about children's lives may not be as informative or reliable as considering household living arrangements and relationships. To date, analyses of the effects of family structure on children have largely ignored cohabitation.

Second, one of the goals of the Personal Responsibility and Work Opportunity Reconciliation Act of 1996 (PRWORA) was to encourage the formation and maintenance of two-parent families. Cohabitation can represent a type of two-parent family, but it was probably not the two-parent family form that was envisioned by the original architects of welfare reform. Thus, it is important to consider the relationship between cohabitation and public assistance. This has become even more important given the new marriage promotion incentives that are being pursued.

In this chapter, I refer broadly to children living in "cohabiting-couple" households. This term may be unfamiliar to some readers so I define it here. Cohabiting-couple households contain a child and at least one biological parent. I call cohabiting-couple households that contain two biological parents "cohabiting-parent" households. Those that have just one biological parent, I call "cohabiting-partner" households.

Cohabiting Arrangements

Cohabitation is becoming more prevalent. The number of unmarried partner households increased from 3.2 million in 1990 to 5.5 million in 2000.[3] Similarly, during this period, there has been an 88 percent increase in cohabiting-couple households with children under fifteen, from 891,000 to 1.675 million.[4] Half of adults have cohabited, and most recent marriages are preceded by cohabitation.[5] Consequently, increasing numbers of children are living with cohabiting adults. According to 1990 Decennial Census data released in the Public Use Microdata Sample (PUMS), 2.2 million children, or 3.5 percent of children, were living in cohabiting-couple households.[6] Findings from the Survey of Income and Program Participation (SIPP) indicate that this living arrangement grew among children. In 1996, 3.3 million children, or 5 percent of children, were living in cohabiting-couple households.[7] This household structure is more common for some racial and ethnic groups than for others. For example, 8 percent of Puerto Rican children were living in cohabiting-couple households, in contrast to only 3 percent of white children.[8] When statistical data are reported, these children are commonly grouped with children living with single, unmarried mothers.

If the scope is narrowed to children in unmarried-mother families, we obtain a slightly different perspective. Consistently (in 1990,
1996, and 1999) just over half of children living with unmarried
mothers reside with just their mother and no other adults, indicating
that a substantial percentage of children in unmarried-mother families do not live with only their biological mother.[9] Data from the
National Survey of America's Families (NSAF) indicate that, in
1999, one-fifth of children who lived with unmarried mothers
lived in cohabiting-couple households, and 11 percent lived with
their parents, and 12 percent lived with other adults (see figure 5.1).[10]
Furthermore, there are racial and ethnic variations in living arrangements.[11] For example, data from the SIPP indicate that nearly
one-quarter of Hispanic children in unmarried-mother families
lived in cohabiting-couple households, whereas 9 percent of African-American children did so.[12]

An increasing number of children are born into cohabiting-couple
households. The percentage doubled between the early 1980s and
early 1990s; 12 percent of children born in the early 1990s were
born into cohabiting-couple households. These levels are higher
among minorities than among non-Hispanic whites. Nearly one-
fifth of African-American and Hispanic (16 percent and 17 percent,

Figure 5.1
Living Arrangements of Children in Unmarried-Mother Families, 1999

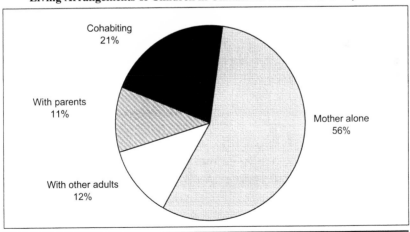

Source: Gregory Acs and Sandi Nelson, *"Honey, I'm Home": Changes in Living Arrangements in the Late 1990s*, Assessing the New Federalism Policy Brief B (Washington, D.C.:
Urban Institute, 2001), available from: http://newfederalism.urban.org/html/series_b/b38/
b38.html, accessed November 19, 2002.

respectively) children were born to cohabiting couples in contrast to only 9 percent of white children. Births to cohabitors represent an increasing proportion of unmarried childbearing. (Among children born to unmarried women in the early 1990s, 39 percent were born into cohabiting-parent households with two biological parents.)[13] This rise is largely due to an increase in the percentage of unmarried women who are cohabiting.[14] These levels are even higher among low-income families.[15] Clearly, these trends require a shift away from standard notions of unmarried-mother families.

Most cohabiting women do not give birth to children while cohabiting. A substantial percentage of women who become pregnant during cohabitation marry (33 percent) or break up (7 percent) before their child is born.[16] In fact, unmarried pregnant women are increasingly cohabiting before the birth of their child. In the early 1990s similar proportions of single pregnant women married (11 percent) or cohabited (9 percent) prior to the birth of their child.[17] Childbearing during cohabitation is more common among Hispanics than whites or African Americans. In fact, the levels of childbearing and intentions for childbearing among Hispanics suggest that cohabitation is a more acceptable arena for family building than among white or African-American women. Thus, cohabitation may be treated as almost equivalent to marriage, particularly among the Hispanic population, which has longstanding cultural support for cohabitation and consensual unions.[18]

Not all children who live in cohabiting-couple households are living with both biological parents. About half (54 percent) of children are living in cohabiting-couple households that are structurally similar to stepfamilies in that they live with only one biological parent and that parent's partner.[19] Among white children, cohabiting-couple households more often appear like stepparent families. Three-fifths (61 percent) of white children in cohabiting-couple households live with only one biological parent in contrast to only one-third (36 percent) of Hispanic children. The biological relationship of children to the adults in the households may be important for our understanding of the implications of cohabitation.

Although many children might not be living in a cohabiting-couple household at any one point in time, a considerable share will eventually spend some of their lives in one. Figure 5.2 illustrates that nearly two-fifths of children in the United States are expected to live in cohabiting-couple households at some point during their childhood.[20] These estimates vary somewhat, depending on the data source and methodology.[21] Cohabitation is expected to be part of some children's lives more than others. More than half (55 percent) of all African-American children are expected to live in a cohabiting-couple household, as are about 40 percent of Hispanic children and about 30 percent of white children.[22]

Implications for Children

One way to establish the importance of distinguishing between cohabiting-couple households and other unmarried-parent or married-couple families is to show that children in cohabiting-couple households fare better or worse than children in other types of families. Cohabitation may be advantageous for children by providing two potential caretakers and income providers, but it may be disadvantageous for children because of the relatively short duration, informal nature of cohabiting unions, and other factors.[23]

Assessing the implications of children's living arrangements is complicated by selection issues. A particular family or household type does not necessarily advantage or disadvantage children. Individuals who choose to enter a specific type of family or household may do so because of particular characteristics related to child outcomes, such as income or education.

Figure 5.2
Children Who Will Ever Live in a Cohabiting Household, 1990–1994 Cohort

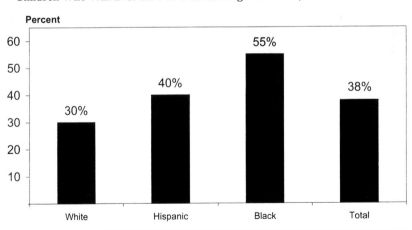

Source: Larry Bumpass and Hsien-Hen Lu, "Trends in Cohabitation and Implications for Children's Family Contexts in the United States," *Population Studies* 54 (2000): 29–41.

Economic Factors

Official poverty estimates are based on family income, and the cohabiting partner is not considered part of the family. Recently, the National Academy of Sciences recommended that the definition of "family" be expanded so that the cohabiting partner's income is included when estimating poverty levels.[24] Each approach represents an extreme. The official estimates assume that the partner provides nothing, and the expanded family definition assumes that the partner shares equally with all family members. It is unlikely that either assumption accurately reflects the circumstances of cohabiting-couple households.[25]

Including the cohabiting parent's or partner's income in family income can make a substantial difference in the poverty level of children in cohabiting-couple households.[26] Manning and Lichter's analysis of Public Use Microdata Samples (PUMS) data indicates that poverty rates of children in cohabiting-couple households in 1990 were quite high, nearly 50 percent. When the male partner's or father's income is treated as part of the family income and he is counted as part of the consuming unit, about 31 percent of children in cohabiting-couple households are living in poverty, compared with 44 percent when the partner or father is excluded from the family. Including the cohabiting partners and fathers draws 40 percent of poor children in cohabiting-couple households out of poverty, and only a small percentage of non-poor children in cohabiting-couple households fall into poverty. Thus, cohabiting partners or fathers do not always provide a net gain in economic well-being. Yet including the cohabiting partner or father as part of the household unit does not change the overall levels of poverty for children in unmarried-mother families: Children in cohabiting-couple households represent only a small share of children, and cohabiting partners and fathers, on average, are not high-income earners.[27]

Children living in cohabiting-couple households fare worse economically than their counterparts in married couple families, but they fare better than children living with other unmarried parent families.[28] Although living with two parents does not guarantee economic security for children, parents in married-couple families possess considerably stronger socioeconomic resources than cohabiting parents. Figure 5.3 compares the poverty rates of children in unmarried-mother families by living arrangement. The poverty rates of chil-

Figure 5.3
Child Poverty Rates in Unmarried-Mother Families
by Living Arrangement, 1989

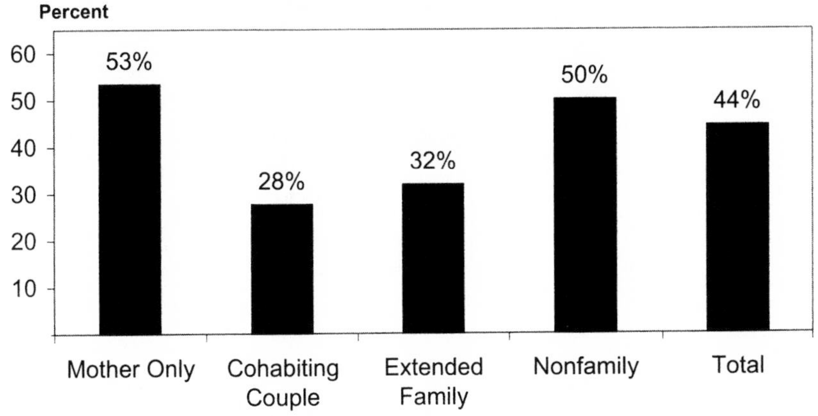

Percent

Mother Only	Cohabiting Couple	Extended Family	Nonfamily	Total

53% — Mother Only
28% — Cohabiting Couple
32% — Extended Family
50% — Nonfamily
44% — Total

Source: Wendy D. Manning and Daniel T. Lichter, "Parental Cohabition and Children's Economic Well-Being," *Journal of Marriage and the Family* 5B (1996): 998–1010.

dren living in cohabiting-couple households are considerably lower than those of children living with only their mother or in non-family households. Figure 5.4 illustrates the gain from cohabitation for children on the basis of their race and ethnicity. For example, Puerto Rican and white children living with just their mother have poverty rates twice that of children living in cohabiting-couple households. Black and Mexican-American children still gain economically from living in cohabiting-couple households, but the benefit is somewhat smaller. Taken together, these results suggest that understanding the economic circumstances of children requires distinguishing cohabiting-couple households from both other unmarried-parent and married-couple families.

Another measure of economic uncertainty is material hardship—whether there were times when a household could not pay its essential expenses. Using SIPP data, Bauman found that income from cohabiting partners and parents did significantly less to alleviate material hardship than did the income from a spouse.[29] These findings suggest that cohabiting-couple households may not share their income in the same manner as married couples. It appears that children in cohabiting-couple households benefit less from their parent's cohabitation than they would if they were married.

Figure 5.4
Child Poverty Rates in Unmarried-Mother Families by Race/Ethnicity, 1989

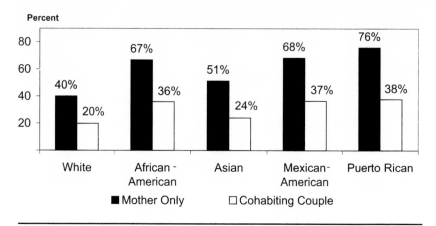

Source: Wendy D. Manning and Daniel T. Lichter, "Parental Cohabition and Children's Economic Well-Being," *Journal of Marriage and the Family* 5B (1996): 998–1010.

An important indicator of economic hardship is receipt of public assistance. Peter Brandon and Larry Bumpass rely on SIPP data to examine differences in rates of public assistance for various types of families.[30] Not surprisingly, predicted levels of Aid to Families with Dependent Children (AFDC) receipt were highest for children living with only their mother (see figure 5.5). Children living with their biological mother and her cohabiting partner (cohabiting-partner households) came in a close second. Their odds of welfare receipt were almost twice as high as those of children living with two biological cohabiting parents (cohabiting-parent household). Children residing in households with two married parents experienced the lowest probabilities of welfare receipt, half as high as two-biological-cohabiting-parent families. These empirical results basically reflect the eligibility rules outlined by Robert Moffitt and colleagues.[31] At the same time, we can see considerable variation in how children in cohabiting-couple households were treated under the former welfare system.

Social Factors

Considerably less research attention has been paid to the social or developmental consequences of cohabitation for children. Until re-

Figure 5.5
Predicted Probability of AFDC Receipt by Family Structure, 1985–1994

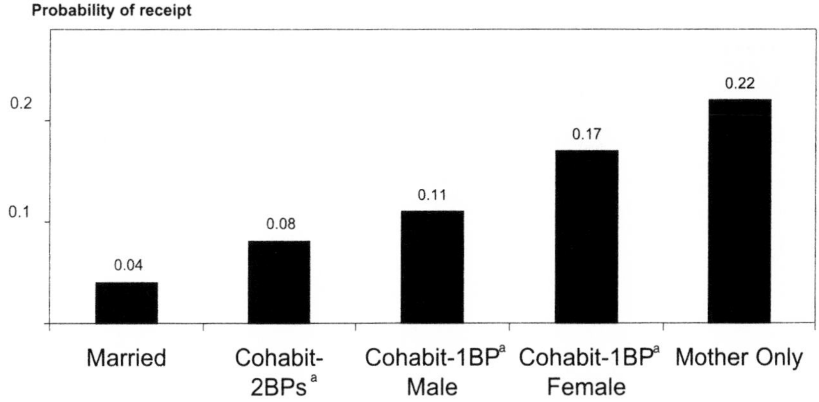

Probability of receipt

Married	0.04
Cohabit-2BPs[a]	0.08
Cohabit-1BP[a] Male	0.11
Cohabit-1BP[a] Female	0.17
Mother Only	0.22

[a]BP = Biological parent.
Source: Peter Brandon and Larry Bumpass, "Children's Living Arrangements, Coresidence of Unmarried Fathers, and Welfare Receipt," *Journal of Family Issues* 22 (2001): 3–26, table 7.

cently, data that include cohabitation as a family type have not been widely available. In addition, sample-size limitations have prevented detailed analyses and hampered the generalizability of results. Policymakers should be cautious about drawing broad conclusions from select small samples. Below, I make comparisons that account for the biological relationship of children to adults in the household and the marital status of the adults.

As in married-parent families, children's emotional and developmental well-being may depend to some extent on their biological relationship to adults in the household. Most of the research that examines how child well-being in cohabiting-parent households contrasts to married-parent families suggests some differences (and a few similarities) in academic achievement, behavior problems, and developmental outcomes.[32] Thus, children living in cohabiting-parent households are generally disadvantaged compared with children in married-parent families. Also, some racial and age differences are evident.[33] We must be cautious about the outcomes we consider because the vast majority of the children in two-biological parent families are under the age of five.[34]

The evidence that contrasts the well-being of children in cohabiting-partner households and married-*stepparent* families indicates that marriage does not necessarily provide a protective buffer. Children living in cohabiting-partner households compared to those living in married-stepparent families share similar levels of well-being for indicators of behavior problems, school engagement, and some measures of academic achievement.[35] Teenagers living in cohabiting-couple households fare equally well as teens living in married-stepparent families in terms of school problems, suspension and expulsion from school, grade point average, and college expectations.[36] Adolescents in cohabiting-couple households fare worse than those in married-stepparent families in terms of delinquency and performance on the Peabody Picture Vocabulary Test.

The research that contrasts the social well-being of children living with only one parent and those in cohabiting-partner households suggests that the latter fare as well as children living with only one parent.[37] Among children living with unmarried mothers, cohabitation appears neither to advantage nor disadvantage children socially. Other evidence indicates that there are advantages and disadvantages of cohabitation that differ according to social outcome and race of the child.[38] Taken together, the evidence suggests that regardless of the comparison group, children from cohabiting-couple households appear to experience some unique social and developmental outcomes. Yet, the evidence is not conclusive and requires further attention to the parenting context in terms of behaviors and relationship quality, age of the child, biological relationship to the child, as well as the stability of marital and cohabiting unions.

Future Considerations

This chapter illustrates the importance of carefully considering definitions of families and households. Children's economic and social well-being vary depending on whom we include in our measures of families and households. We must be explicit about the meaning of family and household types when analyzing welfare and family structure. The complexity and shifting nature of family life make it difficult to create enforceable policies, but we need to think beyond marital status when we consider children's social and economic well-being.

This increase in cohabitation does not mean that cohabitation is replacing marriage. It is important to note that virtually all Americans marry at some point. The delay in marriage is evident from the increases in the age at marriage. Thus, marriage is not being eliminated; it is simply being postponed. Young adults expect to get married and continue to hold the institution of marriage in high regard. Despite the strength of marriage, children are increasingly being born and raised outside of married two-biological parent families. The link between marriage and parenthood has weakened.

Racial and ethnic differences in family formation have received considerable attention. In particular, concern has been raised about lower marriage rates among African Americans. Yet this racial gap in marriage cannot be adequately addressed without consideration of cohabitation. In fact, half of the racial gap in union formation disappears when the definition of union formation is expanded to include both marriage and cohabitation.[39] Also, greater percentages of black men and women who are in unions are cohabiting than whites or Hispanics.[40] Similarly, Hispanics have high cohabitation rates and more frequently bear children while cohabiting than whites or blacks.[41] The role of cohabitation in the marriage process and children's lives appears to differ according to race and ethnicity. The empirical evidence suggests that the meaning of cohabitation is not consistent for racial and ethnic groups. Thus, understanding family patterns among minorities requires attention to cohabitation and the recognition that uniform interpretations of the meaning of cohabitation may not exist.

Married couples are presumed to share equally in all family and household resources. This assumption is probably not completely true and depends to some extent on the power dynamics of the families. It remains unclear how to treat the issue of income pooling for cohabiting-couple households. They do not appear to share resources in the same way as married couples. Further investigation of intrahousehold income distribution is required, as well as an analysis of parenting roles.

Most of the research reviewed in this chapter cannot account for the effects of transitions into and out of cohabiting-couple households on children's well-being. The data requirements are somewhat strict, requiring complete children's residence histories or prospective data that include cohabitation as a living arrangement. There appears to be increased awareness that the greater the number of family transitions that children experience, the more negatively their lives are influenced.[42] If children are born to unmarried mothers living alone, they are expected to spend about half of their childhood living with only their mother; if they are born into cohabiting-couple households, they are expected to spend only one-quarter of their childhood living with only their mother.[43]

We must focus our attention on treatment of cohabiting-couple households in our new system of welfare. This issue is complicated: States have extensive control over their welfare programs, so more variation and flexibility will exist than under the Aid to Families with Dependent Children system. In an environment of rapid policy change and shifts in control to local areas, it will be difficult to capture how children in cohabiting households are treated, even as new marriage promotion initiatives may draw attention to children in such households.

Larger samples or targeted subsamples will allow us to learn more about variation in the meanings of family and household living arrangements among race and ethnic groups and income groups. Cohabitation is more common among minorities and individuals with weak economic prospects; as a consequence, it sometimes has been viewed as an adaptive family-formation strategy among the disadvantaged.[44] Family ties and kinship are defined differently depending in part on the long-standing cultural traditions of racial and ethnic groups. Thus, to assume that policy levers to encourage one type of family form will have the same implications for all children is misguided.

Notes

1.   Rebecca London, "Trends in Single Mothers' Living Arrangements from 1970 to 1995: Correcting the Current Population Survey," *Demography* 35 (1998): 125–131.

2.   See, for example, Gregory Acs and Sandi Nelson, *The Kids Are Alright? Children's Well-Being and the Rise of Cohabitation,* Assessing the New Federalism Policy Brief B-48 (Washington, D.C.: Urban Institute, 2002); Kurt Bauman, "Shifting Family Definitions: The Effect of Cohabitation and Other Nonfamily Household Relationships on Measures of Poverty," *Demography* 36 (1999): 315–325; Eirik Evenhouse and Siobhan Reilly, "Pop Swapping? Welfare and Children's Living Arrangements," paper presented at the meeting of the Population Association of America, New York, 1999; Wendy D. Manning and Daniel T. Lichter, "Parental Cohabitation and Children's Economic Well-Being," *Journal of Marriage and the Family* 58 (1996): 1998–2010; Robert A. Moffitt, Robert Reville, and Anne E. Winkler, "Beyond Single Mothers: Cohabitation and Marriage in the AFDC Program," *Demography* 35 (1998): 259–278; and Elizabeth Thomson, Thomas Hanson, and Sara S. McLanahan, "Family Structure and Child Well-Being: Economic Resources vs. Parental Behavior," *Social Forces* 73 (1994): 221–242.

3.   Tavia Simmons and Grace O'Neill, *Households and Families: 2000,* Census 2000 Brief C2KBR/01-8 (Washington, D.C.: U.S. Census Bureau, September 2001).

4.   U.S. Census Bureau, "Unmarried-Couple Households, by Presence of Children: 1960 to Present," June 29, 2001, available from: http://www.census.gov/population/socdemo/hh-fam/tabUC-1.txt, accessed October 16, 2002.

5. Larry Bumpass and Hsien-Hen Lu, "Trends in Cohabitation and Implications for Children's Family Contexts in the United States," *Population Studies* 54 (2000): 29–41.

6. Manning and Lichter, 1996.

7. Jason Fields, *Living Arrangements of Children,* Current Population Reports (P70–74) (Washington, D.C.: U.S. Census Bureau, 2001).

8. Ibid.

9. Gregory Acs and Sandi Nelson, *"Honey, I'm Home": Changes in the Living Arrangements in the Late 1990s,* Assessing the New Federalism Policy Brief B-38 (Washington, D.C.: Urban Institute, 2001); Fields, 2001; and Wendy D. Manning and Pamela Smock, "Children's Living Arrangements in Unmarried-Mother Families," *Journal of Family Issues* 18 (1997): 526–544.

10. Acs and Nelson, 2001.

11. Manning and Smock, 1997.

12. Fields, 2001.

13. Bumpass and Lu, 2000; and R. Kelly Raley, "Increasing Fertility in Cohabiting Unions: Evidence for the Second Demographic Transition in the United States," *Demography* 38 (2001): 59–66.

14. Raley, 2001.

15. Sara McLanahan, Irwin Garfinkel, Nancy Reichman, and Julien Teitler, "Unwed Parents or Fragile Families? Implications for Welfare and Child Support Policy," in *Out of Wedlock: Trends, Causes, and Consequences of Nonmarital Fertility*, edited by Lawrence L. Wu and Barbara Wolfe (New York: Russell Sage Foundation, 2001), pp. 201–228.

16. Wendy D. Manning, "Childbearing in Cohabiting Unions: Racial and Ethnic Differences," *Family Planning Perspectives* 33 (2001): 217–223.

17. Raley, 2001.

18. Manning, 2001.

19. Fields, 2001.

20. Bumpass and Lu, 2000.

21. See Deborah Roempke Graefe and Daniel T. Lichter, "Life Course Transitions of American Children: Parental Cohabitation, Marriage, and Single Motherhood," *Demography* 36 (1999): 205–217.

22. Estimates are drawn from Bumpass and Lu, 2000.

23. This topic is explored more fully in Wendy Manning, "The Implications of Cohabitation for Children's Well-Being," in *Just Living Together: Implications for Children, Families, and Public Policy*, edited by Alan Booth and Ann C. Crouter (Mahwah, N.J.: Lawrence-Erlbaum, 2002), pp. 121–152.

24. Constance F. Citro and Robert T. Michael, editors, *Measuring Poverty: A New Approach* (Washington, D.C.: National Academy Press, 1995).

25. Bauman, 1999.

26. Acs and Nelson, 2002; Marcia Carlson and Sheldon Danziger, "Cohabitation and the Measurement of Child Poverty," *Review of Income and Wealth* 2 (1999): 179–191; and Manning and Lichter, 1996.

27. See also Bauman, 1999; Carlson and Danziger, 1999; Lingxin Hao, "Family Structure, Private Transfers, and the Economic Well-Being of Families with Children," *Social Forces* 75 (1999): 269–292; and Manning and Smock, 1997.

28. Manning and Lichter, 1996.

29. Bauman, 1999.

30. Peter Brandon and Larry Bumpass, "Children's Living Arrangements, Coresidence of Unmarried Fathers, and Welfare Receipt," *Journal of Family Issues* 22 (2001): 3–26.

31.   Moffitt, Reville, and Winkler, 1998.
32.   Susan L. Brown, "Child Well-Being in Cohabiting Unions," paper presented at the annual meeting of the Population Association of America, Washington D.C., March 2001; Thomas L. Hanson, Sara S. McLanahan, and Elizabeth Thomson, "Economic Resources, Parental Practices, and Children's Well-Being," in *Consequences of Growing Up Poor*, edited by Greg J. Duncan and Jeanne Brooks-Gunn (New York: Russell Sage Foundation, 1997), pp. 190–238; Sandi Nelson, Rebecca Clark, and Gregory Acs, *Beyond the Two-Parent Family*, New Federalism National Survey of American Families B-31 (Washington, D.C.: Urban Institute, 2001); Thomson et al., 1994.
33.   See Brown, 2001; and Nelson, Clark, and Acs, 2001.
34.   Brown, 2001.
35.   Donna R. Morrison, "Child Well-Being in Step Families and Cohabiting Unions Following Divorce: A Dynamic Appraisal," paper presented at the annual meeting of the Population Association of America, Chicago, March 1998; and Donna R. Morrison, "The Costs of Economic Uncertainty: Child Well-Being in Cohabiting and Remarried Unions Following Parental Divorce," paper presented at the Annual Meeting of the Population Association of America, Los Angeles, March 2000.
36.   Wendy D. Manning and Kathleen Lamb, "Parental Cohabitation and Adolescent Well-Being," Working Paper 02-03, Center for Family and Demographic Research, Bowling Green State University, 2002.
37.   Morrison, 1998; and Manning and Lamb, 2002.
38.   Rachel Dunifon and Lori Kowaleski-Jones, "Who's in the House? Race Differences in Cohabitation, Single Parenthood, and Child Development," *Child Development* 73 (4), (July/August 2002): 1249–1264 and Nelson, Clark, and Clark, 2001.
39.   R. Kelly Raley, "A Shortage of Marriageable Men? A Note on the Role of Cohabitation in Black-White Marriage Differences," *American Sociological Review* 61 (1996): 973–983.
40.   Lynne M. Casper and Suzanne M. Bianchi, *Continuity and Change in the American Family* (Thousand Oaks, Calif.: Sage Publications, 2002).
41.   Manning, 2001.
42.   See, for example, Lawrence L. Wu and Bruce C. Martinson, "Family Structure and the Risk of a Premarital Birth," *American Sociological Review* 58 (1993): 210–232.
43.   Bumpass and Lu, 2000.
44.   Nancy S. Landale and Renata Forste, "Patterns of Entry into Cohabitation and Marriage among Mainland Puerto Rican Women," *Demography* 28 (1991): 587–607.

References

Acs, Gregory, and Sandi Nelson. 2001. *"Honey, I'm Home": Changes in the Living Arrangements in the Late 1990s.* Assessing the New Federalism Policy Brief B-38. Washington, D.C.: Urban Institute.

———. 2002. *The Kids Are Alright? Children's Well-Being and the Rise of Cohabitation.* Assessing the New Federalism Policy Brief B-48. Washington, D.C.: Urban Institute.

Bauman, Kurt. 1999. "Shifting Family Definitions: The Effect of Cohabitation and Other Nonfamily Household Relationships on Measures of Poverty." *Demography* 36: 315–325.

Brandon, Peter, and Larry Bumpass. 2001. "Children's Living Arrangements, Coresidence of Unmarried Fathers, and Welfare Receipt." *Journal of Family Issues* 22: 3–26.

Brown, Susan L. 2001. "Child Well-Being in Cohabiting Unions." Paper presented at the annual meeting of the Population Association of America. Washington, D.C. March.

Bumpass, Larry, and Hsien-Hen Lu. 2000. "Trends in Cohabitation and Implications for Children's Family Contexts in the United States." *Population Studies* 54: 29–41.

Carlson, Marcia, and Sheldon Danziger. 1999. "Cohabitation and the Measurement of Child Poverty." *Review of Income and Wealth* 2: 179–191.

Casper, Lynne M., and Suzanne Bianchi. 2002. *Continuity and Change in the American Family.* Thousand Oaks, Calif.: Sage Publications.

Citro, Constance F., and Robert T. Michael. Editors. 1995. *Measuring Poverty: A New Approach.* Washington, D.C.: National Academy Press.

Dunifon, Rachel, and Lori Kowaleski-Jones. 2002. "Who's in the House? Race Differences in Cohabitation, Single Parenthood, and Child Development." *Child Development* 73 (4) (July/August): 1249–1264.

Evenhouse, Eirik, and Siobhan Reilly. 1999. "Pop Swapping? Welfare and Children's Living Arrangements." Paper presented at the meeting of the Population Association of America. New York.

Fields, Jason. 2001. *Living Arrangements of Children.* Current Population Reports (P70–74). Washington, D.C.: U.S. Census Bureau.

Graefe, Deborah Roempke, and Daniel T. Lichter. 1999. "Life Course Transitions of American Children: Parental Cohabitation, Marriage, and Single Motherhood." *Demography* 36: 205–217.

Hanson, Thomas L., Sara S. McLanahan, and Elizabeth Thomson. 1997. "Economic Resources, Parental Practices, and Children's Well-Being." In *Consequences of Growing Up Poor.* Edited by Greg J. Duncan and Jeanne Brooks-Gunn. New York: Russell Sage Foundation: 190–238.

Hao, Lingxin. 1996. "Family Structure, Private Transfers, and the Economic Well-being of Families with Children." *Social Forces* 75: 269–292.

Landale, Nancy S., and Reneta Forste. 1991. "Patterns of Entry into Cohabitation and Marriage among Mainland Puerto Rican Women." *Demography* 28: 587–607.

London, Rebecca A. 1998. "Trends in Single Mothers' Living Arrangements from 1970 to 1995: Correcting the Current Population Survey." *Demography* 35: 125–131.

Manning, Wendy. 2002. "The Implications of Cohabitation for Children's Well-Being." In *Just Living Together: Implications for Children, Families, and Public Policy.* Edited by Alan Booth and Ann C. Crouter. Mahwah, N.J.: Lawrence-Erlbaum: 121–152.

Manning, Wendy D. 2001. "Childbearing in Cohabiting Unions: Racial and Ethnic Differences." *Family Planning Perspectives* 33: 217–223.

Manning, Wendy D., and Kathleen Lamb. 2002. "Parental Cohabitation and Adolescent Well-Being." Center for Family and Demographic Research. Bowling Green State University. Working Paper 02-03.

Manning, Wendy D., and Daniel T. Lichter. 1996. "Parental Cohabitation and Children's Economic Well-Being." *Journal of Marriage and the Family* 58: 998–1010.

Manning, Wendy D., and Pamela Smock. 1997. "Children's Living Arrangements in Unmarried-Mother Families." *Journal of Family Issues* 18: 526–544.

McLanahan, Sara, Irwin Garfinkel, Nancy Reichman, and Julien Teitler. 2001. "Unwed Parents or Fragile Families? Implications for Welfare and Child Support Policy." In *Out of Wedlock: Trends, Causes, and Consequences of Nonmarital Fertility.* Edited by Lawrence L. Wu and Barbara Wolfe. New York: Russell Sage Foundation: 201–228.

Moffitt, Robert A., Robert Reville, and Anne E. Winkler. 1998. "Beyond Single Mothers: Cohabitation and Marriage in the AFDC Program." *Demography* 35: 259–278.

Morrison, Donna R. 1998. "Child Well-Being in Step Families and Cohabiting Unions Following Divorce: A Dynamic Appraisal." Paper presented at the annual meeting of the Population Association of America. Chicago. March.

————. 2000. "The Costs of Economic Uncertainty: Child Well-Being in Cohabiting and Remarried Unions Following Parental Divorce." Paper presented at the Annual Meeting of the Population Association of America. Los Angeles. March.

Morrison, Donna R., and Amy Ritualo. 2000. "Routes to Children's Economic Recovery after Divorce: Are Maternal Cohabitation and Remarriage Equivalent?" *American Sociological Review* 65: 560–580.

Nelson, Sandi, Rebecca Clark, and Gregory Acs. 2001. *Beyond the Two-Parent Family.* New Federalism National Survey of American Families B-31. Washington: D.C.: Urban Institute.

Raley, R. Kelly. 1996. "A Shortage of Marriageable Men? A Note on the Role of Cohabitation in Black-White Marriage Differences." *American Sociological Review* 61: 973–983.

————. 2001. "Increasing Fertility in Cohabiting Unions: Evidence for the Second Demographic Transition in the United States." *Demography* 38: 59–66.

Simmons, Tavia, and Grace O'Neil. 2001. *Households and Families: 2000.* Census 2000 Brief C2KBR/01-8. Washington, D.C.: U.S. Census Bureau. September.

Thomson, Elizabeth, Thomas Hanson, and Sara S. McLanahan. 1994. "Family Structure and Child Well-Being: Economic Resources vs. Parental Behavior." *Social Forces* 73: 221–242.

U.S. Census Bureau. 2001. "Unmarried-Couple Households, by Presence of Children: 1960 to Present." Available from: http://www.census.gov/population/socdemo/hh-fam/tabUC-1.txt. Accessed October 16, 2002.

Wu, Lawrence L., and Bruce C. Martinson. 1993. "Family Structure and the Risk of a Premarital Birth." *American Sociological Review* 58: 210–232.

6

Fatherhood, Cohabitation, and Marriage

Wade F. Horn

A new consensus has developed that fatherlessness is a significant risk factor leading to poor developmental outcomes for children. Research consistently finds that, even after controlling for income and other sociodemographic variables, children who grow up without the active involvement of a committed and responsible father, compared with those who do, are more likely to fail at school, develop behavioral and emotional problems, get into trouble with the law, engage in early and promiscuous sexual activity, or become welfare dependent later in life.[1] The question no longer is whether fatherlessness matters, but what to do about it.

Despite this important shift in thinking about the importance of fathers to child well-being, fathers received little mention in the historic 1996 welfare reform legislation, except in the tougher child support enforcement measures and a new grant program supporting visitation by noncustodial parents. The underlying assumption of this legislation seems to be that when it comes to welfare reform, the only fathers worth caring about are nonresident fathers.

But three categories of fathers are relevant to a discussion of welfare reform and child well-being: nonresident fathers, cohabiting fathers, and married fathers. What do we know about these three types of fathers and the influence of each on the well-being of children?

Nonresident Fathers

Today, nearly four of every ten children in the United States are growing up in homes without their biological fathers. In low-income households, the percentage of children growing up without their biological fathers is even higher (although many are living with relatives, boyfriends, or others). Indeed, nearly 90 percent of all households receiving welfare are headed by a single mother.

The historical policy answer to the problem of absent fathers has been child support enforcement—and for good reason. Any man who fathers a child ought to be held responsible for helping to support that child financially. Moreover, research generally substantiates that child well-being is improved when nonresident fathers pay child support.[2] Nevertheless, child support enforcement alone is unlikely to improve substantially the well-being of children for several reasons.

First, although receipt of child support has been consistently associated with improvements in child outcomes, the magnitude of the effects tends to be quite small because the average level of child support is quite modest, only about $3,000 per year.[3] Such a modest amount of additional income, although certainly helpful, is unlikely to change significantly the life trajectory of most children.

Second, many fathers of children residing in low-income households are undereducated and underemployed themselves, and as such they may lack the resources to be able to provide meaningful economic support for their children. Too strong a focus on child support enforcement may lead many of these already marginally employed men to drop out of the paid labor force altogether in favor of participation in the underground economy. It is difficult to be an involved father when one is in hiding. Thus, the unintended consequence of strong child support enforcement policies may be to decrease, not increase, the number of children growing up with the active involvement of their father, proving once again that no good public policy goes unpunished.

Third, an exclusive focus on child support enforcement ignores the many noneconomic contributions that fathers make to the well-being of their children. If we want fathers to be more than cash machines for their children, we need public policies that support their work as nurturers, disciplinarians, mentors, moral instructors, and skill coaches—and not just as economic providers. Doing otherwise is to downgrade fathers to, in the words of Barbara Dafoe Whitehead, "paper dads."[4]

Dissatisfaction with the results of child support enforcement alone as the primary strategy for dealing with nonresident fathers has led some analysts to advocate enhanced visitation as the mechanism for improving the well-being of children. In a meta-analysis of sixty-three studies, however, Paul Amato, professor in Pennsylvania State University's Department of Sociology, and Joan Gilbreth, assistant professor in Nebraska Wesleyan Univeristy's Sociology, Anthropology, and Social Work Department, question whether frequency of visitation is the most important aspect of a nonresident father's relationship with his children.[5] Rather, they argue, the quality of the father-child relationship and the degree to which nonresident fathers engage in authoritative parenting (that is, not only encouraging their children but also monitoring their children's behavior and enforcing age-appropriate limits) are more important to child well-being.

For example, Amato and Gilbreth found that children who report feeling close to their fathers were more likely to succeed in school and evidenced fewer internalizing and externalizing problems. But once a father no longer lives with his children, his involvement with his children declines rapidly.[6] Indeed, 40 percent of children in father-absent homes have not seen their father in more than a year. Of the remaining 60 percent, only one in five sleeps even one night per month in the father's home. Only one in six children living without his or her father sees him an average of once or more per week.[7]

The strongest predictor of child well-being—even stronger than payment of child support—was the degree to which nonresident fathers engaged in authoritative parenting. Children whose nonresident fathers listened to their problems, gave them advice, provided explanations for rules, monitored their academic performance, helped with their homework, engaged in mutual projects, and disciplined them were significantly more likely to do well in school and to evidence greater psychological health, compared with children whose fathers mostly engaged them in recreational activities, such as going out to dinner, taking them on vacations, and buying them things.

Unfortunately, other research has found that nonresident fathers are far less likely than in-the-home fathers to engage in authoritative parenting.[8] One reason, as Amato and Gilbreth point out, is the constraints inherent in traditional visitation arrangements. Because time with their children is often severely limited, many nonresident fathers strive to make sure their children enjoy themselves when they are with them. As a result, nonresident fathers tend to spend less time than in-the-home fathers helping their children with homework, monitoring their activities, and setting appropriate limits and more time taking them to restaurants or the movies, activities that have not been found to be associated with enhanced child outcomes. Thus, although visitation by nonresident fathers is certainly something to be encouraged, the context of visitation discourages nonresident fathers from engaging in the kinds of behaviors most associated with improvements in child well-being.

Cohabiting Fathers

Cohabitation is one of the fastest growing family forms in the United States today. In 1997, 4.13 million couples were cohabiting outside of wedlock, compared with fewer than 0.5 million in 1960.[9] Of cohabiting couples, 1.47 million, or about 36 percent, have children younger than age eighteen residing with them, up from 21 percent in 1987. Of unmarried couples in the twenty-five to thirty-four-year age group, nearly 50 percent have children living with them.[10] Larry Bumpass, professor in the University of Wisconsin Department of Sociology, and Hsien-Hen Lu, an assistant professor at Columbia University's Mailman School of Public Health, estimate that nearly half of all children today will spend some time in a cohabiting household before age sixteen.[11] Cohabitation also appears to be quite common among the poor. According to recent research by Sara S. McLanahan, professor in Princeton University's Department of Sociology, and Irv Garfinkel, professor at Columbia University's School of Social Work, with so-called "fragile families," at the time a child is born out of wedlock, more than half of low-income parents are cohabiting.[12]

Some argue that cohabitation is the equivalent of marriage. But cohabitation is a weak family form, especially compared with marriage. Cohabiting couples break up at much higher rates than do married couples, and although 40 to 50 percent of couples who have a child while cohabiting go on to get married, they are more likely to divorce than are couples who get married before having children.[13] Three-quarters of children born to cohabiting parents will see their parents split up before they reach sixteen, compared with only about one-third of children born to married parents.[14]

The fact is that children born to cohabiting couples are likely, before too long, to see their fathers transformed into occasional visitors. Extrapolating from the research literature on attachment theory, it may be that children whose fathers are involved early on but then disappear have worse outcomes than children whose fathers are continuously absent. If so, focusing on strengthening cohabitation may, in reality, be making a bad situation worse.

Moreover, many men in cohabiting relationships are not the biological fathers of the children in the household, or at least are not the biological fathers of all the children in the household. By one estimate, 63 percent of children in cohabiting households are born not to the cohabiting couple but to a previous union of one of the adult partners, most often the mother.[15] This situation is problematic in that substantial evidence indicates that cohabitation with a man who is not biologically related to the children substantially increases the risk of both physical and sexual child abuse.[16] Thus, cohabitation not only is unlikely to deliver a long-term father to a child but also puts children at an increased risk for child abuse if they are cohabiting with a man other than their biological father.

Married Fathers

Although speaking about the importance of fathers to the well-being of children is becoming increasingly popular, speaking about the importance of marriage to the well-being of fatherhood or of children is still out of fashion. Yet, the empirical literature clearly demonstrates that children do best when they grow up in an intact, married-parent household. We know, for example, that children who grow up in a household with continuously married parents do better at school, have fewer emotional problems, are more likely to attend college, and are less likely to commit crime or develop alcohol or illicit drug problems. That these results are not simply a result of differences in income is attested to by the fact that stepfamilies, which have household incomes nearly equivalent to continuously married households, offer few of these benefits to children.[17]

The empirical evidence also is quite clear that married adults—women as well as men—are happier, healthier, and wealthier than their single counterparts. Married adults also report having more satisfying sex than nonmarried adults, and married men show an earnings boost that is not evident in cohabiting relationships.[18] Married fathers also, on average, are more likely to be actively engaged in the lives of their children and, perhaps just as important, are more accessible to them.

In contrast, research consistently finds that unwed fathers are unlikely to stay connected to their children over time. Longitudinal research by Robert Lerman and Theodora Ooms, for example, found that 57 percent of unwed fathers visited their child at least once per week during the first two years of their child's life, but by the time the child reached age seven and one-half that percentage dropped to less than 25 percent.[19] Other research suggests that three-quarters of fathers who are not living with their children at the time of their birth never subsequently live with them. Marriage may not be a certain route to a lifetime father, but it is a more certain route than any other.

Of course, some married households, especially in which domestic violence and child abuse are present, are horrible places for both children and adults. But contrary to the stereotypes perpetuated by the media and some advocacy groups, domestic violence and child abuse are substantially *less* likely to occur in intact, married households than in any other family arrangement. The truth is that if we really care about the well-being of children, public policy needs to do a better job of encouraging marriage.

Why Not Marriage?

Given that marriage is good for children and adults, why is everyone not rushing to the altar to get married? First, the past forty years have seen an extraordinary shift in cultural norms concerning sex, marriage, and childbearing. With the advent of effective birth control in the 1960s, sex became separated from marriage. Then, as increasing numbers of women entered the paid labor force, childbearing became separated from marriage. As the data on cohabitation indicate, living together is increasingly becoming separated from marriage as well.

As a result of these cultural and social changes, there is simply less pressure today to get and stay married than there was just two or three generations ago. Forty years ago, there existed an extraordinary consensus that couples in troubled marriages should "stay together for the sake of the kids." Today, couples are increasingly likely to say, "We're getting divorced for the sake of the kids." One can hardly imagine a more dramatic cultural shift.

Second, when couples do get married, public policy frequently punishes them economically. The marriage penalty within the U.S. tax code for higher wage earners is well known. Somewhat less well known is the financial penalty for marriage found in the Earned Income Tax Credit (EITC). The EITC is an income supplement that provides up to $4,000 a year to a low-income working parent with children. This tax credit is now the largest federal antipoverty program. The good news is that the EITC, unlike the old welfare system it is beginning to replace, encourages work because only those with earnings are eligible. The bad news is that it can make marriage prohibitively expensive. That is so because the EITC is pegged to wages, not to family structure. Thus, two low-wage earners would be far better off, at least as far as the EITC is concerned, if they stay single than if they marry.

Suppose, for example, a single mother is working full-time at a minimum-wage job. This mother will have take-home pay of less than $7,000 after paying taxes and child-care expenses. With the help of the EITC, her take-home pay increases to about $10,000, still not enough to escape poverty. If she marries the father of her children, it can make all the difference—even if he, too, has few work skills and only a minimum-wage job. But marriage will cost this woman about $1,800 in EITC benefits, or almost 20 percent of her net income. Making low-income women choose between $1,800 in tax benefits or a husband and a father for her children simply makes no sense.

According to calculations by Eugene Steuerle of the Urban Institute, when one takes into account the full package of welfare benefits, the marriage penalty for a single mother who chooses to marry an employed man can be quite severe.[20] For example, when an unemployed single mother marries a man working at minimum wage, the total marriage penalty is $2,688. When a single mother working full-time at minimum wage marries an $8-per-hour full-time worker, the marriage penalty is a shocking $8,060. In such circumstances, marriage simply makes no economic sense.

A legitimate question is whether there is clear evidence that low-income couples change their behavior because of the marriage penalties in the EITC. The honest answer is no. Little evidence indicates that low-income communities are filled with mini-economists busily calculating the extent of the EITC marriage penalty before deciding to get married. But anecdotal evidence suggests that people in low-income communities have a sense that if they get married they "lose stuff." They may not know exactly how much "stuff" they lose when they marry, but they know marriage is a bad deal. And they are right.

Bringing Back the "M" Word

The evidence that marriage, on average, is good for children, adults, and communities is beyond debate. The empirical literature is quite clear that marriage is the most stable and healthy environment for raising children. In addition, men and women who are married and stay married have been shown to be happier and healthier, and to make more money over time than their single counterparts. Moreover, communities with more households headed by married couples are beset by fewer social ills, such as crime and welfare dependency, than communities where marriage is less prevalent.

Given that healthy marriages are good for children, good for adults, and good for communities, it seems reasonable to conclude that government has a stake in helping couples who choose marriage for themselves form and sustain healthy marriages. There are, of course, those who suggest we do not know enough about how to support healthy marriages to warrant government action in this area. To some extent, these critics have a point. There is still much we need to know. But while acknowledging that there is much to learn about the most effective ways to support healthy marriage, we should also acknowledge that there is much we *do* know. We know, for example, that healthy marriages are a result, not of luck or chance, but of hard work and skills, and that these skills *can* be taught. We also know that premarital education programs can help couples form and sustain a healthy marriage by teaching communication and problem-solving skills. We also know that programs that assign mentoring couples to newlyweds can help young couples adjust to their new marriage in healthy ways. Finally, we know that programs designed to save even the most troubled marriages *can* work. Yes, there is much we need to learn about supporting healthy marriages, but we already know more than enough to get started.

What Government Ought Not to Do

Still, there are limits on government action even when seeking to promote a social good, such as healthy marriages. Hence, before considering what government ought to do, I would first like to emphasize what government ought *not* do when it comes to encouraging and supporting marriage.

First, government ought not merely to strive for neutrality, but should positively support healthy marriages. Government is neutral about many things. For example, government is neutral about what flavor of ice cream we buy because there is no evidence that one choice is better for us than another. But government is not neutral about many other things—home ownership or charitable giving, for example—because both are believed to contribute to the common good. For that reason, the government makes it easier for us to buy a house or to give to charities by providing tax incentives. In much the same way, government can—and should—provide support for healthy marriages precisely because it can be shown that healthy marriages contribute to the common good.

Second, promoting healthy marriages ought not to be about telling anybody to get married. Choosing to get married is a private decision. Government should not get into the business of telling people whom, or even whether, to marry. No one believes that the proper role of government in this arena should include the creation of a Federal Dating Service.

Third, promoting healthy marriage ought not to result, intentionally or otherwise, in policies that encourage anyone to enter into, or trap anyone in, an abusive relationship. Seeing more Americans enjoying healthy marriages should be the goal. That is so because healthy marriages are good for children and adults alike. Abusive marriages, on the other hand, are not good for anyone—neither adults nor children. Abuse of any sort by a spouse or parent cannot be tolerated under any circumstances, and marriage promotion efforts ought not to provide comfort to spouse or child abusers.

Fourth, providing support for healthy marriages ought not to be equated with withdrawing supports and services for single-parent families. Government should encourage and support healthy marriages because that is what the data say are best for children. There are no data suggesting that taking away support from single mothers helps children. Indeed, many single parents make heroic efforts, often with great success, to raise their children well. Promoting healthy marriages and supporting single parents are not, and must not be, mutually exclusive. Together, they are part of an integrated effort to promote child well-being.

Finally, government ought not to seek to promote marriage by being afraid to speak its name. There is no evidence that cohabitation confers the same benefits on children, adults, or communities as marriage does. In fact, much of the evidence indicates that cohabitation may be no different from living with only one parent. For example, Mignon R. Moore, assistant professor in Columbia University's Department of Sociology, and P. Lindsay Chase-Lansdale, professor at Northwestern University's School of Education and Social Policy, found that "the presence of a cohabiting partner did not significantly affect the likelihood of intercourse or pregnancy [in the children of the household], suggesting that it is the marital union rather than the added household adult that acts as a protective factor against early sexual intercourse for adolescents in two-parent households."[21] If the policy objective is the betterment of the lives of children, there is no evidence to suggest we will do so by equating cohabitation with marriage.

What Government Should Do

With these constraints in mind, what *should* government do when it comes to marriage? First, government ought to make clear that it is in the business of promoting healthy marriages and not just in increasing marriage rates. That's because healthy marriages are an effective strategy for improving the well-being of children, whereas unhealthy marriages are not. Government has no interest in encouraging couples to remain in marriages that are good for no one, neither adults nor children—nor society, for that matter.

Second, government needs to be more willing to bring up the topic. Anyone who has ever spent time in welfare offices can attest to the striking absence of any posters, literature, or conversation promoting the virtues of marriage. Our reluctance even to bring up the topic of marriage sends the not-so-subtle message that marriage is neither expected nor valued. The wonder is not that so few go on to get married, but that some actually do. If we want more marriages in low-income communities, we have to be more willing to bring up the topic.

For example, when faced with a nonmarital birth, hospitals should ask about both paternity establishment and marriage. Today, in most cases hospital personnel ask unwed fathers to establish paternity. Doing so is extremely important. But hospital personnel should also ask the simple question, "Have you considered getting married?" If the answer is yes, the couple can be referred to helpful services, such as premarital education. If the answer is no, that is fine. But if we never ask the question, we will never be in the position to help those couples who are contemplating marriage form and sustain a healthy one.

In addition, social programs dedicated to strengthening families should offer marriage enrichment opportunities. Head Start provides an example. Many children in Head Start live with a married mother and father. While Head Start centers routinely provide parenting education classes, few, if any, Head Start programs currently offer marriage education classes. Head Start represents a perfect opportunity not only to teach parents parenting skills, but also to teach married couples healthy marital skills.

Government also can create public education campaigns highlighting the benefits of healthy marriages. The government funds numerous public education campaigns promoting various healthy behaviors. Marriage can and should be added to this list. In doing so, however, the message should never make single parents feel somehow "second best." The point is to offer supports for healthy marriages, not to make single parent families feel bad.

Third, public policy has to stop punishing couples when they get married. Under current law if couples, especially low-income couples, marry, our tax code and social welfare system punish them. Removing as many of these marriage disincentives as possible from our laws and policies is a very important first step. It seems patently unfair to promote the value of marriage and then impose a financial penalty of between $2,000 and $8,000 on couples who get married. At the very least, the EITC needs to be reformed to ensure that it does not punish low-income couples who choose to marry.

Fourth, states should do more to promote the employment of low-income men so that they are seen as better "marriage material." Some evidence indicates that women—especially women living in low-income communities—are reluctant to marry males whom they consider to have lower economic prospects than themselves.[22] In fact, the availability of a suitable potential husband, primarily defined as employed and not in jail or prison, has been found to have a greater effect on marriage and nonmarital fertility than Aid to Families with Dependent Children benefit levels.[23] One way to encourage marriage, then, is to expand participation in welfare-to-work programs to include low-income men as a means of increasing not only their own life prospects but their marriageability as well.

In expanding employment services to low-income males, however, care should be taken *not* to condition receipt of services on having fathered a child out of wedlock. To do so would only introduce perverse incentives for men to father children out of wedlock, in much the same way that the current system provides perverse incentives for unmarried women to bear children.

Finally, states should take affirmative steps to enhance the marital and parenting skills of high-risk families. Marriage alone is not sufficient to improve the well-being of children. For marriage to have a

---

Box 6.1
Examples of Marriage Promotion Activities

- Encourage hospitals, when faced with a nonmarital birth, to ask about both paternity establishment and marriage. Today, in most cases hospital personnel ask unwed fathers to establish paternity. Doing so is extremely important. But hospital personnel should also ask about the couple's marriage plans.

- Develop a referral system for premarital education. Schools, clinics, job training sites, and welfare offices, all offer an opportunity to provide a referral to premarital education. Such referrals should always be voluntary, not mandatory, and should never be made in such a way as to make those who are not considering marriage feel obligated to do so.

- Encourage social programs dedicated to strengthening families to offer marriage enrichment opportunities.

- Create public education campaigns highlighting the benefits of healthy marriages. The government funds numerous public education campaigns promoting various healthy behaviors. Marriage can and should be added to this list. In doing so, however, the message should never make single parents feel somehow "second best." The point is to offer supports for healthy marriages, not to make single parent families feel badly.

- Increase support for intervention services, including mentoring programs, so that troubled marriages can be made whole and strong once again. Often, when couples are having trouble in their marriages, they think they have only two options: get divorced or stay miserable. The truth, however, is that there is a third option: participate in marital therapy, which can help them repair their marriage. Offering this third option gives couples hope that things can—and often do—get better, if the couples work at it.

---

positive impact on the development of children, parents must have the skills both to sustain a marriage and to be good parents. Unfortunately, many men and women lack the necessary skills to sustain a marriage and raise children well. Some may have grown up in broken homes and never experienced positive marital role models. Others may have had inadequate or abusive parents themselves. To help couples sustain a marriage and be good parents, states should encourage religious and civic organizations to offer parenting and marriage enrichment classes to mothers and fathers applying for public assistance. Although results vary according to the specific curriculum, a substantial body of literature indicates the success of parent skills training and marital enrichment programs.[24]

Conclusion

I am aware that there are those who counsel resignation when it comes to nonmarriage in low-income communities, believing that marriage is a "middle class value" that is not necessarily shared by low-income communities. New data from Sara S. McLanahan and Irwin Garfinkel, however, indicate that at the time of the child's birth, 80 percent of low-income, urban couples are involved in an exclusive romantic relationship with each other and two-thirds want—and expect—to get married. Half believe their chances of marrying—not some time to somebody, but to each other—are "certain" or "near certain."[25] It is not a question, therefore, of imposing middle-class "marriage values" on reluctant couples but of helping them achieve something they say they want for themselves—lasting, stable marriages.

The new consensus is that fathers do matter to the well-being of children. Regrettably, welfare reform has yet to take this consensus fully into account. Doing so will require that clear distinctions be made between nonresident, cohabiting, and married fathers. Although it is certainly important to help all three categories of fathers be a positive influence in the lives of their children, both experience and research teach us that the category of fathers most likely to improve the well-being of children is married fathers.

Notes

1. For a review of this literature, see Wade F. Horn, *Father Facts,* 3d ed. (Gaithersburg, Md.: National Fatherhood Initiative, 1999).
2. For a review, see Irwin Garfinkel, Sara S. McLanahan, Daniel R. Meyer, and Judith A. Seltzer, editors, *Fathers under Fire: The Revolution in Child Support Enforcement* (New York: Russell Sage Foundation, 1998).
3. U.S. House of Representatives, Committee on Ways and Means, *1996 Green Book* (Washington, D.C.: Government Printing Office, 1996), p. 578.
4. Personal communication from Barbara Dafoe Whitehead to Wade Horn.
5. Paul R. Amato and Joan G. Gilbreth, "Non-Resident Fathers and Children's Well-Being: A Meta-Analysis," *Journal of Marriage and the Family* 61 (1999): 557–573.
6. Valarie King, "Non-Resident Father Involvement and Child Well-Being," *Journal of Family Issues* 15 (1994): 78–96; and Judith A. Seltzer, "Relationships between Fathers and Children Who Live Apart: The Fathers' Role after Separation," *Journal of Marriage and the Family* 53 (1991): 79–101.
7. Frank F. Furstenberg and Christine W. Nord, "Parenting Apart: Patterns of Child Rearing after Marital Disruption," *Journal of Marriage and the Family* 47 (1985): 893–905.

8.   E. Mavis Heatherington, "An Overview of the Virginia Longitudinal Study of Divorce and Remarriage with a Focus on Early Adolescence," *Journal of Family Psychology* 7 (1993): 39–46; and Furstenberg and Nord, 1985, p. 896.

9.   Lynne Casper and Ken Bryson, *Household and Family Characteristics: March 1997* (Washington, D.C.: U.S. Census Bureau, 1998).

10. Ibid. See also Wendy D. Manning and Daniel T. Lichter, "Parental Cohabitation and Children's Economic Well-Being," *Journal of Marriage and the Family* 58 (1996): 998–1010.

11. Larry Bumpass and Hsien-Hen Lu, "Trends in Cohabitation and Implications for Children's Family Contexts in the United States," *Population Studies* 54 (2000): 29–41.

12. *See* Bendheim-Thomas Center for Research on Child Wellbeing, "Dispelling Myths about Unmarried Fathers," *Fragile Families Research Brief 1* (2000), available from: http://crcw.princeton.edu/fragilefamilies/, accessed September 19, 2001.

13. Kristin A. Moore, "Executive Summary: Nonmarital Childbearing in the United States, in *Report to Congress on Out-of-Wedlock Childbearing*, DHHS Publication PHS 95–1257 (Washington, D.C.: U.S. Department of Health and Human Services, 1995), p. vii.

14. David Popenoe and Barbara Dafoe Whitehead, *Should We Live Together? What Young Adults Need to Know about Cohabitation before Marriage* (New Brunswick, N.J.: National Marriage Project, 1999), p. 7.

15. Deborah R. Graefe and Daniel T. Lichter, "Life Course Transitions of American Children: Parental Cohabitation, Marriage, and Single Motherhood," *Demography* 36 (1999): 205–217.

16. Robert Whelan, *Broken Homes and Battered Children: A Study of the Relationship between Child Abuse and Family Type* (London: Family Education Trust, 1993), p. 29. See also Martin Daly and Margo Wilson, "Evolutionary Psychology and Marital Conflict: The Relevance of Stepchildren," in *Sex, Power, Conflict: Evolutionary and Feminist Perspectives*, edited by David M. Buss and Neil Malamuth (New York: Oxford University Press, 1996); and Leslie Margolin, "Child Abuse by Mothers' Boyfriends: Why the Over-Representation?" *Child Abuse and Neglect* 16 (1992): 541–551.

17. Horn, 1999.

18. Steven Stack and J. Ross Eshleman, "Marital Status and Happiness: A 17-Nation Study," *Journal of Marriage and the Family* 60 (1998): 527–536. See also Maggie Gallagher, *The Abolition of Marriage*, (Washington, D.C.: Regnery, 1996); and Linda Waite, "Does Marriage Matter?" *Demography* 32 (1995): 483–501.

19. Robert Lerman and Theodora Ooms, *Young Unwed Fathers: Changing Roles and Emerging Policies* (Philadelphia: Temple University, 1993): 45.

20. C. Eugene Steuerle, "The Effects of Tax and Welfare Policies on Family Formation," paper presented at the Conference on Strategies to Strengthen Marriage, Family Impact Seminar, Washington, D.C., June 1997.

21. Mignon R. Moore and P. Lindsay Chase-Lansdale, "Sexual Intercourse and Pregnancy among African-American Girls in High Poverty Neighborhoods: The Role of Family and Perceived Community Environment," *Journal of Marriage and Family* 63 (November 2001): 1146–1157.

22. Mark A. Fossett and K. Jill Kiecolt, "Mate Availability and Family Structure among African-Americans in U.S. Metropolitan Areas," *Journal of Marriage and the Family* 55 (1993): 288–302; Lawrence H. Ganong, Marilyn Coleman, Aaron Thompson, and C. Goodwin-Watson, "African American and European American College Students' Expectations for Self and Future Partners," *Journal of Family Issues* 17 (1996): 758–775; Kim M. Lloyd and Scott J. Smith, "Con-

textual Influences on Young Men's Transition to First Marriage," *Social Forces* 74 (1996), pp. 1097–1119; and Devendra Singh, "Female Judgment of Male Attractiveness and Desirability for Relationships: Role of Waist-to-Hip Ratio and Financial Status," *Journal of Personality and Social Psychology* 69 (1995): 1086–1101.

23. William J. Darity, Jr., and Samuel L. Myers, "Family Structure and the Marginalization of Black Men: Policy Implications," in *The Decline in Marriage among African-Americans,* edited by M. Belinda Tucker and Claudia Mitchell-Kernan (New York: Russell Sage Foundation, 1995). See also Randall Stokes and Albert Chevan, "Female-Headed Families: Social and Economic Context of Racial Differences," *Journal of Urban Affairs* 18 (1996): 245–268.

24. *See* Michael J. McManus, *Marriage Savers: Helping Your Friends and Family Avoid Divorce* (Grand Rapids, Mich.: Zondervan, 1995).

25. James Devitt, "Columbia, Princeton Research Suggests Changes in Welfare and Child Support Policies Can Promote Stable Families," press release, Columbia University, New York, July 2, 2001, available from http://www.columbia.edu/cu/news/01/07/welfare_reform_2001.html, accessed March 27, 2003.

References

Amato, Paul R., and Joan G. Gilbreth. 1999. "Non-Resident Fathers and Children's Well-Being: A Meta-Analysis." *Journal of Marriage and the Family* 61: 557–573.

Bendheim-Thomas Center for Research on Child Wellbeing. 2000. "Dispelling Myths about Unmarried Fathers." *Fragile Families Research Brief 1.* Available from: http://crcw.princeton.edu/fragilefamilies/. Accessed September 19, 2001.

Bumpass, Larry, and Hsien-Hen Lu. 2000. "Trends in Cohabitation and Implications for Children's Family Contexts in the United States." *Population Studies* 54: 29–41.

Casper, Lynne, and Ken Bryson. 1998. *Household and Family Characteristics: March 1997.* Washington, D.C.: U.S. Census Bureau.

Daly, Martin, and Margo Wilson. 1996. "Evolutionary Psychology and Marital Conflict: The Relevance of Stepchildren." In *Sex, Power, Conflict: Evolutionary and Feminist Perspectives.* Edited by David M. Buss and Neil Malamuth. New York: Oxford University Press: 9–28.

Darity, William J., Jr., and Samuel L. Myers. 1995. "Family Structure and the Marginalization of Black Men: Policy Implications." In *The Decline in Marriage among African-Americans.* Edited by M. Belinda Tucker and Claudia Mitchell-Kernan. New York: Russell Sage Foundation: 263–309.

Devitt, James. 2001. "Columbia, Princeton Research Suggests Changes in Welfare and Child Support Policies Can Promote Stable Families." Press Release. Columbia University. New York. July 2. Available from http://www.columbia.edu/cu/news/01/07/welfare_reform_2001.html. Accessed March 27, 2003.

Fossett, Mark A., and K. Jill Kiecolt. 1993. "Mate Availability and Family Structure among African-Americans in U.S. Metropolitan Areas." *Journal of Marriage and the Family* 55: 288–302.

Furstenberg, Frank F., and Christine W. Nord. 1985. "Parenting Apart: Patterns of Child Rearing after Marital Disruption." *Journal of Marriage and the Family* 47: 893–905.

Gallagher, Maggie. 1996. *The Abolition of Marriage.* Washington, D.C.: Regnery.

Ganong, Lawrence H., Marilyn Coleman, Aaron Thompson, and C. Goodwin-Watson. 1996. "African American and European American College Students' Expectations for Self and Future Partners." *Journal of Family Issues* 17: 758–775.

Garfinkel, Irwin, Sara S. McLanahan, Daniel R. Meyer, and Judith A. Seltzer. Editors. 1998. *Fathers under Fire: The Revolution in Child Support Enforcement.* New York: Russell Sage Foundation.

Graefe, Deborah R., and Daniel T. Lichter. 1999. "Life Course Transitions of American Children: Parental Cohabitation, Marriage, and Single Motherhood." *Demography* 36: 205–217.

Heatherington, E. Mavis. 1993. "An Overview of the Virginia Longitudinal Study of Divorce and Remarriage with a Focus on Early Adolescence." *Journal of Family Psychology* 7: 39–46.

Horn, Wade F. 1999. *Father Facts.* 3d edition. Gaithersburg, Md.: National Fatherhood Initiative.

King, Valarie. 1994. "Non-Resident Father Involvement and Child Well-Being." *Journal of Family Issues* 15: 78–96.

Lerman, Robert, and Theodora Ooms. 1993. *Young Unwed Fathers: Changing Roles and Emerging Policies.* Philadelphia: Temple University.

Lloyd, Kim M., and Scott J. Smith. 1996. "Contextual Influences on Young Men's Transition to First Marriage." *Social Forces* 74: 1097–1119.

Manning, Wendy D., and Daniel T. Lichter. 1996. "Parental Cohabitation and Children's Economic Well-Being." *Journal of Marriage and the Family* 58: 998–1010.

Margolin, Leslie. 1992. "Child Abuse by Mothers' Boyfriends: Why the Over-Representation?" *Child Abuse and Neglect* 16: 541–551.

McManus, Michael J. 1995. *Marriage Savers: Helping Your Friends and Family Avoid Divorce.* Grand Rapids, Mich.: Zondervan.

Moore, Kristin A. 1995. "Executive Summary: Nonmarital Childbearing in the United States." In *Report to Congress on Out-of-Wedlock Childbearing.* DHHS Publication PHS 95–1257. Washington, D.C.: U.S. Department of Health and Human Services.

Moore, Mignon R., and P. Lindsay Chase-Lansdale. 2001. "Sexual Intercourse and Pregnancy among African-American Girls in High Poverty Neighborhoods: The Role of Family and Perceived Community Environment." *Journal of Marriage and Family* 63 (November): 1146–1157.

Popenoe, David, and Barbara Dafoe Whitehead. 1999. *Should We Live Together? What Young Adults Need to Know about Cohabitation before Marriage.* New Brunswick, N.J.: The National Marriage Project.

Seltzer, Judith A. 1991. "Relationships between Fathers and Children Who Live Apart: The Fathers' Role after Separation." *Journal of Marriage and the Family* 53: 79–101.

Singh, Devendra. 1995. "Female Judgment of Male Attractiveness and Desirability for Relationships: Role of Waist-to-Hip Ratio and Financial Status." *Journal of Personality and Social Psychology* 69: 1086–1101.

Stack, Steven, and J. Ross Eshleman. 1998. "Marital Status and Happiness: A 17-Nation Study." *Journal of Marriage and the Family* 60: 527–36.

Steuerle, C. Eugene. 1997. "The Effects of Tax and Welfare Policies on Family Formation." Paper presented at the Conference on Strategies to Strengthen Marriage. Family Impact Seminar. Washington, D.C. June.

Stokes, Randall, and Albert Chevan. 1996. "Female-Headed Families: Social and Economic Context of Racial Differences." *Journal of Urban Affairs* 18: 245–68.

U.S. House of Representatives. Committee on Ways and Means. 1996. *1996 Green Book.* Washington, D.C.: Government Printing Office.

Waite, Linda J. 1995. "Does Marriage Matter?" *Demography* 32: 483–501.

Whelan, Robert. 1993. *Broken Homes and Battered Children: A Study of the Relationship between Child Abuse and Family Type.* London: Family Education Trust.

7

Teenage Sex, Pregnancy, and Nonmarital Births

Isabel V. Sawhill

When Congress enacted the new welfare law in 1996, it put at least as much emphasis on reducing teen and nonmarital childbearing as it did on requiring work. It did so for a very good reason: A high proportion of children living in single-parent families are poor (see figure 7.1), and the growth of single-parent families has contributed to the rise in child poverty over the past few decades. So anything that stems the growth of such families could be beneficial to children.

Poverty Trends in Family Structure

Poverty in the United States, especially child poverty, is increasingly associated with family structure. In the mid-1960s, only 35 percent of all poor children lived in female-headed families. Today, that figure stands at 63 percent. The proportion being raised by single parents is even higher when we exclude children affected by short spells of poverty of the kind typically associated with brief periods of joblessness and focus just on children who spend most of their formative years in poverty.

The proportion of all American children who are poor increased from 15 percent in 1970 to 21 percent in 1994 (and then declined). Virtually all of this increase was associated with the growth of single-parent families (see figure 7.2). The arithmetic behind this conclusion is straightforward. Because child poverty is five times higher in single-parent than in two-parent families and because the proportion of all children living in fatherless families increased dramatically, child poverty rates increased by about five percentage points

Figure 7.1
Child Poverty Rates by Living Arrangement, 1998

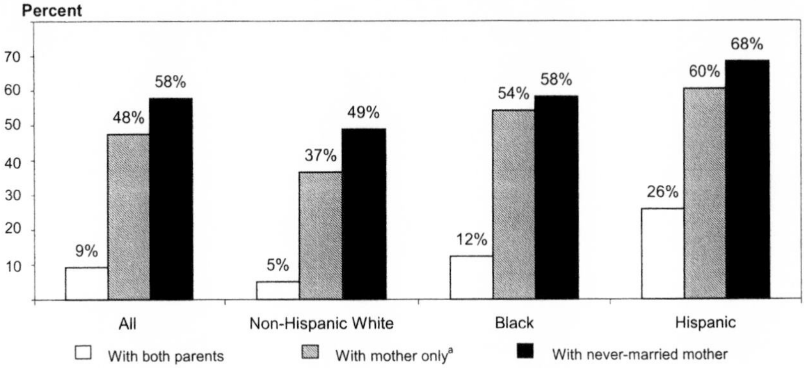

Percent

aIncludes mothers who are divorced; married, spouse absent; widowed; and never married. *Source*: U.S. Census Bureau, *Marital Status and Living Arrangements: March 1998 (Update) Current Population Reports P20-514* (Washington, D.C.: U.S. Census Bureau, December 1998), pp. 37–55, table 6, "Living Arrangements of Children Under 18 Years, by Marital Status and Selected Characteristics of Parent: March 1998," available from: http://www.census.gov/prod/99pubs/p20-514u.pdf, accessed November 18, 2002.

over this period. This phenomenon begs the question of why marriage has collapsed, but the simple facts about the breakdown of families and their implications for children are indisputable.

Not only the growth of female-headed families but also shifts in the composition of the group of single parents have contributed to greater poverty and welfare dependency. In the 1960s and 1970s, most of the growth of single-parent families was caused by increases in divorce. In the 1980s and 1990s, almost all of the increase has been driven by nonmarital childbearing (see figure 7.3). Currently, 33 percent of all children in the United States are born outside of marriage. The proportion is more than half in many of our largest cities and nearly half now in several states (such as Louisiana and Mississippi). Unmarried mothers tend to be younger and more disadvantaged than their divorced counterparts. As a result, they and their children are even more likely to be poor. Poverty is not the only consequence of growing up in a single-parent home; research by Sara McLanahan, professor in Princeton University's Department of Sociology, and others has shown that such children are disadvantaged in other ways as well, but the economic consequences are the most obvious and to many people the most compelling.[1]

Figure 7.2
Increase in Child Poverty Attributable to the Growth of
Female-Headed Families, 1970–1996

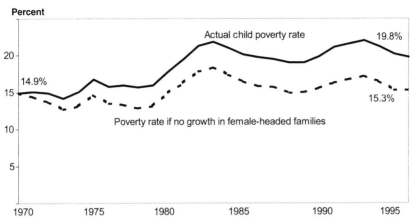

Source: Author's calculations based on data from U.S. Census Bureau, *Historical Poverty Tables—People* (Washington, D.C.: U.S. Census Bureau, June 4, 1999), table 10, "Related Children in Female Householder Families as a Proportion of All Related Children, by Poverty Status: 1959 to 2001," available from: http://www.census.gov/hhes/poverty/histpov/ hstpov10.html, accessed November 18, 2002.

Figure 7.3
Children in Female-Headed Families Whose Mothers Are
Divorced vs. Never-Married

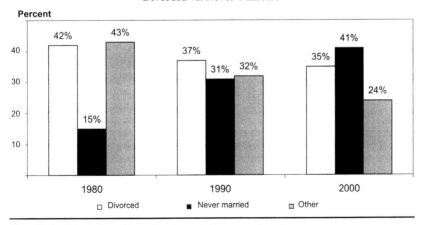

Note: "Other" includes widowed, and married, spouse absent.
Source: U.S. Census Bureau, *Families and Living Arrangements* (Washington, D.C.: U.S. Census Bureau, June 9, 2001), table CH-5. "Children Under 18 Years Living With Mother Only, by Marital Status of Mother: 1960 to Present," available from: http://www.census.gov/ population/socdemo/hh-fam/tabCH-5.txt, accessed November 18, 2002.

The good news is that the rise in the fraction of all children born out of wedlock—and the concomitant rise in single-parent families— appears to have slowed or stabilized since about 1994 (see figure 7.4). This trend happens to coincide with the welfare rolls' sharp decline but precedes the enactment of the national welfare reform law by two years. Although the reasons for the slowdown remain murky, some data will put the changes in context.

First, we should be clear that, statistically, most nonmarital births occur among women in their twenties, especially their early twenties (see figure 7.5). Nonmarital childbearing is not, as many people seem to think, synonymous with teenage childbearing. Moreover, there is nothing magic about age twenty. A woman who has a birth at age eighteen or nineteen is not very different from one who has a

Figure 7.4
Percent of Births to Unmarried Women, 1980–2000

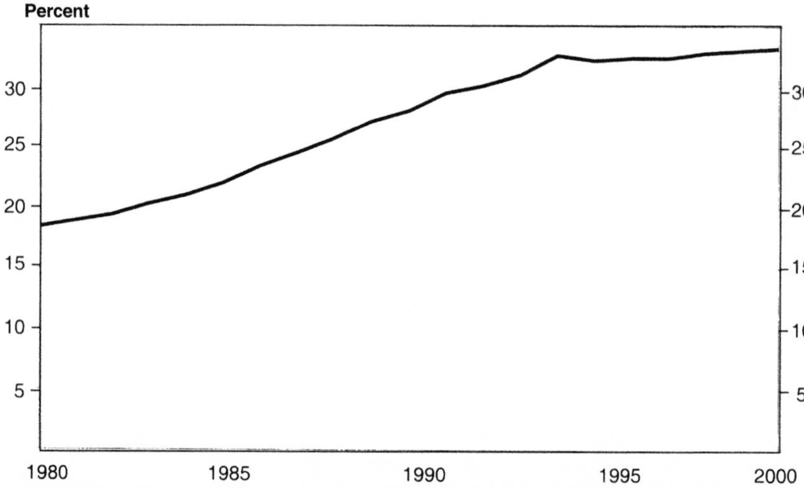

Source: For 1980–1999, National Center for Health Statistics, *Nonmarital Childbearing in the United States, 1940–99*, National Vital Statistics Reports 48 (16) (Hyattsville, Md: National Center for Health Statistics, October 18, 2000), p. 17, table 1, "Number, rate, and percent of births to unmarried women and birth rate for married women: United States, 1940–99," available from: http://www.cdc.gov/nchs/data/nvsr/nvsr48/nvs48_16.pdf, accessed November 18, 2002; for 2000, National Center for Health Statistics, *Births: Final Data for 2000*, National Vital Statistics Reports 50 (5) (Hyattsville, Md.: National Center for Health Statistics, February 12, 2002), p. 46, table 17, "Number, birth rate, and percent of births to unmarried women by age, race, and Hispanic origin of mother: United States, 2000," available from: http://www.cdc.gov/nchs/data/nvsr/nvsr50/nvsr50_05.pdf, accessed September 16, 2002.

Figure 7.5
Nonmarital Births by Mother's Age, 2000

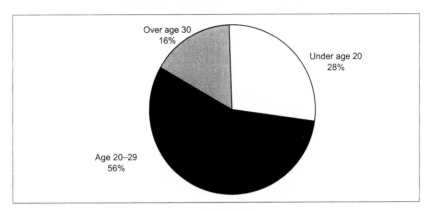

Over age 30
16%

Under age 20
28%

Age 20–29
56%

Source: National Center for Health Statistics, *Births: Final Data for 2000*, National Vital Statistics Reports 50 (5) (Hyattsville, Md.: National Center for Health Statistics, February 12, 2002), p. 46, table 17, "Number, birth rate, and percent of births to unmarried women by age, race, and Hispanic origin of mother: United States, 2000," available from: http://www.cdc.gov/nchs/data/nvsr/nvsr50/nvsr50_05.pdf, accessed September 16, 2002.

birth at age twenty or twenty-one. A high proportion (about half) of nonmarital births are second or higher-order births; if we look just at the *first* birth a woman has outside of marriage, the importance of the teenage years looms larger. Specifically, half of all nonmarital childbearing starts during the teen years (see figure 7.6). So if we want to reduce nonmarital childbearing and the poverty that accompanies it, the adolescent years are a good time to start. Young girls who have children, often before completing their education, are less likely to marry and more likely to have additional children than those who delay parenting to a later age. One study compared teens who delayed childbearing because of a miscarriage with those who did not and found that those in the latter group were not particularly disadvantaged by the birth.[2] They did, however, spend longer as single parents and had more births before age thirty than those who miscarried. This study relied on a very small sample in which more than half of the control group (that is, the girls who miscarried) got pregnant again and went on to give birth before age twenty. Moreover, children of the young mothers suffer a variety of adverse consequences, including poorer health, less success in school, and more behavior problems.

Figure 7.6
Nonmarital Birth by Mother's Age, 1995

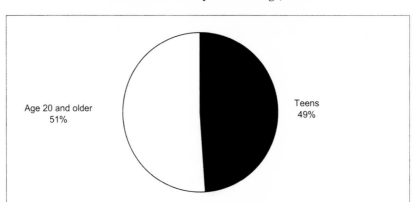

Age 20 and older
51%

Teens
49%

Source: U.S. House of Representatives, Committee on Ways and Means, *1998 Green Book: Background Materials and Data on Programs within the Jurisdiction of the Committee on Ways and Means* (Washington, D.C.: Government Printing Office, 1998), p. 539, figure 7-4, "Births to Unmarried Women in 1995: Live Births by Age of Mother and Previous Births."

I want to say a word here about culture. Both early childbearing and nonmarital childbearing vary enormously among population subgroups (see figure 7.7). Some of the differences are a result of differences in socioeconomic status, but one would be hard-pressed to explain all of them in this way. Note, for example, that early childbearing rates and nonmarital childbearing rates are much lower among immigrant than among native-born women, despite the fact that immigrants have much less education.

The increasing number of children born out of wedlock is the proximate result of three factors: later marriage, a higher birth rate among young unmarried women, and a lower birth rate among older married women. Some people believe the solution is to encourage marriage even among the very young, and others believe the solution is to encourage postponement of childbearing to later ages. Without delving too deeply into this controversy, let me simply suggest that the goal among those concerned about child poverty should be to discourage both too early childbearing and childbearing outside of marriage. Very early childbearing, even were it to occur within marriage, is inconsistent with the growing requirements of the economy for workers with high levels of education. In addition, teenage marriages are highly unstable. But we should also recognize

Figure 7.7

Teen and Nonmarital Births by Race/Ethnicity and Immigrant Status, 2000

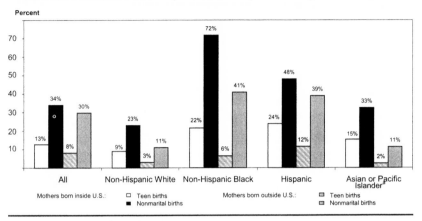

[a]Includes some Hispanic mothers.

Source: National Center for Health Statistics, *Births: Final Data for 2000*, National Vital Statistics Reports 50 (5) (Hyattsville, Md.: National Center for Health Statistics, February 12, 2002), p. 43, table 13, "Total number of births, rates (birth, fertility, and total fertility), and percent of births with selected demographic characteristics, by detailed race of mother and place of birth of mother: United States, 2000," available from: http://www.cdc.gov/nchs/data/nvsr/nvsr50/nvsr50_05.pdf, accessed September 16, 2002.

that the breakdown of marriage as the normative context for raising children may have consequences for our society that are at least as profound as the age at which childbearing begins. Indeed, the teen birth rate is far lower now than it was in the 1950s. What is new is the proportion of very early births that occur to unmarried women and the much broader acceptance of single parenting.

For whatever reasons, marriage is being replaced by what a team of researchers from Columbia and Princeton Universities call "fragile families." Preliminary evidence from this team's work in several cities, as well as other research, suggests that about half of young mothers who give birth out of wedlock are cohabiting with the father of their child at the time of birth and that another 30 percent are "romantically involved." Past research suggests that such ties are not very durable. If this research is any guide, within a year or two, many of the fathers will have disappeared. But some believe that the outcome could change if we intervened at the time of the child's birth in ways that encouraged more father involvement.

High rates of cohabitation raise another issue: Are our estimates of child poverty too high because we fail to capture the income available from men who live with single mothers? On the one hand, such income may be substantially underreported or incompletely measured in standard tabulations of family income. On the other hand, that income may not be consistently or reliably available to the women and children living in such households. We need more research on this important question.

The Decline in Teen Births

Returning to the question of trends in early nonmarital childbearing, one reason that nonmarital childbearing appears to have stabilized is that teen birth rates have declined. Because such a high proportion of teen births (more than three-quarters) occur outside of marriage (see figure 7.8) and because teen mothers often go on to have additional children without marrying, any decline in teenage childbearing will eventually reduce the proportion of all births that occur outside of marriage. The decline in teen birth rates dates from the early 1990s (see figure 7.9), but it appears to have accelerated in recent years and can be expected to have a lagged effect on nonmarital childbearing and single parenting more generally.

Why are teen birth rates declining? In the past, any progress in this area was entirely a result of the greater availability of abortion.

Figure 7.8
Percent of Nonmarital Births by Mother's Age, 2000

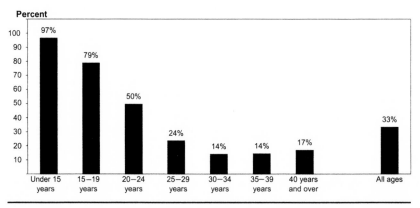

Source: National Center for Health Statistics, *Births: Final Data for 2000*, National Vital Statistics Reports 50 (5) (Hyattsville, Md.: National Center for Health Statistics, February 12, 2002), p. 46, table 17, "Number, birth rate, and percent of births to unmarried women by age, race, and Hispanic origin of mother: United States, 2000," available from: http://www.cdc.gov/nchs/data/nvsr/nvsr50/nvsr50_05.pdf, accessed September 16, 2002.

Figure 7.9
Teen Birth Rates, Age 15–19, 1972–2000

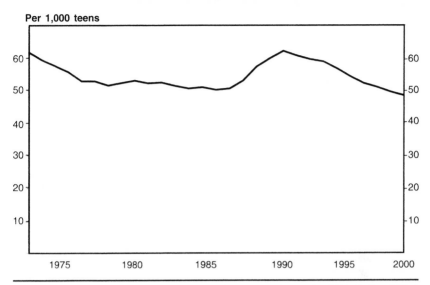

Source: National Center for Health Statistics, *Births: Final Data for 2000*, National Vital Statistics Reports 50 (5) (Hyattsville, Md.: National Center for Health Statistics, February 12, 2002), p. 30, table 4, "Total fertility rates and birth rates by age of mother: United States, 1970-2000, and by age and race of mother: United States, 1980–2000," available from: http://www.cdc.gov/nchs/data/nvsr/nvsr50/nvsr50_05.pdf, accessed September 16, 2002.

What is new in the 1990s is that teen birth rates are declining because of fewer pregnancies, not because an increasing fraction of teen pregnancies are being aborted (see figure 7.10).

The decline in the teen pregnancy rate raises the question of what is causing fewer teens to become pregnant. Some analysts contend that the major reason is that more of them are abstaining from sex, and some say that greater use of contraception is the primary reason. Most people who have reviewed the data and the associated controversies have suggested that a reasonable conclusion is that teens are both engaging in less sex and using more protection.[3] The reasons for these changes in their behavior are not clear, but they probably stem from five developments.

First, some indirect evidence suggests that the changes are related to a growing awareness of AIDS and other sexually transmitted diseases (STDs), which now affect more than 3 million teens per year. The proportion of adolescents who have received formal education

Figure 7.10
Teen Pregnancy and Abortion Rates, Age 15–19, 1972–1996

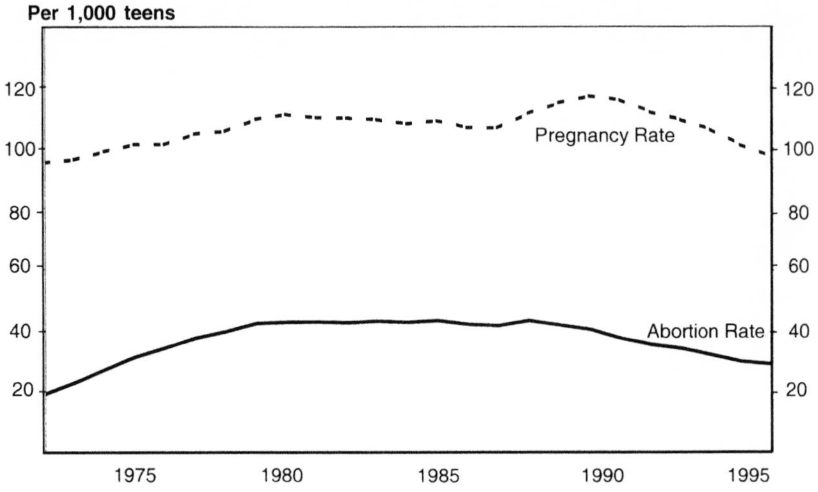

Per 1,000 teens

Source: National Campaign to Prevent Teen Pregnancy, *Special Report: U.S. Teenage Pregnancy Statistics with Comparative Statistics for Women Aged 20–24* (June 1999), p. 9, available from: http://www.teenpregnancy.org/findfact.pdf, accessed November 21, 2001.

about these dangers has increased during the past decade, a fact that has had an effect on the extent of sexual activity among this group, according to at least one study.[4] In addition, condom use among teens has increased sharply, although benefits from condom use have been partially offset by a decline in the use of the pill. This substitution of one birth control method for another undoubtedly reflects the relative efficacy of the two methods in protecting against STDs. Finally, the threat of AIDS may explain why rates of sexual activity among young males appear to have declined faster than for females. The new health risks associated with sexual activity have put males and females on a slightly more level playing field.

A second possible reason for the decline in teen pregnancy is more conservative attitudes. Various polls and surveys suggest that the youngest generation is less accepting of casual sex than are their older brothers and sisters. According to the General Social Survey, in 1972 only 10 percent of eighteen- to twenty-four-year-olds said that it was "always wrong to have sex before marriage," whereas in 1998 this proportion had more than doubled, to 23 percent. More conservative attitudes do not always translate into more conservative behavior, but at least one study, done by a group of researchers at the Urban Institute, found that more than half of the decline in sexual activity among seventeen- to nineteen-year-old urban males between 1988 and 1995 was directly attributable to the more conservative attitudes that emerged during this period.[5]

Among the teens who remain sexually active, a third factor that appears to have lowered pregnancy rates is the availability of more effective forms of contraception, such as injectables and implants. Failure rates for more traditional forms of contraception (including the pill) are high—especially given the tendency of teens to use them inconsistently—so the small but growing use of Depo-Provera and Norplant appears to be making a real difference.

A fourth possible source of the decline in teen pregnancy is welfare reform itself in combination with new supports for the working poor. Not only does the new welfare system provide less long-term assistance to unmarried women, but during the past decade, Congress has increased supports for the working poor by expanding the Earned Income Tax Credit (EITC), Medicaid, and some other programs. In 1986, a single mother who took a low-paying job was little better off than she had been on welfare. But by 1997, she was able to double her income by going to work, and not surprisingly, the employment rates of young, unmarried mothers have increased dramatically in recent years. Work is, I would suggest, a great contraceptive.

We should also keep in mind that the 1996 welfare law included new tools for establishing paternity and enforcing the child support obligations of absent fathers. As the word spreads that fathering a child out of wedlock brings ongoing financial responsibilities, some pregnancies and births could be deterred.

But what about the emphasis in the new law on reducing nonmarital and teen births? If the new welfare system is having an effect, it is probably more because of the new signals it is sending than because local offices are doing anything differently, such as referring women to family-planning clinics. Field studies conducted by the Manpower Demonstration Research Corporation as well as the Rockefeller Institute at the State University of New York-Albany have found few changes in local practice to match the emphasis in the law on reducing teen and nonmarital births, although many states are devoting additional funds to abstinence education or are using the abstinence funds included in the bill for more broadly oriented programs that provide mentoring, after-school programs, or media campaigns directed at reducing teen pregnancy. In addition, many states have capped welfare benefits for those who have additional children while on welfare; although one recent study suggests that the caps may have had an effect, more research is needed before we can come to any firm conclusions on this issue.[6] As an important footnote here, I want to add that child sexual abuse is more common than most people realize; evidence suggests that as many as one-third of women on welfare were sexually abused as children, usually by male relatives or friends. Such abuse puts these women at much greater risk of early pregnancy and makes them distrustful of other people, leading to a variety of other problems later in life.[7]

Finally, the decline in teen pregnancy rates could be related to the recent strength of the economy. Although I know of no data or evidence that would support this hypothesis in a concrete way, it stands to reason that young people may have more reasons to complete their education and more opportunities to enter the job market. In combination with the incentives provided by the EITC and other supports for the working poor, a strong economy has probably played some role.

In conclusion, I would summarize the evidence about recent trends as follows: First, the growth of single-parent families and nonmarital births to young mothers slowed or declined during the late 1990s; this trend should have positive effects on child poverty rates and child well-being in the future. Second, what has produced this good news is probably a combination of fear of AIDS, changes in welfare and other policies, improvements in contraceptive technology, and more conservative attitudes.

Notes

1. Sara McLanahan, "Parent Absence or Poverty: Which Matters More?" in *Consequences of Growing Up Poor*, edited by Greg Duncan and Jeanne Brooks-Gunn (New York: Russell Sage Foundation, 1997), pp. 35–48.
2. V. Joseph Hotz, Susan Williams McElroy, and Seth G. Sanders, "The Impacts of Teenage Childbearing on the Mothers and the Consequences of those Impacts for Government," in *Kids Having Kids*, edited by Rebecca A. Maynard (Washington, D.C.: Urban Institute Press, 1997), pp. 55–94.
3. At the National Campaign to Prevent Teen Pregnancy, we have carefully reviewed all the data on this question, and our conclusion is that both have played a role. I would caution against any attempt to be much more specific than that in terms of allocating the credit, given the uncertainties in the data. Obtaining good measures of sexual activity and contraceptive use is extremely difficult, and one's answer to the question about the relative importance of abstinence versus contraception is highly sensitive to technical questions about the data and methods used. For example,

although the National Survey of Family Growth (NSFG) reported a decline in sexual activity from 1990 to 1995, many researchers are unwilling to rely on that data because the 1990 data came from a telephone rather than an in-person interview and thus are not strictly comparable to data from earlier years. And although some data sources, such as the National Survey of Adolescent Males, show a decline in sexual activity among males (at least among white males), other data sources, such as the Youth Risk Behavioral Survey and the NSFG, indicate that this decline was not accompanied by a statistically significant decline in sexual activity among females, at least over the period for which comparable data exist. Because only females can get pregnant, it is not clear what we should make of this finding.

4.   Leighton Ku, Freya L. Sonenstein, Laura D. Lindberg, Carolyn H. Bradner, Scott Boggess, and Joseph H. Pleck, "Understanding Changes in Sexual Activity among Young Metropolitan Men: 1979–1995," *Family Planning Perspectives* 30 (November–December 1998): 256–262.

5.   Ibid.

6.   For a more extended discussion of welfare reform and the decline in teen pregnancy, see Isabel V. Sawhill, "Welfare Reform and Reducing Teen Pregnancy," *Public Interest* 138 (Winter 2000): 40-51; and Isabel V. Sawhill, *What Can Be Done to Reduce Teen Pregnancy and Out-of-Wedlock Births?* Welfare Reform and Beyond Policy Brief No. 8 (Washington, D.C.: Brookings Institution, October 2001).

7.   See Jason DeParle, "Early Sex Abuse Hinders Many Women on Welfare," *New York Times,* November 28, 1999.

References

Acs, Gregory, and Megan Gallagher. 2000. *Income Inequality among America's Children.* New Federalism: National Survey of America's Families Policy Brief B-6. Washington, D.C.: Urban Institute. January.

DeParle, Jason. 1999. "Early Sex Abuse Hinders Many Women on Welfare." *New York Times.* November 28.

Edin, Katheryn, and Laura Lein. 1997. *Making Ends Meet: How Single Mothers Survive Welfare and Low-Wage Work.* New York: Russell Sage Foundation.

Hotz, V. Joseph, Susan Williams McElroy, and Seth G. Sanders. 1997. "The Impacts of Teenage Childbearing on the Mothers and the Consequences of those Impacts for Government." In *Kids Having Kids.* Edited by Rebecca A. Maynard. Washington, D.C.: Urban Institute Press.

Ku, Leighton, Freya L. Sonenstein, Laura D. Lindberg, Carolyn H. Bradner, Scott Boggess, and Joseph H. Pleck. 1998. "Understanding Changes in Sexual Activity among Young Metropolitan Men: 1979–1995." *Family Planning Perspectives* 30 (November–December): 256–262.

McLanahan, Sara. 1997. "Parent Absence or Poverty: Which Matters More?" In *Consequences of Growing Up Poor.* Edited by Greg Duncan and Jeanne Brooks-Gunn. New York: Russell Sage Foundation.

Sawhill, Isabel V. 2000. "Welfare Reform and Reducing Teen Pregnancy." *Public Interest* 138 (Winter): 40–51.

———. 2001. *What Can Be Done to Reduce Teen Pregnancy and Out-of-Wedlock Births?* Welfare Reform and Beyond Policy Brief No. 8. Washington, D.C.: Brookings Institution. October.

8

Child Maltreatment and Foster Care

Richard J. Gelles

In January 1996, preliminary findings from the Third National Study of the Incidence of Child Abuse and Neglect of the U.S. Department of Health and Human Services (HHS) began to circulate in government and professional circles. The preliminary results indicated a substantial increase in the rates of most forms of child maltreatment between the time of the second survey, conducted in 1986, and the third survey, conducted in 1993. Although the data for the third survey had been collected between September and December 1993, and the preliminary results were available in January 1996, it took nine more months for HHS to release the final report of the survey. The report opened with the finding that the number of abused and neglected children doubled between 1986 and 1993. The data were made public only one month after President Clinton signed the Personal Responsibility and Work Opportunity Reconciliation Act of 1996 (PRWORA), or what is conventionally called "welfare reform." Coincidence or not, the publication of the results of the federal government's decennial survey of child maltreatment suggested that welfare reform would lead to an even larger increase in the number of children abused and neglected by parents and caretakers.

The fact that the federal government collects incidence and prevalence data on child maltreatment suggests that the occurrence of child maltreatment and child placements could be tracked over time to determine whether federal and state welfare reform legislation does have an impact on the frequency and severity of child maltreatment. Unfortunately, this notion is far too optimistic. The status of government statistics on the occurrence of child maltreatment is comparable to the Woody Allen commentary about a bad Catskills resort: the food is bad and the portions are small. Trend data on child

maltreatment and children placed in out-of-home care as a consequence of child maltreatment are meager, and the quality of the data
is quite variable.

This chapter first examines the sources of data on child maltreatment and children placed in foster care. Second, it presents findings
on the extent of maltreatment and the number of children placed in
foster care. Third, it examines trend data on abuse, neglect, and foster care placements. The data, as of yet, show no evidence that
PRWORA is producing an increase in abuse, neglect, or foster care
placements.

Data Sources

No single data source provides reliable and valid data on the occurrence of child abuse and neglect or on the number of children in
foster care and their status over time. A variety of data sources collectively present a rough portrait of maltreated children and their
placements; the most recent data are for 2000. The data sources are
as follows:

- *National Incidence Survey of Reported and Recognized Child Maltreatment (NIS).* The Child Abuse Prevention and Treatment Act of
1974 (PL 93-247) established the National Center on Child Abuse and
Neglect (NCCAN) and instructed it to "make a full and complete study
and investigation of the national incidence of child abuse and neglect. . . ." (Section 2b [6]). NCCAN (now the Office on Child Abuse
and Neglect) has conducted three national surveys of recognized and
reported child maltreatment. The studies, conducted in 1979–1980,
1986, and 1993,[1] surveyed nationally representative samples of professionals who come into contact with suspected cases of child maltreatment. The survey extrapolates information from those reports to
develop a national estimate of the incidence of child abuse and neglect. A fourth survey is in the process of being designed.

- *National Child Abuse and Neglect Data System (NCANDS).* The
NCCAN/Office of Child Abuse and Neglect of HHS also sponsors the
collection of state data on official reports of child abuse and neglect,
dispositions, victims, services, and perpetrators as part of the NCANDS.
The data can be derived from Summary Data Component reports filed
by states. Fifty states and the District of Columbia submitted reports
for 2000.[2] Thirty-four states reported child-specific data.

- *Prevent Child Abuse America Reports from the States.* The private,
nonprofit group Prevent Child Abuse America (formerly the National
Committee to Prevent Child Abuse, or NCPCA) conducts its own an-

nual survey of child abuse reporting and child abuse fatalities. The data are derived from states that voluntarily participate in the survey.[3]

- *The Voluntary Cooperative Information System (VCIS).* The Voluntary Cooperative Information System of the American Public Human Services Association (formerly the American Public Welfare Association) collected data on children residing in out-of-home care until 1995.

- *The Child Welfare League of America (CWLA), Child Abuse and Neglect: A Look at the States: 1999 CWLA Stat Book.* This volume provides national and state-by-state data on child welfare, including child abuse and neglect reports and investigations, child maltreatment fatalities, children in out-of-home care, and children adopted. The sources for the Stat Book are the NIS, NCANDS, VCIS, and CWLA's own state agency survey.[4]

- *The Adoption and Foster Care Analysis and Reporting System (AFCARS)* is a system developed for collecting data on children in foster care and children who have been adopted under the auspices of the state child welfare agency. There are two components, the state component and the federal component. The state component consists of the information system used to collect case management information, and transmits the AFCARS data to the federal system. The federal system consists of the information system that receives the data, processes the data, and checks it for compliance and quality, and develops reports. Data collection began in the states October 1, 1994, with data submitted to the federal system beginning June 15, 1995. Data from the AFCARS system cover the period from 1998 to 2000.

- *The State Automated Child Welfare Information System (SACWIS)* is the final data system. State SACWIS systems must do the following, at a minimum: (1) Meet the AFCARS data collection and reporting requirements; (2) Provide for intrastate electronic data exchange with data collection systems operated under the Temporary Assistance for Needy Families program, Medicaid, child support enforcement, and the NCANDS (unless not practicable for certain reasons); (3) Provide for automated data collection on all children in foster care under the responsibility of the state child welfare agency to support implementation of statutory child protections and requirements; (4) Collect and manage information necessary to facilitate delivery of child welfare services, family preservation and family support services, family reunification services, and permanent placement; (5) Collect and manage information necessary to determine eligibility for the Foster Care, Adoption Assistance, and Independent Living Programs and to meet case management requirements for these programs; (6) Monitor case plan development, payment authorization and issuance, and review and management including eligibility determinations and redeterminations; and (7) Ensure confidentiality and security of information. The SACWIS system is operational only in a handful of states and is not yet yielding data.

Trends

This section describes the data sources that provide information on the extent of and trends in child maltreatment and foster care placements.

National Incidence Survey (NIS) Estimates

According to the third NIS survey (NIS-3), the number of recognized and/or reported cases of child maltreatment increased between 1986 and 1993.[5]

The rates and number of children who are recognized as maltreated were compared on the basis of two definitions of maltreatment. Using the general definition of child maltreatment, the number of cases increased from 1,424,400 (22.6 per 1,000 children) to 2,815,600 (41.9 per 1,000).[6] Under the more stringent *harm definition,* which required that an act of commission or omission result in demonstrable harm, the number of abuse and neglect cases increased 67 percent, from 931,000 (14.8 per 1,000) in 1986 to 1.5 million (23.2 per 1,000) in 1993 (see figures 8.1 and 8.2).[7]

Figure 8.1
Prevalence of Maltreatment under the Harm Standard, 1980, 1986, and 1993

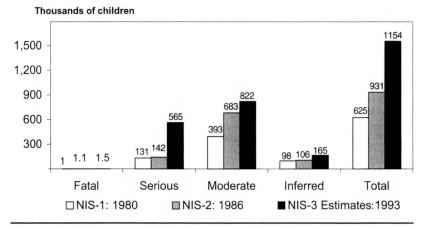

Thousands of children

□ NIS-1: 1980   ▨ NIS-2: 1986   ■ NIS-3 Estimates: 1993

Source: National Center on Child Abuse and Neglect, *Study Findings: Study of National Incidence and Prevalence of Child Abuse and Neglect: 1993* (Washington, D.C.: U.S. Department of Health and Human Services, 1996).

NCANDS Estimates

The NCANDS data system did not begin tabulating state child abuse and neglect reports until 1990. Before that, state data on child abuse and neglect reports—including data on fatalities—were collected by the NCPCA (now Prevent Child Abuse America) and the American Association for Protecting Children/American Humane Association.

Data from NCANDS record only the cases actually reported to state agencies and then reported to NCANDS. In 2000, more than 2.79 million children were reported to state agencies for investigation, according to data submitted by fifty states and the District of Columbia.[8] The actual number of confirmed child victims increased from 790,526 in 1990 to 879,000 in 2000, an increase of 11.2 percent. (Note: Forty-four states participated in the survey in 1990, and fifty states and the District of Columbia submitted data in 2000.)

Although the number of victimized children increased between 1990 and 2000, the rate of confirmed child maltreatment increased from 13.4 per 1,000 in 1990 to a peak of 15.3 per 1,000 in 1993. Thereafter, the rate of child abuse victimization declined (see figure 8.3). The steepest declines were for the two years following the enactment of welfare reform legislation. In 1996, the rate was 14.7 per 1,000 children; it dropped to 13.9 per 1,000 in 1997 and to 12.2 per 1,000 in 2000.[9] The rate of victimization was the lowest in 1999, 11.8 per 1,000.

Figure 8.2
Rates from Maltreatment under the Harm Standard, 1980, 1986, and 1993

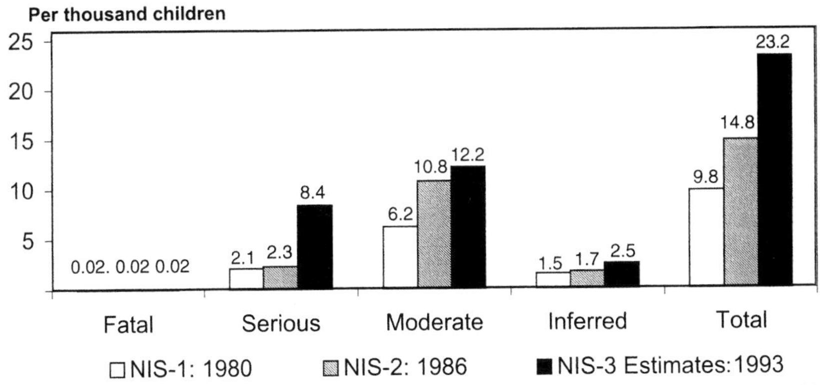

Per thousand children

	Fatal	Serious	Moderate	Inferred	Total
NIS-1: 1980	0.02	2.1	6.2	1.5	9.8
NIS-2: 1986	0.02	2.3	10.8	1.7	14.8
NIS-3 Estimates: 1993	0.02	8.4	12.2	2.5	23.2

☐ NIS-1: 1980   ▨ NIS-2: 1986   ■ NIS-3 Estimates: 1993

Source: National Center on Child Abuse and Neglect, *Study Findings: Study of National Incidence and Prevalence of Child Abuse and Neglect: 1993* (Washington, D.C.: U.S. Department of Health and Human Services, 1996).

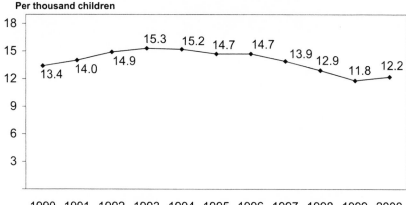

Figure 8.3
Child Victimization Rates, 1990–2000

Source: U.S. Department of Health and Human Services, Administration on Children, Youth and Families, *Child Maltreatment 2000* (Washington, D.C.: Government Printing Office, 2002), p. 24, figure 3-2, "Victimization Rates, 1990–2000," available from: http://www.acf.hhs.gov/programs/cb/publications/cm00/cm2000.pdf, accessed November 22, 2002.

Fatalities

Prevent Child Abuse America projected that nationwide 1,201 child abuse fatalities occurred in 2000,[10] an increase from 1,143 in 1990 and a decrease from a high of 1,261 in 1992 (see figure 8.4). The rate of child maltreatment fatalities was 1.78 per 100,000 children in the population in 1997 and 1.84 per 100,000 children in 1990.[11] No changes occurred in the rate of child maltreatment fatalities between 1995 and 1997 (see figure 8.5). NCANDS data on child fatalities place the number of child maltreatment fatalities at 935 in 1996; 979 in 1997; 1,098 in 1998; 1,089 in 1999; 960 in 2000 (with a revised figure for 2000 at 1,201 based on data from states providing information on child fatalities from agencies other than child welfare agencies—for example, coroner's offices or fatality review boards). The rates for the period 1996 to 2000 are presented in figure 8.5. The NCANDS report for 2000 notes that the increase in reported deaths appears to be a result of increased reporting from additional sources.[12]

Children in Foster Care

The VCIS estimate on the number of children in foster care on the last day of 1990 was 400,000. The new federal AFCARS data system's initial report on children in foster care was for the year

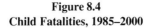

Figure 8.4
Child Fatalities, 1985–2000

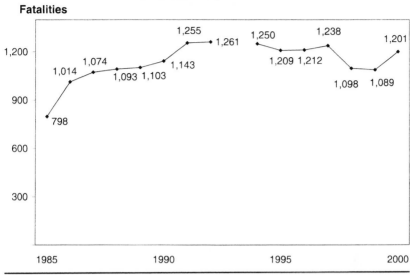

Source: For 1985 and 1994–1997, Ching-Tung Wang and Kathryn Harding, *Current Trends in Child Abuse Reporting and Fatalities: The Results of the 1998 Annual 50 State Survey, Prevent Child Abuse America,* 1999; for 1998–2000, U.S. Department of Health and Human Services, Administration on Children, Youth and Families, *Child Maltreatment 2000* (Washington, D.C.: Government Printing Office, 2002), p. 56, table 5-1, "Child Fatality Rates per 100,000 Children, 1996–2000," available from: http://www.acf.hhs.gov/programs/cb/publications/cm00/cm2000.pdf, accessed November 22, 2002.

1998. The number of children in out-of-home care in 1998 was 560,000. This number increased to 581,000 in 1999. On September 30, 2002, there were 556,000 children in foster care. Thus, for the first time in close to two decades, the foster care population declined.[13] Preliminary estimates for 2001 show a slight increase to 565,000, but this number is still below the peak in 1999.

Reliability and Validity

The picture that emerges from existing data sources is that child abuse and neglect appear to have increased substantially between 1990 and 2000. On the surface, both the number of cases and the rate of child maltreatment have increased, as has the number of children in out-of-home care. However, readers should be cautious in accepting the apparent increases at face value.

Data on recognized and reported child maltreatment are not data on the actual or true occurrence of abuse and neglect. Rates and

Figure 8.5
Child Fatality Rates, 1985 and 1994–2000

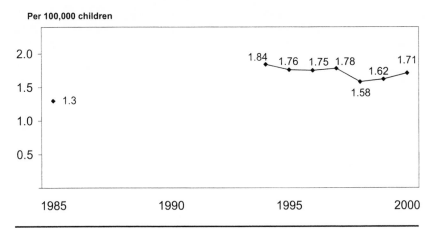

Per 100,000 children

Source: For 1985 and 1994–1997, Ching-Tung Wang and Kathryn Harding, *Current Trends in Child Abuse Reporting and Fatalities: The Results of the 1998 Annual 50 State Survey, Prevent Child Abuse America,* 1999; for 1998–2000, U.S. Department of Health and Human Services, Administration on Children, Youth and Families, *Child Maltreatment 2000* (Washington, D.C.: Government Printing Office, 2002), p. 56, table 5-1, "Child Fatality Rates per 100,000 Children, 1996–2000," available from: http://www.acf.hhs.gov/programs/cb/publications/cm00/cm2000.pdf, accessed November 22, 2002.

numbers of reporting and recognition depend on a variety of factors, not the least of which is the definition of what constitutes abuse and neglect. First, state definitions vary quite a bit, and over the past thirty years, states have revised and expanded their legal definitions of child maltreatment.

Second, standards for screening reports vary. Some states investigate nearly all reports, whereas other states require investigation of only a portion of reports. In 2000, Florida, for example, screened out only 2.2 percent of its 117,523 reports of child abuse and neglect, while Washington State screened out 28.2 percent of its 67,152 reports.[14]

Third, state data management information systems vary. Not all states actually participate in annual NCANDS or NCPCA tabulations. Within states, changes in state laws and incidents of child abuse fatalities can influence rates of recognition and reporting. A widely reported incident of abuse can result in a spike in reports. In addition, for the past three decades, ongoing training efforts have aimed at increasing reports of abuse and neglect. At the same time, staffing and resources can "cap" how many reports a state child protective system can actually handle.

Finally, the data themselves are subject to inaccuracies. Consider the inaccuracies noted during the discovery and monitoring stages of a class action suit against a county department of child welfare. As part of the monitoring of the consent decree, the department was required to select sixty case files for external review. One of the sixty files was on a child who had been dead for ten years. Worse, the file included a risk assessment supposedly conducted two years before the review—eight years after the child had died. Three other files were of children who had been adopted and thus were no longer part of the child welfare system.

This error rate is rather substantial, especially in light of the fact that the department itself selected the cases that would be reviewed externally. As a rule, criminologists consider homicide and fatality data to be the most reliable and valid. Yet, even child fatality data are subject to variability. Some states and jurisdictions routinely autopsy all child deaths, but others autopsy only a fraction of child deaths. Experts generally assume that many child abuse fatalities are misclassified as accidents, suicides, or sudden infant death syndrome.[15]

Data on out-of-home care have the same problems as other child welfare data. AFCARS data are available only since 1998 and are not comparable to the VCIS or CWLA data collected prior to the implementation of the federal system.

The national data on child maltreatment reporting and children in foster care depend on cooperation of local and state administrators. In some years, the response rate is actually 100 percent (for example, in 2000), whereas in other years the rate is as low as 80 percent.

Implications and Recommendations

The nation still lacks a reliable and valid means of measuring the occurrence of child abuse and neglect and tracking the travel of children through the various services and placements that exist in the national child welfare system. The AFCARS system and the forthcoming SACWIS system may improve the reliability and validity of data sources. Many states, however, remain unable or unwilling to participate fully in those systems. Rather than comply with SACWIS regulations, some states are considering accepting the monetary penalty for nonparticipation. The lack of a national data system is particularly problematic, because child welfare is a nearly $20 billion system.

Data systems that assess the occurrence of child abuse and neglect need to be developed. Just as the U.S. Department of Justice has implemented the National Survey of Crime Victims to augment official crime data reports collected by the Uniform Crime Statistics, the federal government needs to develop or fund a direct measure of child abuse and neglect. Given the Department of Justice's experience in this area, the Bureau of Justice Statistics could be funded to collect such information.

States need to develop information systems that are user-friendly and provide reliable data. Legacy management information systems, such as AFCARS or SACWIS, should be replaced with real-time, Internet-based management information systems. Agencies and organizations that report on the occurrence of child abuse and neglect should be encouraged not to equate child abuse reporting with the actual occurrence of child abuse. Federal and state reports, as well as press releases to the media, should carefully qualify data by pointing out that reported and recognized cases are not the same as actual cases of child maltreatment. (All government publications on child abuse and neglect and foster care should include the rate of occurrence per 1,000 children. All tables and figures in such reports should also include rates.)

Data that actually track children in the child welfare system are needed. The current data source merely provides a snapshot of children in out-of-home care and documents entrances and exits from such care. Caution should be exercised in reporting on existing data sources. Fluctuations in child abuse and neglect reports, foster care placements, and even child abuse fatalities do not necessarily reflect changes in the actual occurrence of abuse and neglect or foster care placements.

The caveats noted above should be acknowledged in considering the current trend data on child abuse and neglect and on children placed in foster care. As of 2000, those data indicated the following:

- Reports of child abuse and neglect have stabilized at about 3 million children per year.

- Rates of confirmed child maltreatment rose from 1990 to 1993, fell slightly between 1993 and 1996, declined steeply between 1996 and 1999, and then rose in 2000.

• Child abuse fatalities remained stable at about 1,200 per year.

• Foster care placements increased each year until 2000. Adoptions were stable at about 22,000 until 1996. New data suggest that adoptions from foster care increased to 36,000 in 1998 and to 51,000 in 2000.[16]

Welfare Reform's Impact

The key question to be addressed is, has welfare reform legislation affected the occurrence of child abuse and neglect and the number of children placed in foster homes? The qualified answer is that no evidence indicates that welfare reform legislation has produced an increase or decrease in child maltreatment reports, child abuse and neglect fatalities, or the number of children placed in foster care.

Given the paucity of relevant data, this answer must be qualified. The data are only as recent as 2000, four years after the passage of federal welfare reform legislation. The downturn in the economy that began in 2000 may be reflected in the reversal of the five-year trend of decreases in child maltreatment victimization. This reversal bears watching in the 2002 data.

More important, because a key component of welfare reform was devolution to the states, state-by-state trend analysis is required to identify the short-term effects of welfare reform legislation. Because data are collected by states, tracking changes in child maltreatment reporting, victimization fatalities, and out-of-home care for each state is possible.

Few data indicate an effect of welfare reform on child abuse and neglect or on placements of children in foster care, but that does not mean that an effect will not be seen in the future. Critics of welfare reform legislation believe that it will ultimately increase the rates of abuse and neglect as well as the number of children placed into out-of-home care. The key impact may occur after individual welfare recipients reach the sixty-month lifetime limit for receiving benefits, which occurred July 1, 2001. Even then, one would expect some kind of lag between the expiration of eligibility for benefits and the onset of maltreatment, recognition of maltreatment, and response by child welfare agencies and the courts.

Conversely, welfare reform may result in a decrease in the occurrence of child abuse, victimization, fatalities, and out-of-home placement. If, as the proponents of welfare reform hoped, welfare reform brings about a reduction in out-of-wedlock births and increases in work and intact families, the changes could be expected to reduce the occurrence of maltreatment and the need for out-of-home placement of maltreated children.

The possibility of welfare reform increasing or decreasing the occurrence of child abuse and neglect notwithstanding, it is important to conclude this chapter by reasserting that—as yet—no evidence indicates that welfare reform has increased the risk of children's being abused and neglected, nor that it has produced a major increase in placements of children into kin, foster, or residential care. What data we have suggest a small reduction in the rate of child victimization and a continued stable (albeit unacceptable) rate of child abuse and neglect fatalities.

Notes

1. Kenneth Burgdorf, *Recognition and Reporting of Child Maltreatment* (Rockville, Md.: Westat, 1980); National Center on Child Abuse and Neglect, *Study Findings: Study of National Incidence and Prevalence of Child Abuse and Neglect: 1988* (Washington, D.C.: U.S. Department of Health and Human Services, 1988); and National Center on Child Abuse and Neglect, *Study Findings: Study of National Incidence and Prevalence of Child Abuse and Neglect: 1993* (Washington, D.C.: U.S. Department of Health and Human Services, 1996).
2. U.S. Department of Health and Human Services, Administration on Children, Youth, and Families, *Child Maltreatment 1998: Reports from the States to the National Child Abuse and Neglect Data System* (Washington, D.C.: Government Printing Office, 2000).
3. Ching-Tung Wang and Kathryn Harding, *Current Trends in Child Abuse Reporting and Fatalities: The Results of the 1998 Annual 50 State Survey* (Chicago: Prevent Child Abuse America, 1999).
4. Child Welfare League of America, *Child Abuse and Neglect: A Look at the States: 1999 CWLA Stat Book* (Washington, D.C.: CWLA Press, 1999).
5. National Center on Child Abuse and Neglect, 1996.
6. The general definition was labeled the *endangerment standard*. This definition includes children who have been harmed by acts of abuse and neglect and children who have not yet been harmed, but who experience abuse and neglect that, according to the view of community professionals, puts them in danger of being harmed. See National Center on Child Abuse and Neglect, 1996, pp. 2–9.
7. The *harm standard* requires that a child has suffered demonstrable harm as a result of maltreatment. See National Center on Child Abuse and Neglect, 1996, pp. 2–9.
8. U.S. Department of Health and Human Services, Administration on Children, Youth, and Families, *Child Maltreatment 2000: Reports from the States to the National Child Abuse and Neglect Data System* (Washington, D.C.: Government Printing Office, 2002).
9. U.S. Department of Health and Human Services, Administration on Children, Youth, and Families, 2000.
10. This projection is based on data from forty-three states. A total of 935 fatalities occurred in those states.

11. Wang and Harding, 1999. No rate or projection is available for 1998 because too few states representing too small a percentage of the U.S. population of children reported data for 1998 to Prevent Child Abuse America.
12. U.S. Department of Health and Human Services, Administration on Children, Youth, and Families, 2000, p. 53, footnote 1.
13. Congressional Research Service, *Background Data on Child Welfare* (Washington, D.C.: Congressional Research Service, 2002).
14. U.S. Department of Health and Human Services, Administration on Children, Youth, and Families, *Child Maltreatment 1997: Reports from the States to the National Child Abuse and Neglect Data System* (Washington, D.C.: Government Printing Office, 1999).
15. Philip W. McLain, Jeffrey J. Sacks, and Robert G. Froehlke, "Estimates of Fatal Child Abuse and Neglect, United States, 1979–1988," *Pediatrics* 91 (1993): 338–343.
16. Congressional Research Service, 2002.

References

Burgdorf, Kenneth. 1980. *Recognition and Reporting of Child Maltreatment*. Rockville, Md.: Westat.

Child Welfare League of America. 1999. *Child Abuse and Neglect: A Look at the States: 1999 CWLA Stat Book*. Washington, D.C.: CWLA Press.

Congressional Research Service. 2002. *Background Data on Child Welfare*. Washington, D.C.: Congressional Research Service.

McLain, Philip W., Jeffrey J. Sacks, and Robert G. Froehlke. 1993. "Estimates of Fatal Child Abuse and Neglect, United States, 1979–1988." *Pediatrics* 91: 338–343.

National Center on Child Abuse and Neglect. 1988. *Study Findings: Study of National Incidence and Prevalence of Child Abuse and Neglect: 1988*. Washington, D.C.: U.S. Department of Health and Human Services.

———. 1996. *Study Findings: Study of National Incidence and Prevalence of Child Abuse and Neglect: 1993*. Washington, D.C.: U.S. Department of Health and Human Services.

U.S. Department of Health and Human Services, Administration on Children, Youth, and Families. 1999. *Child Maltreatment 1997: Reports from the States to the National Child Abuse and Neglect Data System*. Washington, D.C.: Government Printing Office.

———. 2000. *Child Maltreatment 1998: Reports from the States to the National Child Abuse and Neglect Data System*. Washington, D.C.: Government Printing Office.

———. 2002. *Child Maltreatment 2000: Reports from the States to the National Child Abuse and Neglect Data System*. Washington, D.C.: Government Printing Office.

Wang, Ching-Tung, and Kathryn Harding. 1999. *Current Trends in Child Abuse Reporting and Fatalities: The Results of the 1998 Annual 50 State Survey*. Chicago: Prevent Child Abuse America.

9

Housing Conditions and Homelessness

John C. Weicher

The Housing Act of 1949 enunciated the national housing goal: "a decent home in a suitable living environment for every American family." That is a useful framework for considering the housing and neighborhoods in which children live: (1) housing—whether children live in decent homes, (2) neighborhoods—whether children live in suitable living environments, and (3) the homeless—the people who do not live in any home at all.

Housing policy is different from other social welfare issues. Housing programs are fundamentally different from the other programs discussed in this volume, and housing policy analysts use different data sources and different measures of well-being. This chapter therefore describes housing data sources in some detail before discussing the substantive questions.

One fundamental difference between housing and other social welfare programs is that housing assistance is not an entitlement. Until the Temporary Assistance for Needy Families program (TANF), housing was the only major low-income benefit program that was not an entitlement, and in the entire history of federal housing programs, going back to the 1930s, it never has been. Less than 30 percent of eligible households with children receive assistance.

We are all familiar with the stereotypical welfare mother living in public housing, so it is worth pointing out that the stereotype is not the norm in either welfare or housing. In 1996, only about 25 percent of the households on Aid to Families with Dependent Children (AFDC) received housing assistance; conversely, only about 25 percent of the households receiving housing assistance were on AFDC. One reason that the last proportion is so low is that about one-third of those who receive housing assistance are elderly. It is also worth noting that families with children have traditionally not been a group of special concern to housing policymakers, unlike the elderly, minority groups, and residents of rural areas. The first separate discussion of their housing appears to be by Kathryn Nelson, an economist at the U.S. Department of Housing and Urban Development (HUD) Office of Policy Development, and Jill Khadduri, a principal associate at Abt Associates Inc.[1] In the past few years, HUD has begun to report them separately from other groups in required annual reports to Congress.[2]

Housing Conditions

American Housing Survey

These facts imply that neither housing program administrative data nor welfare program administrative data are adequate to describe the housing circumstances and neighborhood environments of low-income families with children. National sample surveys are the first data source.

The most useful is the American Housing Survey (AHS), which is conducted by the Census Bureau for HUD.[3] It has come out biennially since 1981, and annually from 1973 to 1981. It is based on a longitudinal national sample of 45,000 households by housing unit (not by household). The current sample has been in use since 1985. The questionnaire and survey technique were changed in 1997, and there appear to be some inconsistencies between the 1995 data and the 1997 data.[4] So, unfortunately, post-welfare reform data will not be directly comparable to pre-reform data. It is certainly true that 1996 was not the year in which welfare reform actually occurred, but for those interested in welfare reform, there could not be a worse year for a discontinuity in the data. In this chapter, I will limit myself almost entirely to pre-reform data so as to describe trends in housing on a reasonably consistent basis. The chapter will thus provide a benchmark against which post-reform housing and neighborhood conditions can be evaluated. I will also provide a brief discussion of the 1997 data, explaining the difficulties in comparing 1995 with 1997, with particular reference to welfare reform.

In addition to detailed housing data, the AHS includes some demographic and economic information on households: composition, including presence of children; and income, including sources and poverty status. It is therefore possible to identify welfare recipients and other low-income households.

The AHS includes separate, smaller surveys of forty-five large metropolitan areas, on a four-year cycle. The metropolitan samples are about 3,000 housing units each. The data could perhaps be used to analyze the effects of different state welfare reforms on the housing of children, but attempts to analyze rent control with them have not been encouraging. Disentangling the effects of the policy from the demographic and economic characteristics that vary across metropolitan areas is difficult.

Assisted households are not easily identified in the AHS. Respondents appear to know whether they live in public housing, but not whether they receive some other type of assistance. Public housing constitutes only about one-third of all subsidized housing, so this situation is obviously unsatisfactory for analytical purposes. HUD has identified subsidized units in the AHS by matching addresses with program records and has published separate national tabulations of them in *Characteristics of HUD-Assisted Renters and Their Units,* published in 1989, 1991, and 1993.[5] The volumes include comparable data for unsubsidized eligible households.

Because the AHS is longitudinal by housing unit, we do not know what happens to individual families when they move. When they move into a surveyed unit, we have some information about the unit they used to occupy and why they moved; when they move out, they are lost. If a welfare household moves out of the survey, we do not know whether the household has moved up because the adults are working and making more money, or whether it has moved down, or onto the streets, because the adults are worse off and cannot afford the rent. We do know what is happening in the aggregate.

Administrative Data

HUD also produces some purely administrative data, which began only in 1996—barely pre-reform. They are published as *A Picture of Subsidized Households.*[6] The data are published down to the project level and include "percentage with children" and "percentage on welfare." As of 1998, welfare constituted more than half of the income for 16 percent of assisted households, and there were children in 47 percent of assisted households. The data can be used for tracking the economic well-being of a subset of families with children but not the conditions of the families' housing.

The data provide some information about the changes since welfare reform was enacted. Between 1996 and 1998, the proportion of subsidized households that were on welfare declined by five percentage points, and the proportion that were working increased by three percentage points. That ratio—3:5, or 60 percent—is roughly the same as the estimated 50 to 60 percent of welfare leavers who seem to be employed.

Children's Circumstances

One important way in which housing programs differ from other social welfare programs is in the matter of income limits. Housing program eligibility is determined by household income relative to the median income of the metropolitan area or nonmetropolitan county, not by dollar income or poverty status. The relevant measures are as follows:

- "Low income": income below 80 percent of local median, the statutory upper limit for assistance.

- "Very low income": income below 50 percent of local median, traditionally defining priority for housing assistance.

- "Extremely low income": income below 30 percent of local median, currently used to establish the proportion of households that must receive different forms of assistance.

To put these measures in a more familiar context, the poverty line is about 33 percent of the national median income for a family of four. That line is roughly similar to extremely low income, although the poverty line is set nationally and adjusted only for inflation, whereas housing eligibility limits are set locally and adjusted for changes in nominal income. About 86 percent of extremely low-income households are poor. Only about 57 percent of very low-income households are poor. (Because the household income distribution has been gradually but steadily becoming more unequal since the late 1960s, this type of measure results in a larger number of households in each low-income category, although not necessarily a larger number of households with children.)

A further difference is that income is measured for different entities: families and unrelated individuals in the Current Population Survey (CPS) and the Decennial Census, and households in the AHS. Among other consequences, the number of individuals below the poverty line varies. It is quite possible for two unrelated people who live together to have incomes below the poverty line, but for their combined income to put them above the line as a household. It is even possible if one of them also has a child, because the poverty threshold for a two-person family is about 32 percent above that for an individual; for a three-person family, it is about 56 percent above the individual threshold. Thus, the incomes of subfamilies are included as part of the household, and the incomes of cohabitors are combined. Both categories have been growing in importance since 1970.[7] In addition, income in the two surveys is measured for different time periods: the previous calendar year for the CPS, the most recent twelve months for the AHS.[8]

Housing policy typically has focused on "very low-income renters." That focus is relevant for this volume. Renters constitute about 80 percent of the nonelderly households who report that welfare or Supplemental Security Income (SSI) accounts for more than half their income. This chapter ignores the small number of homeowners who are on welfare.

Traditionally, the key indicators of housing circumstances have been quality and space. More recently, affordability has been added to the list.

Housing Quality

The official measure of housing quality used by HUD, the Congressional Budget Office, and most independent analysts categorizes housing units as having "serious physical problems" or "moderate physical problems." The criteria are complicated (see box 9.1). As an approximation, severe physical problems are those that will probably cost more to remedy than it is worth to do so. Moderate physical problems can probably be remedied cost-effectively.

Among very low-income renters with children, 2.0 percent (127,000 households) lived in housing with severe physical problems as of 1995. As figure 9.1 shows, the incidence of severe physical problems has been declining steadily at least since 1978 (and surely much longer), when it was 7.5 percent.[9] These figures exclude households receiving housing assistance from the numerator, but not the denominator, of the ratios. A total figure can be obtained for 1993 by including the data on assisted households for that year: 164,000 unassisted and 53,000 assisted households lived in housing with severe physical problems, about 2.5 percent of the total.

Box 9.1
Housing Quality Measures

Severe Physical Problems

A unit has severe physical problems if it has any of the following five problems:

1. Plumbing: lacking hot or cold piped water or a flush toilet, or lacking both bathtub and shower, all inside the structure for the exclusive use of the unit.

2. Heating: having been uncomfortably cold last winter for twenty-four hours or more because the heating equipment broke down, and it broke down at least three times last winter for at least eight hours each time.

3. Electric: having no electricity, or all of the following three electric problems: exposed wiring; a room with no working wall outlet; and three blown fuses or tripped circuit breakers in the last ninety days.

4. Upkeep: having any five of the following maintenance problems: water leaks from the outside, such as from the roof, basement, windows or doors; leaks from inside structure, such as pipes or plumbing fixtures; holes in the floors; holes or open cracks in the walls or ceilings; more than eight by eleven inches of peeling paint or broken plaster; or signs of rats or mice in the last ninety days.

5. Hallways: having all of the following four problems in public areas: no working light fixtures; loose or missing steps; loose or missing railings; and no elevator.

Moderate Physical Problems

A unit has moderate physical problems if it has any of the following five problems, but none of the severe problems:

1. Plumbing: on at least three occasions during the last three months or while the household was living in the unit if less than three months, all the flush toilets were broken down at the same time for six hours or more.

2. Heating: having unvented gas, oil, or kerosene heaters as the primary heating equipment.

3. Upkeep: having any three of the overall list of problems mentioned above under severe physical problems.

4. Hallways: having any three of the problems mentioned above under severe physical problems.

5. Kitchen: lacking a sink, range, or refrigerator for the exclusive use of the unit.

Source: U.S. Department of Housing and Urban Development, *Rental Housing Assistance—The Worsening Crisis: A Report to Congress on Worst Case Housing Needs* (Washington, D.C.: U.S. Department of Housing and Urban Development, 2000), appendix D, A-28, A-29.

My preference is to exclude assisted households because their housing circumstances are not likely to be affected by a change in their income or welfare status; at least, their housing quality and space are not likely to be affected, although their rent burden might be.

Severe physical problems have become uncommon to the point that the percentage is about the same for all income categories of renters with children. Measuring income relative to the median for the area, as HUD does for program purposes, the incidence of severe physical problems in 1995 was about 2 percent for every income category from the lowest (0 to 20 percent of area median) to the highest (above area median). It also was about the same for all households as for very low-income renters with children: 2.0 percent for the latter, compared with 2.1 percent for all households, both renters and owners, of all incomes in all demographic categories. In 1978, the difference was large: 7.5 percent for unassisted very low-income renters with children, compared with 3.4 percent for all households.

Space

The most common measure of adequacy is the ratio of people living in the unit to the number of rooms in it. A household is "overcrowded" if it has more than one person per room.

Figure 9.1
Housing Quality, 1978–1995

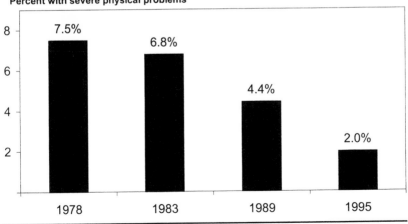

Percent with severe physical problems

Source: U.S. Census Bureau and U.S. Department of Housing and Urban Development, *American Housing Survey for the United States in [various years]*, Current Housing Reports, Series H150 (Washington, D.C.: Government Printing Office, various years).

The incidence of overcrowding among unassisted very low-income renters with children was about 8.1 percent in 1995 (527,000 households), which represents a percentage decline from 10.8 percent in 1978 (450,000 households), as figure 9.2 shows.[10] The incidence of crowding among all renters has been declining since at least 1950, when it was first reported in the Decennial Census using the current criterion, and it is reasonable to assume that crowding has been declining for very low-income renters with children over that longer period as well.[11] In 1950, about 24 percent of renters were crowded; in 1995, about 8 percent were. This comparison excludes single-person households, which by definition cannot be crowded.

Overcrowding among very low-income renters with children is much higher than among the general population: 8.1 percent versus 3.5 percent (again excluding single-person households). In 1978, the difference was similar: 10.8 percent versus 5.3 percent.

Affordability

The 1990 Cranston-Gonzalez National Affordable Housing Act added affordability to the national housing goal: "The Congress affirms the national goal that every American family *be able to afford* a decent home in a suitable environment."[12] Affordability is typi-

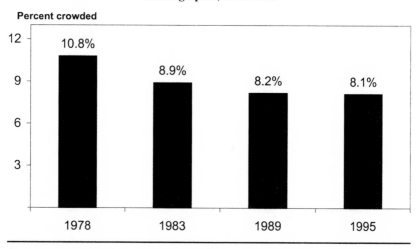

Figure 9.2
Housing Space, 1978–1995

Percent crowded

Source: U.S. Census Bureau and U.S. Department of Housing and Urban Development, *American Housing Survey for the United States in [various years]*, Current Housing Reports, Series H150 (Washington, D.C.: Government Printing Office, various years).

cally measured as the ratio of rent to income; public policy is primarily concerned with renters. A ratio of 30 percent or less generally is considered acceptable and is the target level in most housing subsidy programs. A ratio of 50 percent or more is a high rent burden, and for the past decade was a federal criterion for priority among households eligible for assistance.

By these ratios, housing affordability for very low-income renters with children is a major problem and has worsened slightly, as figure 9.3 shows. In 1995, about 29.6 percent (about 1.9 million households) paid more than half their income for rent, up from 28.0 percent in 1978. More than half (51.1 percent, or 3.3 million households) paid more than 30 percent, about the same percentage as in 1978 (50.9 percent, or 2.1 million households.) The 1983 spike in the data results from the twin recessions of 1980 and 1981–1982. The changes in affordability are not large, but they stand in noticeable contrast to the improvements in housing quality and space during the same period.

High rent burden is strongly correlated with income. More than 40 percent of extremely low-income renters with children (those with incomes below 30 percent of the area median) paid more than half of their income for rent. Among those with very low but not ex-

Figure 9.3
Housing Affordability, 1978–1995

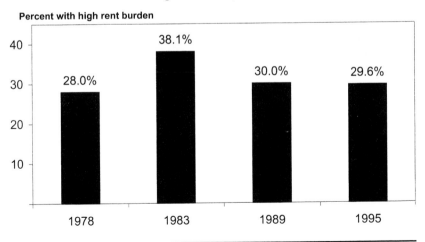

Percent with high rent burden

Source: U.S. Census Bureau and U.S. Department of Housing and Urban Development, *American Housing Survey for the United States in [various years]*, Current Housing Reports, Series H150 (Washington, D.C.: Government Printing Office, various years).

tremely low incomes (between 30 percent and 50 percent of the area median), only 13 percent had a high rent burden. Among those with low but not very low incomes (between 50 percent and 80 percent of the area median), only about 1.5 percent had a high rent burden. There were virtually no households with a high rent burden at higher incomes.

Subjective Rating

The AHS also includes a different kind of housing measure: the subjective opinion of the household. In 1995, about 10 percent (629,000) of all very low-income renters with children rated their housing as "poor" (defined as a score of 1 to 4 on a scale of 10).[13]

Housing ratings are correlated with income, although not as strongly as with rent burden. About 11 percent of extremely low-income renters with children rate their housing as poor, compared with 8 percent of those with very low but not extremely low incomes and 5 percent of those with low but not very low incomes. In this case, however, the incidence of poor ratings does not particularly decline among households with higher incomes.

Less than 3 percent of all households (2.9 percent) considered their housing poor as of 1995. This percentage has actually increased since 1978, when the percentage was 2.5 percent. The subjective rating has not moved in the same direction as nearly all objective measures of housing quality. At least two explanations are possible: Either subjective standards have risen as our society has become richer, or households are considering other aspects of their housing beyond those measured in the AHS. The former appears to be more likely, given the large number of attributes in the survey.

The 1997 Data

The most recent data generally show a deterioration in housing conditions for all households. An increased number of units present severe physical problems for renters (not owners), and units increasingly are crowded and have high cost burdens for both owners and renters at all income levels. The incidence of households reporting that they live in poor housing is also higher, but this may simply be because nonresponse is higher and the offsetting reduction comes almost entirely from those rating their housing as a "10." Among unassisted very low-income renters with children, the incidence of severe physical problems is up to 2.8 percent, a somewhat larger increase than among all renters, but the incidence of crowding is down slightly and the incidence of high rent burden is up slightly, to 31.0 percent. The latter changes are smaller than the corresponding changes among all renters. It seems likely that the differences between the 1995 and 1997 data reflect the survey differences mentioned earlier rather than any reaction to welfare reform; any effect of welfare reform is overwhelmed by the technical differences.

Interpreting the Data

By almost every objective measure, housing quality steadily improved through 1995 for virtually every identifiable demographic group of interest for as long as we have data: since 1974, according to the AHS, and since at least 1940 for the smaller number of attributes reported in the Decennial Census. (Unfortunately, changes in the questionnaire and survey in 1997 make it difficult to make valid comparisons after 1995.) This trend includes low-income families with children. Affordability, however, has not been improving; indeed, earlier data suggest that this problem was worse in 1995 than in 1974, and probably worse in 1974 than earlier.

A possible explanation is that people are choosing to spend more of their income on housing as their economic situation improves. Decent housing may have become more affordable, however. From 1974 to 1995, the median renter income quadrupled, whereas the rent component of the Consumer Price Index—which measures the rent on the same quality unit over time—tripled. Nonetheless, the typical unsubsidized, poor, renter family in 1995, which had an income of about $6,600, reported paying about $4,700 for housing. Even allowing for food stamps and Medicaid, that sum does not leave much for anything else.

It is also possible that the calculated rent burden may be in part the result of data problems. For example, households may be underreporting their income. The AHS tabulations of assisted households show that about 20 percent of residents in public housing and other subsidized projects report rent-to-income ratios above 40 percent, even though the program rules specify a rent-to-income ratio of no more than 30 percent. For that matter, about 10 to 15 percent report rent-to-income ratios below 20 percent. The best explanation appears to be that gross incomes are understated and rents are overstated.[14] This explanation, however, does not account for the rising trend in high rent burden. A second data problem is nonresponse. In the 1991 AHS, 24 percent of surveyed households did not answer the question about their income. The Census Bureau has not published nonresponse rates for earlier surveys, so there is no way of identifying any trend in AHS nonresponse rates or relating nonresponse to reported rent burden over time. Renters do have a slightly higher response rate than owners (78 percent versus 76 percent).

My judgment is that the best housing indicator of changes in the well-being of welfare recipients and former recipients is likely to be the rent burden, despite the measurement problems. That burden is strongly correlated with income, more so than the other measures, and can be measured fairly easily in survey research. The drawback is that rent burden has been increasing over time, so it may be hard to disentangle any effects of welfare reform from the long-term trend. Crowding is probably the second-best indicator; it, too, is easy to measure, and has been declining over time.

The main shortcoming of these measures is likely to be the absence of pre-reform benchmark data in the post-reform surveys, especially for rent burden.

Neighborhoods

Data Sources

The national AHS has little useful geographic information, and not much more is in the metropolitan area surveys, because of the Census Bureau's confidentiality rules. The surveys, however, do include information on the characteristics of the neighborhoods in which people live, even though they do not identify the neighborhoods. The data include subjective ratings of the neighborhood on a scale of 1 to 10, which corresponds to the subjective ratings of housing. They also include respondent or enumerator identification of some neighborhood problems.

The most detailed, relevant data come from the HUD reports, *Characteristics of HUD-Assisted Renters and Their Units,* which include information on all very low-income renters. The most recent data are for 1993. Because the reports go back only to 1989, there is not much to be gained by looking at trends.

For extensive neighborhood data, we must turn to the Decennial Census, which is almost the converse of the AHS. The Census offers much geographic and demographic information and makes it easy to determine neighborhood characteristics, but it has limited information on housing quality. Much non-Census information is available by tract, such as data on schools and crime. Census data are reported by income or poverty status, not by the HUD measure of "low income," and it is a difficult task for anyone outside HUD to convert one to the other.

A Picture of Subsidized Housing lists the Census tract so that the project neighborhood can be located. Sometimes the project is the tract; more often, the project is a substantial but minor fraction of the housing and population in the tract. Project data can be combined with neighborhood data from other sources, including the Decennial Census.

Neighborhood Ratings

The best currently available measure of neighborhood circumstances is the AHS subjective ratings. In 1995, 16 percent (1.0 million) of all very low-income renters with children rated their neighborhood as poor.

Neighborhood ratings, like housing ratings, are correlated with income, although not as strongly as rent burden. About 19 percent of extremely low-income renters with children rate their neighborhood as poor, compared with 12 percent of those with very low but not extremely low incomes. Higher-income groups give lower ratings, in the range of 6 to 10 percent. Renters with children, in all income ranges, are less satisfied with their neighborhood than with their housing.

The same is true for all households. About 5.4 percent of all households considered their neighborhoods poor as of 1995. This percentage also has increased since 1978, when it was 3.6 percent. In this case, the AHS does not have much objective information about the neighborhood. The enumerator describes the neighborhood with respect to the type of housing or other land use, the condition and age of nearby buildings (including whether windows are barred), and the condition of the streets, including the presence of trash, litter, or junk. There is no particular reason to assume that residents consider these the most important attributes of their neighborhood. Published tabulations for "poor renters," just over half of whom are households with children, identify the biggest problem as "people" (unspecified) at 18 percent of all households, followed by crime at 15 percent and noise at 12 percent. All of these problems are identified on the basis of the opinion of the household interviewee, not the observation of the enumerator. This ranking of problems is not very different from the opinions expressed by all surveyed households.

Interpreting the Data

In one sense, it is perhaps surprising that very many households give a poor rating to their neighborhood or, for that matter, their housing. People who dislike their housing or neighborhood, even very low-income households, have the option of moving. Low-income renters have high mobility into and out of poverty areas. Given their mobility, they should be able to find neighborhoods that are at least "fair" or satisfactory.

Residents of subsidized housing, particularly those in public housing, are not so mobile. They are unable to move without losing their subsidy, and they do not move often. The Decennial Census, as well as anecdotal evidence, indicates that quite a few public housing projects are in very undesirable neighborhoods. Public housing residents give their neighborhoods substantially worse ratings than other very low-income renters. Among nonelderly public housing residents (two-thirds of whom are families with children), 39 percent rate their neighborhood as poor. Residents like their housing much better; 13 percent rate it as poor, not very different from the 11 percent of all very low-income renters with children.

Past Census data provide some basis for believing that the neighborhood environments of welfare recipients and other very low-income renters have changed for the worse. The geographic extent of poverty is spreading within urban areas because nonpoor households tend to move out of poverty areas and near-poverty areas faster than poor households do. (It is important to remember that "poverty areas" are officially defined as Census tracts with at least 20 percent of the population below the poverty threshold. Most of the urban poor live in poverty areas, but most people in poverty areas are not poor.) The traditional poverty neighborhoods—those identified from the 1960 Census—have been losing population because both poor and nonpoor residents have been moving out. Roughly speaking, in the 1960s, white nonpoor households moved out of poverty neighborhoods; in the 1970s, black nonpoor households moved out; in the 1980s, anyone who could moved out.[15] The remaining adults were typically not in the labor force; they lived on income-conditioned transfers, such as welfare or Social Security. In addition, in most of those neighborhoods the housing stock has been shrinking as units have been abandoned or razed. Anyone who has lived in one of these neighborhoods for a decade or more is indeed likely to have felt that the neighborhood has deteriorated. (These data refer to all poor people, not just poor families with children.) Anecdotal evidence suggests that the deterioration continued in the 1990s.

The 2000 Decennial Census will provide the information we need to analyze changes in neighborhoods for very low-income renters with children, including present and former welfare recipients, although numerous problems are posed by the fact that welfare reform was passed about halfway through the decade. The Census information will lose its freshness within a few years, but it can still be used to study welfare reform. Specifically, Census data can be used in combination with surveys of current and former welfare recipients. If the households have moved since welfare reform, it should be possible to form some opinion about whether their neighborhoods are better or worse. The 2000 Census provides socioeconomic and demographic characteristics of the neighborhoods, such as the income level and distribution, the proportion of families that are intact, and the proportion of adults employed or at least in the labor force. Local governments' administrative data can be used to provide relevant information on public services and community problems, which are perhaps the most important indicators of neighborhood conditions, particularly data on crime and schools. The Census data are less useful for describing households that have not moved since welfare reform, but some of the local government data will still be relevant and important.

The best indicator of the neighborhood environment is probably the crime rate, which may be the easiest data to obtain as well as the most timely. It is relevant both for those who move and those who remain in their old neighborhood and is especially useful over time, as the socioeconomic and demographic composition of neighborhoods changes. School achievement is certainly at least as important, but it is less timely and often more difficult to obtain.

Homelessness

Data Sources

Data about the homeless are extremely important for analyzing welfare reform. If welfare recipients lose their benefits, can they still pay the rent? If not, where do they go?

Unfortunately, reliable data on the homeless are very difficult to come by, even more so if the purpose is to track the experience of that group over time. The AHS misses them. As a longitudinal survey of housing units, it is not designed to find people with no residence. The 1990 Census made a special effort to count them, and the 2000 Census included another such effort. The 1990 survey, although criticized by homeless advocates, has been the basis for much analysis and some policy making in the decade since.

Otherwise, we have only special surveys of various kinds. The most recent is the National Survey of Homeless Assistance Providers and Clients, conducted by the Census Bureau in 1996. (The data were analyzed by the Urban Institute.)[16] This survey is the successor to a similar 1987 study.[17] It is based on a geographic sample that includes the twenty-eight largest metropolitan areas, with smaller metropolitan areas and rural areas sampled on a random basis. Interviews were conducted with the operators of some 12,000 programs and facilities, such as homeless shelters and soup kitchens; through these programs, a sample of program clients was identified and interviewed. Most of the clients were homeless at the time of the interview or had recently been homeless. The survey is not designed to reach homeless people who are not served by programs for the homeless.

The survey comes at a convenient time, coinciding with welfare reform. The fact that there were nine years between surveys suggests that it may be a long time before similar data are available on what has happened under TANF.

Some localities have attempted to count the homeless population. Those studies are useful for local policy purposes, but they are of mixed quality and difficult to use for national policy purposes or analysis. Local administrative data on shelter use are available, but interpreting them over time is complicated by the growth in shelters and other programs to serve the homeless.

Homelessness among Families with Children

The available data indicate that families with children are not a large share of the homeless population.

The Urban Institute estimated the number of homeless individuals at two different times in 1996, finding a substantial variation. The estimate was 440,000 in an average week in October 1996, and 842,000 in an average week in February 1996.[18] The homeless comprised 0.17 to 0.32 percent of the total population at the two dates, or about 1.2 percent to 2.3 percent of the impoverished population. The 1987 Urban Institute study estimated that about 500,000 to 600,000 people were homeless, including those on the streets who were not being served by shelters, soup kitchens, or other programs.[19] Martha R. Burt of the Urban Institute and her coauthors judge that the higher 1996 figure is more comparable to the 1987 numbers.[20] If so, then the number of homeless increased during the period.

These figures include about 50,000 to 100,000 homeless families with children, which contain about 100,000 to 200,000 children. In all, about one-sixth to one-third of the homeless are members of homeless families with children.

The Urban Institute also estimates the number of individuals who are homeless at any time during a year. Those figures are larger: 0.9 percent to 1.3 percent of the total population, or 6.3 percent to 9.6 percent of the poverty population.[21]

Interpreting the Data

The data perhaps provide a baseline for studies of welfare reform, but the numbers are not large, and the seasonal variation is high. For both reasons, it is probably difficult to measure the effects of welfare reform or any other policy change on homelessness among families.

Some studies have indeed asked whether former recipients are now homeless or have been homeless since they went off welfare. A joint Hudson-Mathematica study of former welfare recipients in Milwaukee found that 8 percent reported being homeless at some time during the preceding year.[22] This figure is within the range for homelessness among the poverty population reported by the Urban Institute. Thus, the Urban Institute data provide a benchmark for homelessness among low-income families and, for what it is worth, suggest that former welfare recipients are about as likely to be homeless during a year as other poor people. Otherwise, unless the study includes a nonwelfare comparison group, there is generally no context in which to evaluate whether the responses show a high or low incidence of homelessness or other housing-related problems.[23] Certainly, we have far too little information to offer any serious opinion on homelessness since welfare reform.

Conclusion

This chapter has been concerned primarily with housing conditions. It has not attempted to relate housing circumstances to measures of child well-being. If an urban reformer of 60 or 100 years ago were to come back today, she or he would be very surprised by the omission. Slums were seen as the location of most urban problems, and were thought to be the breeding grounds of physical disease, mental illness, juvenile delinquency, and crime. Urban reformers believed that these problems were not only located in the slums, but also were caused by poor housing. If the slums were razed and replaced with decent housing, the problems of their poor residents would be solved. Public housing was seen as a war on poverty, all by itself.

Obviously these views have not been borne out by events. Within twenty years, erstwhile supporters of public housing became bitter critics. By 1961, Jane Jacobs could refer to "low-income projects that have become worse centers of delinquency, vandalism and general social hopelessness than the slums they were supposed to replace" without attracting much criticism.[24] At the same time, more sophisticated academic studies in various disciplines were concluding that housing was a much less important contributor to the medical and social problems of the poor than were education, income, and other socioeconomic characteristics. An exhaustive review of this literature in the mid-1970s found virtually no evidence that better housing by itself had any beneficial effect.[25] Since then, the subject has died from the literature.

Nonetheless, housing circumstances are important for the well-being of children and their families. The affordability data certainly indicate that the cost of housing leaves very little for other goods and services and makes it difficult for poor families to achieve any minimally adequate standard of living.

Notes

1.   Kathryn P. Nelson and Jill Khadduri, "To Whom Should Limited Housing Resources Be Directed?" *Housing Policy Debate* 3 (1992): 1–55.
2.   U.S. Department of Housing and Urban Development, Office of Policy Development and Research, *Rental Housing Assistance—The Crisis Continues: The 1997 Report to Congress on Worst Case Housing Needs* (Washington, D.C.: U.S. Department of Housing and Urban Development, 1998).
3.   U.S. Census Bureau and U.S. Department of Housing and Urban Development, *American Housing Survey for the United States in [various years],* Current Housing Reports, Series H150 (Washington, D.C.: Government Printing Office, various years).
4.   The 1997 survey differs from that of previous years in several ways. The 1997 American Housing Survey (AHS) was conducted using "computer-assisted personal interviewing," meaning that the interviewer brought a computer to the interview that contained the household's responses from the 1995 survey; the 1997 responses were entered into the computer during the interview. Also, the 1997

questionnaire was reorganized, and the Census Bureau changed computer plat-
forms and processing software/language, so all the software had to be rewritten.

5. U.S. Department of Housing and Urban Development, Office of Policy Develop-
    ment and Research, *Characteristics of HUD–Assisted Renters and Their Units in
    [various years]* (Washington, D.C.: U.S. Department of Housing and Urban De-
    velopment, various years).

6. U.S. Department of Housing and Urban Development, Office of Policy Develop-
    ment and Research, *A Picture of Subsidized Households* (Washington, D.C.: U.S.
    Department of Housing and Urban Development, various years).

7. New data on the changes in cohabitation have recently been calculated by three
    Census analysts. See Lynne M. Casper, Philip N. Cohen, and Tavia Simmons,
    "How Does POSSLQ Measure Up? Historical Estimates of Cohabitation," paper
    presented at the annual meeting of the Population Association of America, New
    York City, 1999.

8. The result can be a substantial difference between the Current Population Survey
    (CPS) and AHS, and even movement in different directions. In 1993, the CPS
    reported a poverty rate of 15.1 percent (39.3 million individuals), while the AHS
    reported 15.0 percent (36.8 million); but in 1995 the CPS poverty rate fell to 13.8
    percent (36.4 million), while the AHS rate rose to 15.3 percent (38.9 million). In
    1997, the CPS rate declined further to 13.3 percent (35.6 million), whereas the AHS
    rate remained at 15.3 percent (39.4 million). The CPS population is larger than the
    AHS population because the AHS includes only "population in housing units"; the
    CPS also includes group quarters such as orphanages, nursing homes, penitentia-
    ries, and dormitories. In 1997, the difference was 14.3 million people.

9. AHS data for all renter families, and for all renters and owners, show a decline in
    severe physical problems since 1974. Prior quality data from the Decennial Census,
    using a different measure, show a sharp decline since 1940 (the earliest year for
    which quality data are available).

10. These figures are lower bounds because the published data do not separately tabu-
    late those renters who are crowded among households with severe physical prob-
    lems or paying more than half their income for rent. In 1995, as many as 71,000 of
    the households with these problems could also have experienced crowding.

11. In the 1940 Census, "crowding" was defined as more than 1.5 persons per room.
    By this criterion, crowding has been declining steadily since 1940.

12. Italics added. Although the act states that it is "affirming" the goal of affordability, in
    reality the statute added affordability to the 1949 goal. No previous legislation
    identified affordability as a housing goal. Public policy discussions have increas-
    ingly centered on affordability since the early 1980s, however.

13. Through 1983, households rated their housing as "excellent, good, fair, or poor";
    after that year, they were asked to use a scale of 1 to 10. The number of responses
    in the 1 to 4 range in 1985 corresponded roughly to the number reported as "poor"
    in 1983.

14. This issue is discussed in detail in the 1989 volume of *Characteristics of HUD–
    Assisted Renters and Their Units*, pp. 11–13, 33–34. Among the hypotheses inves-
    tigated that did not make a noteworthy difference in the rent-to-income ratio distri-
    bution were allocation procedures for missing data, calculation of utility allowances,
    state welfare rules governing rent payments, and inclusion of nonrent costs (such as
    garbage collection and property insurance) as part of rent. Adjustment for each of
    these factors did reduce the incidence of high rent-to-income ratios in subsidized
    housing, but only marginally; as reported in the text, the incidence of high ratios
    (and also low ones) remains unexpectedly large, and the explanation appears to be
    underreporting of income and, perhaps, overreporting of utilities.

15. John C. Weicher, "How Poverty Neighborhoods Are Changing," in *Inner-City Poverty in the United States,* edited by Laurence E. Lynn Jr. and Michael G. H. McGeary (Washington, D.C.: National Academy Press, 1990). The data reported in my 1990 study cover only the years from 1960 to 1980. When I was at HUD in the first Bush administration, I analyzed the 1990 data on urban poverty neighborhoods and found that population in the traditional poverty areas had declined sharply since 1980.
16. Martha R. Burt, Laudan Y. Aron, Toby Douglas, Jesse Valente, Edgar Lee, and Britta Iwen, *Homelessness: Programs and the People They Serve: Findings of the National Survey of Homeless Assistance Providers and Clients,* Summary Report (Washington, D.C.: Urban Institute, December 7, 1999), available from: http://www.urbaninstitute.org/housing/homeless/homeless.html, accessed September 26, 2001.
17. Martha R. Burt and Barbara E. Cohen, *America's Homeless: Numbers, Characteristics, and the Programs That Serve Them* (Washington, D.C.: Urban Institute Press, 1989).
18. Renu Shukla, "Millions Still Face Homelessness in a Booming Economy," press release, Urban Institute, Washington, D.C. February 1, 2000.
19. Ibid.
20. Ibid.
21. Ibid.
22. Rebecca Swartz, Jacqueline Kauff, Lucia Nixon, Tom Fraker, Jay Hein, and Susan Mitchell, *Converting to Wisconsin Works: Where Did Families Go When AFDC Ended in Milwaukee?* (Indianapolis: Hudson Institute, 1999).
23. The Urban Institute's National Survey of America's Families is an exception. It does have a comparison group, and it reports a higher incidence of housing problems for former welfare recipients than for other low-income women.
24. Jane Jacobs, *The Death and Life of Great American Cities* (New York: Vintage Books, 1961).
25. Stanislav V. Kasl, "Effects of Housing on Mental and Physical Health," in *Housing in the Seventies, Working Papers,* U.S. Department of Housing and Urban Development, National Housing Policy Review (Washington, D.C.: Government Printing Office, 1976). Exceptions may exist for very specific housing attributes. Ingestion of lead-based paint in large enough doses by small children, for example, can result in lead poisoning and serious mental and physical damage. Lead paint, however, is not a special problem for poor families with children. It was widely used in housing of all qualities between the 1900s and the 1950s, and then to a diminishing extent until it was prohibited by the Consumer Product Safety Commission in 1978, under federal statute. The most extensive survey of lead paint concluded that it was found about equally in housing built before 1978 at all price ranges, and about equally in housing occupied by households in all income ranges. See U.S. Department of Housing and Urban Development, Office of Policy Development and Research, *Comprehensive and Workable Plan for the Abatement of Lead-Based Paint in Privately Owned Housing: Report to Congress* (Washington, D.C.: U.S. Department of Housing and Urban Development, 1990). Lead paint was found in about three-quarters of all housing built before 1980 and in about 55 percent of the total housing stock.

References

Burt, Martha R., Laudan Y. Aron, Toby Douglas, Jesse Valente, Edgar Lee, and Britta Iwen. 1999. *Homelessness: Programs and the People They Serve: Findings of the*

National Survey of Homeless Assistance Providers and Clients. Summary Report. December 7. Washington, D.C.: Urban Institute. Available from: http://www.urbaninstitute.org/housing/homeless/homeless.html. Accessed September 26, 2001.

Burt, Martha R., and Barbara E. Cohen. 1989. *America's Homeless: Numbers, Characteristics and the Programs That Serve Them.* Washington, D.C.: Urban Institute Press.

Casper, Lynne M., Philip N. Cohen, and Tavia Simmons. 1999. "How Does POSSLQ Measure Up? Historical Estimates of Cohabitation." Paper presented at the 1999 annual meeting of the Population Association of America. New York City.

Jacobs, Jane. 1961. *The Death and Life of Great American Cities.* New York: Vintage Books.

Kasl, Stanislav V. 1976. "Effects of Housing on Mental and Physical Health." In *Housing in the Seventies, Working Papers,* by U.S. Department of Housing and Urban Development. National Housing Policy Review. Washington, D.C.: Government Printing Office.

Nelson, Kathryn P., and Jill Khadduri. 1992. "To Whom Should Limited Housing Resources Be Directed?" *Housing Policy Debate* 3: 1–55.

Shukla, Renu. 2000. "Millions Still Face Homelessness in a Booming Economy." Press release. Washington, D.C.: Urban Institute. February 1.

Swartz, Rebecca, Jacqueline Kauff, Lucia Nixon, Tom Fraker, Jay Hein, and Susan Mitchell. 1999. *Converting to Wisconsin Works: Where Did Families Go When AFDC Ended in Milwaukee?* Indianapolis: Hudson Institute.

U.S. Census Bureau and U.S. Department of Housing and Urban Development. Various years. *American Housing Survey for the United States in [various years].* Current Housing Reports, Series H150. Washington, D.C.: Government Printing Office.

U.S. Department of Housing and Urban Development. Office of Policy Development and Research. Various years. *Characteristics of HUD-Assisted Renters and Their Units in [various years].* Washington, D.C.: U.S. Department of Housing and Urban Development.

———. Various years. *A Picture of Subsidized Households.* Washington, D.C.: U.S. Department of Housing and Urban Development.

———. 1990. *Comprehensive and Workable Plan for the Abatement of Lead-Based Paint in Privately Owned Housing: Report to Congress.* Washington, D.C.: U.S. Department of Housing and Urban Development.

———. 1998. *Rental Housing Assistance—The Crisis Continues: The 1997 Report to Congress on Worst Case Housing Needs.* Washington, D.C.: U.S. Department of Housing and Urban Development.

———. 2000. *Rental Housing Assistance—The Worsening Crisis: A Report to Congress on Worst Case Housing Needs.* Washington, D.C.: U.S. Department of Housing and Urban Development.

Weicher, John C. 1990. "How Poverty Neighborhoods Are Changing." In *Inner-City Poverty in the United States.* Edited by Laurence E. Lynn Jr. and Michael G. H. McGeary. Washington, D.C.: National Academy Press.

10

Child Health

Lorraine V. Klerman

Welfare reform might affect the health of children positively or negatively through several pathways. This chapter first examines those pathways. Then it considers whether existing federal data sets can be used to measure the changes that might occur.

How Welfare Reform Might Affect Child Health

When considering the impact of welfare reform on child health or any of the other numerous child outcomes of interest to policymakers, it is important to understand that: (1) welfare reform is not a single entity, and (2) effects may differ by the age and gender of the child.[1] There is considerable state variation in the implementation of the federal welfare reform initiative. The effects of welfare reform can be expected to differ by approach. For example, those policies that focus on financial work incentives might lead to improved child outcomes while those that focus on mandatory work-related activities might worsen them. It is also possible that welfare policies will have different impacts on children depending on their stage of development and their gender. Some approaches might have favorable impacts on preschoolers but adverse effects on adolescents. Similar differences by gender may be found.

Researchers have begun to develop models of the possible linkages between welfare reform and child outcomes.[2] They expect that welfare reform will have a direct effect on income, work, family structure, child care, and educational attainment. These changes will, in turn, affect parental psychological well-being, parent-child interaction, the children's socialization, and access to health and related services. These direct and intermediate changes might affect a number of child outcomes, including cognitive development, behavioral and emotional adjustment, school achievement and attainment, behavior, safety, and physical and mental health.

Focusing on health outcomes, welfare reform generally might create or worsen financial or other barriers to the availability of medical care to children. It also might affect health in more subtle ways through its effect on other benefit programs, on child care, on children with special health care needs, and on poverty generally.

Medical Care

Welfare reform could make medical care less available if families lose their access to Medicaid, the major federal health program for poor children. But Congress was aware of this danger and included in the welfare reform legislation a provision that families who would have been eligible for Medicaid under Aid to Families with Dependent Children (AFDC) would remain eligible for Medicaid. Moreover, the welfare reform law did not alter the expanded Medicaid eligibility adopted in earlier years. In addition, a year after the welfare reform law was passed, the State Children's Health Insurance Program (SCHIP) was passed, increasing the number of children who are eligible for federal-state programs of health insurance. Thus, although few women leaving welfare for work are likely to find employment that offers private health insurance, public health insurance will still be available for their children if they take appropriate action.

Eligibility alone, however, does not guarantee that children will be insured. Prior to welfare reform, women and children enrolled in AFDC were automatically eligible for Medicaid, that is, no additional application was needed. As a result of welfare reform, women must apply for Medicaid directly. Some reports have suggested that this process led to many Medicaid-eligible children not being enrolled either because mothers did not realize that separate enrollment now was necessary, because mothers lacked the time or interest to engage in this process, or because welfare workers incorrectly interpreted the new law.[3] The federal government has urged states to take aggressive action to ensure that all Medicaid-eligible children are enrolled. The latest figures suggest that the decline between 1995 and 1998 in Medicaid enrollment of families, children, and pregnant women has been reversed and that enrollment is beginning to increase, suggesting that federal and state efforts to increase the percentage of enrolled children are succeeding.[4]

Insurance is not the only resource necessary to obtain medical care. The mother or some other family member must have the time to take the child to a provider. The various activities associated with seeking employment or with employment itself might make it difficult to find time to apply for Medicaid. Having a job, looking for a job, or engaging in job training might also mean that the mother is not available to take a child for health supervision examinations or care for acute or chronic conditions.

Other Benefit Programs

Similar problems arise with other benefit programs, especially food stamps. Welfare workers are not aggressively linking families to all the services to which they might be entitled. Enrollment in the food stamp program has declined markedly since the implementation of welfare reform, despite the fact that few former welfare recipients have earnings that place them over the food stamp eligibility cutoff (130 percent of the federal poverty level).[5] In fact, a 1999 U.S. General Accounting Office report detailed cases in which states were making it difficult to apply for food stamps, not informing families that they were still eligible for food stamps even if they left the welfare rolls, or even taking illegal actions regarding food stamp eligibility.[6] Welfare reform could have an adverse impact on children's health if it makes it more difficult to provide them with the nourishment they need.

Child Care

Welfare reform requires states to make child care available to working mothers. High-quality child care might have a positive effect on child health by detecting health problems early and helping families obtain care, as Head Start does by providing healthy foods and teaching mothers about health-promoting activities for themselves and their children. Child care of poor quality can lead to illness and injury, as well as deprive children of the emotional support and intellectual stimulation that they need. Welfare reform is challenging states and local communities to develop and fund child care that meets high standards or the federal government to fund a universal preschool program, perhaps by expanding Head Start.

Children with Special Health Care Needs

Some women have been on the welfare rolls because they were caring for children with special health care needs, such as asthma or cerebral palsy, or who were in wheelchairs or dependent on a venti-lator. Preschool children with such conditions might need round-the-clock care, and their school-age counterparts who are integrated into regular or special classes might still need after-school supervi-sion. Women with little or no income have often sought help from welfare to enable them to stay at home and care for such children. Although such women should be exempt from the requirements of the welfare reform act, apparently some are being pressured to seek employment. It will be important to determine whether the health of children with special needs is affected by welfare reform.

Poverty-Related Conditions

Welfare reform might affect child health by improving or worsen-ing the conditions associated with poverty. The data overwhelm-ingly indicate that children whose families fall below or close to the federal poverty line have poorer health than do more well-to-do chil-dren, even when both have health insurance. Granted, access to medical care might be more difficult to obtain for the poorer child with Medicaid than for the more well-to-do child with private health insurance, but the differences appear to be the result of other factors as well: less adequate housing, more dangerous and unhealthy neigh-borhoods, inadequate child care facilities, and behaviors and prac-tices by children and parents that are less conducive to health pro-motion. For example, poor mothers—because of inadequate infor-mation, time pressures, or insufficient funds—might select less healthy foods for their children, allow them to be sedentary, not use child restraints in automobiles, or not provide them helmets for bi-cycle riding. Their homes might lack working smoke detectors or have peeling lead paint or molds and other airborne particles that cause asthma attacks. Food might not be stored safely if refrigera-tion is inadequate or absent.

If obtaining employment allowed mothers to move their children to safer and healthier housing and environments and put the moth-ers and children in contact with others who might model healthier behaviors, welfare reform might have a positive effect on child health. If, as seems likely, mothers make little money from their jobs, or if they are forced off welfare and have no new source of income, pov-erty will continue to take its toll on the health of children through limited access to high-quality health care, inadequate housing, poor food, and health-compromising behaviors.

Measuring Changes in Child Health

Lack of Medicaid coverage will affect how often children are seen by a physician, especially for preventive care, and it might affect immunization rates unless the "safety-net" providers pick up the slack. So the impact of welfare reform in the short run will be on utilization measures rather than on mortality and morbidity. A reduction in Medicaid coverage or an increase in the percentage of uninsured children might increase the pain and suffering experienced by children. Children who do not see a physician when they need care and children who do not go to a dentist for preventive care will probably suffer more than children with easier access because they are insured.

It is too early to tell if the decline in Medicaid in 1995 and 1996 had any effect on children's health. First, the lag in obtaining data, at least from the National Health Interview Survey (NHIS), is too long. Second, if children lost coverage for only a year or two, most would not have been affected, at least the relatively healthy ones. Third, many, if not most, of the children who lost Medicaid coverage probably still received care from the safety-net providers who care for the uninsured. (However, those safety-net providers might have become less financially healthy as a result of the children being uninsured.) Finally, the absence of Medicaid coverage was unlikely to affect mortality, with the possible exception of women being unable to obtain prenatal care or pre-term infants not being accepted by neonatal intensive care units, neither of which appears to have happened. And lack of Medicaid coverage probably did not affect the number of illnesses children experienced, although it might have influenced how long they were sick and whether they suffered any long-term effects.

Needed Data

The information required to measure the impact of welfare reform would need to have several features:

- Measures sensitive to the aspects of children's physical and emotional health that might be affected by welfare reform.

- Ability to determine present and past economic status, including welfare receipt and, possibly, the reasons that the mother left the welfare rolls.

- A sample that includes enough poor children to permit valid conclusions.

- Inclusion of a sample of children with similar characteristics who were not affected by welfare reform to serve as a comparison group (enabling the researchers to avoid the error of attributing to welfare reform changes that were already occurring, such as the decline in teenage births).

- Inclusion of measures during a period before implementation of welfare reform (or early in that process) in order to provide before-and-after data.

- Periodic data collection in order to trace trends over time.

- Aggregation of data by state (if state comparisons are wanted).

- Ability to provide information within a year of its collection.

Child Health Measures

The effects of welfare reform on child health could be measured by health status, health-related behaviors, or medical care access or utilization. The traditional measures of health status are deaths, illnesses, and injuries. These measures are probably too crude to be able to detect welfare reform's effects. Mortality is declining for children of all ages, although injuries and violence among adolescents still cause many deaths. With the exception of asthma and diabetes, illnesses are also declining, although sexually transmitted infections remain a problem among adolescents. Non-fatal injuries also are declining. It is unlikely that welfare reform will have any effect on these traditional measures or, if it does, that the effect can be determined, given the strong time trends. As Kristin Moore, president of Child Trends, has noted:

> Multiple determinants of health exist, including genetic factors and the social and physical environment. In addition, most children are pretty healthy. If rates of child health problems are low and welfare reform is no more than a distal influence on children's health, why would we expect to find any effects of welfare reform that are big enough to be measurable?[7]

A reversal in the generally favorable trends coinciding with the implementation of welfare reform, however, would be worrisome.

Another health status measure is the parent's perception of the child's health. The National Center for Health Statistics' (NCHS) ongoing NHIS asks parents whether they think the health of a child is, in general, excellent, very good, good, fair, or poor. Welfare reform probably would not affect this measure.

Alternative ways to measure health status involve examining physical and mental functioning. For example, the health of the elderly is often measured by their ability to perform the activities of daily living, that is, can they do the things that one ordinarily does on a daily basis without assistance? Also, the NHIS asks a representative sample of the population whether they are unable to carry on their *usual* activity. The usual activity of school-age children is attending school; for preschool children, it is play. Another example is the question on the 1994 National Health Interview Survey on Disability that asked about children's difficulty in performing *everyday* activities in the area of learning, communication, mobility, and self-care. But even these measures might not be sensitive to welfare reform; moreover, the questions on everyday activities have not been incorporated into the ongoing NHIS.

Welfare reform might affect health-related behaviors related to safety, nutrition, or sexual behavior. Because they have more money, employed mothers might provide their children with booster seats, bicycle helmets, or more nutritious foods (for example, they might meet the "five a day" standard for fruits and vegetables). Or, on the negative side, the absence of the mother from the home because of employment might provide more opportunities for adolescent sexual activity.

Experts agree on few measures of children's emotional health. Many of these measures cannot be administered using survey methods. More work in this area will be needed.

Welfare reform might affect access to and use of medical care, as described earlier in this chapter. Some of the traditional measures of medical care are usual source of care and frequency of physician visits during a defined period. The latter is a poor measure of medical care adequacy because children with a chronic condition, such as asthma, might need to see a physician often, while children who are healthy might not.

The problem of how to measure child health and child well-being is being pursued in many quarters, not just by those interested in welfare reform. The Federal Interagency Forum on Child and Family Statistics issues an annual report entitled *America's Children: Key National Indicators of Well-Being* that includes measures of economic security, behavioral and social environment, and education, in addition to health. The Office of the Assistant Secretary for Planning and Evaluation in the U.S. Department of Health and Human Services (HHS) also issues a report, *Trends in the Well-Being of America's Children & Youth*, that uses a larger set of indicators, including mortality, health conditions, health care, social development, behavioral health, and teen fertility. The Annie E. Casey Foundation's annual *Kids Count Data Book* presents state profiles of child well-being and is one of the few publications that provides state-level data. In addition, several groups—such as the Children and Adolescent Health Measurement Initiative, a collaborative effort of the Foundation for Accountability and the National Committee for Quality Assurance—are now working to develop new measures of child health.

Federal Data Systems

The federal government operates several data collection systems that contain information about children's health status, health-related behaviors, and medical care access and utilization. Health status can be measured using the Vital Statistics system (characteristics of births and deaths), NHIS, National Health and Nutrition Examination Survey, and the National Hospital Discharge Survey. (All these surveys are the responsibility of the NCHS.) The Centers for Disease Control and Prevention (CDC) publishes data on communicable diseases, including those diagnosed in children and youth.

Health-related behaviors can be studied using data from the NHIS, the Youth Risk Behavior Surveillance System (a CDC survey), the National Household Survey on Drug Abuse (sponsored by the Substance Abuse and Mental Health Administration), and Monitoring the Future (a survey of youth substance abuse). Information on adult behaviors that might influence child health is collected in the Behavior Risk Factor Surveillance System, a CDC survey.

Medical care access and utilization can be measured by examining data from the NHIS, the Medical Expenditure Panel Survey (an Agency for Healthcare Research and Quality survey), the National Immunization Survey (an NCHS survey), the State and Local Area Integrated Telephone Survey (SLAITS, an NCHS survey), the March supplement to the Current Population Survey (CPS), and the Survey of Income and Program Participation (SIPP) (the latter two are Census Bureau surveys). Administrative data, such as Medicaid files from the Centers for Medicare and Medicaid Services, also are useful. This list is not exhaustive.

All these federal data sets contain measures of child health and are either ongoing or collect information periodically and have been doing so since before welfare reform was implemented. Yet, none is totally adequate to the task of assessing the impact of welfare reform. Few ask about welfare status, and some have no indicator of economic status. In most of the studies, the sample of poor children is not large enough to reach valid conclusions. Moreover, the poor, who are most likely to be affected by welfare reform, are often among those whom federal studies are unable to contact or convince to cooperate, leading to low response rates in this group. Few federal data sets can be disaggregated to the state level or to smaller geographical areas. Because of variations in state welfare policies, policymakers might want to obtain data at the state or county level. Also, policymakers might want a quicker turnaround time than is now available from many of the federal data systems.

The NHIS is the most likely to show changes in children's health *after* welfare reform, because it collects information on a large enough sample of poor children (not just those on welfare). NHIS sampling methods, moreover, provide data only for the nation as a whole and for a few large states. The CPS can provide information on changes in health insurance status by state and relatively quickly, but its estimates have been questioned, especially for the smallest states. The SIPP is another possibility.

Federal data collection efforts would need to be modified to make them more responsive to monitoring the effects of welfare reform. Survey samples would have to be enlarged, oversample the poor, and permit disaggregation of results to at least the state level. Reports would have to be generated more expeditiously and questions added on the aspects of child health most likely to be affected by welfare reform. These modifications seem unlikely, however, because of their cost. And even if Congress approved additional funds, the magnitude of the changes would probably mean that the revised surveys would not be fielded for several years, so that baseline data would not be available.

Similar suggestions for modifying or expanding the federal statistics systems were made by the Committee on National Statistics of the National Research Council as a result of a 1996 workshop. The report noted, "The changes that are occurring in health and social welfare programs require new or modified survey questions on a wide range of topics."[8] Other themes are still relevant today:

- Modifying the sampling schemes of existing surveys is important to meet data needs for program analysis and monitoring. The workshop noted that devolution of responsibility for social welfare programs to state governments increased the need for state-level estimates and that none of the national surveys provided complete and reliable estimates at the state level.

- Creating a comprehensive, regularly updated, accessible database that provides detailed information about program features for states (and localities, where applicable) is essential.

Another possibility would be a federally sponsored survey specifically designed to examine the effects of welfare reform on the entire country as well as by state. Such a survey could be built on the SLAITS, which already calls many households to request information about children. But even the SLAITS would need to be modified to oversample those most likely to be affected by welfare reform and, because it is a telephone survey, it might miss the poorest families who are most likely to lack phone service. (The SLAITS attempts to compensate for this problem by weighting.) Again, this approach would be expensive, but it probably could begin relatively soon after authorization. Even so, baseline data would not be available.

On the positive side, a group of largely independent studies of welfare families is being used to determine the effects of welfare reform on child health. Some of the studies are funded by the federal government, and others by states and foundations. Several started early enough so that baseline data are available, and some have comparison groups. Fortunately, the directors of these studies realized the advantages that might accrue from using the same set of child health and well-being measures. With support from the John D. and Catherine T. MacArthur Foundation and HHS, they worked with Child Trends to develop measures of child well-being that include: health and safety, social and emotional adjustment, use of health and human services, child care, and home environment and parenting practices.

Conclusion

Measuring the health and well-being of children after welfare reform will be difficult, but not impossible. Some federal data sets will provide trends on a limited group of indicators for poor children nationally and for the largest states, but most federal data collection efforts are not adequate to the task. Their indicators of child health are not sensitive enough to detect the types of changes in child well-being that welfare reform might produce; they do not have a large enough sample of welfare families; they ask too few questions about welfare status; and they can not provide state-level data, which might provide insights into whether different welfare reform policies had different effects.

For example, it is unlikely that welfare reform would have a measurable impact on infant mortality. Most children who are going to die in the first year of life die in the first week. Most of these children die because of congenital anomalies incompatible with life or from extreme prematurity, that is, being born too soon. Our knowledge of how to prevent these two conditions is very weak. Urging women to take folic acid supplements before they become pregnant could reduce some congenital defects. How would welfare reform encourage such supplementation? Convincing women to stop smoking during pregnancy would affect low birth weights but, again, how would welfare reform encourage smoking cessation? Some believe that reducing stress might improve pregnancy outcomes. Does welfare reform increase or decrease stress? The few infants who die between one month and one year of life usually die of SIDS or injuries. Will welfare reform affect these conditions? Moore has suggested:

> Because health conditions are infrequent among children and take time to develop, researchers should identify "crocuses" and "miners' canaries" that might serve as harbingers of good or poor child health outcomes. Possible outcomes include health status, infectious diseases, accidents, injuries, or poisonings. Such problems could result from poor supervision, monitoring, or care on the part of parents or child care workers. Child health outcomes also could improve if family income, parent education, or household organization improve in ways that enhance children's health and safety.[9]

The problem of detecting changes resulting from a 1996 law that is still being implemented is compounded by the 1997 passage of SCHIP legislation. The impact of SCHIP, particularly on access and utilization of health care, may be greater than that of welfare reform.[10] Distinguishing between the effects of SCHIP and welfare reform will be almost impossible using federal data sets.

The country, however, will have the results of several well-designed individual studies, mostly at the state level. If the studies are well executed, they will provide the necessary information for selected areas and it should be possible to extrapolate, cautiously, from these studies to the entire country.

Notes

1.   For a synthesis of the results of welfare reform by type of program, child outcome, and age, see Jeffrey Grogger, Lynn A. Karoly, and Jacob A. Klerman, *Consequences of Welfare Reform: A Research Synthesis*, DRU-2676-DHHS (Santa Monica, Calif.: RAND, July 2002).
2.   Greg J. Duncan and P. Lindsay Chase-Lansdale, "Welfare Reform and Children's Well-Being," in *The New World of Welfare*, edited by Rebecca M. Blank and Ron Haskins (Washington, D.C.: Brookings Institution Press, 2001).
3.   Bowen Garrett and John Holahan, "Health Insurance after Welfare," *Health Affairs* 19 (2000): 175–184.
4.   Eileen R. Ellis, Vernon K. Smith, and David M. Rousseau, *Medicaid Enrollment in 50 States, December 2001 Data Update* (Washington, D.C.: Kaiser Commission on Medicaid and the Uninsured, 2002).
5.   Sheila R. Zedlewski, and Sarah Brauner, *Are the Steep Declines in Food Stamp Participation Linked to Falling Welfare Caseloads?* Assessing the New Federalism Project, Series B, No. B-3 (Washington, D.C.: Urban Institute, 1999).
6.   U.S. General Accounting Office, *Food Stamp Program—Various Factors Have Led to Declining Participation* (Washington, D.C.: Government Printing Office, 1999).
7.   Kristin Moore, comments on "Child Health and Well-Being," by Lorraine V. Klerman, in *Family Well-Being after Welfare Reform*, edited by Douglas J. Besharov, 2002, available from: http://www.welfareacademy.org/pubs/familywellbeing/familywellbeing-ch9klerman.pdf, accessed November 18, 2002.
8.   Constance F. Citro, Charles F. Manski, and John Pepper, editors, *Providing National Statistics on Health and Social Welfare Programs in an Era of Change, Summary of a Workshop* (Washington, D.C.: National Academy Press, 1998).
9.   Moore, 2002, pp. 9-11–9-12.
10.   Peter G. Szilagyi, Jack Zwanziger, Lance E. Rodewald, Jane L. Holl, Dana B. Mukamel, Sarah Trafton, Laura P. Shone, Andrew W. Dick, Lynne Jarrell, and Richard F. Raubertas, "Evaluation of a State Health Insurance Program for Low-Income Children: Implications for State Child Health Insurance Programs," *Pediatrics* 105 (2000): 363–371.

References

Citro, Constance F., Charles F. Manski, and John Pepper, editors. 1998. *Providing National Statistics on Health and Social Welfare Programs in an Era of Change, Summary of a Workshop*. Washington, D.C.: National Academy Press.

Duncan, Greg J., and P. Lindsay Chase-Lansdale. 2001. "Welfare Reform and Children's Well-Being." In *The New World of Welfare*. Edited by Rebecca M. Blank and Ron Haskins. Washington, D.C.: Brookings Institution Press.

Ellis, Eileen R., Vernon K. Smith, and David M. Rousseau. 2002. *Medicaid Enrollment in 50 States, December 2001 Data Update*. Washington, D.C.: Kaiser Commission on Medicaid and the Uninsured.

Garrett, Bowen, and John Holahan. 2000. "Health Insurance after Welfare." *Health Affairs* 19: 175–184.

Grogger, Jeffrey, Lynn A. Karoly, and Jacob A. Klerman. 2002. *Consequences of Welfare Reform: A Research Synthesis.* DRU-2676-DHHS. Santa Monica, Calif.: RAND. July.

Moore, Kristin. 2002. Comments on "Child Health and Well-Being," by Lorraine V. Klerman. In *Family Well-Being after Welfare Reform.* Edited by Douglas J. Besharov. Available from: http://www.welfareacademy.org/pubs/familywellbeing/familywellbeing-ch9klerman.pdf. Accessed November 18, 2002.

Szilagyi, Peter G., Jack Zwanziger, Lance E. Rodewald, Jane L. Holl, Dana B. Mukamel, Sarah Trafton, Laura P. Shone, Andrew W. Dick, Lynne Jarrell, and Richard F. Raubertas. 2000. "Evaluation of a State Health Insurance Program for Low-Income Children: Implications for State Child Health Insurance Programs." *Pediatrics* 105: 363–371.

U.S. General Accounting Office. 1999. *Food Stamp Program—Various Factors Have Led to Declining Participation.* Washington, D.C.: Government Printing Office.

Zedlewski, Shelia R., and Sarah Brauner. 1999. *Are the Steep Declines in Food Stamp Participation Linked to Falling Welfare Caseloads?* Assessing the New Federalism Project, Series B, No. B-3. Washington, D.C.: Urban Institute.

11

Nutrition, Food Security, and Obesity

Harold S. Beebout

The dramatic reduction in welfare caseloads has been accompanied by surprisingly steep declines in participation in the Food Stamp Program (FSP). Because most families leaving welfare remain eligible for food stamps, many policymakers and program officials are questioning whether the safety net is working as intended. In the Personal Responsibility and Work Opportunity Reconciliation Act of 1996 (PRWORA), which eliminated the entitlement to Aid to Families with Dependent Children (AFDC) and converted cash assistance into block grants to states, Congress clearly intended to maintain a safety net for food assistance and health insurance coverage. After deliberations concerning the role of the FSP and whether it should be folded into the Temporary Assistance for Needy Families (TANF) block grant, Congress left the FSP intact as an entitlement for low-income families, albeit not without imposing some limits on eligibility and benefits, as discussed in the next section.

This chapter examines how welfare reform has affected the access of low-income families with children to food stamps, the largest source of food assistance and the only one substantially affected by welfare reform. This chapter also takes a broader look at nutrition and hunger as they affect the well-being of children, including the troubling trends in obesity among adolescents in low-income families.

The first section of this chapter reviews measures of access to FSP benefits, focusing on how those benefits have changed under welfare reform and indicating several areas of policy concern. The second section looks at the federal government's effort to measure food security and hunger and explores the question of whether food insecurity and hunger have become more acute with welfare reform.

Nutrition and related health outcomes as an important dimension of child well-being are discussed in the third section. The final section discusses the implications of these trends for policy and research priorities.

Access to Food Stamps

Access to food stamps changed in two ways with welfare reform. First, PRWORA and subsequent legislation limited FSP eligibility for two types of households and reduced benefits modestly for all FSP households. The second change, and the one with the larger impact, is the indirect effect of the decline in TANF caseloads as a result of PRWORA on FSP participation.

Changes in Food Stamp Program Policy

Welfare reform legislation changed FSP eligibility and benefits in four ways:

- It limited eligibility for able-bodied adults without dependents (ABAWDs) not working twenty hours per week.

- It disqualified most legal immigrants (elderly and disabled immigrants as well as children were later grandfathered in).

- It reduced benefits for all families by a modest amount.

- It provided for coordination of benefits with TANF sanctions. Previously, when states sanctioned TANF recipients for noncompliance with work requirements, the sanction would be partially offset by increases in food stamp benefits. This federal legislation allowed states to eliminate the offset and to sanction FSP benefits for individuals sanctioned under TANF.

Although these changes reduced the number of people receiving food stamps, as discussed below, they were not the major impetus for the sharp decline in the FSP rolls. In particular, they were not the leading factor in the large drop in the number of participating families with children.

Decline in Food Stamp Participation

Between August 1995 and July 2000, the number of FSP participants declined sharply: by 8.0 million, or 31 percent.[1] This drop is largely the result of three factors: (1) PRWORA provisions that limited FSP eligibility for ABAWDs and legal immigrants; (2) families achieving employment success with earnings above the FSP eligibility threshold as a result of the booming economy and welfare reform; and (3) families who left or were diverted from TANF and who, despite their eligibility, did not participate in the FSP.

Perhaps 20 percent of the decline in the number of FSP participants can be attributed to the PRWORA policy changes limiting FSP eligibility for ABAWDs and legal immigrants.[2] Most of those losing eligibility as a result of those policy changes were not children, but the limits on legal immigrants did affect some families with children. Most of the other 80 percent of the decline occurred among households with children.[3]

The drop in the number of participants can also be attributed to the fact that some families lost eligibility because they moved from welfare to work, raising their family income above the eligibility threshold—that is the good news arising from a combination of welfare reform and a strong economy. We do not yet have good estimates, but that number might account for half of the remaining decline in participation.

Finally, eligible families leaving TANF participated in the FSP at a lower rate once they left TANF, despite the fact that they were still eligible for food stamps.[4] Between August 1995 and February 1999, the number of AFDC/TANF recipients, largely in single-parent families, declined by 5.7 million, a 44 percent drop.[5] The lower rates of participation among TANF leavers and among those diverted from TANF might account for roughly the other half of the remaining decline in participation.

Declines among Single-Parent Households

Among households with children, nearly two-thirds of the decline in participation occurred among single-parent households.[6] The rate of decline was similar for single-parent and for other households with children.[7] The reasons for the decline between the two types of households probably differ, however, with welfare reform being a key factor for single-parent families and the economy a more important factor for other households with children.

Among single-parent households, policy concern differs by vulnerability. The policy concern about the decline in FSP participation differs according to the vulnerability of three categories of single-parent households. The first category consists of families continuing to receive TANF benefits. Their link to the cash assistance system means that the traditional access from within the welfare system to Medicaid and food stamps is intact. Given these links, they will probably continue to participate in FSP and Medicaid under welfare reform at the same relatively high rates as they did before welfare reform. With welfare reform, however, the number of single-parent households continuing to receive both cash assistance and food stamp benefits has dropped sharply. Although cash assistance recipients still represent more than half of all single-parent FSP households, the proportion is declining. In addition, many more of the TANF–FSP households are working—the percentage of single-parent households with earnings has doubled since welfare reform.

The second group consists of low-income, working, single-parent families eligible for FSP benefits but not receiving TANF: welfare leavers, families diverted from TANF, and others. Because many of these families participated in the FSP before leaving TANF, many observers expected their participation in the FSP to hold steady at relatively high rates. However, studies of families leaving TANF show surprisingly low rates of participation in the FSP and lower-than-expected rates of participation in Medicaid.[8] In fact, the rates of participation for those eligible for food stamps among this group will probably resemble those of the working poor in the past.[9] Whether this is an access problem and a policy issue of concern depends on the reasons for the low participation rate. If families know about their eligibility for food assistance, and the cost of applying for and receiving benefits is not unduly burdensome (including the need to take time off work and to confront other hassles), then current policies and program operations may be appropriate, and access may not be a problem. The fact that participation rates appear to vary widely by state, however, does give rise to concern that some states are offering greater access to food assistance than others.[10]

The third group of single-parent families who may be cause for concern consists of those who have left welfare but report little or no earnings. According to the Urban Institute's National Survey of America's Families (NSAF), about a quarter of the families leaving TANF do not have earnings, and about half of those without earnings report having no income.[11] This group makes up about 10 or 12 percent of all households leaving welfare. According to the NSAF, only about half of the families leaving welfare that have an income below 50 percent of the poverty rate participate in the FSP. The low rates of participation among what appear to be very vulnerable families with children—those with little or no earnings and an income of less than half of the poverty threshold—are a matter of substantial policy concern.

Later parts of this chapter discuss more fully what these program access concerns mean for research and policy priorities, but first the chapter reviews some of the most relevant research on nutrition and hunger, which is also likely to factor into these priorities.

Nutrition

Nutrition and dietary factors are associated with poor nutrition in vulnerable groups, including children in low-income families, women of child-bearing age, and the elderly, as well as those with chronic health conditions. Poor diets, poor nutrition, and nutrition-related health conditions are especially prevalent among low-income families:[12]

- According to data from the National Health and Nutrition Examination Survey (NHANES), 12 percent of low-income children ages one to two, and 29 percent of low-income pregnant women are iron deficient.[13] The nation had great success in reducing iron deficiency during the 1970s, but the rate has remained constant since then.

- According to data from the Continuing Survey of Food Intake for Individuals data, only 33 percent of people ages two and older meet the dietary guidelines for percent of calories from fat.[14]

- According to NHANES data, 16 percent of low-income adolescents are overweight or obese.[15] This rate is double that for higher-income adolescents.

Most Americans do not have a healthy diet, get enough exercise, or follow other guidelines for good health. The trend of rising levels of obesity and of being overweight, particularly the high rate for low-income adolescents, is a high priority problem with serious long-term consequences. As David Murray writes:

During the past decade, however, the number of children who are overweight has more than doubled. Approximately 11 percent of American children are overweight. An additional 14 percent have a body mass index between the 85th and 95th percentiles, which puts them at increased risk for becoming overweight and experiencing a variety of serious health problems.[16]

Murray's latest data reflect the period from 1988 to 1994. More recent data for 1999 and 2000 indicate that the prevalence of overweight among adolescents has continued to rise, reaching 15 percent.[17]

Food Security and Hunger

In 1995, the federal government launched a major effort to measure food security and hunger. Food security measures are based on a set of questions included annually in the Current Population Survey (CPS) since 1995 (a related set of food sufficiency questions was included in the NHANES starting in 1988 and updated to the CPS questions in 1999). The measures from the CPS are based on the household respondent's perception about whether the household had adequate access to food or whether it did not have enough food as a result of a lack of money or other resources. Responses to the questions are used to assign each household to one of three categories: (1) food secure, (2) food insecure without hunger, and (3) food insecure with hunger.

The CPS-based food security measures show that approximately 32 percent of all low-income households (130 percent of the poverty level) have some degree of food insecurity, meaning that the household respondents perceived that they had some problems getting enough food. Roughly 11 percent of all low-income households fall into the more severe range, "food insecure with hunger."[18]

These food security measures have been criticized because they are based on the perceptions of respondents and thus have an unclear relationship to more objective measures of nutrition or health status. For example, as Richard Bavier notes:

In the CPS data reported in *Household Food Insecurity in United States in 1995*, 38 percent of the households that were classified as "food insecure with moderate hunger" answered "no" every time they were asked a direct question about hunger. All household respondents were asked Question 35: "In the last twelve months, since May 1994, were you ever hungry but didn't eat because you couldn't afford enough food?" In addition, households with children were asked Question 47: "In the last twelve months, (was CHILD'S NAME/were the children) ever hungry but you just couldn't afford more food?"

Moreover, only about 38 percent of the households with "moderate hunger" on the twelve-month scale had calendar year 1994 pretax incomes below the poverty line. Fewer than half (46 percent) of the households with "severe hunger" were poor in 1994. What's more, more than one-third of the "moderate hunger" household and more than one-fourth of the "severe hunger" households had money incomes above 185 percent of their poverty lines, meaning that they were not even in the poorest third of all households. Around 15 percent of the "moderate hunger" households and around 10 percent of the "severe hunger" households seemed to have 1994 incomes above the median for all households![19]

Neither I nor the general policy community knows exactly what to make of the food security measures. Research to better identify how food security and insecurity correlate with nutritional status and other things we care about is a high priority.

Nevertheless, measures like this are often reasonably reliable for showing change, even if they are not terribly good at measuring the level. So I still think that the finding of no change is valid. And we absolutely need to know more about why we have this apparent lack of correlation between the amount of food assistance people are getting and their status on the measure. For example, at 130 percent of the poverty line, those receiving food stamps are more likely to report food insecurity than those not receiving them.[20]

In any event, if welfare reform had a substantial effect on food security or hunger, these measures should be capable of discerning the impact. Between 1995 and 2001, no appreciable change occurred in these measures for low-income households or for households as a whole.[21] This absence of change leads to the conclusion that at least by these measures, welfare reform has not significantly changed the hunger and food-insecurity status of low-income families.

Implications and Recommendations

This review of children's well-being based on nutrition-related outcomes, suggests that five areas are in urgent need of further research.

How Are Highly Vulnerable Families Faring?

With welfare reform and a strong economy, the nation has made great strides in moving families off welfare and into work, leading to greater self-sufficiency. Recognizing this substantial achievement, we now need to be concerned about how the most vulnerable families are faring.

Perhaps the vulnerable group of greatest concern is families with children who report having little or no employment and very little income and who receive no cash assistance, or, in many cases, other safety-net benefits such as food stamps. The national surveys raise concerns about this apparently vulnerable group, but they do not really answer the question about how they are coping. We need detailed case studies of a sample of these families to understand the extent to which their well-being—especially the well-being of their children—is threatened. The case studies would address the following questions:

- How are these families living with little or no reported income? Do they have unreported earnings or other income? Are they being supported by family, friends, or charity?

- Why are these families not working? What are their barriers to work? How severe are they?

- Why are these families not participating in the safety-net programs such as food stamps? Do they think they are not eligible for benefits? Have they been sanctioned? Do they think the hassle is too great?

Why is Participation in Safety-Net Programs Higher in Some States?

Some states appear to be more successful than others at moving families *off* welfare while keeping those who remain eligible and in need of assistance *on* food stamps and Medicaid. Why are those states more successful? Is their success connected with messages that they convey to families and welfare offices, training of the workers, better support from their automated eligibility systems, or other factors? Work now underway should help answer these questions.[22]

How Are All Low-Income Families Faring?

Now that welfare reform has moved a large proportion of families off the rolls, and that welfare diversion policies are common, we should focus not on how welfare families are faring but on how low-income families in each state are faring. It no longer is useful to look at the former group because a large portion of it has left the rolls. It also is becoming not particularly useful to look at how welfare leavers are faring because many families are being diverted before they file a welfare application. Although the national surveys help tell us how low-income families are faring on average, the survey samples are generally too small to give us reliable, state-specific information. And because policies have become so diverse across states, we need to be able to measure the well-being of low-income families at the state level under a given state's particular set of policies. Doing so could mean incorporating state-level estimates for large states within national surveys or conducting separate state surveys.

How Do Food Insecurity Measures Relate to More Direct Measures of Well-Being?

It is important to study how the relatively new measures of food insecurity relate to more direct measures of well-being, such as diet quality, nutritional status, and health. Early research has raised questions about the relationship between measures of food insecurity and measures of diet and nutrient intake. Similarly, we need to know more about how measured food insecurity is related to health outcomes. Findings are just starting to emerge from research based on the NHANES III, which contains a set of questions related to food security as well as information on nutrition and health status.[23] Finally, we need to know more about what is going on in households reporting more severe levels of food insufficiency, how they are coping, and the degree of the threat to the well-being of the children in these households. For example, in households receiving food stamps who report being "food insecure with hunger," is the hunger the result of food stamps being exhausted before the next month's allotment is available?

What Are the Trends in Regard to Overweight and Obesity?

As mentioned earlier, most Americans do not have a healthy diet, get enough exercise, or follow other guidelines for good health. The rising levels in being overweight and in obesity, particularly among low-income adolescents, is a high-priority problem with serious long-term consequences. They lead to higher rates of diabetes, high blood pressure, and other health problems. Dietary and health habits begun in childhood can have a strong positive or negative effect on later health.

More attention needs to be given to improving dietary and health behaviors in children and adolescents. How this goal can be accomplished and the roles the FSP, the schools, and other institutions will play in accomplishing it are important questions.

Notes

1. Estimated changes in Food Stamp Program (FSP) caseloads are based on administrative data on the number of individuals and households receiving food stamps during a month. From August 1995 to May 1999, the number of people receiving food stamps dropped from 26.0 million to 18.0 million. The choice of August 1995 as the pre-reform point is somewhat arbitrary. States were then rapidly reforming their Aid to Families with Dependent Children (AFDC) programs under waivers prior to the passage of the Personal Responsibility and Work Opportunity Reconciliation Act (PRWORA) in late 1996. (The number of food stamp recipients declined to 16.9 million in July 2000, but then grew to 19.7 million in July 2002.)
2. Characteristics of recipient households are based on information from a sample of cases collected each month to estimate payment error rates. The data on able-bodied adults without dependents (ABAWDs) and permanent resident aliens are from unpublished tables prepared by Laura Castner and Randy Rosso of Mathematica Policy Research, Inc., from the fiscal year 1996 and 1998 samples. From the Au-

gust–September 1996 average of 1.01 million, the number of ABAWDs dropped to 0.46 million by August–September 1998, a difference of 0.55 million. From the August–September 1996 average of 1.43 million, the number of legal immigrants dropped to 0.32 million by August–September 1998, a gross difference of 1.11 million. However, we need to adjust for the increase in naturalized citizens of 0.15 million, for a net difference of 0.96 million. This calculation assumes, as an approximation, that all the change in these two groups was a result of the legislated limits and not the economy or other factors.

3.   Suzanne Smolkin and Robert Howard, *Characteristics of Food Stamp Households, Fiscal Year 1995* (Alexandria, Va.: U.S. Department of Agriculture, Food and Consumer Service, April 11, 1997), table B2; and Laura Castner and Randy Rosso, *Characteristics of Food Stamp Households, Fiscal Year 1998* (Alexandria, Va.: U.S. Department of Agriculture, Food and Nutrition Service, Office of Analysis, Nutrition, and Evaluation, February 2000), table A-26. In 1995 there were 21.85 million participants in households with children compared with 16.07 million in 1998 for a decline of 5.78 million. The decline among all participants from FY 1995 to FY 1998 was 6.99 million. The 5.78 million decline plus the 1.5 million reduction in ABAWDs and aliens more than accounts for the total decline of 6.99 million, but the time period is slightly different, and there is double counting since some aliens were children. See Laura Castner and Scott Cody, "Trends in FSP Participation Rates: Focus on September 1997," draft report, Mathematica Policy Research, Inc., Washington, D.C., 1999.

4.   Castner and Cody, 1999. On the basis of 1997 data, the number of eligible people in households with children fell by 1.24 million, from 19.50 million to 18.26 million. With a participation rate of 83 percent, the estimated rate for 1997 for this group, the change in the number of eligible people would account for 40 percent of the decline of 2.56 million in the number of participants in households with children.

5.   The number of Temporary Assistance for Needy Families (TANF) recipients fell from 13.10 million in August 1995 to 7.38 million in February 1999.

6.   Smolkin and Howard, 1997, table 3.3; and Castner and Rosso, 2000, table 3.3.

7.   Single parents constituted nearly 70 percent of all FSP households with children in both 1995 and 1998. See Smolkin and Howard, 1997, table 3.3; and Castner and Rosso, 2000, table 3.3.

8.   See Sheila Zedlewski and Sarah Brauner, *Declines in Food Stamp and Welfare Participation: Is There a Connection?* Assessing the New Federalism Discussion Paper 99-02 (Washington, D.C.: Urban Institute, 1999). According to Zedlewski and Brauner, only 42 percent of former welfare recipients with an income level below the FSP eligibility line were participating in the program. FSP participation rates, defined as the proportion of FSP–eligible households actually receiving FSP benefits, are one measure of program access. Estimates of the number of eligible households are based on data from national surveys such as the current Current Population Survey (CPS), the Survey of Income and Program Participation (SIPP), and the National Survey of America's Families (NSAF) or on surveys of families who have left welfare. Estimates of the number of participants usually come from administrative data but may come directly from survey data.

9.   Single parents constituted 68 percent of all FSP households in both 1995 and 1998. See Smolkin and Howard, 1997, table C2; Castner and Rosso, 2000, table C2.

10.   Participation declines in the FSP for the two-year period between August 1996 and August 1998, for example, range from 5 percent in Nebraska to 48 percent in Vermont. Some portion of this difference might be explained by more households' losing eligibility, but substantial differences remain.

11. Zedlewski and Brauner, 1999.
12. Measures of diet quality, nutrition, and health status are based largely on the National Health and Nutrition Examination Survey (NHANES) and the Continuing Survey of Food Intakes by Individuals. The NHANES is a representative sample of the U.S. noninstitutionalized population and consists of two components: (1) a household interview and (2) an interview and examination conducted in a mobile examination center. Both surveys collect detailed information on dietary intake, food security, and participation in food programs (Food Stamp Program; Women, Infants, and Children Program; National School Lunch Program; and National School Breakfast Program).
13. U.S. Department of Health and Human Services, *Healthy People 2010*, vol. 2, conference edition (Washington, D.C.: U.S. Department of Health and Human Services, 2000), p. 19-37.
14. Ibid., p. 19-27.
15. Ibid., p. 19-14.
16. David Murray, comments on "Nutrition, Food Security, and Obesity," by Harold S. Beebout, in *Family Well-Being after Welfare Reform*, edited by Douglas J. Besharov, 2002, available at http://www.welfareacademy.org/pubs/familywellbeing/familywellbeing-ch10beebout.pdf, accessed September 30, 2002.
17. National Center for Health Statistics, *Prevalence of Overweight Among Children and Adolescents: United States, 1999–2000*, available from: http://www.cdc.gov/nchs/products/pubs/pubd/hestats/overwght99.htm, accessed November 19, 2002.
18. Mark Nord, Margaret Andrews, and Steven Carlson, *Household Food Security in the United States 2001* (Washington, D.C.: U.S. Department of Agriculture, Economic Research Service, 2002).
19. Richard Bavier, comments on "Nutrition, Food Security, and Obesity," by Harold S. Beebout, in *Family Well-Being after Welfare Reform*, edited by Douglas J. Besharov, 2002, available at http://www.welfareacademy.org/pubs/familywellbeing/familywellbeing-ch10beebout.pdf, accessed September 30, 2002.
20. Nord et al., 2002.
21. William L. Hamilton, John T. Cook, William W. Thompson, Lawrence F. Buron, Edward A. Frongillo, Jr., Christine M. Olson, and Cheryl A. Wehler, *Household Food Security in the United States in 1995: Summary Report of the Food Security Measurement Project* (Washington, D.C.: U.S. Department of Agriculture, 1997); Nord et al., 2002.
22. A Mathematica Policy Research, Inc., study directed by LaDonna Pavetti and sponsored by the U.S. Department of Health and Human Services and the Robert Wood Johnson Foundation is looking at these issues.
23. See, for example, Katherine Alaimo, Christine M. Olson, Edward A. Frongillo, and Ronette R. Briefel, "Food Insufficiency, Poverty, and Health in U.S. Pre-School and School-Age Children," paper presented at American Public Health Association Conference, Chicago, November 1999; Christine M. Olson, "Nutrition and Health Outcomes Associated with Food Insecurity and Hunger," *Journal of Nutrition* 129 (1999): 521S–524S; Katherine Alaimo, Ronette R. Briefel, Edward A. Frongillo, and Catherine M. Olson, "Food Insufficiency Exists in the United States: Results from the Third National Health and Nutrition Examination Survey," *American Journal of Public Health* 88 (1998): 419–426; and Ronald E. Kleinman, J. Michael Murphy, Michelle Little, Maria Pageno, Cheryl A. Wehler, Kenneth Regel, and Michael S. Jellinek, "Hunger in Children in the United States: Potential Behavioral and Emotional Correlates," *Pediatrics* 101 (1998): 1–6.

References

Alaimo, Katherine, Ronette R. Briefel, Edward A. Frongillo, and Christine M. Olson. 1998. "Food Insufficiency Exists in the United States: Results from the Third National Health and Nutrition Examination Survey." *American Journal of Public Health* 88 (3): 419–426.

Alaimo, Katherine, Christine M. Olson, Edward A. Frongillo, and Ronette R. Briefel. 1999. "Food Insufficiency, Poverty, and Health in U.S. Pre-School and School-Age Children." Paper presented at American Public Health Association Conference. Chicago. November.

Bavier, Richard. 2002. Comments on "Nutrition, Food Security, and Obesity," by Harold S. Beebout. In *Family Well-being after Welfare Reform*. Edited by Douglas J. Besharov. Available at http://www.welfareacademy.org/pubs/familywellbeing/familywellbeing-ch10beebout.pdf. Accessed September 30, 2002.

Brauner, Sarah, and Pamela Loprest. 1999. *Where Are They Now? What States' Studies of People Who Left Welfare Tell Us.* New Federalism Issues and Options for States, Series A, No. A-32. Washington, D.C.: Urban Institute.

Castner, Laura, and Scott Cody. 1999. *Trends in FSP Participation Rates: Focus on September 1997.* Draft report. Washington, D.C.: Mathematica Policy Research, Inc.

Castner, Laura, and Randy Rosso. 2000. *Characteristics of Food Stamp Households, Fiscal Year 1998.* Alexandria, Va.: U.S. Department of Agriculture, Food and Nutrition Service, Office of Analysis, Nutrition, and Evaluation.

Hamilton, William L., John T. Cook, William W. Thompson, Lawrence F. Buron, Edward A. Frongillo, Jr., Christine M. Olson, and Cheryl A. Wehler. 1997. *Household Food Security in the United States in 1995: Summary Report of the Food Security Measurement Project.* Washington, D.C.: U.S. Department of Agriculture.

Kleinman, Ronald E., J. Michael Murphy, Michelle Little, Maria Pageno, Cheryl A. Wehler, Kenneth Regel, and Michael S. Jellinek. 1998. "Hunger in Children in the United States: Potential Behavioral and Emotional Correlates." *Pediatrics* 101 (1): 1–6.

Loprest, Pamela. 1999. *How Families That Left Welfare Are Doing: A National Picture.* Assessing the New Federalism. Series B, No. B-1. Washington, D.C.: Urban Institute.

Murray, David. 2002. Comments on "Nutrition, Food Security, and Obesity," by Harold S. Beebout. In *Family Well-Being after Welfare Reform*. Edited by Douglas J. Besharov. Available at http://www.welfareacademy.org/pubs/familywellbeing/familywellbeing-ch10beebout.pdf. Accessed September 30, 2002.

National Center for Health Statistics. 2002. *Prevalence of Overweight among Children and Adolescents: United States, 1999–2000.* Available from: http://www.cdc.gov/nchs/products/pubs/pubd/hestats/overwght99.htm. Accessed November 19, 2002.

Nord, Mark, Margaret Andrews, and Steven Carlson. 2002. *Household Food Security in the United States 2001.* Washington, D.C.: U.S. Department of Agriculture, Economic Research Service.

Olson, Christine M. 1999. "Nutrition and Health Outcomes Associated with Food Insecurity and Hunger." *Journal of Nutrition* 129: 521S–524S.

Smolkin, Suzanne, and Robert Howard. 1997. *Characteristics of Food Stamp Households Fiscal Year 1995.* Alexandria, Va.: U.S. Department of Agriculture, Food and Consumer Service. April 11.

U.S. Department of Health and Human Services. 2000. *Healthy People 2010,* vol. 2. Conference edition. Washington, D.C.: U.S. Department of Health and Human Services.

Zedlewski, Sheila, and Sarah Brauner. 1999. *Declines in Food Stamp and Welfare Participation: Is There a Connection?* Assessing the New Federalism Discussion Paper 99-02. Washington, D.C.: Urban Institute.

12

Crime and Juvenile Delinquency

Lawrence W. Sherman

If we could measure the connection between violent crime and welfare reform properly, we might find that it has more to do with neighborhoods than with households or individuals. If welfare reform is affecting behavior or quality of life, it is probably doing so through group context and the cumulative or synergistic effects of changes in the economies of families concentrated in space. Behavioral effects correlated with being on welfare tend to disappear when you change the neighborhood context. To understand crime in relation to welfare—to understand crime and violence in this country at all—you have to disaggregate it.

The following example illustrates this point. The Australian homicide rate is 2 per 100,000. The U.S. homicide rate is now about 6 per 100,000, or only about three times higher. The homicide rate in the state of Maryland is about 10 per 100,000, but the homicide rate in Baltimore is about 40 per 100,000. In the rest of Maryland, the homicide rate is lower than it is in Australia—about 1.2 per 100,000.

Most of Maryland has a homicide rate lower than Australia's. The fact that Baltimore has a homicide rate of about 40 per 100,000, or forty times that of the rest of Maryland, is an accident of political geography based on the proportion of the suburbs that is encompassed by the city limits. Dallas, for example, has a much lower homicide rate than Baltimore, but it has a history of annexing suburbs, which Baltimore does not. Hence, it is misleading to compare homicide rates across cities or to look at national homicide rates without disaggregating them by the factors that are most strongly correlated with their existence. Some of those factors—like age, gender, race, and income—are at the individual level, but the effects of those characteristics are magnified by location and space.

That the City of Baltimore has a homicide rate of 40 per 100,000 is not important to this discussion. What is important is the fact that in East Baltimore, the homicide rate is probably on the order of 200 to 300 per 100,000 and is heavily concentrated among males ages fifteen to thirty, whose murder rates could be in excess of 400 or 500 per 100,000.

Neighborhood-level homicide rates are not reported by the FBI, but they are just the kind of numbers that we ought to be tracking in a systematic way from year to year. If we want computerized statistics to help us see how our indicators are working from month to month, we need to get below the national and city-level data and zero in on where the problems are most heavily concentrated.

It is not possible to determine what percentage of welfare cases occurs in what percentage of the Census tracts in the United States from administrative data. According to the U.S. Department of Health and Human Services, only about ten states have the information systems that would be necessary to locate welfare recipient households by Census tract. Fortunately, those ten states have about half the population of the country, so it may be possible to study welfare issues spatially.

An even better opportunity exists with the distribution of crime data. Only fifty cities account for about 50 percent of the homicides in this country, and every one of those fifty cities has computerized crime records that show the location of the crime by the address of occurrence, thus allowing the identification of high-crime places like East Baltimore.

Including homicide rates by Census tract in national statistics for all the high-crime areas or high-welfare areas would not involve a large proportion of the Census tracts within the fifty largest cities. Baltimore, for example, has 200 Census tracts, 50 of which account for more than half the homicides. Those 50 Census tracts have an average labor force participation of people over age eighteen of about 25 percent; put another way, that is 75 percent nonemployment.

Including other information, such as child welfare cases and school statistics, would provide another basis for looking at the effects of government programs in poverty areas. Such programs often are crafted as though for the whole country, but they actually are based on a handful of urban neighborhoods.

Examining a subgroup organized by space and then by the demographic categories of age, gender, and race within those spatial areas would perhaps be the most informative way to investigate many

St. Louis Community College

kinds of questions. For example, the national homicide rate has declined steadily since 1993. The rate is now 17 percent below where it was in 1984, the year it began to rise and subsequently rose quite a bit. What are the components of that decrease?

If a big drop-off in the homicide rate of the baby boom generation has occurred, it would hide any increase in the rate for the rest of the population. In fact, there is reason to believe that 1998 saw a slight increase in homicides in inner-city areas. The baby boom generation not only is aging but is dying at an accelerating rate, as violent baby boomers are getting killed themselves in domestic homicides and other violent events. The baby boom generation has a huge effect on the average rate of anything in this country. It is important to distinguish the typical baby boomer situation from that of an inner-city teenager to understand what is going on with children, poverty, welfare, and the country as a whole.

One could argue that we do not have a homicide problem in the country as a whole, given the low rates. Frank Zimring, professor at the University of California, Berkeley, School of Law, and Gordon Hawkins, professor emeritus at the University of Sydney, actually argue the opposite.[1] They say that even if one excludes certain groups, we still have a pretty high homicide rate, but their argument predated the big drop.

Many theories attempt to explain why the homicide rate has decreased. One of the more compelling correlations is the following: The year in which the homicide rate started to decrease consistently was the first year in which police increased their enforcement of laws against carrying concealed weapons and started taking guns off the street at a higher rate. That rate is about seventy-five times higher than the rate of gun seizures in Latin American countries with high homicide rates, like Colombia. By raising the gun seizure rate in relationship to the homicide rate, police activity may have contributed substantially to the drop in the homicide rate.[2]

It is difficult to know whether that is a cause-and-effect relationship, in large part because of the aggregation problem. The data from the poorest 1,000 or 2,000 Census tracts (out of about 50,000 Census tracts in the country), which can be obtained only by getting fifty police departments to give you their data, show whether, in fact, large increases in arrests for gun carrying occurred. Those data would provide a much stronger basis for inference about what is happening if someone were able to collect it all.

Likewise, hospital data focused on the small number of poverty areas can provide information on some of the critical data issues. For example, the Hospital of the University of Pennsylvania reported that every gunshot-wound injury in that hospital is recorded by the emergency department; more serious cases are sent to the trauma department. What gets recorded in the emergency department is important because one of the useful databases is the National Electronic Injury Surveillance System (NEISS), which is a sample of emergency departments.

I audited the claim that the emergency department data record every case and that the trauma cases are recorded in addition to the emergency data. The NEISS does not survey the trauma departments. It only surveys emergency departments, which are separate departments within hospitals. The trauma department at the hospital is reporting more cases than the emergency department, which is obviously not the only referral. Thus, complete counts of shootings require careful checks on separate data sets.

A National System

A national inner-city statistics system would allow us to go to the handful of hospitals serving those neighborhoods, work out the quirks, and compile medical data on violence and key issues like gunshot wounds and, for example, children who are rendered paraplegic. This is exactly the kind of thing that does not get revealed in a national survey because it is a rare event. But if you go to the streets of Baltimore on a summer night, you will be astonished at how many young men you see out on the streets in wheelchairs.

Rare events nationally are highly concentrated in poverty areas. Tragedies like crippling gunshot wounds are the kind of thing that needs to be measured, regardless of welfare reform, and that could be measured if the data resources were applied where the problem is concentrated. By spreading out the data resources, we do the same thing we do with national crime intervention: Of $4 billion in crime prevention money handed out by the federal government every year, Vermont gets $1 million per homicide and inner-city Baltimore gets about $5,000 per homicide—because of the difference in their homicide rates.

If we were to create a national inner-city poverty area index of crime, violence, and related data, what would it look like? To answer that question, we must start with the presently available national- and city-level data and then break those data down by neighborhood or Census tract.

Police Data

The primary indicators of crime problems involving children in poverty areas come from police records. They include: homicide victims by age and weapon, arrests for all offenses by age, and total violent crime in high-poverty Census tracts.

The data are generally available only from one police department at a time. Only the homicide data are reported with consistency at the national level by the FBI. The FBI also reports arrest data from differing numbers of reporting jurisdictions annually. It does not report data by poverty Census tracts. Annual *Vital Statistics* reports based on death certificates also include homicide victimization data, but not by Census tract, and not with the consistency when matched with police data. A painstaking effort to assemble those data from one police department at a time could smooth out differences in recording practices and create a national census of crime officially reported in neighborhoods where welfare was or is highly prevalent.

Victimization Survey Data

The National Crime Victimization Survey is conducted twice annually by the Census Bureau for the Bureau of Justice Statistics, U.S. Department of Justice. It estimates both the age and the income characteristics of victims and offenders. In theory, the data in this survey could be analyzed to focus on children in poverty; in practice, the data have never been reported this way. The values of the data are limited for tracking poverty areas, given the national sampling frame. The sampling system prevents estimates from even being drawn at the state level, let alone Census tracts.

Drug Abuse Data

The annual high school survey of drug abuse by the University of Michigan's Institute of Social Research covers a wide range of substance abuse measures, including prevalence and frequency of use by drug type. This survey has the same problem as the victimization survey in that it cannot be used to track rare events in poverty areas.

Other Dysfunctional Behaviors

The National Youth Survey estimates a number of high-risk behaviors, including crime, drug abuse, alcohol use, and sexual activity. Once again, it cannot be used to measure behaviors in specific neighborhoods.

The Data

Some useful things can be learned from the data, but most of the conclusions are already widely reported, raising more questions than they answer.

Homicide

The FBI reports that the number of murders of people under age eighteen dropped from 2,521 in 1994 to 1,598 in 1998, a 24 percent drop. The decline was almost entirely found among murders of juveniles committed with firearms, which went from 1,512 in 1994 to 769 in 1998 (down 51 percent). The numbers, however, reflect a shifting population base, as different numbers of agencies are included in different years, with different populations. In the latest FBI report (on 1998), for example, comparative 1994–1998 data are reported only for about 60 percent of the nation's population. More than half of the police agencies reported no data on who gets arrested for what offense at what age. Similarly, the data on the age of homicide victims omit about 20 percent of the homicides, for which police report no demographic characteristics. Because the FBI's reporting program is voluntary, participation in the program fluctuates from year to year, making data on arrestee and victim characteristics especially difficult to obtain with any consistency.

Nonetheless, a major drop in juvenile homicides has certainly occurred. The key question of how much of that drop has happened in poverty areas will remain unanswered until the necessary data collection system is assembled from the major police agencies.

Violent Crime Arrests

The FBI also reports 1994–1998 reductions in juvenile arrests for other violent crimes among the 60 percent of the population for which data are available in both years. The juvenile arrest reductions, however, are not nearly as large as the homicide arrest reductions. Juvenile robbery arrests are down by 29 percent (compared with 48 percent for murder in those agencies), juvenile rape arrests are only down 8 percent, and aggravated assault arrests are down 13 percent. Given the problems in the compilation of arrest data in each agency, the numbers may contain substantial errors that could change the picture. Arrest data, of course, also are a reflection of police practices, perhaps more so than a reflection of juvenile criminal conduct.

Other Crime by Census Tracts

Although police data are not published by Census tract, most police agencies can supply arrest and offense data identified by the location of the crime or the address of the victims and arrestees. They can do this on a monthly basis, so a timely national discussion of the implications of the data is possible. The data have never been aggregated by Census tract, but they could be, and then linked to many other social indicators for the same tracts. The 500-odd Census tracts where most homicide occurs could be the focus for most welfare reform impact and intervention analyses. Unfortunately, the national survey data do not sample micro-geographically and could not serve the purpose of tracking serious juvenile crime in the places where it is most concentrated.

Implications and Recommendations

The pathway between welfare reform and measures of crime is likely to be at the neighborhood level because welfare affects individual households as well as the surrounding households, and it maybe even has effects at the block level. I live two blocks away from high concentrations of welfare families, and if welfare reform is going to change behavior in that area, which has a high homicide rate, it is likely to do so through group effects in the neighborhood.

The changes in crime are likely to have cascading effects. What contributes to those cascades, we do not know. The only way we are going to find out is to look in the concentrated neighborhoods, because that is where we could measure changes in other things that co-vary with changes in violence and crime. We are not going to pick them up at the aggregate level. We are going to have to find them street by street, or Census tract by Census tract.

Even though cocaine use might be down nationally, it could be up in certain neighborhoods. By going to the emergency rooms as well as the police departments for measures about those neighborhoods, we could be putting those data together. That has never been done. Adele Harrell, a principal research associate at the Urban Institute's Justice Policy Center, explains why this approach is so important:

> Studies of the effects of welfare reform on juvenile delinquency and victimization need to look instead at the effects of reform on delinquency risk factors. Actual changes in juvenile arrest rates may take longer to appear and will be more difficult to attribute to welfare reform. In a study of a program called "Children at Risk," the Urban Institute focused on the development of delinquency and drug use among adolescents in severely distressed neighborhoods, which were defined as having high levels of crime, poverty, unemployment, and social problems of all kinds. As youths move from childhood to adolescence, the importance of the family begins to decrease and the importance of neighborhood and peer groups begins to increase. From the youth risk factor literature, we identified four groups of risk factors—environmental, family, peer group, and individual.
>
> Hypotheses about the effects of welfare reform should focus on its impact on these risk factors, and not hypothesize measurable direct effects on juvenile offending rates. The environmental risk factors consist of low-socioeconomic-status, crowded, crime-ridden, transient neighborhoods. Family risk factors are family history of alcoholism, family involvement in drugs and crime, and poor and inconsistent parenting. Across multiple studies, those factors have been identified as predictors. What do they predict? They predict adolescent involvement in drug use and crime and poor outcomes.[3]

Based on these neighborhood realities and possible sources of data, I would make the following recommendations:

Focus on the hot spots. Tracking the crime and misconduct issues for children in poverty cannot be done cheaply by piggybacking onto existing data systems. Those systems have been impervious to such uses for many years, and minor tweaking will be unable to change that. The goal of reporting "national" rates of crime and arrest interferes with good measurement of problems in hard-to-measure populations. But good measurement remains possible through collaboration with a small number of big cities. Identification of certain high-poverty rural counties could cover an even higher portion of all children in poverty and identify sheriff's agencies that could provide key data.

Support monthly data transfers. Virtually all big-city police agencies would provide monthly data transfers that would be limited to poverty areas and financially supported by a third party. They would be even more eager to help if they were supported with in-kind services, such as equipment and analytic tools. The growth of crime analysis in policing over the past decade has made this possible in places where it was once inconceivable, such as Philadelphia (with 2 percent of the nation's murders). Similar data systems could be established with hospital emergency rooms, under state laws requiring doctors to report gunshot wounds to police. Those requirements often are ignored by urban hospitals because of cost factors, but financial support for such reporting could give both local and national policymakers important information—especially on such issues as repeat shooting victimization, Medicaid enrollment, and the relationship of changing welfare support to changing patterns of shooting victimization. Although there are more hospitals than police agencies, the major trauma centers treat a large portion of all gunshot wounds in most cities; in Philadelphia, for example, only eight hospitals treat 80 percent of the ambulance cases for firearm injury.

Merge crime and misconduct data with other indicators in the same census tracts. An ongoing monitoring system for a small number of poverty areas could be created to merge indicators of welfare rolls, new hiring and unemployment claims, health, educational achievement, student discipline cases, teen pregnancy, and other measures of both possible causes and outcomes. Given the disproportionately large investment that the nation makes in social services for those areas, it is striking that no comparable investment has been made in measuring the correlates of those services. A monthly or quarterly national report focused on the relationship between services and problems would be far more useful than the overly aggregated administrative data to which we are currently limited.

Notes

1. Franklin E. Zimring and Gordon Hawkins, *Crime Is Not the Problem: Lethal Violence in America* (New York: Oxford University Press, 1997).
2. Lawrence W. Sherman, "Gun Carrying and Homicide Prevention," *Journal of the American Medical Association* 283 (2000): 1193–1195.
3. Adele Harrell, comments on "Crime, Juvenile Delinquency, and Dysfunctional Behavior," by Lawrence W. Sherman, in *Family Well-Being after Welfare Reform*, edited by Douglas J. Besharov, 2002, available from: http://www.welfareacademy.org/pubs/familywellbeing/familywellbeing-ch11sherman.pdf, accessed November 18, 2002, *citing* Adele Harrell, Shannon Cavanagh, and Sanjeev Sridharan, *Impact of the Children at Risk Program: Comprehensive Final Report II,* submitted to the National Institute on Drug Abuse (Washington, D.C.: Urban Institute, May 1998). The study was funded in part by the Annie E. Casey Foundation.

References

Harrell, Adele. 2002. Comments on "Crime, Juvenile Delinquency, and Dysfunctional Behavior," by Lawrence W. Sherman. In *Family Well-Being after Welfare Reform.*

Edited by Douglas J. Besharov. Available from: http://www.welfareacademy.org/pubs/ familywellbeing/familywellbeing-ch11sherman.pdf. Accessed November 18, 2002.

Harrell, Adele, Shannon Cavanagh, and Sanjeev Sridharan. 1998. *Impact of the Children at Risk Program: Comprehensive Final Report II*. Submitted to the National Institute on Drug Abuse. Washington, D.C.: Urban Institute. May.

Sherman, Lawrence W. 2000. "Gun Carrying and Homicide Prevention." *Journal of the American Medical Association* 283: 1193–1195.

Zimring, Franklin E., and Gordon Hawkins. 1997. *Crime is Not the Problem: Lethal Violence in America*. New York: Oxford University Press.

13

Drug Use

Peter Reuter

Welfare rolls and illicit drugs are connected in at least two ways. First, drug use can serve as a barrier to exit from welfare by reducing the ability to find and retain a job. Second, welfare recipiency of the mother can affect drug use among the children, through any of a number of mechanisms. Given the focus of this volume, the chapter deals with maternal drug use, which is also the much better studied of the two.

The chapter is primarily about illicit drugs; alcohol gets only passing mention. Although the latter causes users health and behavioral problems comparable to those of cocaine, heroin, etc., the illegality of the other drugs gives them a particular place in social policy. The need to obtain large sums of money for purchase, the risk of imprisonment and loss of privileges, as well as the effect on popular attitudes toward the welfare population increase the importance of understanding the extent of illegal drug use among welfare recipients.

I begin with a description of the available data sets concerning drug use generally and discuss trends in drug problems over the past two decades, since drug use in the welfare population is not isolated from the broader changes. This is followed by a review of recent evidence on the relationship of maternal drug use to welfare participation around the time of the passage of the Personal Responsibility and Work Opportunity Reconciliation Act of 1996 (PRWORA) and of the evidence as to whether the problem has increased with the implementation of the Temporary Assistance for Needy Families program (TANF). The final section speculates about the likely path of drug use in the adult welfare population.

The broad indicators tell a consistent story of declines in the use of cocaine and heroin, not yet compensated for by increases in the use of other dangerous, addictive, and expensive drugs such as methamphetamine. Drug use among welfare recipients has been above that among the general population, but dependence and abuse make a modest contribution to keeping mothers (the vast majority of adult recipients) on welfare. The indicators suggest that drugs may be a fairly marginal factor in outcomes for the welfare population in the foreseeable future; relatively few women will enter TANF or remain in TANF as a result of their drug use.

Data Sets

Four major data sets are familiar to those who study this topic. All of them can be accessed through the website of the Inter-University Consortium on Political and Social Research, which also contains the published reports and tables.[1]

Monitoring the Future (MTF), a survey of high school students' use of alcohol, tobacco, and other drugs, has been operating for twenty-five years. In addition to its cross-section, MTF also has about twenty-five active panels, since 2,500 respondents are recruited out of each year's high school senior class to participate in panels that now extend to age forty. Through this period, the same three principal investigators have been asking the same questions; as a result, they have produced a very stable high-quality data set. However, the survey principals have demonstrated little interest in exploring special topics.

There are no data on the welfare status of the household in MTF, either cross-sectional or longitudinal. The income questions in the annual cross-sections are not very useful because the data are self-reported by students, with limited knowledge of their parents' earnings. The best proxy for the economic status of the household is the education of parents, which is hardly adequate for analysis of welfare status.

The second broad survey is the National Household Survey on Drug Abuse (NHSDA), now carried out every year. The sample size has grown from about 10,000 in 1990 to approximately 70,000 in 1999. The sample is now large enough to produce state-level estimates of drug use for broad age groups; those might allow for analysis of differences among states, but no pre–PRWORA baseline exists at the state level. The NHSDA contains quite detailed information on household and personal income, including welfare and poverty status, and has been used extensively to study drug use and welfare participation prior to 1996. Analysis is complicated by the fact that question wording has changed in important ways across years. Sheldon Danziger, professor at the University of Michigan School of Social Work, and colleagues have begun using the data for analyses of this relationship post-PRWORA.[2]

The third relevant data set is the Drug Abuse Warning Network (DAWN), which provides figures on emergency room admissions causally related to use of specific illegal drugs. Unfortunately, this data set is thin, providing only age, sex, and race of the person, and the data set makes it difficult to do neighborhood-level analyses because of the catchment areas of many emergency rooms. However, some ecological analyses should be possible, relating emergency room admissions to welfare participation by neighborhood.

Of potential interest is a relatively new data set called Arrestee Drug Abuse Monitoring (ADAM), which contains data on biological assays (as well as self-report) for drug use in a sample of arrestees in about thirty-five counties. Eventually, the Department of Justice hopes to have seventy participating counties. ADAM includes a detailed survey instrument about criminal and noncriminal earnings and sociodemographic variables. Though females constitute less than one-quarter of arrestees, the ADAM sample is large enough to provide useful data on earnings, family responsibility, welfare participation, and drug use in the criminally active female population.

These data sets are underutilized. One director of the NHSDA thought that 50 percent of the items had never been looked at. The topic came up when he was queried as to whether it would be possible to add some items; he responded that it would certainly be possible to subtract some. All the data are becoming increasingly accessible for public use but there has been little funding for secondary analyses of some of them.

Changing Patterns

Drug use in the general population rose rapidly in the late 1970s, maybe even into the early 1980s, after which a substantial decline took place. Figure 13.1 illustrates the trend; it reports past-year use of any illicit drug and of marijuana from 1979 to 2001 for the household population over age twelve. Drug-use rates in this population have remained stable since the end of the 1980s. In particular, the epidemic of cocaine use came to an end in the 1980s.

Figure 13.1
Past-Year Drug Use, 1979–2001

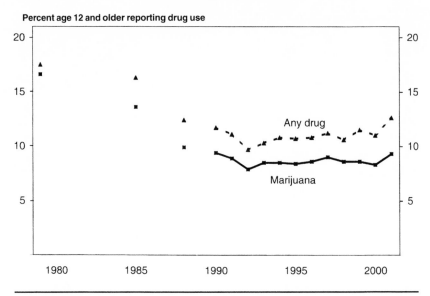

Percent age 12 and older reporting drug use

Source: U.S. Department of Health and Human Services, Substance Abuse and Mental Health Services Agency, *National Household Survey on Drug Abuse* (Rockville, Md.: National Institute on Drug Abuse, various years).

Age-specific patterns turn out to be distinct, however. In particular, the aggregate stability in marijuana use since about 1988 masks sharp increases in adolescent prevalence. As shown in figure 13.2, large increases in marijuana use in the late 1970s among high school seniors were followed by an extended decline over nearly fifteen years. Then in 1992 a dramatic upturn in use began among high school students, effectively doubling the rate by 1998, since when it has plateaued.

How does one account for this recent upturn in adolescent marijuana use? In 1992, candidate Bill Clinton said that he did not inhale, thus making it clear that he had at least tried the drug. But it is difficult to believe that his moral authority, even back then, was so great that it led to a profound change in adolescent behavior. But apart from some throwaway line like that, there are no stories except that attitudes changed, and that merely shifts the mystery: Why did attitudes change?

Could the changes in prevalence be accounted for by movements in poverty rates or other economic indicators? The very smooth long-

Figure 13.2
Daily Marijuana Use and 30-Day Cocaine Prevalence of Use, 1975–2000

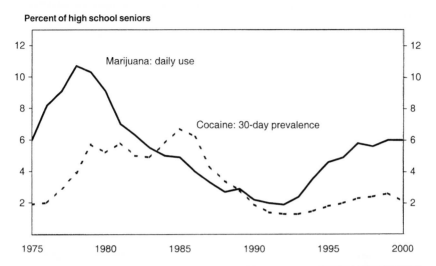

Source: Lloyd Johnson, Patrick M. O'Malley, and Jerald G. Bachman, *Monitoring the Future: National Results on Adolescent Drug Abuse, Overview of Key Findings,* 2001 (Bethesda, Md.: National Institute on Drug Abuse, 2000).

term population patterns through the recession of the early 1990s and the subsequent boom make this implausible. The fact that the recent rise in youthful marijuana use has occurred in almost all Western nations over the same period provides a further basis for skepticism that economic conditions are an important contributor to changes.[3]

If one looks beyond drug use in the general population, which captures mostly occasional use of less dangerous drugs, the indicators tell a different story. For example, according to the latest estimates of the Office of National Drug Control Policy (ONDCP), the number of frequent cocaine users has declined substantially, from about 4 million in 1988 to 2.7 million in 2000.[4] On the other hand, data from the DAWN show dramatic increases in emergency room and medical examiner indicators during approximately the same period (see figure 13.3), apparently inconsistent with the prevalence data. The same is true for heroin: A decline in the number of dependent users and roughly stable prevalence in the household population but sharp and continuing increases in the number of Emergency Department and Medical Examiner mentions of the drug.[5]

Figure 13.3
Cocaine and Heroin Emergency Room Mentions, 1982–2001

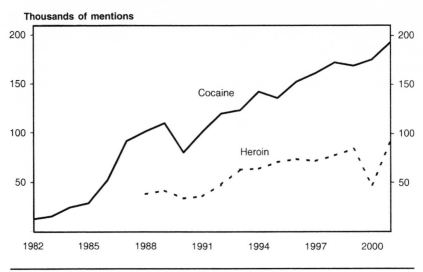

Source: U.S. Department of Health and Human Services, Substance Abuse and Mental Health Services Agency, *National Household Survey on Drug Abuse* (Rockville, Md.: National Institute on Drug Abuse, various years).

The apparent inconsistencies among population surveys, estimates of the number of dependent users, and emergency room data do not necessarily reflect conflict or inaccuracy. Rather, they point to a need to recognize cocaine and heroin use as a career rather than as an event. During the late 1970s and early 1980s, many individuals in their late teens and early twenties experimented with cocaine. Some became regular, but occasional, users; a smaller group went on to become regular and frequent users. By the mid-1980s, the percentage of first-time users had fallen substantially and remained low through the mid-1990s. But the total number of cocaine users did not begin to decline because a modest share (perhaps one-third) of the earlier initiates continued to use the drug. The story with heroin is probably very similar.

As the dangers (medical rather than legal) of cocaine use became more apparent and widely known, regular users who were not dependent and generally using only occasionally became increasingly likely to quit. But as cocaine became cheaper and more addictive in the form of crack, users who had not quit were more likely to become dependent. They were also more likely to be among the urban poor, whose drug use has serious consequences both for themselves and for society. As a result, the association between cocaine use and health problems on the one hand (as reflected in the DAWN's rise) and crime, on the other hand, is now stronger. Jonathan Caulkins, professor at Carnegie Mellon University's Heinz School of Public Policy and Management, and his colleagues are developing models that capture these internal dynamics of epidemics.[6]

More direct indicators illustrate the continued low levels of cocaine and heroin use in youth populations. Figure 13.4 is perhaps the most relevant to the discussion here. It shows drug use among juvenile arrestees (a very high-risk population for drug abuse) in the District of Columbia.[7] It is striking that in the late 1980s, criminally active adolescents still had moderately high rates of use of serious drugs, including PCP—a nasty hallucinogen—and cocaine. Twenty-five to 30 percent had used those drugs shortly before being arrested. However, use of these drugs has almost ceased. There is a spike for PCP in 1995, but, otherwise, today there is little use of illicit drugs other than marijuana.

Arrest is not a rare event for young urban minority males; perhaps as many as a third experience arrest before age eighteen. Ado-

Figure 13.4
Drug Use among D.C. Juvenile Arrestees, 1987–2000

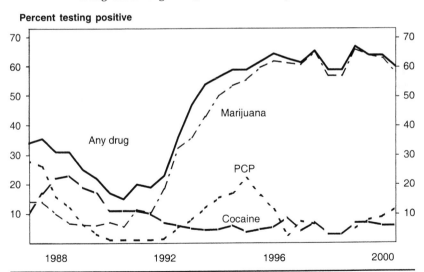

Percent testing positive

Source: District of Columbia Pretrial Services Agency, *Drug Test Statistics for DC Arrestees* (Washington, D.C.: DC Pretrial Services Agency, monthly).

lescent marijuana use may lead to later cocaine, heroin, or methamphetamine use, but little evidence so far points to an incipient epidemic of any of these drugs, notwithstanding media reports. Andrew Golub and Bruce Johnson, researchers at the National Development and Research Institutes, have shown that the probability of
transitioning from marijuana use to cocaine, heroin, or methamphetamine use by age twenty-six has declined substantially in the past
decade, from 39 percent (for the 1962–1963 birth cohort) to 24 percent (1970–1971 birth cohort).[8]

I have referred so far almost exclusively to cocaine, heroin, and
marijuana. Synthetic drugs are often mentioned now. However, only
methamphetamine shows signs of becoming a problem comparable
to cocaine or heroin in terms of the numbers affected, the severity of
the problems, and the duration of the addiction. Even methamphetamine may have peaked as a problem, at least according to the latest
estimates from ONDCP.

Drugs and Welfare Receipt

Pre-PRWORA

At the time of enactment of PRWORA, many welfare professionals believed that for a substantial fraction of clients, substance abuse
and dependence were major contributing factors to their welfare status. Illicit drugs were seen as comparable to, if not more important
than, alcohol. In the pre–PRWORA era, more emphasis was given
the contribution of substance abuse to welfare entry. Post–PRWORA,
the emphasis has been on its role as a barrier to exit through employment.

The National Center on Addiction and Substance Abuse (CASA),
headed by Joseph Califano, former secretary of Health, Education,
and Welfare, published a short report in 1994[9] apparently based on
the 1991 NHSDA, asserting that "[m]others receiving AFDC are three
times more likely to abuse or be addicted to alcohol and drugs than
mothers not receiving AFDC (27 percent compared to 9 percent)."[10]
It concluded that "[a]t least 1.3 million adult welfare recipients currently abuse or are addicted to drugs and alcohol."[11] With fewer
than 5 million adult welfare recipients, this was an alarming number.

The CASA estimate seemed far too high as an estimate of the
prevalence of a serious problem in this population, given that the
vast majority of the drug users in the NHSDA consumed only mari-

juana. Moreover, the fraction of non–AFDC recipients said to be abusers was also higher than found in other surveys. Nonetheless, the estimate received wide circulation even five years later. For example, a 1999 National Governors Association report continued to cite the CASA study, among others. Califano continued to make similar claims in 2002.[12]

In 1996, an analysis of the 1992 National Longitudinal Alcohol Epidemiologic Survey (NLAES)[13] concluded that only 3.6 percent of AFDC recipients over eighteen were drug dependent or drug abusers and that 7.6 percent were alcohol dependent.[14] Moreover the authors concluded that rates for welfare recipients were "comparable to rates of heavy drinking (14.8 percent), drug use (5.1 percent), alcohol abuse and/or dependence (7.5 percent), and drug abuse and/or dependence (1.5 percent) among the subpopulation of the United States not receiving welfare benefits."[15]

Rukmalie Jayakody, an assistant professor in Pennsylvania State University's Department of Human Development and Family Studies, Sheldon Danziger, and Harold Pollack, a professor at the University of Michigan's School of Public Health, provide a careful analysis of the 1994 and 1995 NHSDAs.[16] They found that, for illegal substances other than marijuana, prevalence among single mothers receiving welfare was higher than among those not on welfare, but that the figures were low: 10 percent and 7 percent. Similar findings held for alcohol dependence: 9 percent in the welfare population and 5 percent for single mothers not on welfare. Having used crack increased the risk of being a welfare recipient substantially, but substance use (including alcohol) was a less important risk factor than either being a high school drop out or having a psychiatric disorder. Adjusting for a number of demographic and family characteristics, a woman on welfare was almost twice as likely as one not on welfare to be classified as a problem drug user, still leaving the proportion quite low.[17]

Dean Gerstein, senior vice president for the National Opinion Research Center's Substance Abuse, Mental Health, and Criminal Justice Department, and his colleagues analyzed the combined 1994–1996 NHSDA files. They again found that AFDC recipients had higher substance abuse rates than the overall working age population (eighteen to sixty-four) and that the differences were modest: 8 percent of AFDC recipients were classified as substance dependent, compared with 5 percent in the broader population.[18]

The principal explanation for the differences between the later studies and that from CASA appears to lie in the definitions. The CASA report never explicitly described how it classified an individual as a drug abuser or drug dependent, but it appears that using an illicit drug at least once per month was sufficient for that diagnosis. A monthly user of marijuana is certainly flouting the law on a regular basis, but there is little basis for asserting that this, if accompanied by no other drug use, is a serious behavioral problem, with important adverse consequences either for the mother or family. Marijuana dependence is a real phenomenon. Approximately 10 percent of users are at some stage dependent on the drug. But most past-month users are not daily users. In contrast, the other research groups used a diagnostic instrument that was imbedded in the NLAES and the NHSDA interview schedule and that focused on behavioral problems related to drug or alcohol use.

That is not to say that rates as low as those reported by the NLAES or the NHSDA should be accepted at face value. These nationwide household surveys are known to underestimate the prevalence of drug abuse and dependence. For example, in recent years the NHSDA has produced estimates of the total number of frequent cocaine users of about 700,000, yet other estimates, including the results of urinalysis of arrestees, generate estimates more than four times that figure.[19] Heroin dependence, estimated to affect about 900,000 persons, cannot be estimated from the NHSDA at all, because of the instability of the lifestyles of heroin addicts. Can one rely solely on these general population surveys for estimates of the extent of drug use and abuse among AFDC recipients?

There were always some discrepant findings, particularly studies of welfare clients in specific programs. For example, Carol Sisco and Carol Pearson, in a study of Maryland AFDC recipients enrolled in a demonstration welfare to work transition program, gave some standardized tests for substance abuse.[20] They found a prevalence rate of 16 to 21 percent for alcoholism and drug abuse and an additional 21 to 31 percent with social problems related to alcohol and drug abuse. A research group in Berkeley has been conducting research on a variety of public program settings in northern California. Constance Weisner, professor in the University of California at San Francisco, Department of Psychiatry, and Laura Schmidt, a scientist at the Alcohol Research Group, found that 21 percent of welfare clients were multiple drug users, on a past year basis.[21]

Post–PRWORA

Since the implementation of TANF, the focus has been on whether drug use has become an important barrier to exit, given the new emphasis on finding employment. Not only might illicit drug use lead to ineffective job search, but with drug testing of job applicants very common, many might be rejected simply for detected drug use. In particular, many expected that an increasing share of the diminishing welfare client population would be drug dependent.

There has been a continuing flow of estimates of the prevalence of substance abuse in the client welfare population in specific counties and states. Typical of the findings in the literature are those recently reported by Jeffrey Merrill, professor at the University of Medicine and Dentistry of New Jersey's Robert Wood Johnson Medical School, and his colleagues, who interviewed a sample of 740 Florida WAGES clients. Nineteen percent of the WAGES respondents admitted to drinking to intoxication at some point in their life (12 percent within the past thirty days). Five percent of the women admitted to using an illegal drug in the past month, while 21 percent said that they had used a drug at least once in their lifetime. Marijuana was the most common drug (3 percent in the past month and 17 percent during their lifetime), followed by cocaine (1 percent and 8 percent, respectively). Only six women (less than 1 percent) admitted to ever having used heroin. Those who had used illicit drugs during their lifetime averaged almost 4.5 years of use.[22]

The authors note that these figures are much lower than those generated by the earlier CASA study also led by Merrill and suggest that the explanation may lie in the deterrent effect of TANF, as compared with AFDC, for women with substance abuse problems. The conjecture is that fewer poor mothers with substance abuse problems are applying for welfare in the new system. Data on entrants are still rare so that conjecture cannot be readily assessed.[23]

Data from five other states[24] are roughly consistent with this. For example, New York state officials reported that use of a modified CAGE instrument led to between 2 and 10 percent positive screens for substance abuse. Sandra Danziger, an associate professor at the University of Michigan School of Social Work, and her colleagues found in a self-report survey of clients in a Michigan county that only 3.3 percent of a sample of 753 TANF recipients were drug dependent and 2.7 percent were alcohol dependent. In New Jersey, a study found only 5 percent who had experienced an episode of binge drinking in the prior thirty days; the figure for frequent use of cocaine, heroin, or amphetamines was very much higher.[25] Sally Satel, the W. H. Brady, Jr., Fellow at the American Enterprise Institute, reports that in New York City a screener for substance abuse detects only 3 to 4 percent as potential problems. Numerous states have reported detecting very few clients with substance abuse problems, frequently less than 2 percent.[26]

A few analyses of the NHSDA post-TANF have appeared. Harold Pollack and his colleagues analyzed the 1998 NHSDA and found less than 5 percent satisfying criteria for drug dependence.[27] Preliminary analyses of the 2000 NHSDA data by Pollack indicate similar figures.[28]

As before PRWORA, there are a few discrepant findings, suggesting that the problem is a serious one. For example, Oregon, with one of the most sophisticated detection systems, has found 19 percent of clients with drug or alcohol problems. Studies of Alameda County, California, have found comparable rates there.[29]

The Future

Are figures as low as 5 percent for drug abuse plausible for a population with as many problems as welfare clients? There is one fragmentary indicator with much more credibility suggesting that drug use rates among welfare recipients is low. For a few months, until an American Civil Liberties Union (ACLU) suit ended it, one county in Michigan tested every welfare recipient for recent drug use. Of 258 recipients tested, only 21 tested positive for any drug; only three of these tested positive for a drug other than marijuana. This is one county, and not one with a major city, but it at least provides some sense of credibility.

Views in the field have changed slowly. The National Governors Association in 1999 reported views and impressions from four states (Kansas, New Jersey, North Carolina, and Oregon); none provided a figure lower than 20 percent. Also cited was a CASAWORKS program statement that "63 percent of state welfare administrators estimate that between 20 percent and 40 percent of TANF recipients need substance abuse treatment."[30]

I think that the weight of the very imperfect evidence is that abuse of illicit drugs affects only a modest share of welfare clients, even after the sharp declines post-PRWORA. That does not imply that it should receive no attention. Harold Pollack and Peter Reuter argue that welfare participation provides an important venue for identifying and helping poor mothers with drug problems.[31] Although, the population of drug-dependent poor women, graphically described in Leon Dash's *Rosa Lee* is aging, their children are at higher risk of also becoming drug dependent.[32]

What is true in 2002 need not be true five years from now. I believe that it depends primarily on changes in drug use in the general population. Although drug abuse is associated with poverty, the direction of causality is unclear and probably bidirectional. Many other factors, such as price, enforcement, prevention, and social attitudes, also influence drug use—as evidenced by the wide fluctuations in prevalence rates over short periods of time.

There has been an aging of the population of dependent drug users, certainly those dependent on expensive drugs. This aging has led to low drug-use initiation rates, particularly in communities that are rich in untreated addicts, who serve as a form of inoculation. Female use of drugs other than marijuana has always been substantially less than that of males, typically only 50 to 60 percent as high. Even the much discussed methamphetamine epidemic still remains primarily a western and mid-western phenomenon; it is much smaller in scale than those for cocaine and heroin. There might be a new drug that leads to large numbers of women becoming addicted and dysfunctional, but it is striking that, despite all the developments in neurochemistry, synthetic illegal drugs have made only modest advances.

I do not mean that a new epidemic of use of expensive, dependency-creating, illegal drugs will never occur, only that it is not likely over the next few years. The most likely near future is a client population in which drug abuse and dependence will be of declining importance.

Notes

1.   See http://www.icpsr.umich.edu/SAMHDA/.
2.   See Rukmalie Jayakody, Sheldon Danziger, and Harold Pollack, "Welfare Reform, Substance Use, and Mental Health," *Journal of Health Politics, Policy, and Law* 25 (2000): 623–651.
3.   Robert MacCoun and Peter Reuter, "Evaluating Alternative Cannabis Policies," *British Journal of Psychiatry* 178 (2001): 123–128.
4.   William Rhodes, Mary Layne, Anne-Marie Bruen, Patrick Johnston, and Lisa Becchetti, *What America's Users Spend on Illicit Drugs, 1988–2000* (Washington, D.C.: Office of National Drug Control Policy, December 2001).

5.   Official estimates of the number of past-week heroin users in a specific year have fluctuated dramatically. Estimates made in 2000 gave a figure for 1988 of 923,000. The 2000 series showed a fall of about 30 percent to 630,000 in 1992 and then a rise to the 1988 level by 1997. An updated series, published by the Office of National Drug Control Policy in 2002 gave a 1988 estimate of 1.15 million, again falling by about 30 percent to 1992, but then continuing to fall, at a slower pace, for the next seven years.

6.   See Doris Behrens, Jonathan Caulkins, Gernot Tragler, Josef Haunschmied, and Gustav Feichtinger, "A Dynamic Model of Drug Initiation: Implications for Treatment and Control," *Mathematical Biosciences* 159 (1999): 1–20.

7.   The District of Columbia has been collecting such data for much longer than any other jurisdiction.

8.   Andrew Golub and Bruce Johnson, "Variation in Youthful Risks of Progression From Alcohol and Tobacco to Marijuana and to Hard Drugs Across Generations," *American Journal of Public Health* 91 (2) (2001): 225–232.

9.   Jeffrey Merrill, Kimberly S. Fox, Jennifer C. Friedman, and Gerald E. Pulver, *Substance Abuse and Women on Welfare* (New York: National Center on Addiction and Substance Abuse, 1994).

10.   Ibid., p. 3. AFDC, or Aid to Families with Dependent Children, was replaced by Temporary Assistance for Needy Families (TANF).

11.   Ibid., p. 7.

12.   Joseph Califano, "To Reform Welfare, Treat Drug Abuse," *Washington Post*, September 18, 2002.

13.   The National Longitudinal Alcohol Epidemiologic Survey was very similar to the National Household Survey on Drug Abuse in scope and sample size at that time.

14.   Bridget F. Grant and Deborah A. Dawson, "Alcohol and Drug Use, Abuse and Dependence among Welfare Recipients," *American Journal of Public Health* 86 (1996): 1450–1454.

15.   Grant and Dawson, 1996, p. 1453.

16.   Jayakody et al., 2000.

17.   Ibid.

18.   Dean Gerstein, Janet Greenblatt, Tara N. Townsend, Julie D. Lane, Carolyn S. Dewa, Angela M. Brittingham, and Michael Pergamit, *Substance Use and Mental Health Characteristics by Employment Status* (Rockville, Md.: Substance Abuse and Mental Health Services Administration, June 1999).

19.   Rhodes et al., 2001.

20.   Carol B. Sisco and Carol L. Pearson, "Prevalence of Alcoholism and Drug Abuse among Female AFDC Recipients," *Health and Social Work* 19 (1994): 75–77.

21.   Oddly enough, when the same researchers followed up these clients in 1995, they found that substance abuse was "not a significant determinant of long welfare stays, repeat welfare, or the total time a person remained on welfare during the six year period." Laura Schmidt, Constance Weisner, and James A. Wiley, "Substance Abuse and the Course of Welfare Dependency," *American Journal of Public Health* 88 (1998): 11. It seems unlikely that on the one hand substance abuse could be a major risk for welfare enrollment but not for length of stay.

22.   Jeffrey C. Merrill, Sara Ring-Kurtz, Delia Olufokunbi, Sherri Aversa, and Jennifer Sherker, *Women on Welfare: A Study of the Florida WAGES Population* (Philadelphia: University of Pennsylvania School of Medicine, Treatment Research Institute, 1999).

23.   Merrill et al., 1994.

24.   The five states are California (Alameda County), Michigan, New Jersey, New York, and Pennsylvania. For New York and Pennsylvania, there was no published study, just an oral report by a senior official.

25. Sandra K. Danziger, Mary Corcoran, Sheldon Danziger, Colleen Heflin, Ariel Kalil, Judith Levine, Daniel Rosen, Kristin Seefeldt, Kristine Siefert, and Richard Tolman, "Barriers to the Employment of Welfare Recipients," in *The Impact of Tight Labor Markets on Black Employment*, edited by R. Cherry and W. Rodgers (New York: Russell Sage Foundation, 2000), pp. 239–269.

26. Sally Satel, "Welfare-to-Work for People with Drug and Alcohol Problems: A Review of New York City's Human Resources Administration Program," unpublished manuscript, American Enterprise Institute, Washington, D.C., 2002.

27. Harold Pollack, Sheldon Danziger, Kristin Seefeldt, and Rukmalie Jayakody, "Substance Use Among Welfare Recipients: Trends and Policy Responses," *Social Service Review* 72 (2) (2002): 256.

28. Harold Pollack and Peter Reuter, "Welfare Enrollment and Substance Abuse Treatment," unpublished manuscript, School of Public Health, University of Michigan, Ann Arbor, Mich., 2002.

29. Rex S. Green, Lynn Fujiwara, Jean Norris, Shanthi Kappagoda, Anne Driscoll, and Richard Speiglman, *Alameda County CalWORKs Needs Assessment: Barriers to Working and Summaries of Baseline Status, Report no. 2* (Berkeley, Calif.: Public Health Institute, March 2000).

30. Merrill et al., 1994, p. 5.

31. Pollack and Reuter, 2002.

32. Leon Dash, *Rosa Lee: A Mother and Her Family in Urban America* (New York: Basic Books, 1996).

References

Behrens, Doris, Jonathan Caulkins, Gernot Tragler, Josef Haunschmied, and Gustav Feichtinger. 1999. "A Dynamic Model of Drug Initiation: Implications for Treatment and Control." *Mathematical Biosciences* 159: 1–20.

Califano, Joseph. 2002. "To Reform Welfare, Treat Drug Abuse." *Washington Post.* September 18.

Danziger, Sandra K., Mary Corcoran, Sheldon Danziger, Colleen Heflin, Ariel Kalil, Judith Levine, Daniel Rosen, Kristin Seefeldt, Kristine Siefert, and Richard Tolman. 2000. "Barriers to the Employment of Welfare Recipients." In *The Impact of Tight Labor Markets on Black Employment.* Edited by R. Cherry and W. Rodgers. New York: Russell Sage Foundation: 239–269.

Dash, Leon. 1996. *Rosa Lee: A Mother and Her Family in Urban America.* New York: Basic Books.

Delva, J.,Y. Neumark, C. Furr, and J. Anthony. 2000. "Drug Use among Welfare Recipients in the United States." *American Journal of Alcohol and Drug Abuse* 26 (2): 335–342.

District of Columbia Pretrial Services Agency. Monthly. *Drug Test Statistics for D.C. Arrestees.* Washington, D.C.: D.C. Pretrial Services Agency.

Gerstein, Dean, Janet Greenblatt, Tara N. Townsend, Julie D. Lane, Carolyn S. Dewa, Angela M. Brittingham, and Michael Pergamit. 1999. *Substance Use and Mental Health Characteristics by Employment Status.* Rockville, Md.: Substance Abuse and Mental Health Services Administration. June.

Golub, Andrew, and Bruce Johnson. 2001. "Variation in Youthful Risks of Progression From Alcohol and Tobacco to Marijuana and to Hard Drugs Across Generations." *American Journal of Public Health* 91(2): 225–232.

Grant, Bridget F., and Deborah A. Dawson. 1996. "Alcohol and Drug Use, Abuse and Dependence among Welfare Recipients." *American Journal of Public Health* 86: 1450–1454.

Green, Rex S., Lynn Fujiwara, Jean Norris, Shanthi Kappagoda, Anne Driscoll, and Richard Speiglman. 2000. *Alameda County CalWORKs Needs Assessment: Barriers to Working and Summaries of Baseline Status, Report no. 2*. Berkeley, Calif.: Public Health Institute. March.

Jayakody, Rukmalie, Sheldon Danziger, and Harold Pollack. 2000. "Welfare Reform, Substance Use, and Mental Health." *Journal of Health Politics, Policy, and Law* 25: 623–651.

Johnson, Lloyd, Patrick M. O'Malley, and Jerald G. Bachman. 2000. *Monitoring the Future: National Results on Adolescnet Drug Abuse, Overview of Key Findings*. Bethesda, Md.: National Institute on Drug Abuse.

MacCoun, Robert, and Peter Reuter. 2001. "Evaluating Alternative Cannabis Policies." *British Journal of Psychiatry* 178: 123-128.

Merrill, Jeffrey, Kimberly S. Fox, Jennifer C. Friedman, and Gerald E. Pulver. 1994. *Substance Abuse and Women on Welfare*. New York: National Center on Addiction and Substance Abuse.

Merrill, Jeffrey, Sara Ring-Kurtz, Delia Olufokunbi, Sherri Aversa, and Jennifer Sherker. 1999. *Women on Welfare: A Study of the Florida WAGES Population*. Philadelphia: University of Pennsylvania School of Medicine, Treatment Research Institute.

Pollack, Harold, Sheldon Danziger, Kristin Seefeldt, and Rukmalie Jayakody. 2002. "Substance Use Among Welfare Recipients: Trends and Policy Responses." *Social Service Review* 76 (2) (June): 256.

Pollack, Harold, and Peter Reuter. 2002. "Welfare Enrollment and Substance Abuse Treatment." Unpublished manuscript. School of Public Health, University of Michigan. Ann Arbor, Mich.

Rhodes, William, Mary Layne, Anne-Marie Bruen, Patrick Johnston, and Lisa Becchetti. 2001. *What America's Users Spend on Illicit Drugs, 1988–2000*. Washington, D.C.: Office of National Drug Control Policy. December.

Satel, Sally. 2002. "Welfare-to-Work for People with Drug and Alcohol Problems: A Review of New York City's Human Resources Administration Program." Unpublished manuscript. American Enterprise Institute. Washington, D.C.

Schmidt, Laura, Constance Weisner, and James A. Wiley. 1998. "Substance Abuse and the Course of Welfare Dependency." *American Journal of Public Health* 88: 11.

Sisco, Carol B., and Carol L. Pearson. 1994. "Prevalence of Alcoholism and Drug Abuse among Female AFDC Recipients." *Health and Social Work* 19: 75–77.

Substance Abuse and Mental Health Services Agency. Annual. *Drug Abuse Warning Network Emergency Department and Medical Examiner Data*. Rockville, Md.: National Institute on Drug Abuse.

———. Annual. *National Household Survey on Drug Abuse*. Rockville, Md.: National Institute on Drug Abuse.

14

Mothers' Work and Child Care

Julia B. Isaacs

This chapter discusses the availability of data to address policy questions about child care for low-income families. Specifically, I attempt to answer the question: How can existing surveys, studies, and other data be used to measure the availability and quality of child care for low-income families? I discuss several sources of data, briefly describing what each source tells us and outlining its strengths and weaknesses. Included in this review are national population-based survey data; federal and state administrative data; state survey data, specifically from studies of families leaving welfare ("leaver studies"); and, very briefly, special child care studies.

National Surveys

It is common for child care policymakers to complain about the lack of good data on child care. As bad as the situation may be, it was worse before the arrival of the Survey of Income and Program Participation (SIPP), which has added considerably to our knowledge of child care. Much of what we know about child care utilization patterns and costs comes from SIPP data. The SIPP will continue to be an important source of information on child care in the future, along with the related Survey of Program Dynamics, which follows a subset of SIPP families for a longer period to study welfare reform longitudinally and which includes questions about child care arrangements.

Another important national population-based survey for the study of child care is the Current Population Survey (CPS). The CPS does not actually provide much direct information about child care arrangements. It does, however, provide considerable information on the labor force participation and income of parents. Those data are important for answering questions about the number of children with working parents and the income of those parents, providing some indication of the potential need for child care and child care subsidies.

A third useful national survey, the National Household Education Survey (NHES), may not be as well-known among welfare reform researchers. Conducted annually by the Department of Education, the NHES includes an Early Childhood Program Participation component in certain years. For example, the 2001 NHES provides useful information about child care arrangements for children under age six and not in kindergarten, including details about the language of the provider, care for sick children, and the distance between the care and the home and job—data not found in the other national surveys. A separate component of the 2001 NHES provides similar information on before- and after-school arrangements for children in kindergarten through eighth grade. One drawback of the NHES for studying child care for low-income children is that the NHES does not collect detailed income information. The survey does, however, try to collect enough income information to determine who is above or below the poverty line.

Other national surveys with relevance for child care policymakers include the National Survey of America's Families (NSAF) and the child development supplement to the Panel Study of Income Dynamics (PSID). Both studies collected data on child care arrangements in 1997, and the NSAF also collected data on arrangements in 1999 and 2002. Finally, I should at least mention the 1990 National Child Care Survey and the related Profile of Child Care Settings as good household and provider surveys, respectively, although the data from those surveys are now quite dated.

To answer the question of what the national survey data tell us, I will briefly highlight three sets of findings: average child care costs, particularly for low-income families; the importance of both informal and formal child care arrangements; and estimates of the need for child care and child care subsidies.

In terms of child care costs, it turns out that child care expenses often are the second- or third-largest item in the budget of a low-income working family. In 1997, for example, child care expenses averaged 20 percent of family income, or $224 per month, for poor working families who paid for child care, according to SIPP data.[1] Only 30 percent of poor families with a child under fifteen and a working mother paid for child care, however. Comparable data for families with a working mother and family income at or above the poverty line indicate that 45 percent paid for care, and that expenses averaged 7 percent of family income ($331 per month) among those who paid for care.

Some families that do not pay for care are benefitting from child care subsidies. Another way in which poor families save on child care costs is by using more informal arrangements—more relative care, less care in centers—than other families. Some evidence of this pattern can be seen in data from the 1999 NSAF, which indicate that 23 percent of child care arrangements for low-income preschool children were in centers, compared with 30 percent of such arrangements for preschool children living in families with incomes above 200 percent of the poverty line. Parents and relatives provided 62 percent of child care arrangements for low-income preschoolers, but only 50 percent of arrangements for children with incomes at or above 200 percent of the poverty line.[2]

Finally, my own work at the U.S. Department of Health and Human Services (HHS) has involved using national surveys to inform policymakers about the number of children eligible for child care assistance under the Child Care and Development Fund (CCDF). Specifically, the estimates are based on data from the CPS, processed through the Urban Institute's TRIM3 micro-simulation model.[3] Although the estimates vary slightly from year to year, depending on population and employment trends, approximately 30 to 32 million children live in families with either a single parent working or both parents working, at all income levels. Roughly 9 to 10 million of those children live in families that are below the eligibility limit for child care subsidies, based on current state policies. The estimate of eligible children could rise to 15 to 16 million if all states raised their eligibility limits to 85 percent of state median income, the maximum allowed under federal law. However, the 9 to 10 million estimate is a better estimate of current eligibility, since it reflects the actual eligibility limits set by the states within the broad parameters of the federal legislation.

An obvious strength of the national population-based surveys is that they provide nationally representative data. An associated weakness, however, is their inability to provide information that is reliable at the state or local level. HHS has been able to provide state-by-state estimates in some analyses, but only by combining three years of CPS data; even then, some state-level data were based on small sample sizes. Another strength of the national data sets is that they often are quite rich in data, providing information about child care arrangements, family income, participation in welfare, and so forth. Some of the surveys, however, have better data on child care arrangements, and some have better information on who is poor, who is on welfare, and how long they have been on welfare. It is hard to find a survey that collects good data on both domains; only the SIPP and the NSAF do so. A final frustration with national survey data is that time lags often occur in the processing of the data and its release for analysis. The fact that the SIPP data on costs are from 1997—and even that did not come out until 2002—is a testament to this particular problem.

Federal and State Administrative Data

Primary among other sources of data are the data on child care subsidies provided through the CCDF. Under the federal child care legislation, states are required to submit various data to the federal government. Using ACF Form 800, states report aggregate numbers of children getting subsidies as well as some characteristics of those subsidies, such as the type of provider and age of the child. Using Form 801, states submit disaggregated, or micro-level, data on children in care, providing more detailed information that includes ages of children, family income level, whether the family receives Temporary Assistance for Needy Families (TANF), and so forth. In addition, each state has its own administrative data system, which often has an even richer set of information than what is sent to Washington, D.C.

The administrative data are useful for telling us about the children who are receiving federally subsidized child care under the CCDF. The federal subsidy data, for example, tell us that an average of 1.75 million children received subsidies in an average month in 2000. Combining this fact with the estimate of 9 to 10 million children who are eligible in an average month, it is possible to calculate a percentage of eligible children served under the CCDF. But, the federal administrative data do not cover the additional children who receive child care under TANF or the Social Services Block Grant (SSBG). Adding these children to the CCDF caseload, HHS recently estimated that 2.45 million children received assistance from the CCDF, the SSBG, or TANF, representing 28 percent of an eligible population of slightly over 9 million.[4]

In addition to caseload counts, the federal administrative data provide more detailed information, such as the types of child care arrangements used, as shown in figure 14.1. Specifically, figure 14.1 shows the types of arrangements that are subsidized through CCDF funding in the United States, Texas, and Michigan.

Texas and Michigan were chosen to illustrate quite different patterns of child care use in two large states. In Texas, over three-fourths (76 percent) of the children are served in center-based arrangements (as figure 14.1 shows). In contrast, in Michigan, only 16 percent of the children are served in centers, and relative care is the arrangement for half (50 percent) of the children subsidized through CCDF funds. Across the nation as a whole, the majority (58 percent) of children served through CCDF funding are in center-based arrangements, but a significant portion (13 percent) are cared for by relatives. The remaining subsidized arrangements include family day care homes (22 percent), group homes (3 percent), and in-home care by non-relatives (4 percent).

The figure distinguishes between settings that are licensed or regulated and those settings that are legally operating. Although most centers are licensed or regulated and most relative care is not, some states provide subsidies to license-exempt centers, such as centers in churches and schools in certain states. And while the majority of family day care homes are licensed or regulated, a significant proportion are exempt from licensing.

Administrative data have the advantage of providing information on the entire population of children receiving subsidies, not just a sample. This characteristic allows results to be reported by state or locality, without encountering the sample size problems of survey data. Another strength is that administrative data are collected longitudinally. A weakness of the federal administrative data sets, however, is that they are limited to subsidies funded under the CCDF. Very little is known about children receiving TANF–funded child care assistance or other forms of subsidized care. Another limitation of administrative data is that they only provide information about the child care arrangements that are subsidized, telling us nothing about the vast number of unsubsidized child care arrangements. Furthermore, administrative data are not very rich in detail. We know whether children are in a center or in a family day care home, but we do not know anything about the quality of the settings. In addition, administrative data are sometimes incomplete or of uncertain reli-

Figure 14.1
Percent of Children Served in All Types of Care, FY 2000

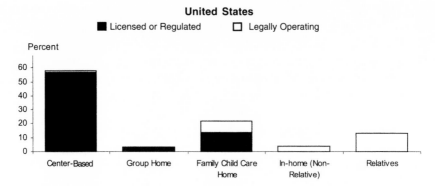

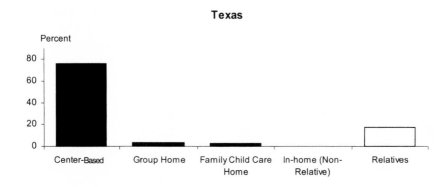

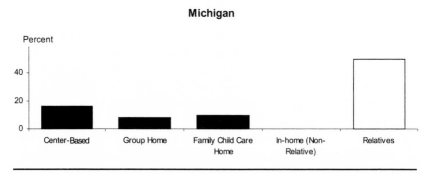

Source: U.S. Department of Health and Human Services, Child Care Bureau, "FFY 2000 CCDF Data Tables and Charts," available from: http://www.acf.dhhs.gov/programs/ccb/research/00acf800/cover.htm, accessed November 21, 2002.

ability, particularly with regard to data elements that are not critical to the administration of the program. Finally, both the states and the federal government are still working on implementing the new data-reporting requirements enacted as part of the 1996 legislation. As is common with new data systems, the first few years of data may be less complete, less reliable, and reported on a less timely basis than should be the case once the system is up and running.

State Surveys of Families Leaving Welfare

A third data source is the information on child care arrangements for families leaving welfare. The Office of the Assistant Secretary for Planning and Evaluation (ASPE) at HHS awarded $2.9 million in grants to fourteen states and large counties in September 1998, to study families leaving welfare. Some additional "leavers" studies were funded a year later. Although each state study was slightly different, the families were generally surveyed about six to twelve months after leaving welfare and were asked a variety of questions about their employment status, household income, use of government programs, child care arrangements, experiences of material hardship, and general child and family well-being. In addition, the states tracked welfare "leavers" through various administrative data sets, including child care subsidy data sets in a few states.

According to an early review of the ASPE-funded leaver-study questionnaires, all studies asked about child care arrangements, including the type of child care provider, if any, used after the family left welfare.[5] However, findings from only four to eight studies were included in the child care section of the final synthesis report on the ASPE-funded leavers studies, because of challenges in comparing findings across states.[6] Data from these states suggest that care by relatives and siblings of the children was the most common type of care, used by 41 to 65 percent of employed leavers with non-parental arrangements. An additional 6 to 13 percent of leavers' children were cared for by friends or neighbors. The percentage of employed leavers families using some kind of center-based care ranged from 8 to 36 percent. These percentages are among families using non-parental care. A significant number of women leaving welfare, particularly those with school-aged children, did not use any non-parental child care arrangements.

Only about half (38 to 61 percent) of employed leavers with child care arrangements reported paying for care, according to the synthesis report on ASPE–funded leavers. A smaller proportion of employed leavers, generally 15 to 25 percent, but ranging across states from 5 to 43 percent, used government subsidies.[7] This percentage rate is consistent with findings from a 1999 review of the earlier state-funded leavers studies, which reported that roughly 10 to 35 percent of leavers who have earnings were using the subsidies.[8] It is lower, however, than some anticipated for a population of low-income working mothers with high priority for access to subsidies in most states. Various explanations have been hypothesized for the lower than expected utilization rate, including low interest in subsidies given the heavy use of unpaid care, problems posed by applications procedures and administrative paperwork, and lack of knowledge of subsidy eligibility.

The state leavers studies add an interesting complement to the data available from national surveys and administrative data. The studies address child care issues for a low-income population of strong policy interest, and they were conducted on a rapid time frame. It is important to recognize their limitations, however. Most surveys of families leaving welfare spend only a few minutes on child care, so they can ask only a few simple questions. Moreover, it is difficult to compare findings across states because of both methodological and policy differences. Finally, some leaver-study surveys suffer from a low response rate because of the difficulty of locating families for the follow-up surveys.

Special Studies

The national and state survey data discussed thus far have been general surveys that include child care questions as only one of many topics. A number of child care studies that focus entirely on child care bear mentioning, particularly the Child Care Bureau's Child Care Research Partnerships, various early child development studies, and the National Study of Low-Income Child Care.

The Child Care Bureau is funding several child care research partnerships, which are multiyear efforts to pull together various partnerships of universities and states to study child care issues. The partnerships are using a variety of data sources. Several are using state administrative data sets, often linked to TANF or wage record administrative data. In Chicago, however, the researchers are collecting data directly from in-person visits to child care providers in local neighborhoods. The research partnerships also are addressing a diverse set of policy-relevant questions. One study is looking at how TANF recipients choose care. Another is looking at subsidy data over time to determine the length of time for which people get subsidies and continuity of care, which is an important element of quality. Another is conducting research on parental measures of quality and examining the correlation between parental perceptions of quality and observations by researchers.

The Child Care Research Partnerships have much to offer to the study of child care among low-income families. They involve multiple projects across multiple states and are using a variety of rich data sets to address a number of policy-relevant research questions. The partnerships already have produced some interesting findings, such as how parental choice is influenced by quality and flexibility and how child care subsidies affect employment rates among welfare recipients. One drawback of the partnerships is that they do not provide a nationally representative examination of child care across the country.

One final source of data is the National Study of Low-Income Child Care. This ongoing five-year study is being conducted by Abt Associates Inc. under the direction of the Office of Research, Planning, and Evaluation of the Administration for Children and Families. It examines low-income child care markets, looking at twenty-five communities in seventeen states. A substudy is looking at family child care markets in five neighborhoods. The study is intended to examine the impact of subsidies on the type, amount, and quality of child care in local markets. The project is still underway, with final reports expected in 2003.

Conclusion

If asked whether we have good child care data, I do not know whether to answer that the glass is half-full or half-empty. We have better child care data than we used to, but we still have many unanswered questions. The complexity and multiplicity of child care arrangements makes it hard to get a comprehensive sense of how children spend their time when they are in nonparental care. Studying the more informal arrangements, which are less visible to the researchers, is particularly challenging. We have a better sense of the various types of child care providers that low-income families use, but we still lack good data on the important question of the quality of these settings. Although advances have been made in measuring quality, measurement challenges still exist. Even for the basic data on child care arrangements, we experience some frustrating time lags in getting the data cleaned up and ready for analysis by researchers. Finally, a tension exists between the need for better national data and the need for data that is representative at the state and local levels, where many policy decisions are made.

Notes

1. Kristin Smith, *Who's Minding the Kids? Child Care Arrangements: Spring 1997*, Current Population Report, P70-86 (Washington, D.C.: U.S. Census Bureau, 2002), p. 17.
2. Freya Sonenstein, Gary Gates, Stefanie Schmidt, and Natalya Bolshun, *Primary Child Care Arrangements of Employed Parents: Findings from the 1999 National Survey of America's Families* (Washington, D.C.: Urban Institute, 2002), p. 18.
3. For description of the model and one set of estimates, see Helen Oliver, Katherin Ross Phillips, Linda Giannarelli, and An-Lon Chen, *Eligibility for CCDF–Funded Child Care Subsidies under the October 1999 Program Rules: Results from the Trim3 Microsimulation Model* (Washington, D.C.: Urban Institute, 2002).
4. U.S. Department of Health and Human Services, *Child Care Eligibility and Enrollment Estimates for Fiscal Year 2000* (Washington, D.C.: U.S. Department of Health and Human Services, 2002), p. 1.
5. Julia B. Isaacs, "Measuring Outcomes for Former Welfare Recipients: A Review of 11 Survey Instruments," paper presented at the National Association for Welfare Research and Statistics (NAWRS), Cleveland, Ohio, August 1999, p. 7.
6. Gregory Acs and Pamela Loprest, *Final Synthesis Report of Findings from ASPE's "Leavers" Grants* (Washington, D.C.: U.S. Department of Health and Human Services, 2001), p. 123. Note that differences in definitions of care categories and populations covered made it challenging to compare child care findings even among the eight studies included in the child care section of the report.
7. Ibid., p. 124.
8. Rachel Schumaker and Mark Greenberg, *Child Care after Leaving Welfare: Early Evidence from Leavers Studies* (Washington, D.C.: Center for Law and Social Policy, 1999), p. 11. Schumaker and Greenberg emphasize the preliminary nature of the findings and the methodological issues affecting the studies.

References

Acs, Gregory, and Pamela Loprest. 2001. *Final Synthesis Report of Findings from ASPE's "Leavers" Grants*. Washington, D.C.: U.S. Department of Health and Human Services.

Isaacs, Julia B. 1999. "Measuring Outcomes for Former Welfare Recipients: A Review of 11 Survey Instruments." Paper presented at the National Association for Welfare Research and Statistics (NAWRS), Cleveland, Ohio.

Oliver, Helen, Katherin Ross Phillips, Linda Giannarelli, and An-Lon Chen. 2002. *Eligibility for CCDF–Funded Child Care Subsidies under the October 1999 Program Rules: Results from the Trim3 Microsimulation Model*. Washington, D.C.: Urban Institute.

Schumaker, Rachel, and Mark Greenberg. 1999. *Child Care after Leaving Welfare: Early Evidence from Leavers Studies*. Washington, D.C.: Center for Law and Social Policy.

Smith, Kristin. 2002. *Who's Minding the Kids? Child Care Arrangements: Spring 1997.* Current Population Reports, P70-86. Washington, D.C.: U.S. Census Bureau.

Sonenstein, Freya, Gary Gates, Stefanie Schmidt, and Natalya Bolshun. 2002. *Primary Child Care Arrangements of Employed Parents: Findings from the 1999 National Survey of America's Families.* Washington, D.C.: Urban Institute.

U.S. Department of Health and Human Services. 2002. *Child Care Eligibility and Enrollment Estimates for Fiscal Year 2000.* Washington, D.C.: U.S. Department of Health and Human Services.

———. 2002. "FFY 2000 CCDF Tables and Charts." Washington, D.C.: U.S. Department of Health and Human Services. Available from http://www.acf.dhhs.gov/programs/ccb/research/00acf800/cover.htm. Accessed November 21, 2002.

15

Activities of the U.S. Department of Health and Human Services

Don Winstead and Ann McCormick

The central goal and purpose of the 1996 welfare reforms can be summarized as giving states the tools and resources they need to improve the lot and prospects of low-income families and children. This theme is predominant in the provisions that made assistance conditional and time-limited to reduce dependency, established strict work standards to help families become self-sufficient, provided unprecedented levels of child care funding to encourage adults to leave welfare for work, sought to reduce nonmarital births in general and teen nonmarital births in particular, which, in turn, reduce the disadvantage of children raised without the active involvement of two parents, strengthened child support enforcement to increase the level of financial support provided by noncustodial parents, and preserved entitlements to health and nutritional assistance to maintain a federal safety net for families experiencing temporary financial problems.

The success of these reforms, anticipated by many and unpredicted by others, is measurable across many dimensions. Since the Personal Responsibility and Work Opportunity Reconciliation Act of 1996 (PRWORA) replaced the Aid to Families with Dependent Children program (AFDC) with the Temporary Assistance for Needy Families program (TANF), caseloads are down; work effort, especially among female-headed households, is up; nonmarital childbearing is down; child support collections are up; and child poverty is down. Unfortunately, success, or even progress, across other dimensions is not always easy to measure.

This chapter briefly describes the major efforts of the U.S. Department of Health and Human Services (HHS) to understand the condition of the low-income population before and after welfare reform. This effort involves many activities across several HHS agencies, most notably the Administration for Children and Families (ACF), the National Institute of Child Health and Human Development (NICHD), and the Office of the Assistant Secretary for Planning and Evaluation (ASPE). Except to the extent that some of the activities and studies mentioned below have been supported jointly by ASPE and funding from other sources, the following discussion highlights primarily the activities of ASPE.[1] The chapter begins with a description of our efforts to study welfare outcomes for families and children, describes some on-going HHS publications addressing family and child well-being, includes a discussion of issues affecting the quality of welfare outcomes research and monitoring of well-being, discusses child well-being in the context of welfare reauthorization, and concludes with a discussion of various approaches to improving the measurement of child well-being.

Outcomes Research

With the help of dedicated policy research funding, ASPE has initiated or participated in a number of activities over the last five years to study the outcomes of welfare reform and assess the impacts of policy changes on the low-income population. These efforts include collecting and using state-specific surveys, as well as state and federal administrative data (including linked administrative data); focusing on assessing the well-being of the low-income population; developing and reporting reliable and comparable state-by-state measures of family hardship and well-being; the utilization of other support programs; and measuring outcomes for a broad population of current, former and potential welfare recipients, as well as other special populations affected by state TANF policies.

Our interest is in covering a wide spectrum of policy interests focusing on welfare outcomes, poverty, working families, supports for low-income populations, the hard-to-serve and other special populations, and effects on children. Our research agenda is designed to assess and monitor welfare outcomes by:

- addressing a wide range of topics related to families and children, including economic and other supports for poor families;

- enhancing state and local capacity for data collection and monitoring studies, including state-level data collection efforts, administrative data linking, and the creation of public-use and restricted-access data files; and

- facilitating states' monitoring of outcomes for their own state and local populations by providing technical assistance to improve the quality of research results, ensuring more uniformity and comparability across studies, and synthesizing results across state and local level monitoring studies.

HHS is concerned with a wide range of individual and family outcomes. While a broad array of research exists about welfare reform being funded by other public and private sources, the Department has created a substantial research, evaluation, and data strategy to study the outcomes of welfare reform. These studies are designed to document the implementation of welfare reform and its effects, and to add to and enhance the information about welfare reform outcomes that is available to the Congress and other interested parties. We have attempted to identify knowledge gaps and, often with other public and private funding partners, we have created a portfolio of research, evaluation, and data activities to increase our understanding of the outcomes of welfare reform. Overall, our focus has been on creating an integrated picture of the low-income population, especially low-income families with children, combined with broader analyses of the economic condition, health and well-being, sociodemographic characteristics, and the social service needs of low-income individuals, families, and children.

Addressing a Wide Range of Topics

Over the years, the Department has studied economic supports for poor families, children and youth, family formation, special populations and local service delivery issues, and some cross-cutting topics. Our research agenda has included competitive grant programs; projects to improve state data collection, comparability or capacity-building; and analytic projects on welfare-related topics. We have funded projects that measure outcomes for welfare leavers, examine diversion practices, study the characteristics of the TANF caseload (or "stayers"), and measure family hardship and well-being including the utilization of other support programs. Projects also are in place to assess the effects of welfare reform on current, former, and potential welfare recipients and other special populations (for example, child-only cases, people with mental health and substance abuse problems and other disabilities, and immigrant families) affected by state TANF policies.

The Department has funded grants to states and large counties to gather a variety of information about individuals and their families who apply for TANF (including those who are formally or informally diverted) and the degree to which TANF applicants receive, or are aware of their potential eligibility for Medicaid, food stamps, and other programs and services that are important in helping low-income families make a successful transition to work. We are funding projects in six states to study the characteristics of their TANF caseloads, with particular attention to the personal, family, and community factors that may present barriers to employment. Together with ACF, we will be testing employment programs for low-income parents with barriers to work under the long-term, multi-site demonstration and evaluation of programs for hard-to-employ low-income parents, in order to identify effective strategies for promoting employment and family well-being and to determine the effects of such programs on employment, earnings, income, welfare dependence, family functioning, and the well-being of children. We also are supporting a National Governors Association project to build state and local capacity to provide work supports that help low-income working parents sustain employment and advance in the labor market.

In addition, we are supporting a supplement to a broader study (Welfare, Children, & Families: A Three-City Study) of the implications of welfare reform for low-income families in three cities that is examining how work participation requirements and time limits are affecting the service utilization, health and development, support networks, parenting and child care arrangements of adults and children with disabilities. We also are providing continuing support for an evaluation of the effectiveness of a substance abuse research demonstration project that includes coordinating screening, referral, and treatment with employment and training or vocational services. Another project is examining trends in the demand for emergency assistance services, such as homeless shelters and food banks, from the mid-1990s to 2000. In recognition of the fact that the highest concentration of populations on TANF is living in neighborhoods where incarceration rates are also the highest, we funded a project that is investigating the effects of incarceration on low-income children, families, and communities.

Our FY 2002 research agenda included several projects that focus broadly on welfare outcomes for the low-income population. One study will focus on families that exit and re-enter welfare, particularly those that return multiple times, in an attempt to identify the demographic characteristics and employment outcomes of "cyclers," whether their patterns of benefit receipt and cycling patterns have changed since the 1996 welfare reforms, and whether cyclers re-entering welfare for the third time are treated differently than other families by local offices. Another project will explore the coordination of TANF and one-stop employment centers and the unique challenges involved in serving welfare and ex-welfare clients, and the low-skilled in general, through one-stop centers designed to serve people at all income and skill levels. A separate project will attempt to better understand the different types of child-only cases, the service needs of these families, and how states are meeting those needs.

The Department has sponsored or conducted a great number of studies designed to document trends in the low-income population (including both adults and children) as well as in the welfare recipient population, despite the substantial challenges for data collection and analysis to monitoring welfare outcomes created by welfare devolution and increased flexibility in the design and delivery of program benefits. To meet these challenges, new and better data are needed at the state and local level. For example, we have supported efforts to build state data capacity and data comparability through our support of monitoring studies, such as studies of families leaving welfare. Activities that support and enhance the collection, use, and linking of federal and state administrative data and state-specific surveys are critical to understanding the outcomes of welfare reform.

Building Capacity for Data Collection and Monitoring Studies

ASPE has devoted substantial resources to supporting state-level data collection efforts and administrative data linking, making certain that national survey instruments are responsive to policy changes and needs, supporting and maintaining a wide range of Census Bureau data collection efforts, and supporting secondary analyses of state and national-level data to add to our understanding of the effects of welfare reform. We also have committed funds for several projects geared toward developing state-level data on hardship and/or program utilization.

We have provided support for an on-going project designed to match Social Security earnings records with samples of adult welfare recipients and non-recipients from Census surveys to help assess employment and earnings patterns and outcomes on the basis of baseline characteristics. Our support for the administration of a welfare participation question in the State and Local Area Integrated Telephone Survey (SLAITS) has contributed to the fielding of a survey data element that, when combined with other data available from the survey, will permit the development of state-level estimates of the incidence of special health care needs of children of current and former welfare recipients, plus the health insurance status (including Medicaid and the State Children's Health Insurance Program, SCHIP) of current and former recipients. We also have provided funds to support the longitudinal New Immigrant Survey, which will collect data on program utilization, health and economic status, and other characteristics among newly arriving low-income immigrant families in different states. ASPE's contribution will help ensure that comprehensive and relevant data are collected and analyzed and that the study focuses on how children in these families are faring. In addition, we have funded a project to advance our understanding of the value and limitations of measures of material hardship as a component of family well-being.

ASPE has funded several projects that are utilizing existing administrative and survey data. For example, we have contributed support to the Manpower Demonstration Research Corporation's Project on Devolution and Urban Change (UC), a multidisciplinary study of the implementation and impacts of welfare reform and welfare-to-work programs on low-income individuals, families, and communities in four large urban areas, using, among other data sources, longitudinal administrative data for all families receiving AFDC/TANF or food stamps dating back to 1992. In another project we are analyzing survey data on the personal characteristics, potential barriers to employment, strengths and resources, and preparation for employment of current TANF recipients in Illinois to explore the relationships of various factors contributing to employment outcomes. We also are supporting a small grant program for young scholars to encourage secondary analyses of new HHS–sponsored administrative and survey data sets to explore aspects of welfare reform. Finally, the competitive grants we awarded to states and large counties to examine welfare leavers, individuals, and their families who apply for TANF (including those who are formally or informally diverted), and the characteristics of TANF caseloads, used or are using various combinations of state and federal administrative and survey data to report on a variety of welfare reform outcomes.

A project building on past ASPE–funded studies of welfare leavers and welfare applicants was funded in FY 2002. This study will focus on the subgroup of TANF families that exit and re-enter welfare, particularly those that return for multiple times. Another project will utilize five federally administered databases to provide state-by-state estimates of important welfare outcomes. Projects such as these support the overall goal of ensuring that good data are available to create an integrated picture of low-income families with children.

Facilitating State Monitoring

HHS is collecting a great amount of state-level survey data and has supported projects to collect data in about half the states. The surveys are state-sponsored and focus on the questions that states themselves feel are important. These efforts collect data on people who either are welfare recipients or have been welfare recipients, allowing the study of a wide variety of outcome measures. We are encouraging states to use comparable measures in at least some areas. Yet, we believe that welfare reform policies demonstrate a clear interest in promoting states' autonomy and ability to ask their own questions. Therefore, we have not attempted to enforce any kind of uniform survey across the states.

Project on "State-Level Child Outcomes." Starting as a way to help states augment their evaluations of state welfare waivers to examine child and family well-being in the context of welfare reform, this project yielded a guidebook for understanding the effects of state welfare policies on children and culminated in five states' carrying out studies of child outcomes as part of their waiver evaluations. State representatives, federal and private researchers, and foundations worked together over a year to identify and agree on a set of child and family variables that could be measured in state welfare evaluations. Twelve states were competitively selected to receive HHS planning grants and technical assistance in developing social indicators of child and family well-being. Through a series of meetings, the group developed a conceptual model for how welfare polices affect child well-being and chose the factors to be assessed in the evaluations. Ultimately, five of the twelve states received additional funding to add child outcome measures to their existing welfare reform evaluations. Survey instruments and procedures for data collection were as similar as possible across all five states: Connecticut, Florida, Indiana, Iowa, and Minnesota. All five evaluations have been completed and reports have been released. A synthesis of findings from the five state evaluations is forthcoming.

Advancing states' child and youth indicators initiatives. With ACF and foundation support, ASPE launched a complementary multi-year effort in 1998 to promote state efforts to develop and monitor indicators of the health and well-being of children in the context of welfare reform and other policy changes. Building and improving state capacity to assess trends in children's well-being, especially for low-income populations, was the fundamental goal of the project. Grants were provided over two years to fourteen states to form partnerships between state welfare agencies and other agencies and councils with responsibilities for children issues and services; some states also included universities, community government agencies, or other partners. States were provided with opportunities to work with one another, experts in various fields, and federal staff. Technical assistance was provided to the grantees in developing and monitoring indicators, including conceptualization and measurement issues in identifying and measuring appropriate sets of child health and well-being indicators within and across states; ways of creating or using survey and administrative data and of combining several data approaches; and ways to involve state policymakers who could help institutionalize data systems for measuring and tracking child indicators and establish procedures for using indicator information to inform policy deliberations. In addition, ASPE sponsored a technical assistance conference for states interested in developing and monitoring indicators of youth health and well-being as changes occur in welfare and other key policies. Inventories of national and state efforts to improve youth measures and other materials also have been created and are being disseminated during major meetings.

HHS Publications

ASPE has long been engaged in research to track the conditions of vulnerable populations, both as a way to assess the need for policy intervention and to monitor the outcomes of existing policies. ASPE is involved in three separate projects—each with a different aim— that monitor the condition of American children, either as a group or as part of families. Each of these projects produces an annual report that addresses the condition of children, although they vary significantly in their scope, the children covered, the presentation style, and the audience.

"Indicators of Welfare Dependence"

Required by the Welfare Indicators Act of 1994, the Department prepares annual reports to Congress on indicators and predictors of welfare dependence. The 2002 edition provides welfare dependence indicators through 1999, reflecting changes that have taken place since enactment of PRWORA in August 1996. As directed by the Welfare Indicators Act, the report focuses on benefits under the AFDC program, now TANF; the Food Stamp Program; and the Supplemental Security Income (SSI) program.

Welfare dependence is difficult to define and difficult to measure. Like poverty, welfare dependence is a continuum, with variations in degree and duration. For purposes of our reports, we examine dependence (measured as a proportion of income during a year derived from non-work-related cash or near cash assistance) in concert with other key indicators of dependence and deprivation. However, existing data collection efforts do not distinguish between cash benefits associated with work activities and non-work-related cash benefits. In addition, there are time lags in the availability of the national data from the detailed surveys that may be best suited to measure dependence. The 2002 report uses data from the Current Population Survey (CPS) and administrative data to provide updated measures through 1999 for several dependence indicators. Other measures are based on the Survey of Income and Program Participation (SIPP), the Panel Study of Income Dynamics (PSID), and other data sources.

In addition to providing a number of key indicators of welfare recipiency, dependence, and labor force attachment, the report also includes a larger set of risk factors associated with welfare receipt since the causes of welfare receipt and dependence are not clearly known. The risk factors are loosely organized into three categories: economic security measures, measures related to employment and barriers to employment, and measures of nonmarital childbearing. The economic security risk factors include measures of poverty and deprivation that are important not only as predictors of dependence, but also as a supplement to the dependence indicators, ensuring that dependence measures are not assessed in isolation. It is important to examine whether decreases in dependency are accompanied by improvements in family economic status or by reductions in family material circumstances. The fifth annual report was published in 2002.[2]

"Trends in the Well-Being of America's Children and Youth"

The Department also publishes annual reports on trends in the well-being of America's children and youth. It presents the most recent and reliable estimates on more than eighty indicators of well-being. It is intended to provide the policy community and other interested parties with an accessible overview of comprehensive data describing the condition of children in the United States. The indicators cover five broad areas: population, family, and neighborhood; economic security; health conditions and health care; social development, behavioral health, and teen fertility; and education and achievement. The sixth edition was published in 2001.[3]

"America's Children: Key National Indicators of Well-Being"

The Federal Interagency Forum on Child and Family Statistics, a collaboration of twenty federal agencies including ASPE and several other HHS agencies that produce or use statistical data on children and families, annually publishes a synthesis of information on the status of children. The report provides a broad annual summary of national indicators of child well-being and monitors changes in these indicators over time. It includes twenty-four key indicators of the well-being of children, covering children's economic security, health, behavior and social environment, and education; it also presents data on eight key contextual measures. The sixth edition was published in 2002.[4]

Data Quality

Under welfare reform, the task of examining outcomes for the low-income population has become more complex. Our knowledge about the outcomes of welfare reform is limited by the wide variation in the design and application of policies across states, between local sites, and even from worker-to-worker; the continuing evolution and devolution of state policies and organizational structures; and the many, often confounding, variables other than welfare policies (such as the economy) that affect the outcomes of welfare reform. The program differences across geographic areas, in particular, mean that the national surveys we have used in the past to measure program outcomes must be supplemented with other data.

The Department continues to evaluate National Academy of Sciences recommendations to enhance the quality of welfare outcomes research.[5] The 2001 final report of the Panel on Data and Methods for Measuring the Effects of Changes in Social Welfare Programs, *Evaluating Welfare Reform in an Era of Transition*, highlighted some factors that need to be considered as the future direction of welfare research is contemplated. The report identified some important data gaps and offered numerous conclusions and recommendations with respect to defining research questions and outcomes of interest for measuring the effects of welfare reform, as well as the appropriate methods for answering those questions and the data needed to carry out these evaluations. It discussed research designs and methods for the study of welfare reform outcomes, and needed areas and topics of research. The report also addressed alternative federal and state data sources, the limitations of currently available data, and appropriate evaluation design and methods for analysis. In short, while applauding the Department for its broad-based welfare reform research agenda, the report highlighted the need for further improvements and expansions in data collection, development of research questions, and methodological work to build up the "science base" of welfare reform research.

The Department has taken, or is taking, steps to address several of the panel's recommendations. For example, our efforts to build capacity for conducting high-quality program evaluations at the state level and for conducting household surveys of low-income and welfare populations continue. We have committed resources to help improve national household survey questions to better measure program participation and benefit receipt. A project to improve the usefulness of state-level administrative data is just getting started. Improvements in state data reporting were included in the president's welfare reauthorization plan, as were changes to broaden the definition of assistance. State-specific data sets produced by each of the grantees studying welfare leavers have been made available for secondary data analyses of welfare outcomes measures. In addition, we have published a synthesis report that includes administrative data findings from all fifteen of the ASPE–funded leavers studies. Study and consideration of other panel conclusions and recommendations will continue.

Survey Data

Most of what we know about the low-income population comes from national data sets, such as the CPS and the SIPP. As noted above, existing national data sets must be improved in order to capture the new variation in welfare programs across the country. HHS has a continuing interest in expanding the types of outcomes captured in national surveys.

The Survey of Program Dynamics (SPD), for example, was created by the Census Bureau in response to a requirement of the 1996 welfare reform law to collect information to enable evaluation of the impacts of TANF on assistance recipients and other low-income families. The SPD was designed to collect longitudinal data on the demographic, social, and economic characteristics of a nationally representative sample of the population, paying particular attention to the issues of out-of-wedlock births, welfare dependency, the beginning and end of welfare spells, and the causes of recent welfare spells, as well as information about the status of children. Data were collected from the 1992 and 1993 SIPP panels each year from 1997 to 2002. Over that period, there has been substantial attrition among sample households, and several design/re-design options are being discussed.

We may not harvest the fruits of our efforts to improve national data for a number of years. Each element involves conceptualizing a measure of well-being, defining appropriate measures, and then collecting the data. Nevertheless, these efforts are crucial if we are to understand the broader issues affecting the low-income population over the long run.

Administrative Data

Using administrative data to increase our understanding of low-income populations under welfare reform both has great potential and presents many challenges.

Advantages of administrative data analysis. One of the great advantages of administrative data is that they capture information about the full population of people involved in a program. As a result, a researcher can examine rare subgroups and understand patterns of service delivery that might not be captured in a survey. Obtaining data on the full population also allows a researcher to detect changes that may not be evident in a small survey sample and to examine small geographic areas, which may be impossible in a survey. Most administrative data systems provide addresses of program recipients, and advances are occurring in the use of data mapping by welfare researchers. For example, as part of the UC, researchers are examining neighborhood clustering of program receipt and how that changes over time.

Another advantage is that administrative data were collected before welfare reform and continue to be collected. Such information can be difficult to obtain from surveys. Although programs (and their data sets) may change over time, administrative data offer the possibility of understanding shifts in how people were connected to programs prior to reform and how they are connected now. This approach has some limitations, however. State computer systems change, and data archiving is not always as complete as researchers would like.

Finally, administrative data often can capture program variation better than surveys. The data show directly which people are affected by "caseload events" such as sanctions. Such information may be more difficult to gather in surveys because respondents may not be aware of their status within the system.

Challenges of administrative data analysis. A clear disadvantage of administrative data is that when clients leave a program, they leave the administrative data set for that program. As caseloads decline, we have fewer of the population of interest in the administrative data. Another challenge with administrative data sets is that they do not always cover the outcomes of interest. Researchers interested in the economic well-being of a child, for example, want to know the total income of the household in which the child is living. Administrative data may only tell us that the mother is employed; discovering whether other people in the household were employed or had income is more difficult. In addition, administrative data typically offer few insights into post-program outcomes. They also offer limited variables for analysis and do not give us rich data on child well-being. One challenge ahead is to make better use of interesting sources of outcome data, such as school records.

Understanding data quality can also be a challenge. Data quality varies from data set to data set as well as across fields within any one data set. For example, a data set may have complete and high-quality data in one field, such as payments, but poor quality in another field, such as household composition or race. Changes in federal reporting requirements also may affect quality. Working with administrative data requires patience and diplomacy to negotiate with data-producing agencies and dig through poor documentation to understand what the data can and cannot provide.

Concerns about confidentiality can also hinder researchers' efforts to use administrative data. While some concerns may be easy to address from legal and technical standpoints, researchers must take seriously the confidentiality concerns raised by state governments and other organizations. However, addressing those concerns can be a time-consuming process. When working with multiple data sources to link records, researchers need to understand and explain what the threats to confidentiality may be and how they will be minimized.

Linking administrative records. One way to deal with the problem of understanding what happens to clients who leave a program is to match data across programs. Clients of one program often are clients of many programs, either at the same time or in sequence. When a woman leaves TANF, for example, she may be covered by unemployment insurance. By creating linked data files, researchers can follow individuals across multiple programs.

Researchers find it difficult to compare administrative data sets from one system or state with data sets from another system or state. Multiple definitions exist across systems and states—a family or case in one system may be defined differently in another. The growing state-to-state (or county-to-county) variation in welfare programs makes comparisons across state systems difficult to understand. Administrative data often do not directly record program variation, so researchers must further investigate the meaning of data fields, population coverage, and policy context.

One challenge to these efforts is the lack of common identifiers across programs and systems. What appear to be subtle distinctions between the programs can lead to different conclusions about cross-state variation. Potential data incompatibilities have to be carefully assessed. Matching records also requires experience with a particular state's data systems to understand their nuances. HHS is supporting efforts to do this kind of data matching in a number of states. One of the key questions is whether, and for which populations, patterns of overlap and sequencing will change under welfare reform.

Child Well-Being and TANF Reauthorization

While welfare policies are generally directed toward adult behaviors, their underlying goal has always been to support children. The AFDC program was established by the Social Security Act of 1935 to enable states to provide support for needy children without fathers. The TANF block grant program was established to provide cash and other benefits to help needy families support their children. A major goal of the program is to help families leave welfare for work to break the cycle of dependency and improve family and child outcomes. The well-being of families and children is one of several important outcomes of welfare reform.

Establish an Overarching Purpose to Improve the Well-Being of Children

President Bush's welfare reauthorization plan, *Working Toward Independence,* encouraged states to increase their efforts to promote child well-being. It proposed to amend the overall purpose of TANF and to establish that the overarching purpose is to improve the well-being of children. This proposed change was based on the recognition that the goals of TANF are important core strategies for improving the well-being of children.

Improve Program Performance

The president's welfare reauthorization plan reflects his focus on governing with accountability. Outcome-based performance measurement is an important component of an overall management and accountability system. In keeping with the basic principle of maintaining state flexibility, state and local administrators seeking to provide increasingly better TANF outcomes would set goals focused on results rather than dollars spent. States would be required to establish clear and measurable program goals and report annually on their success in meeting those goals.

Set performance goals. Under the president's proposal, the general structure of the state plan provisions would be retained, but new attention would be focused on performance goals and measurement. States would be required to establish specific numerical performance goals for accomplishing each of the TANF purposes. They would have the flexibility to define their own performance goals, but would have to define in their state plans how each of the TANF purposes will help to improve the well-being of children. States also would be required to describe in their state plans the strategies and programs they are employing to address some important TANF challenges related to family and child well-being, including employment retention and advancement; outreach to, and services for, struggling and non-compliant families; services and programs for clients with special problems; and youth development.

Measure and report performance. States would have to take necessary actions to achieve their performance goals and measure their annual performance relative to those goals. States would have the flexibility to define their measurement methodology for accomplishing each of the TANF purposes. States would have to prepare annual performance reports updating their progress in achieving their numerical goals.

Conduct Research and Provide Technical Assistance

Under this proposal, the Department would research the best ways to construct performance measures that relate to the various goals of the TANF program. HHS would collaborate with states to identify key measures and build uniform data support and reporting methodologies to help states better measure their progress toward achieving the goals of TANF. In addition, state data reporting requirements would be modified to focus on the data that are most useful in helping state and local program administrators improve management and performance, as well as useful for federal oversight and research. Data would include information on TANF–funded services and supports, including federal and state expenditures and expenditures for major categories of activities.

Improving the Measurement of Child Well-Being

As noted above, a number of survey design/re-design options are being considered to improve the measurement of child well-being in general, and to enhance the capability of the Census Bureau to capture information on child well-being in particular.

Enhance Current Census Activities

The Census Bureau's SIPP is built around a "core" of labor force, program participation, and income questions designed to measure the economic situation of persons in the United States. The survey is also designed to provide a broader context for analysis by adding questions on a variety of topics not covered in the core section. These questions are assigned to "topical modules" and include personal history, child care, wealth, program eligibility, child support, disability, school enrollment, taxes, and personal income. The SPD, as noted above, expanded on the SIPP and pays particular attention to out-of-wedlock births, welfare dependency, the beginning and end of welfare spells, causes of recent welfare spells, and the status of children. Data have been collected from the 1992 and 1993 SIPP panels each year for six years. Design options are being discussed to overcome some of the attrition among sample households and to provide more reliable state level estimates, including new samples and expanded survey panels with oversamples of low income households with children.

Enhance Longitudinal Tracking Abilities

Welfare reauthorization legislation passed by the House of Representatives in May 2002 (H.R. 4737, Personal Responsibility, Work, and Family Promotion Act of 2002, Section 116) continues annual funding at $10 million for 2003–2007 and incorporates some new language requiring the Census Bureau to implement a new longitudinal survey of program dynamics. The survey would be developed in consultation with HHS and would allow for the assessment of outcomes of continued welfare reform on the economic and child well-being of low-income families with children. To the extent possible, the survey would provide state representative samples. The survey content would include information on out-of-wedlock childbearing, marriage, welfare dependency and compliance with work requirements, the beginning and ending of spells of assistance, work, earnings and employment stability, and the well-being of children.

While still in the early conceptualization phase, several ideas for design of the longitudinal survey are being considered. These include adding to the already rich data collected under the Census Bureau's SIPP program and developing a new annual longitudinal survey by following a subsample of households in the CPS. Additions to the SIPP could include: increasing the sample size of the 2004 SIPP panel to include more low-income households; providing larger samples in selected states to produce better state-level estimates; supplementing the SIPP sample in selected states with an oversample of current TANF recipients using a dual frame sampling strategy; and/or extending for an additional year the three years of data collection currently planned for the 2004 SIPP panel. Another alternative would be to administer annual follow-up surveys to a subsample of households that have responded to the March Annual Demographic Survey of the CPS. The content of these annual follow-up surveys could be modeled on the current annual SPD instrument.

Develop State-Level Indicators

Another approach to monitoring child well-being, included in the welfare reauthorization legislation passed by the Senate Finance Committee in June 2002 (H.R. 4737, The Work, Opportunity and Responsibility for Kids Act of 2002), would assess child well-being at the state level by developing statistical indicators of child well-being. Arguing that monitoring the well-being of children should be on a par with monitoring economic indicators, some researchers have proposed developing an indicator-based system for tracking child and youth well-being at both the national and state levels. They recommend creation of a bipartisan committee to provide advice to the secretary of HHS on the constructs, measures, and data collection methods needed to develop a rigorous system of reliable and valid indicators of child and youth well-being, particularly the well-being of children in low-income families. State-level indicators across multiple domains, including educational outcomes, health and safety, social and emotional development, and family well-being (including family structure, income, employment, child care, and family processes), have been proposed.

Conclusion

The Department is committed to advancing a research, evaluation, and data agenda dedicated to understanding the condition of the low-income population, especially families with children, before and after welfare reform. This includes our welfare outcomes research agenda designed to track the condition of low-income families and children and our annual publications reporting on measures of family and child well-being. We are engaged in a number of activities to improve the quality of welfare outcomes research and well-being monitoring in order to improve our understanding of the complex set of outcomes for low-income Americans in the era following welfare reform. We continue to provide leadership in national-level survey work and are working to facilitate greater comparability in state and local level studies and increase state and local capacity for data collection efforts.

As of this writing, it is not clear which direction or mechanism for improving the measurement of child well-being will be included in welfare reauthorization. What is clear, however, is that improving our knowledge and measurement of child well-being is a topic of interest to all concerned.

Notes

1. The Administration for Children and Families supports welfare reform and social services research and evaluation studies that include examining the impacts of welfare reform on families and children, issues affecting affordability and quality of child care, and access to other supports that facilitate labor force attachment for low-income families. Studies have also been initiated to increase understanding of the effects of transitions in health and human services on other special populations (teens, Native Americans, victims of domestic violence, and rural populations among others).

    The National Institute of Child Health and Human Development supports research on family and child well-being and family and household demography, including studies of the determinants of trends in marriage, divorce, and cohabitation; the formation and changes in household structures, fatherhood, patterns of child support and visitation with absent parents; the use of child care services; the relationship between changing fertility, family patterns, and the well-being of children; intergenerational demography; and the implications of welfare and health policies on families.

2. See U.S. Department of Health and Human Services, *Indicators of Welfare Dependence: Annual Report to the Congress 2002*, available from: http://aspe.hhs.gov/hsp/indicators02/, accessed November 22, 2002.

3. See U.S. Department of Health and Human Services, *Trends in the Well-Being of America's Children and Youth*, available from: http://aspe.hhs.gov/hsp/01trends/, accessed November 22, 2002.

4. See U.S. Department of Health and Human Services, *America's Children: Key National Indicators of Well-Being*, available from: http://www.childstats.gov/americaschildren/, accessed November 22, 2002.

5. Conference report language accompanying the Department's fiscal year 1998 and 1999 appropriations included the recommendation that the Department "submit its research plan to the National Academy of Sciences (NAS) to provide further guidance on research design and recommend further research." Accordingly, ASPE provided a total of over $1 million to the NAS to convene an expert panel to evaluate current and future welfare reform research.

References

Hotz, V. Joseph, Robert Goerge, Julie Balzekas, and Francis Margolin. Editors. 1998. *Administrative Data for Policy-Relevant Research: Assessment of Current Utility and Recommendations for Development*. Executive Summary. Evanston, Ill.: Northwestern University/University of Chicago Joint Center for Poverty Research.

Moffitt, Robert A., and Michele Ver Ploeg. Editors. 2001. *Evaluating Welfare Reform in an Era of Transition*. Washington, D.C.: National Academy Press.

Moore, Kristin Anderson, Matthew Stagner, and Shepherd Smith. 2002. *Child Well-Being: The Overarching Goal of Welfare Reform: How Would We Know It Worked?* Washington, D.C.: Child Trends.

U.S. Census Bureau. 1998. *Overview of the Survey of Income and Program Participation (SIPP)*. 1998. Washington, D.C.: U.S. Census Bureau. Available from http://www.sipp.census.gov/sipp/sippov98.htm. Accessed October 16, 2002.

U.S. Department of Health and Human Services. 2001. *Trends in the Well-Being of America's Children and Youth*. Available from: http://aspe.hhs.gov/hsp/01trends/. Accessed November 22, 2002.

———. 2002. *America's Children: Key National Indicators of Well-Being*. Available from: http://www.childstats.gov/americaschildren/. Accessed November 22, 2002.

———. 2002. *Indicators of Welfare Dependence: Annual Report to the Congress 2002*. Available from: http://aspe.hhs.gov/hsp/indicators02/. Accessed November 22, 2002.

White House. 2002. *Working Toward Independence: The President's Plan to Strengthen Welfare Reform*. Washington, D.C.: White House. Available from http://www.whitehouse.gov/infocus/welfarereform/. Accessed October 16, 2002.

16

Conclusion

Douglas J. Besharov and Peter H. Rossi

The 1990s were a tumultuous time in welfare. The beginning of the decade saw the national welfare caseload rise about 35 percent to reach an all-time high of 5.1 million families in March 1994. Then, the caseload began a more than seven-year, 59 percent decline. By July 2001, only 2.1 million families remained on welfare. Neither the proponents nor the opponents of welfare reform expected a decline of this magnitude.

This volume has examined research on this decline and on its effects on the well-being of low-income children and families. In this chapter, we provide a summary assessment of this research and recommendations for future welfare research.

Disappointing Research

About two years into this massive caseload decline, a major federal welfare reform law, the Personal Responsibility and Work Opportunity Reconciliation Act of 1996 (PRWORA), was passed. It replaced the unpopular Aid to Families with Dependent Children program (AFDC) with the Temporary Assistance for Needy Families program (TANF), which ended the legal entitlement to benefits, mandated that a large percentage of recipients work, and imposed a five-year time limit on the receipt of federally funded benefits.

Few opponents of the 1996 welfare reform bill defended the dependency sustained by the old AFDC program, but they did not think that the approach taken by the new law would work, and they worried that it would hurt many poor children—by forcing families off welfare and into extreme poverty. Hence, they were eager to document the ill effects of welfare reform so that there would be a strong case for changing the new law. Supporters of welfare reform believed that most families would be helped by the new law, but they were also concerned that some families would suffer under the new regime, and they, too, supported efforts to evaluate the consequences of welfare reform.

The result was the initiation of an unprecedented number of research projects—some very large—to evaluate welfare reform's impact on low-income children and their families.[1] Private foundations and the federal government together spent over a quarter of a billion dollars on this effort. The four largest projects were discussed by Peter Rossi in chapter 3:

- The New Federalism Project, and its National Survey of America's Families (NSAF), of the Urban Institute ($84 million between 1996-2002);[2]

- The Survey of Program Dynamics (SPD) of the U.S. Census Bureau ($76 million between 1996-2002);[3]

- The Project on Devolution and Urban Change (UC) of the Manpower Demonstration Research Corporation (MDRC) ($13 million between 1996-2002);[4] and

- The Child Impact Waiver Experiments sponsored by the U.S. Department of Health and Human Services (HHS) ($13 million between 1996-2002).[5]

The decline in welfare caseloads coincided with three major developments: welfare reform, an especially strong economy for low-skilled workers, and massively increased aid to low-income, working families. All three factors arguably were responsible for the caseload decline. Hence, a fundamental issue in evaluating welfare reform is to gauge the relative or separate impact of each factor. Unfortunately, as explained by Rossi, the findings of most of the studies funded as part of this effort suffer from one or more serious problems. The nonexperimental studies are based on designs that, except in rare instances, cannot support estimates of the net effects of welfare reform. There are also weaknesses stemming from unrepresentative samples, low response rates or high attrition rates, and limited external validity (that is, generalizability). As a result, these surveys are unable to parse out these separate impacts and, thus, are unable to assess whether welfare reform improved or harmed the well-being of low-income children and their families.

Here is the problem: Most data sources indicate that poor families, *on average*, suffered little or no substantial additional hardship after welfare reform. Many assume that this means that welfare reform had a benign, if not positive, effect. However, although many more low-income families seem to be doing better since welfare reform, some poor families seem to be doing worse. It is possible that welfare reform caused the latter, and that the strong economy and the large increases in aid to the working poor caused the former—in effect, countering welfare reform's negative effect. The research simply cannot unbundle these impacts with the requisite certainty.

In addition, the SPD and the NSAF have such low response rates that their data may be biased and unrepresentative of the population they were intended to describe, especially the poor, the very group most affected by welfare reform. Although researchers have attempted to compensate for this problem by devising weighting schemes for the data to reflect the probability of nonresponse, it is unclear how successful they have been, leaving the integrity of the data open to question. This undermines these surveys' usefulness even for monitoring the well-being of low-income families and children.

The UC project is designed to avoid the pitfalls inherent in surveys like the SPD and the NSAF, but its usefulness will depend on the success of extremely sophisticated modeling and the existence of relatively large impacts. The UC project is a cohort analysis that assesses the impact of welfare reform by comparing different cohorts of welfare recipients over time. Using survey and administrative data from four major urban areas (Cleveland, Los Angeles, Miami, and Philadelphia), MDRC researchers will compare the outcomes for cohorts of welfare and food stamp recipients receiving welfare under welfare reform to those for cohorts selected from the welfare and food stamp rolls before welfare reform was enacted. In doing so, MDRC hopes to combine the advantages of a cross-sectional and a before-and-after design. So far, however, MDRC staff have not been able to develop modeling techniques that closely reproduce findings in randomized experiments. Consequently, they have concluded that their methodology may be able to detect only very large impacts, larger than almost any of the impacts found in prior research. Thus, it seems unlikely that the UC project will produce findings that will be anything more than suggestive, no matter how sophisticated the statistical modeling.

Finally, the Child Impact Waiver Experiments use a rigorous methodology and represent perhaps the best attempt at measuring the impact of welfare reform in selected states. They, however, also have problems. Given the widespread publicity accompanying welfare reform, it is possible that many families in the control group believed that they, too, were subject to the new welfare rules and changed their behavior accordingly. As a result, the evaluation would not capture the full impact of the reforms. More important, generalizing the findings to other states is problematic, since the welfare reform programs tested in such states as Connecticut, Florida, Indiana, Iowa, and Minnesota differed not only from each other, but also from the TANF programs adopted in most other states.

Given the importance of these research efforts—and their cost—it is especially disappointing that, as Rossi describes, so little will be learned from them. Others have come to the same conclusion. For example, the National Academy of Sciences' Panel on Data and Methods for Measuring the Effects of Changes in Social Welfare Programs concluded that: "Despite the large number of studies that have been and are being conducted on welfare reform, the record on evaluation . . . is not impressive."[6]

At this writing, it seems unlikely that any of these projects will be continued, either because of their problems or because they have run their course. In addition, serious consideration should be given to options ranging from releasing the data sets with strong warnings about their limitations to suppressing their release entirely.

Monitoring Child and Family Well-Being

Given the moral and political implications of blaming—or crediting—welfare reform for the changing condition of the poor, more research on the subject can be expected, even though it is unlikely to be more successful than past efforts. But the desire to conduct such research should not obscure the overriding importance of monitoring the well-being of low-income children and families. Society has a deep and abiding interest in how they are doing—regardless of the cause. For example, a sudden increase in homelessness among children, whether or not due to welfare reform, could signal a need for remedial action. (Careful monitoring of the well-being of families could also help identify gaps in research.)

An important purpose of this volume is to help policymakers, advocates, and scholars with this monitoring. The contributors to this volume raise many of the key questions regarding family and child well-being (and identify various sources of data to answer the questions): What happened to the financial well-being of low-income mothers after welfare reform? What are the implications of the recent rise in cohabitation, and how is child well-being affected by whether the father is living at home and whether he is married to the mother? Are nonmarital and teenage births increasing or decreasing? Has the incidence of child abuse and the number of foster care placements changed? How have housing conditions and homelessness changed? Have there been any significant changes in children's physical and mental health? What have been the trends in hunger, nutrition, and related health outcomes? Can the impact of welfare reform on crime be measured? If so, how? What are the trends in drug use generally and among welfare mothers, and what impact does drug use have on welfare dependency? And, last, what is known about the utilization of child care and early childhood development programs and their impact on children?

Recognizing the importance of monitoring the well-being of low-income families and children, both political parties offered bills to reauthorize TANF in 2002 that contained provisions on the subject. The House-passed, Republican-backed bill to reauthorize TANF added "improving child well-being" to the list of state goals and authorized $10 million per year for the Census Bureau to carry out a "*new* longitudinal survey of program dynamics."[7] Similarly, the Senate, Democrat-backed version authorized $15 million for HHS to conduct a *new* national survey using comprehensive indicators to assess child well-being in each state, using measures such as school achievement and adjustment, social and emotional development, health and safety, and family well-being (including family structure, income, employment, child care arrangements, and family relationships).[8] Hence, it is almost certain that the final TANF reauthorization will include provisions that make monitoring and improving the well-being of children a primary goal of state programs and that provide additional funding specifically to assess well-being at the state level.

These provisions are a welcome demonstration that Congress understands the importance of monitoring the well-being of low-income families. Both proposals have weaknesses, however, that we hope will be addressed in the final TANF reauthorization bill. First, if these efforts lead to the development of a new survey or surveys, rather than build on existing ones, the proposed funding could be inadequate if the tasks assigned to the surveys are too ambitious. Second, they will probably need new instruments that will require extensive development work, for which there appears to be insufficient provision. Third, they may divert funds and energies away from other, possibly more useful efforts such as building on existing surveys. Finally, the biggest weakness of both proposals is that they are too short-term.

Welfare reform's real impact—positive or negative—is likely to be much more long-term than can be measured by studies that last only five or six years. It will probably take a decade or more before we can measure the impact of reduced welfare dependency on conditions that took root over many generations. Working at a regular job may change a mother's outlook on life, but earning enough to make ends meet would surely help—and that may take time as she accrues work experience. A successfully employed mother may be an important role model for her children, but it may take ten years or more before a change in the children's behavior is evident.

That means that any effort to monitor the well-being of low-income children and families will have to be likewise long-term, which, in turn, suggests that the primary means of assessing the well-being of low-income children and families should be through well-established and on-going, national surveys. All contributors to this volume use *existing data sources* to help assess the well-being of children and families.

Nevertheless, all the contributors recognize the shortcomings of these data sources, and often suggest ways to improve or supplement them. As Rossi writes, "[S]erious consideration ought to be given to bolstering . . . ongoing large-scale surveys."[9] Technical research is needed on how to raise response rates and obtain answers from every respondent on sensitive issues such as income and welfare receipt, and on new survey measurement instruments on topics of interest, such as child well-being and family functioning.

Improving the quality and coverage of existing data sources is the approach most likely to provide reliable and continuing information about child and family well-being, but it will not be a simple or inexpensive endeavor, as suggested by what will be needed to improve the two key surveys—the Current Population Survey (CPS) and the Survey of Income and Program Participation (SIPP).

Current Population Survey (CPS)

Over the years, the CPS has provided reasonably good monitoring data on the condition of the nation's poor. As concluded by the Panel on Data and Methods for Measuring the Effects of Changes in Social Welfare Programs:

> The CPS is probably the best all-around national data set for monitoring the well-being of the adult population at the national level because it contains sufficient measures of most income and employment outcomes for individuals and families, is reasonably representative of the overall population and major subgroups of interest, is produced on a timely basis, and is available prior to PRWORA.[10]

The CPS is the main source of information on the employment status of the civilian noninstitutional population sixteen years of age and older, including monthly estimates of unemployment released by the Bureau of Labor Statistics. Although the main purpose of the survey is to collect data on employment-related outcomes, each March a supplement to the CPS (with a sample of 78,000 households, beginning in 2001) collects detailed information on the nation's families, including family income, poverty status, living arrangements, and participation in social insurance and welfare programs. Most of the income and welfare data are for the previous calendar year. However, beginning in March 2000, the Census Bureau started collecting information about the receipt of welfare within the past thirty days. This permits more accurate comparisons to administrative data and allows researchers to examine some transitions on and off welfare. Other supplements to the CPS focus on food security, fertility and marital history, and other topics. A major advantage of the CPS relative to other surveys is its timeliness, with data generally available within six months of collection.

Nevertheless, the CPS also has problems that limit its usefulness for monitoring the well-being of low-income families.[11] First, except in the largest states, its sample size is too small to measure reliably state-level outcomes for welfare recipients, or other populations of interest, such as employed low-income mothers, urban teenagers, and so on. Second, welfare receipt is seriously underreported. For example, Richard Bavier, a policy analyst at the Office of Management and Budget, estimates that, in 2001, the CPS captured just 59 percent of the average monthly TANF recipients compared with administrative records.[12] This reporting problem has steadily worsened over the past decade. Compared with administrative data, the percentage of welfare recipients identified in the CPS fell from 80 percent in 1991 to 59 percent in 2001. Third, the survey does not capture information on many aspects of child well-being. For example, while it provides detailed information regarding the employment patterns of parents, it does not provide direct information about child care arrangements (as do some other surveys, such as the SIPP). Fourth, its ability to track families over time is limited.[13] Thus, it cannot reliably assess the well-being of welfare leavers, examine reasons for exiting welfare, or address other important policy questions.

The CPS is likely to remain the primary data set for monitoring conditions after welfare reform, and therefore the Census Bureau should consider several options for improving it. Sample sizes could be increased to support analysis at the state level. To minimize costs, data collection could be limited to the largest states, with low-income populations oversampled. Greater attention could be devoted to addressing the problem of underreporting of welfare receipt through technical research on how best to capture information on welfare receipt. Linking survey data to administrative data ought to be explored further. The survey's content could be expanded to include more information on how families with children are faring. This could be achieved by expanding the March demographic supplement or by adding other supplements. Finally, the longitudinal component of the survey could be expanded to examine the dynamics of welfare receipt and other topics requiring observations on the same families over time.

Survey of Income and Program Participation (SIPP)

The SIPP is also an important data source for monitoring trends in the well-being of families. Like the CPS, the SIPP collects information on demographic characteristics, income, labor force participation, participation in social insurance and welfare programs, and living arrangements. The SIPP data, however, are generally more detailed, and the survey's topical modules cover a wider range of topics relevant to child well-being, such as parental child care arrangements. The SIPP's most important feature is that it has a substantial longitudinal component, that is, the same households are repeatedly interviewed over an extended period. The 1996 panel had 36,700 participating households, which were interviewed twelve times over a four-year period. The 2001 panel has 35,097 participating households, which are interviewed nine times over a three-year period.

But the SIPP, too, has problems, and these must be addressed if it is to fulfill a useful monitoring function. According to the Panel on Data and Methods for Measuring the Effects of Changes in Social Welfare Programs:

> The SIPP has the advantage of more frequent periodicity of data collection and more extensive program participation coverage, but it has the significant disadvantage of being extremely slow in release, which greatly diminishes its usefulness for monitoring welfare reform. Another issue for monitoring is that the 1996 SIPP panel does not include some new entrants into the sample frame (primarily immigrants and those who move from the institutional to the noninstitutional population). The 1996 SIPP also has differential attrition of higher and lower income sample members, which is a problem for monitoring income and poverty.[14]

Perhaps the most serious problem is the survey's relatively high attrition rate. As Daniel Weinberg, chief of the Census Bureau's Housing and Household Economics Statistics Division, describes, "Attrition rates for the 1996 panel were higher than expected and have soared for the 2001 panel."[15] By the twelfth wave of the 1996 SIPP panel, over one-third of the sample had dropped out and after just the third wave of the 2001 panel, about one-quarter of the sample had dropped out (compared with an 18 percent drop-out rate for the 1996 panel after the third wave).

In addition, the SIPP's longitudinal capacities have recently been constrained. The 2001 and 2004 SIPP panels have been shortened from four years to three years, making it more difficult to analyze welfare dynamics. And, as with the CPS, the underreporting of income, including welfare income, is a serious problem. Bavier observes that by the tenth wave of the 1996 SIPP (representing the period from December 1998 to March 1999), "around one-third of eligible households were providing no information, and around half of those still in the sample had some income imputation."[16] The SIPP's sample sizes are also smaller than those of the CPS, making state-level data even more unreliable. Finally, the data are not made available in a timely fashion. For example, the child care data collected in the spring of 1997 were not published for five years, much too late to be the basis for judgments about current conditions.

If the SIPP is to be continued, its basic data collection capacity must be improved. First and foremost, efforts must be undertaken to reduce the increasing problem of attrition. If this and other needed improvements are successful, consideration could be given to expanding the scope of the survey and its longitudinal capacity. For example, the follow-up period for the 2004 SIPP panel could also be extended from three to four years. A longer follow-up period, among other benefits, would allow researchers to identify more welfare leavers or track them for a longer period after leaving. In addition, the sample of low-income households could be expanded, perhaps in the ten to fifteen states that contain most of the poor, to permit reliable state-level estimates of family and child well-being.

Other Specialized Surveys or Data Sets

Other specialized surveys with information on specific outcomes, many of which are identified in this volume, may be better tools for monitoring some aspects of the well-being of low-income families. Although these data sets also have problems, many of them are better suited to answering some questions than is either the CPS or the SIPP. For example, the National Survey of Family Growth (NSFG), an extensive nationwide survey of women ages fifteen to forty-four, provides reliable national estimates of births, pregnancies, living arrangements, and related behaviors.[17] Interviewers obtain a complete history of each woman's pregnancies, marriages, periods of cohabitation, contraceptive use, work, education, early sexual experiences, and childhood living arrangements—as well as demographic information and data on sources of income, including welfare. This level of detail makes the NSFG particularly useful in monitoring family and fertility-related trends.

Administrative Data

Most national surveys are unable to provide meaningful data about program participation at the state and local levels, which is increasingly important with the devolution of welfare to the state and local levels. State administrative data can often fill this gap. States are required to submit detailed administrative data to the federal government for most major programs, such as TANF, food stamps, and Medicaid. The data often include state summaries, such as caseloads and total spending, as well as detailed information about the characteristics of public assistance recipients, including their age, sex, race or ethnicity, income, employment, and the number and characteristics of other people living in the home. Administrative data contain information on program participants, a great advantage for studying subgroups and small geographic areas. These data can be used to develop reasonably good estimates of family or household income, by linking welfare data with data on earnings from Unemployment

Insurance records and noncash benefits from other program records. In many states, administrative data are available for many years, allowing researchers to examine trends in various outcomes over time.

Administrative data also have weaknesses, however. They may be inaccurate or incomplete, as described by Don Winstead and Ann McCormick (chapter 15). Moreover, they usually have little information on child well-being measures and on outcomes after people leave welfare.

Program Improvement Experiments

TANF is a bundle of program components, and existing data sets cannot determine which measures are important or efficacious, and which are ineffective or even harmful. Nor can we assume that the existing programmatic mixtures, varying by state and sometimes by county, are all alike in how they work. And yet, improvements in policies and programs are undoubtedly possible—if the optimal combinations can be determined.

The preferred evaluation methodology of most social scientists is experimental design, in which individuals are randomly assigned to an experimental or a control group. Randomized experiments are probably the best way to "unbundle" TANF programs to discern such optimal programmatic arrangements. If properly planned and implemented, they should result in experimental and control groups that have comparable measurable and unmeasurable aggregate characteristics (within the limits of chance variation). And, from the moment of randomization, both groups will be exposed to the same outside forces, such as economic conditions, social environments, and other events—allowing any subsequent differences in average outcomes to be attributed to the intervention.

In the past thirty years, experimental designs have been used to evaluate a wide range of social interventions, including evaluations of welfare-to-work programs. When researchers have used less rigorous methodologies, the findings of such research are often questioned. With experimental findings, policymakers can focus on the implications of findings, rather than, as Gary Burtless has observed, "become entangled in a protracted debate about whether the findings of a particular study are statistically valid."[18]

HHS has long been a major supporter of randomized experiments, especially in the welfare field. In addition to various smaller studies, it is now conducting four major, multi-year experiments on employment retention and advancement services,[19] enhanced services for the hard-to-employ, rural welfare-to-work strategies, and efforts to build strong families (see box 16.1). Although each of these areas is important to the further development of welfare reform strategies, we would have preferred to see projects that tested how best to implement the major—and still problematic—aspects of TANF, such as mandatory work ("workfare") and time-limited benefits.

With the exception of "work first" programs, relatively little is known about the impact of most other mandatory programs—a major issue in TANF's reauthorization. For example, there is no recent research on the impact of a "full-engagement" workfare program as operated in New York City. There have been many experiments of state welfare programs that include mandatory work requirements, expanded financial incentives, time limits, and other reform policies. These evaluations have typically measured the impact of the combination of policies. Questions about the effectiveness of mandatory workfare programs could best be answered by conducting randomized experiments in which the experimental group is subject to mandatory work and the control group is not. Or the test could be between alternative strategies, such as mandatory work versus mandatory education and training.

Similarly, there is little research on the impact of time-limited benefits, even though it is a central aspect of TANF. Randomized experiments could be used to assess the relative impact of alternative time-limit policies, such as the length of the time limit, any exemption and extension policies that surround it, and various approaches to counseling and similar services for families about to exhaust their time-limited benefits.

Reasonable people, however, can disagree about the components selected for testing, especially since the final decision is unavoidably the product of a process that weighs both substantive and political considerations as well as feasibility. In any event, the decision has been made and at this time there is no funding available for additional large-scale experiments.

The larger problem with these projects, however, must be noted: They will lack sufficient generalizability to help identify welfare policies that enhance child and family well-being. In each of these experiments, the state is expected to define and develop the needed services. Although it is possible that the states may decide on essentially the same set of services, it is more likely that each state will end up with a different mix of services. That means that whatever the findings may be, they will be restricted to the particular state or locality and to the particular mix of services chosen. If, for example, there are eight states involved, there will be eight experiments—each of limited generalizability. A more productive strategy (probably not possible at this stage of program knowledge) would have been to require all of the cooperating states to adopt essentially the same intervention. Then, if the findings from a number of states using the same intervention are consistent, they may be regarded as relatively robust and more generalizable to all states.

Therefore, although the evaluations of each of these projects has as a goal assessing child well-being,[20] they will add little to our understanding of that important question. As mentioned above, the absence of a common programmatic intervention across the projects means that any findings will be suggestive only, and will require replication in multiple sites. Furthermore, they will not shed any light on the impacts of welfare reform's core elements, such as mandatory work requirements and time limits.

Competing Analyses

In the final analysis, all data sets have limitations, and different analytic approaches often lead to quite different findings. Often enough, advocates on either side emphasize the findings of approaches that support their viewpoints, as exemplified by the debate about whether the incomes of single-mother families rose or fell in the wake of welfare reform. Several studies compared income trends before and after welfare reform, focusing on the poorest single-mother families. These studies arrayed single-mother families from poorest to richest by their incomes (or consumption levels) and then divided them into groups of equal size (generally fifths, or quintiles). They then compared the average income (or consumption) of families in the respective quintiles across several years. As Bavier reports, using different measures of income, examining different household units, considering different time periods, and using expenditure data rather than income data each led to quite different conclusions about the income trends.

Bavier used a comprehensive definition of income that included regular money income, plus noncash food and housing benefits, and the effect of direct taxes. Using the CPS, he found that from

---

Box 16.1
Major HHS Welfare Reform Experiments

Employment Retention and Advancement Project. This project examines the impact of various strategies designed to improve job retention and advancement for low-income parents, including former TANF recipients. The strategies being tested have varying objectives, target populations, and services. Some are "advancement programs" that help low-income workers advance into better jobs by offering services such as "career counseling, targeted job search assistance, close linkages with employers to identify or build career ladders, and education and training to help participants upgrade their skills while working." Others are "placement and retention programs" that seek to assist "'hard-to-employ' people, such as welfare recipients with disabilities or substance abuse problems, find and hold jobs," with advancement remaining a longer-term objective. Finally, some are mixed programs that provide both retention and advancement services sequentially.

The project is a five-year random assignment study conducted by MDRC. (The actual project period is nine years, from September 1, 1998, to September 30, 2007.) As of December 2002, random assignment was underway in thirteen of the fifteen sites (in eight states). The total projected budget is $24 million, with $4.5 million spent in fiscal year (FY) 2002.

Enhanced Services for the Hard-to-Employ Demonstration and Evaluation Project. This project will test the impact of programs designed to help current and former TANF recipients (and other low-income parents) who have experienced problems "entering and sustaining employment." This includes those with low skills, little work experience, health or substance abuse problems, or a criminal record. The range of services to be tested includes:

> supported work, in which people are given subsidized jobs along with training and job search assistance until they find regular jobs; initiatives that combine mental health treatment and employment services; efforts to improve identification of people with serious employment barriers, to increase participation and retention in mental health or substance abuse treatment, and to link treatment with employment services; and "two-generation" interventions that offer services for preschool-aged children or adolescents in parallel with employment services for their parents.

The project is a random assignment study conducted by MDRC. (The actual project period is nine years, from September 29, 2001, to September 28, 2010.) Site selection is planned for 2003, with plans to conduct random assignment in six sites. The total projected budget for the "core" study is $24 million, with $1.5 million spent in FY 2002. Several options to expand the evaluation may be exercised, including options to expand the number of sites (which would cost an additional $10.6 million), conduct a second survey after seventy-two months ($3.4 million), and enlarge the survey sample ($1.2 million). Thus, the total project cost could reach $39.2 million.

Rural Welfare-to-Work Strategies Demonstration and Evaluation Project. This project is designed to measure the effectiveness of rural welfare-to-work strategies.

Box 16.1 (cont.)
Major HHS Welfare Reform Experiments

Many rural areas have exceptionally high poverty rates, and jobs are often far from home. As a result, there may be barriers created by the absence of reliable transportation, limited child care opportunities, and few available social and educational services. The three projects now being tested have taken three distinct approaches for dealing with these problems. The Illinois Future Steps program offers intensive case-management services designed to help participants find employment. The Building Nebraska Families program provides "individualized, home-based education and mentoring to help participants develop life skills and overcome barriers, thus indirectly enhancing their employability." The Tennessee First Wheels program focuses on providing affordable transportation by offering no-interest car loans and helping participants maintain their cars.

The evaluation plan includes random-assignment designs, if possible, to determine the impact of these interventions on employment and family well-being outcomes. Nonexperimental analysis would be used to estimate program impacts when random assignment is not feasible. Mathematica Policy Research, Inc., evaluated an early implementation phase of demonstration. Random assignment has begun in the three sites. (The actual project period is from September 30, 2000, to September 28, 2005.) The total budget over five years is $6 million.

Building Strong Families Project. This project would experimentally evaluate programs designed to promote healthy marriage among unmarried couples, recruited when the mother is pregnant or at the time of the child's birth. The programs "will be designed to help such couples strengthen their relationship, achieve a healthy marriage if that is the path they choose, and thus enhance child and family well-being." They will not only provide instruction and counseling about marriage and relationship skills but will offer services to improve parenting skills and address employment, physical and mental health, or substance abuse problems. Some may include policy changes to enhance financial incentives (or reduce disincentives) to marry.

Mathematica Policy Research, Inc., is the evaluator of the project. HHS intends to conduct random assignment in six sites. (The actual project period is from September 27, 2002, to September 26, 2011.) The total budget for the core study is $19.7 million, with an option to conduct a five-year followup of families, adding about $4.5 million. The cost estimate for the first year is $3.5 million.

Sources: Manpower Demonstration Research Corporation, "Enhanced Services for the Hard-to-Employ," available from: http://www.mdrc.org/project_20_8.html, accessed January 11, 2003; Dan Bloom, Jacquelyn Anderson, Melissa Wavelet, Karen N. Gardiner, and Michael E. Fishman, *New Strategies to Promote Stable Employment and Career Progression: An Introduction to the Employment Retention and Advancement Project* (New York: Manpower Demonstration Research Corporation, February 2002), available from: http://www.mdrc.org/Reports2002/era_conferencerpt/era_exsummary.htm, accessed January 11, 2003; Andrew Burswick and Alicia Meckstroth, *Rural Welfare-to-Work Strategies Demonstration Evaluation: A Summary of the Evaluation Design and Demonstration Programs* (Princeton, N.J.: Mathematica Policy Research, Inc., October 9, 2002), p. 2, available from: http://www.mathematica-mpr.com/PDFs/summaryofeval.pdf, accessed January 12, 2003; U.S. Department of Health and Human Services, Administration for Children and Families, "Building Strong Families," undated draft paper.

1995 to 1998 female-headed families in the bottom quintile experienced a decline in family income of about $617 (in 2001 dollars), or about 7 percent. (All dollars henceforth will be in 2001 dollars.) Other researchers, using alternative definitions of income, report consistent but somewhat different results. For example, some researchers adjust income for family size and attempt to correct for the underreporting of welfare income. When Bavier examined income trends by using household income, rather than family income, he found a smaller decline, just $270, or about 3 percent. The magnitude of these changes also varies depending on the data used. Bavier repeated his analysis using the SIPP, and found somewhat larger declines in family and household income during this period: 9 percent and 12 percent, respectively.

The trend in income is also very sensitive to the time period chosen. For example, when Bavier extended his analysis by using the CPS through 2000, he found an increase in family income of $543, or about 7 percent, and an even larger increase in household income of $1,186, or over 12 percent. And using 1994, the year the caseload began to decline, as the base resulted in gains of $946 in family income (12 percent) and $1,717 in household income (19 percent). Updating further to examine the period from 1994 through 2001 showed a decline in family income of $127 (2 percent), but an increase in household income of $396 (4 percent).

On the other hand, Bavier's analysis of consumption data suggests a steady improvement in the well-being of the poorest female-headed families (throughout the 1995 to 2000 period). Using the Consumer Expenditure Survey (CE), Bavier found that quarterly spending by female family heads in the bottom quintile increased 9 percent between 1995 and 1998 and 15 percent between 1995 and 2000.

As this example illustrates, divergent findings about a host of issues can be expected. Thus, any conclusions about changes in family and child well-being after welfare reform should be based on careful analysis of multiple studies, with a full assessment of each study's data and methodology.

The defects of some studies will be quite obvious. For example, comparisons that are limited to just two—arbitrarily selected—points in time may obscure important trends. As Bavier shows, extending the time frame for analysis from 1995–1998 to 1994–2000 results in a strikingly different picture of income trends. Equally misleading are studies that fail to recognize and adjust for data problems, such as the increasing tendency of families to underreport welfare receipt. And, of course, too many studies make causal inferences from trend data, without adequately accounting for potentially confounding forces, such as the economy.

But the limitations of many studies will not be obvious—even though they will be at variance with others on the same topic. Resolving the differences among them will usually involve a long and contentious debate about competing analyses. Studies based on data with small samples, low response rates, or high levels of missing data should be appropriately discounted. Those that limit their analysis to a narrow time frame should be compared with others with longer or alternative time frames, with recognition of the many other forces that may also affect well-being, such as the economy.

Estimates of child and family well-being that are consistent across several data sets and methodological approaches will be especially credible. But no matter how much we may desire to obtain an unequivocal understanding of the findings of research, different approaches will almost inevitably yield different results. It is important, therefore, to encourage competing analyses and open discussion of different and inconsistent findings. Both the policy and the research communities will benefit from such competition. Researchers will learn the virtues and vices of different methods, and policy analysts will learn about the complexities of the social world, and thus, we hope, learn how to design programs most efficiently.

Persistence, open-mindedness, and a sharp eye will surely be needed. But disadvantaged children and families deserve no less.

Notes

1.   Douglas J. Besharov, Peter Germanis, and Peter H. Rossi, *Evaluating Welfare Reform: A Guide for Scholars and Practitioners* (College Park, Md.: University of Maryland School of Public Affairs, 1997), available from: http://www.welfareacademy.org/pubs/ewr/, accessed December 18, 2002.
2.   Personal communication from Alan Weil, director of the Assessing New Federalism Project, to Peter Germanis, December 11, 2002. This figure includes all costs associated with the project, including other qualitative and quantitative data collection, all publications, management, and dissemination. In addition, the topics covered by the project go beyond welfare reform.
3.   Personal communication from Daniel Weinberg, chief, Housing and Household Economics Statistics Division, U.S. Census Bureau, to Peter Germanis, December 11, 2002.
4.   Personal communication from Charles Michalopoulos, senior research associate, Manpower Demonstration Research Corporation (MDRC), to Peter Germanis, October 31, 2002.

5.   Personal communication from Howard Rolston, director of Planning, Research, and Evaluation in the Administration for Children and Families, U.S. Department of Health and Human Services (HHS), to Peter Germanis, November 1, 2002.

6.   Robert A. Moffitt and Michele Ver Ploeg, editors, *Evaluating Welfare Reform in an Era of Transition* (Washington, D.C.: National Academy Press, 2001), pp. 98–99. See also Moffitt and Ver Ploeg, 2001, pp. 2–3, stating: "The panel finds that studies of welfare reform to date have done a reasonable job of monitoring the progress of the low-income and welfare populations—that is, tracking the well-being of these populations over time, although usually only after reform. More useful studies of this type are under way. However, monitoring studies are only the first step in assessing the effects of welfare reform. The second, more critical step is to evaluate the effects of welfare reform—that is, how it has changed the outcomes for families and individuals relative to what would have happened in the absence of reform. The panel finds that the evaluation studies that have been done are only able to address a small number of questions. There are many important questions that have not been addressed. Little is known about the effects of specific individual reform strategies, for example, a human capital approach versus a work-first approach or a set of relatively strict work requirements versus a set of less strict work requirements. Evaluations of other questions have been limited by weaknesses in data. These weaknesses are particularly limiting for studies that have assessed the overall effect of welfare reform and for national-level studies of broad components of the reform, such as any time limit versus no time limit or work requirements versus no work requirements. Consequently, many important evaluation questions have not been adequately answered."

7.   *Personal Responsibility, Work, and Family Promotion Act of 2002*, 107th Cong., 2d sess., H.R. 4737. Emphasis added.

8.   Senate Committee on Finance, *Description of the "Work, Opportunity, and Responsibility for Kids (WORK) Act of 2002,"* 107th Cong., 2d sess., June 24, 2002, available from: http://finance.senate.gov/leg/leg062602mark.pdf, accessed January 16, 2003.

9.   Peter H. Rossi, "Ongoing Major Research in Welfare Reform: What Will Be Learned," in *Family Well-Being after Welfare Reform*, edited by Douglas J. Besharov, 2002, available from: http://www.welfareacademy.org/pubs/familywellbeing/familywellbeing-ch3rossi.pdf, accessed November 18, 2002.

10.   Moffitt and Ver Ploeg, 2001, p. 116.

11.   See, for example, Moffitt and Ver Ploeg, 2001, p. 116, writing for the Panel on Data and Methods for Measuring the Effects of Changes in Social Welfare Programs: the CPS "has many weaknesses as well. . . . Further, welfare receipt is significantly underreported in the CPS. Finally, it is too small for state-level monitoring of welfare programs because there are too few observations of low-income, single-mother groups to produce estimates with acceptable levels of error."

12.   Personal communication from Richard Bavier, a policy analyst with the U.S. Office of Management and Budget, to Peter Germanis, January 3, 2002.

13.   In the Current Population Survey (CPS), households are interviewed for four consecutive months, then are out of the survey for eight months, and then return to the survey for four months. Because these sets of four monthly observations are one year apart, the CPS has a longitudinal component. In particular, about half the sample interviewed each March as part of the annual demographic survey was interviewed the previous March (and the other half will be interviewed the next March), so longitudinal socioeconomic data covering two years are available for some families, but there are many difficulties in linking these data to make them useful.

14. Moffitt and Ver Ploeg, 2001, p. 116.
15. Daniel H. Weinberg, "The Survey of Income and Program Participation—Recent History and Future Developments," SIPP Working Paper no. 232, U.S. Census Bureau, Washington, D.C., June 20, 2002, p. 18, available from: http://www.sipp.census.gov/sipp/workpapr/wp232.pdf, accessed December 18, 2002.
16. Richard Bavier, "Welfare reform data from the Survey of Income and Program Participation," *Monthly Labor Review* 124 (7) (July 2001): 14. (Income is estimated from household characteristics if the respondent is unable or unwilling to report that information.)
17. The 2002 National Survey of Family Growth (NSFG) was expanded to include interviews with men ages fifteen to forty-four.
18. Gary Burtless, "The Case for Randomized Field Trials in Economic and Policy Research," *Journal of Economic Perspectives* 9 (Spring 1995): 69.
19. These projects build on the Post-Employment Services Demonstration (PESD), a project that tested case management services for welfare recipients who found jobs. The PESD evaluation found that the programs typically did not improve employment outcomes, so the current projects have been designed to target more carefully groups that could benefit and provide a wider range of services.
20. See, for example, U.S. Department of Health and Human Services, Administration for Children and Families, "Enhanced Services for the Hard-to-Employ Demonstration and Evaluation Project," available from: http://www.acf.dhhs.gov/programs/opre/hteweb.htm, accessed January 14, 2003, stating: "In addition to measuring programmatic effects on adults' employment and earnings, the project will evaluate family functioning, child well-being (from early childhood through adolescence), and two generation programs, which provide employment services to adults and direct services to children or youth. The project will also examine the issues and challenges in implementing and operating different approaches that promote employment among the hard-to-employ, the services included in such programs, how programs meet the needs of participants with multiple employment or family challenges, the primary sources of funding for various program models, and the benefits and costs of programs studied."

References

Bavier, Richard. 2001. "Welfare Reform Data from the Survey of Income and Program Participation." *Monthly Labor Review* 124 (7) (July): 13–24.

Besharov, Douglas J., Peter Germanis, and Peter H. Rossi. 1997. *Evaluating Welfare Reform: A Guide for Scholars and Practitioners.* College Park, Md.: University of Maryland School of Public Affairs. Available from: http://www.welfareacademy.org/pubs/ewr/. Accessed December 18, 2002.

Bloom, Dan, Jacquelyn Anderson, Melissa Wavelet, Karen N. Gardiner, and Michael E. Fishman. 2002. *New Strategies to Promote Stable Employment and Career Progression: An Introduction to the Employment Retention and Advancement Project.* New York: Manpower Demonstration Research Corporation. February. Available from: http://www.mdrc.org/Reports2002/era_conference/era_exsummary.htm. Accessed January 11, 2003.

Burswick, Andrew, and Alicia Meckstroth. 2002. *Rural Welfare-to-Work Strategies Demonstration Evaluation: A Summary of the Evaluation Design and Demonstration Programs.* Princeton, N.J.: Mathematica Policy Research, Inc. October 9. Available from: http://www.mathematica-mpr.com/PDFs/summaryofeval.pdf. Accessed January 12, 2003.

Burtless, Gary. 1995. "The Case for Randomized Field Trials in Economic Policy Research." *Journal of Economic Perspectives* 9 (Spring): 63–84.

Manpower Demonstration Research Corporation. "Enhanced Services for the Hard-to-Employ." Available from: http://www.mdrc.org/project_20_8.html. Accessed January 11, 2003.

Moffitt, Robert A., and Michele Ver Ploeg. Editors. 2001. *Evaluating Welfare Reform in an Era of Transition*. Washington, D.C.: National Academy Press.

Personal Responsibility, Work, and Family Promotion Act of 2002. U.S. House. 107th Cong., 2d sess., H.R. 4737.

Rossi, Peter H. 2002. "Ongoing Major Research in Welfare Reform: What Will Be Learned." In *Family Well-Being after Welfare Reform*. Edited by Douglas J. Besharov. Available from: http://www.welfareacademy.org/pubs/familywellbeing/familywellbeing-ch3rossi.pdf. Accessed November 18, 2002.

Senate Committee on Finance. 2002. *Description of the "Work, Opportunity, and Responsibility for Kids (WORK) Act of 2002."* 107th Cong., 2d sess. June 24. Available from: http://finance.senate.gov/leg/leg062602mark.pdf. Accessed January 16, 2003.

U.S. Department of Health and Human Services, Administration for Children and Families. "Building Strong Families." Undated draft paper.

U.S. Department of Health and Human Services, Administration for Children and Families. "Enhanced Services for the Hard-to-Employ Demonstration and Evaluation Project." Available from: http://www.acf.dhhs.gov/programs/opre/hteweb.htm. Accessed January 14, 2003.

Weinberg, Daniel H. 2002. "The Survey of Income and Program Participation—Recent History and Future Developments." SIPP Working Paper No. 232. U.S. Census Bureau. Washington, D.C. June 20. Available from: http://www.sipp.census.gov/sipp/workpapr/wp232.pdf. Accessed December 18, 2002.

Contributors

Richard Bavier is a policy analyst with the U.S. Office of Management and Budget with concentration in distributional analysis of federal spending, poverty measurement, and evaluation of means-tested programs. He is the author of several articles on the impact of welfare reform.

Harold S. Beebout is a senior fellow at Mathematica Policy Research, Inc., and chief information officer, Child and Family Services Agency, District of Columbia. Beebout's policy expertise spans welfare, employment, and nutrition, and he is also an expert in micro-simulation modeling techniques. Among his publications is *The Food Stamp Program: Design Tradeoffs, Policy and Impacts* (with James Ohls, 1993).

Douglas J. Besharov is the Joseph J. and Violet Jacobs Scholar in Social Welfare Studies at the American Enterprise Institute and a professor at the University of Maryland School of Public Affairs, where he directs its Welfare Reform Academy. Earlier, he was director of the U.S. National Center on Child Abuse and Neglect. Among his publications are *Rethinking WIC: An Evaluation of the Women, Infants, and Children Program* (with Peter Germanis, 2001); *America's Disconnected Youth* (1999); *Enhancing Early Childhood Programs: Burdens and Opportunities* (1996); and *Recognizing Child Abuse: A Guide for the Concerned* (1990).

Richard J. Gelles holds the Joanne and Raymond Welsh Chair of Child Welfare and Family Violence in the School of Social Work at the University of Pennsylvania. He is director of the Center for the Study of Youth Policy and co-director of the Center for Children's Policy, Practice, and Research. Among his publications are *The Book of David: How Preserving Families Can Cost Children's Lives* (1996); *Intimate Violence in Families*, 3d ed. (1997); and *The Violent Home* (1974).

Peter Germanis is assistant director of the University of Maryland Welfare Reform Academy. Before joining the Academy, he was director of the Division of Program Evaluation, Office of Family Assistance, U.S. Department of Health and Human Services. He also served in the White House under the Reagan and Bush administrations. Among his publications are *Rethinking WIC: An Evaluation of the Women, Infants, and Children Program* (with Douglas J. Besharov, 2001) and *Evaluating Welfare Reform: A Guide for Scholars and Practitioners* (with Peter H. Rossi and Douglas J. Besharov, 1997).

Wade F. Horn is assistant secretary for children and families, U.S. Department of Health and Human Services (HHS). At the time his chapter was written, he was president of the National Fatherhood Initiative. From 1989 to 1993, he was commissioner for Children, Youth, and Families and chief of the Children's Bureau, HHS. Before that, he served as director of Outpatient Psychological Services at the Children's Hospital National Medical Center in Washington, D.C., and as an associate professor of psychiatry and behavioral sciences at George Washington University. Among his publications are *The Better Homes and Gardens New Father Book* (1998) and *The Better Homes and Gardens New Teen Book* (1999).

Julia B. Isaacs directs research and analyzes human services policies at the Office of the Assistant Secretary for Planning and Evaluation (ASPE), U.S. Department of Health and Human Services. As director of the Data and Technical Analysis Division in ASPE's Human Services Policy office, she has a particular interest in the collection and analysis of data related to welfare, child care, and other programs serving low-income populations.

Lorraine V. Klerman is a professor at the Heller School for Social Policy and Management, Brandeis University. At the time her chapter was written, she was a professor in the Department of Maternal and Child Health of the University of Alabama's School of Public Health at Birmingham. A health services researcher and health policy analyst, her major research areas are family planning, teenage pregnancy, prenatal care, and the impact of socioeconomic status on maternal and child health. Among her publications is *Alive and Well? A Research and Policy Review of Health Programs for Poor Young Children* (1991).

Wendy D. Manning is an associate professor of sociology at Bowling Green State University and director of the Center for Family and Demographic Research. She is a family demographer whose research focuses on the role of cohabitation in the American family system in terms of marriage, childbearing, and child well-being.

Ann McCormick is a social science analyst at the U.S. Department of Health and Human Services, with policy experience in welfare, nutrition assistance, and health policy, and the interactions of means-tested programs as they affect the low-income population.

Peter Reuter is a professor at the School of Public Affairs and the Department of Criminology at the University of Maryland. Since 1999 he has been editor of the *Journal of Policy Analysis and Management*. He is also senior fellow at RAND. Among his publications are *Drug War Heresies: Learning from Other Vices, Times, and Places* (with Robert MacCoun, 2001) and *Disorganized Crime: Illegal Markets and the Mafia* (1985).

Peter H. Rossi is S. A. Rice Professor Emeritus at the University of Massachusetts (Amherst). He is past president of the American Sociological Association and has received numerous awards for work in evaluation from the American Evaluation Association, the American Sociological Association, and the Policy Studies Organization. Among his publications are *Evaluation: A Systematic Approach* (with Howard Freeman and Mark Lipsey, 1993); *Down and Out in America* (1989); *Money, Work, and Crime: Experimental Evidence* (1981); and *Why Families Move* (1955).

Isabel V. Sawhill is a senior fellow in economic studies at the Brookings Institution, where she co-directs the Welfare Reform and Beyond project and directs the Brookings Roundtable on Children. She is president of the National Campaign to Prevent Teen Pregnancy. From 1993 to 1995, she served as an associate director at the Office of Management and Budget. Among her publications are *Updating the Social Contract: Growth and Opportunity in the New Century* (with Rudolph Penner and Timothy Taylor, 2000); *Challenge to Leadership: Economic and Social Issues for the Next Decade* (1988); *The Reagan Experiment: An Examination of Economic and Social Policies under the Reagan Administration* (with John

Logan Palmer, 1982); and *Time of Transition: The Growth of Families Headed by Women* (with Heather Ross, 1975).

Lawrence W. Sherman is director of the Jerry Lee Center of Criminology and the Albert M. Greenfield Professor of Human Relations in the Department of Sociology at the University of Pennsylvania. Among his publications are *Preventing Crime: What Works, What Doesn't, What's Promising* (with David P. Farrington and Brandon Welsh, 1997); *Policing Domestic Violence: Experiments and Dilemmas* (with Janell D. Schmidt and Dennis P. Rogan, 1992); and *Scandal and Reform: Controlling Police Corruption* (1978).

John C. Weicher is assistant secretary for housing and federal housing commissioner at the U.S. Department of Housing and Urban Development (HUD). At the time his chapter was written, he was director of urban policy studies with the Hudson Institute. Before joining Hudson in 1993, he served for four years as assistant secretary for HUD's Office of Policy Development and Research. Earlier he served on the Committee on Urban Policy of the National Academy of Sciences, and the Advisory Committee on Population Statistics of the U.S. Census Bureau. He is a past president of the American Real Estate and Urban Economics Association. Among his publications are *Federal Housing Policy: Problems and Solutions* (2000); *Entitlement Issues in the Domestic Budget* (1985); and *Distribution of Wealth: Increasing Inequality?* (1996).

Don Winstead is the deputy assistant secretary for human services policy for the U.S. Department of Health and Human Services (HHS). Prior to joining HHS in December 2001, he was Welfare Reform Administrator in the State of Florida's Department of Children and Families. He has over thirty years of experience in administering human services, primarily in the area of welfare reform and family self-sufficiency.

Index